**monsoonbooks**

# BANDIT SAINTS OF J

George Quinn holds a BA from                                    ) and
a PhD from the University of Sydney. Between 2001 and retirement in
2008 he was Head of the Southeast Asia Centre in the Faculty of Asian
Studies at the Australian National University. He has a native-speaker
level command of Indonesian and Javanese. He is the author of *The
Novel in Javanese* (KITLV Press, 1991) and *The Learner's Dictionary of
Today's Indonesian* (Allen & Unwin, 2001), plus many scholarly papers
and an English translation of the Indonesian-language novel *The Rape of
Sukreni* (Lontar, 2003).

Learn more about the author and his visits to the Islamic pilgrimage
sites of Java and Madura at www.saintsofjava.net.

### Praise for *Bandit Saints of Java*

"A brilliant book – one of the most engaging, memorable and
genuinely insightful works on Indonesia published in recent
years." Tim Hannigan, *Asian Review of Books*, Hong Kong

"This is the most entertaining book in English on the mystery
and magic of Indonesia since Elizabeth Pisani's *Indonesia Etc.*"
Duncan Graham, *Jakarta Post*, Indonesia

"George Quinn is a master storyteller."
Seno Joko Suyono, *TEMPO*, Indonesia

"The author is a superb, witty and entertaining writer who vividly
records what he saw and felt close-up on the ground. Erudite and
well-researched." Bill Dalton, *Bali Advertiser*, Indonesia

"A scholarly, intelligent and subtle book, written for the general
public." Henri Chambert-Loir, *Archipel*, Paris

# BANDIT SAINTS
# OF JAVA

GEORGE QUINN

**monsoon**

**monsoon**books

First published in 2019
by Monsoon Books Ltd
www.monsoonbooks.co.uk

No.1 The Lodge, Burrough Court, Burrough on the Hill,
Melton Mowbray LE14 2QS, UK

This second edition published in 2020.

ISBN (paperback): 9781912049448
ISBN (ebook): 9781912049455

Cover design by Cover Kitchen.
Cover painting©The British Library Board. "Hadji. (Pelerin). A pilgrim.
Inhabitant of Indonesia. 1781" from Pers, A. Van "Nederlandsch Oost-
Indischen Typen."

All photographs©George Quinn unless stated otherwise. The copyright
owner of "The Five Pandåwå brothers" on page 175 is unknown.
All maps©Australian National University.

A Cataloguing-in-Publication data record is available from the British
Library.

Printed and bound in Great Britain by Clays Ltd, Elcograf S.p.A.
22 21 20          2 3 4

For

EMMY

who has been with this book from the beginning,

a long time ago

"If, say, a Christian really wants to understand the Muslims who attend the mosque down the street, he shouldn't look for a pristine set of values that every Muslim holds dear. Rather, he should enquire into the catch-22s of Muslim culture, those places where rules are at war and standards scuffle. It's at the very spot where Muslims teeter between two imperatives that you'll understand them best."

Yuval Noah Harari *Sapiens: A Brief History of Humankind* (2014)

When I was a small boy, I heard
you couldn't become a Muslim just by doing your prayers.
Where you lived didn't make you a Muslim,
you didn't become a Muslim by fasting,
you weren't a Muslim by the clothes you wear
and your headwear didn't make you a Muslim.
What I heard was ...
it is difficult to say what a Muslim is,
but you are not a Muslim simply because you refuse
what is forbidden and choose what is permitted.

*Suluk Malang Sumirang* (Java, 17th – 18th century)

# Contents

# A note on sources, spelling, names and translations

With readability in mind I have banished bibliographic references and footnotes from the pages of this book (a few obstinate footnotes managed to survive). All quoted or directly consulted sources are recorded in narrative form under Sources at the end of the book. The exact location of pilgrimage sites visited, as well as directions for accessing them, are detailed on the book's website: www.saintsofjava.net. The website also lists general and contextual studies on Javanese religion plus further readings on particular pilgrimage sites.

The vocabulary and texts of Javanese loom large in *Bandit Saints of Java*. Today Javanese is written in Roman script. Roman letters may represent different sounds in Javanese texts from the sounds they represent in English or Indonesian, so the spelling of Javanese words deviates a little from the conventions of English and Indonesian. Here are some pointers to help you voice Javanese words.

/c/ is pronounced "ch" as in "Charlie"

/dh/ is like "d" with the tongue curled up into the roof of the mouth

/th/ is like "t" with the tongue curled up into the roof of the mouth

/å/ is pronounced "o" as in the British English "block"

/a/ is pronounced as in the British English "father"
/ĕ/ is weak as in "kebab"; /é/ is pronounced as in "day",
/è/ as in "bed"


I had no way of tracking down casually encountered informants to ask them for permission to use their names. Following a protocol now becoming general in the social sciences I have given them generic names to protect their privacy and safeguard them from embarrassment or hárassment by those who may find features of this book provocative. Anonymity does not apply, however, to historical figures and public office holders, including tomb custodians. I use their real names.

Modern place names are spelled as they appear in modern maps, and people's personal names are spelled as they themselves spell them. Pre-modern place names and personal names, as well as the titles of Javanese-language texts from times when the Roman alphabet was unknown, are transcribed into the orthography of modern Javanese using the spelling conventions sketched above. Depending on context, a few names appear in variant spellings. Java's great fourteenth century state, for example, is spelled Måjåpait in Javanese, Majapahit in Indonesian, and Madjapahit or Modjopahit in Dutch texts and some older Indonesian texts.

Unless otherwise indicated, translations from Javanese, Indonesian and Dutch are my own. My translations of verses from the Holy Qur'ān are also my own, but rely a lot on other translations in English and Indonesian.

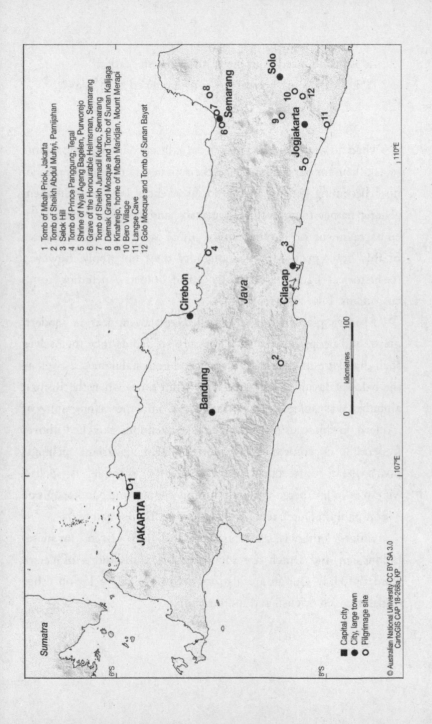

Sumatra

Java

JAKARTA

Bandung

Cirebon

Cilacap

Semarang

Solo

Jogjakarta

1 Tomb of Mbah Priok, Jakarta
2 Tomb of Sheikh Abdul Muhyi, Pamijahan
3 Selok Hill
4 Tomb of Prince Panggung, Tegal
5 Shrine of Nyai Ageng Bagelen, Purworejo
6 Grave of the Honourable Heimsman, Semarang
7 Tomb of Sheikh Jumadil Kubro, Semarang
8 Demak Grand Mosque and Tomb of Sunan Kalijaga
9 Kinahrejo, home of Mbah Maridjan, Mount Merapi
10 Bero Village
11 Langse Cave
12 Golo Mosque and Tomb of Sunan Bayat

107°E    110°E

8°S    8°S

6°S

■  Capital city
●  City, large town
○  Pilgrimage site

0        100
kilometres

© Australian National University CC BY SA 3.0
CartoGIS CAP 18-266a_KP

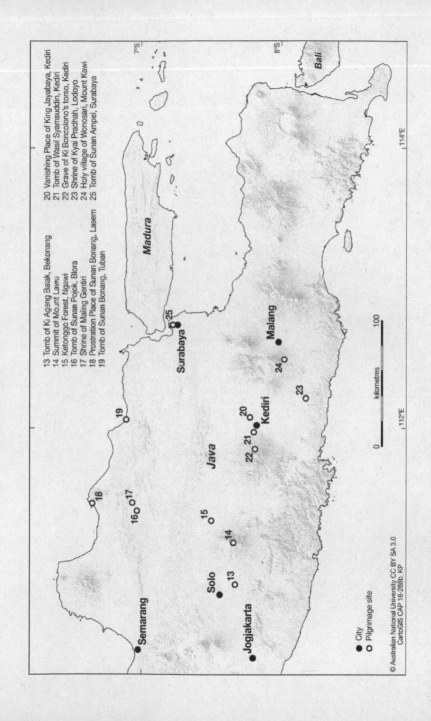

13 Tomb of Ki Ageng Balak, Bekonang
14 Summit of Mount Lawu
15 Ketonggo Forest, Ngawi
16 Tomb of Sunan Pojok, Blora
17 Shrine of Maling Gentiri
18 Prostration Place of Sunan Bonang, Lasem
19 Tomb of Sunan Bonang, Tuban

20 Vanishing Place of King Jayabaya, Kediri
21 Tomb of Wasil Syamsuddin, Kediri
22 Grave of Ki Boncolono's torso, Kediri
23 Shrine of Kyai Pradhah, Lodoyo
24 Holy village of Wonosari, Mount Kawi
25 Tomb of Sunan Ampel, Surabaya

• City
○ Pilgrimage site

© Australian National University CC BY SA 3.0
CartoGIS CAP 18-268b. KP

# Java's inner archipelago

## WHERE ISLAMIC FAITH MEETS LOCAL HISTORY

I stood trembling in the chill of dawn on the summit of Mount Lawu, three thousand metres above the rice fields of Central Java. In the east the sun was rising in a corona of brassy haze. The blue-white porcelain of the sky curved above me. Below, a plain of tumbled cloud stretched to the fast withering smudge of night on the western horizon. The shadow of the mountain lay flung across it like an abandoned blanket.

Scores of young men and women in beanies and hooded windcheaters were milling around or squatting among rocks and tufts of rough tussock. Many were huddled together for protection against the cold. A few were lifting their cameras to take photographs. Some were trying to chat and laugh.

They were Muslim pilgrims.

Somewhere among the jagged knolls of the summit there were sacred places – pools, a cave, a holy boulder, a rough-hewn shrine – but I didn't wait around to visit them. After climbing through the night I was exhausted. Probably I was dazed by the effects of altitude. By 8 am, I was glad to be heading down again.

It was 2001. I had been foolish enough to forget my age (fifty-seven at the time) and join a mass pilgrimage to the peak of the sacred volcano. The pilgrimage happens annually on the eve of the Islamic New Year's Day, the first of Muharram. I estimate between 5,000 and 10,000 people took part.

I started out from a roadside base station at two o'clock the previous afternoon. Labouring through foothills under a blackening sky I came across another pilgrim, Kusnadi from Surabaya, aged around thirty. Like me he was alone so we teamed up. By five o'clock breakers of mist were rolling in slow-motion down the mountain. Visibility shrank to less than a hundred metres. Everywhere water was dripping from the scrubby slopes into puddles along the rock-strewn path. We reached the end of the easy walking at an altitude of two thousand metres where we dined on rice crackers and squashed bread rolls from our backpacks. Then, as night fell, we headed up a steep track into a rain squall.

I still see my companion's pain-twisted face squinting into the darkness above.

Kusnadi sinks to the ground beside the track. He squats grimacing in the mud in the dim ring of illumination from my flashlight. His right leg is cramping. He slaps at his calf. He hammers his thigh with his fists. He tries to flex his leg in front of him. He reaches forward and eases his left trainer-shoe off. Rain sparkles in the beam of the flashlight as he rolls a muddy sock away from his foot and examines his toes. They are raw with blood. The nail on his big toe has split. One half of it is hanging off the toe. Red flesh glistens beneath it.

He takes a damp handkerchief from his pocket and wraps it carefully around the toe. He puts his sock and shoe back on. As he struggles to his feet he gasps and his breath billows before him in the frigid air. He looks up at the dark angle of the mountain. "Let's go," he says. There is a new edge of determination in his voice.

As he heads for the summit through the rain-sodden night, he is not really articulate about why he is doing it. The most he can say is the annual climb is a significant event. He hopes that by doing it he can put behind him the disappointments of the past and lock in a better future. He has been unemployed for the last four years. He hopes to set up a small business with friends, cultivating fish in artificial ponds. He also hopes to marry the girl he is engaged to.

On the treacherous rubble of the volcano I sense Kusnadi's longing for an inner foothold. It is the first time he has been on a pilgrimage. He takes it seriously. In his backpack he is carrying an Indonesian translation of the *Nahjul Balaghah*, the sayings of the Caliph Ali (in office 656 – 661 CE).

The summit is a remote place, or as remote as you can get in densely populated Java. Kusnadi is uncertain what he will do when he gets there. The hard walls of religious orthodoxy lie hidden far below, but as a good Muslim he is nervous about the "pagan" elements in the pilgrimage ritual. He has heard there is a shrine up there much visited by non-Muslims, especially Chinese. He knows that the saint of the mountain, Sunan Lawu, is a problematic Muslim who was in fact the last Hindu-Buddhist king of Måjåpait, the state that dominated Java in the fourteenth century.

Four hundred metres short of the summit Kusnadi's leg is cramping again. His left foot throbs. We are now above the rain clouds. It is 11 pm. Flint-sharp stars fill the sky. The air is near freezing, far colder than he has ever known air to be. Under his breath, over and over as he pulls himself upwards, he breathes one consoling phrase: "Your Will be done." (*Aku pasrah marang Kěrså Paduk*å.)

Kusnadi's fervour wasn't exceptional that night, but it wasn't universal either. Most of the thousands on the mountain were young, and many were there for the fun of a night climb with friends. Some, like Kusnadi, were novice mountaineers. They had no idea what they were letting themselves in for. Around eight o'clock a group of five young men whooped past us wearing rain-drenched t-shirts, jeans and rubber flip-flops. They didn't get far. We met them again an hour later as they stumbled down, shocked and shivering. One of them, now barefoot, was sagging between two friends with his arms around their shoulders. Near the summit we passed a group of three teenage girls squatting in the icy mud. They were sobbing into their *hijab* scarves. One of them was wailing and calling on Allah for help. Standing over them, two young men were pleading with them: "Get up and come with us down to base ... if you don't you won't survive the night."

The climb up rain-slicked tracks was tough but the slithering descent was tougher. Without the reassurance of walking poles or mountaineering footwear, I slipped and fell a dozen times. I sprained both knees ... painfully, but I was still able to walk. Luckily the tracks were patrolled by mini-squads of students from the Eleventh of March University in nearby Solo. They were carrying first aid kits. They propped me up, put bandages around my knees, and patched my abrasions. They told me (laughing) that I kept falling because I had been disrespectful to Sunan Lawu. They noticed I had urinated against the side of the mountain without apologising to him.

"Pilgrim numbers have jumped," one female student told me. She was standing outside a tent among trees at the base of the mountain where she and fellow students were treating the injured and handing out free food. "Now we have to deal with broken legs, sprains, exhaustion and hypothermia. It's amazing! It simply wasn't like this ten years ago."

In 2001 there was even a ramshackle eatery doing a busy trade not far below the summit. After a night of climbing I breakfasted there on instant noodles and tepid tea. I've never eaten a more delicious meal.

Back at the base-station, Kusnadi allowed volunteers to treat his bloodied foot. Before he limped off – a very relieved man – he gave me his copy of the *Nahjul Balaghah*. I have it before me as I write. Its covers are blistered by rainwater, its spine warped, its pages foxed and buckled. There is a passage in it highlighted in blue ballpoint. In a letter to one of his sons, dated around 657 CE, the Caliph Ali wrote:

"Pilgrims have willingly accepted the sufferings, troubles and hazards of The Way, leaving behind their friends, enduring scarcities of food and comfort during the pilgrimage so they may reach the journey's end – a happy place. They willingly bear all discomforts and do not begrudge any expenditure by way of alms and charities, and helping the poor and the needy. Every step they take towards their goal, however tiring and exhausting, is a happy event in their lives."

On Mount Lawu that night I was one face in a shadowy snapshot of Java's pilgrimage culture. It is a dense, batik-like pattern of contradictions. Seriousness collides with laughter, curiosity with bewilderment, piety with scepticism, hope with resignation, escapism with nuts-and-bolts practicality, stoicism with exuberance, individualism with the comfort of a crowd, intense spirituality with (in many places, but not on Mount Lawu) the joy of shopping.

Java's pilgrimage culture, with its diversity and multitude of contradictions, is a rebuke to the standardised fundamentalism that has been gaining ground in Indonesia's religious landscape since the 1980s. In the rhetoric of this orthodoxy the "real" Islam is pure and exclusive. Piety comes from obedience to religious authority and its rules.

Local pilgrimage is anything but pure and exclusive, or rigidly authoritarian. It is powerfully Islamic but it fuses Islam with local history, the ancient power of place and a pastiche of devotional practices with roots deep in the pre-Islamic past. Quietly but tenaciously – just outside the great echo chamber of public space – it is growing as fast as the higher profile neo-orthodoxy.

The ritual centre and historical beginning point of Islam is in the *haram ain*, the twin holy cities of Mecca and Medina in modern Saudi Arabia. Around this ancient centre brilliant civilisations have sprouted and wilted from roots in the revelations of the Prophet Muhammad. At various times their brilliance has dominated the Arab Middle East, Turkey and the Balkans, large parts of Africa, greater India, Central Asia, Iran, even Iberian Europe, once known as Al-Andalus.

In the early decades of the twenty-first century a quiet revolution is happening. The centre of Islamic energy is shifting – has *already* shifted – far to the east. Indonesia is the new Andalus. It was once a peripheral land in the world of Islam, but no longer. With Islam at its centre, it is building unprecedented prosperity within well-established democratic institutions.

Like the old Andalus, Indonesia is multi-religious. Hinduism, Christianity, Confucianism and Buddhism, plus some indigenous primal religions, manage a *modus vivendi* side-by-side with the majority faith of Islam. True, Indonesia is no utopia of religious tolerance. But despite spot-fires of communal conflict and the smouldering of old ethnic tensions, despite regular reports of religious bigotry and periodic acts of religiously inspired terrorism, and despite growing Islamic conservatism, slowly and precariously a social order is emerging based on a secular constitution, the rule of law, and flawed, but resilient, religious tolerance that is adapting well to the environment of modernity.

This is not because Indonesians are blessed with some special generosity of spirit. Rather it is a gift of colonial rule. When European greed staked its claim over the islands of Southeast Asia it embraced a variety of cultures and religious traditions. The arbitrary boundaries of the Dutch East Indies took in Bali, Flores, Manado, Papua and Timor where Muslims are a minority. Today, if aggressive Islamic fundamentalism were to be left unchecked – the movement to establish an Islamic state, for example – it could trigger a secessionist backlash in the regions where Muslims remain a minority, putting at risk Indonesia's hard-won and essentially artificial unity. Nationalism would not allow that to happen.

Another guarantor of tolerance (admittedly a flaky guarantor) is the country's rising prosperity. From the beginning, commerce in the islands of Southeast Asia has been multi-ethnic and multi-religious. The old ports of Melaka, Banten, Surabaya, Makassar and Batavia were filled with indigenous Indonesians speaking a score of different languages, plus Europeans, Chinese, Arabs and Indians. The economic miracle of Singapore is their modern descendant. Today the booming tourist island of Bali is a case study in the productivity – indeed the commercial necessity – of inter-communal trust underpinned by religious tolerance. In 2002 and 2005, Muslim fanatics killed a total of 222 people in bomb attacks that hit hard at the Balinese economy. But today Muslim investors, entrepreneurs, managers and rank-and-file workers continue to make money in Bali side-by-side with Balinese Hindus. Contrary to popular belief, Bali is not primarily a playground for foreign tourists. Rather, it is crowded with millions of cashed-up Muslim tourists, most of them from the neighbouring islands of Indonesia. The tallest annual spike in visits to the island coincides not with the holidays of Europe, East Asia and Australia, but with the Muslim festival of Idul Fitri (*Aid ul-Fitr*).

And as the pages of this book will show, there is an influential legacy of tolerance that, in Java at least, springs from the ancient, inclusive power of place, and finds expression in the stories and practices of local pilgrimage.

Indonesia's population is now around 260 million of whom close to 90% are Muslims, making it easily the biggest Muslim country in the world. This is a statistical commonplace that has slipped under the radar of academia and the mainstream media beyond Southeast Asia. Most Islam-watchers are stuck in a kind of time warp, fixated on the hatreds and decay of the old Muslim heartland in the Middle East. Sure, Indonesia is part of the global Islamic community – the *ummah* – so to some degree it reflects the grandeur, diversity, turbulence, piety and the moral squalor of the Islamic world at large. But the mirror it holds up to that wider world is surprisingly small. There is much beyond its frame that the world does not see. The fact is, Indonesian Islam has a personality that sets it apart from the ancient hub of the Islamic world. Even Indonesia's island-strewn geography – a world of twisting seaways, thick forests, water-filled rice fields, heavy rain and tropical humidity – contrasts with the vast land masses of Islam's old heart with their deserts, oases, arid uplands, mountains, grassland steppes and dry air.

Indonesian Islam sources much (but far from all) of its uniqueness in the ancient civilisation of Java. Populated today by well over 130 million people, Java is the demographic keel of Indonesia, also its cultural and political heart. It hosts three major ethno-linguistic groups: the Sundanese in the west, the Javanese in central and most of east Java, and the Madurese in east Java and the adjacent island of Madura. Layered over these indigenous peoples are the migrants who have flocked to Java from the country's thousands of outer islands, even from beyond the borders of Indonesia. Java's peoples, whether indigenous or migrant, are overwhelmingly Sunni Muslims following the Shafi'i school of law.

The shrine custodian stooped, lifted the hem of a thick batik curtain and crawled under it into the darkness beyond. I followed on my hands and knees. We sat cross-legged on the floor inside. A few scratches of light crept through the roof tiles filling the space with faint phosphorescence. In front of me stood an indistinct bell-shaped mass. The custodian flicked at a cigarette lighter. With a pair of tongs he picked up a lump of incense and held it over the flame. After a few seconds the incense flared dragging shaky fingers of shadow across the copper mask of his face. He placed the smouldering lump on a small clay brazier. Muscles of white smoke rippled up into the wide-open mouth of an iron chimney pipe that disappeared into the dimness above. The air filled with the sharp sweet scent of rose-perfumed charcoal.

The custodian cleared his throat and leaned forward as if collecting his thoughts. Looking at the floor, he sent a sidelong glance in my direction.

"What's your name again?" he asked in a low voice.

"George. From Australia."

"Ah, yes, I remember. And your purpose?"

"Good fortune for my family and a safe journey home for me."

He sat up straight and adjusted his tight-fitting batik head cloth.

He poked at the incense with his tongs and took a deep breath. Looking ahead he spoke firmly in ultra-respectful high Javanese.

"My humble apologies, Your Grace. I come before you to introduce Your Grace's grandson ..."

He paused.

"Your name again ...?" he whispered.

"George."

"... Your Grace's grandson George."

I was in the shrine of Nyai Agĕng Bagĕlèn, the Grand Lady of Bagelen, mythic matriarch of the Bagelen region sixty kilometres west of Jogjakarta in Central Java. It was a small, brick and plaster building, austere but picturesque, with whitewashed walls, glossy moss-green tiled floors and a brown tiled roof above the green and yellow paint-work of its doors and shuttered windows. Opposite the entry door, at the end of a short, roofed walkway, stood a simple open-sided rest pavilion, and beyond it a carefully tended garden with a canopy of trees shading its neat, sandy yard.

Minutes earlier I had been sitting in the shrine's porch chatting with Ibu Astuti, a thirty-year-old mother of two from the nearby city of Purworejo. Her four-year-old son, Alfian, had been tumbling about the porch, playing with visitors. Astuti grabbed his arm and pulled him down beside her. Her face – framed in a bright blue *hijab* headscarf – was radiant as she folded down his collar and pinched away an imaginary speck of dust on his cheek.

"We first came here five years ago," she said, nodding towards her husband who was staring at his mobile phone. "After four years of marriage we were still childless so we came here and I paid my respects to the Grand Lady. Shortly afterwards I fell pregnant and our son was born ... and here he is. Now we have a baby daughter too."

JAVA'S INNER ARCHIPELAGO 25

She didn't seem at all perturbed that I was scribbling details of her personal life into my notebook.

"When I woke up this morning I felt someone calling me. It was an inner call, but it came from somewhere beyond me. I think it came from the Grand Lady. Anyway, that's why we're here. We came at once by motorbike. We couldn't say no. She is like the head of our family."

In packets of terse, earthy language Ibu Astuti told me the story of Nyai Agĕng Bagĕlèn.

"The Grand Lady had very pendulous breasts. This was a problem when she sat at her loom. Her nipples might get tangled in the threads of her weaving, which would be painful ..." she pursed her lips at her small son and raised her eyebrows "... wouldn't it?"

Alfian gazed up at her with round eyes and nodded.

"So she flipped her breasts over her shoulders and her children were able to suckle from behind as she worked. One day as she was weaving she sensed that one of her children was suckling from behind. She looked around and was startled to see that a black calf was drinking from her breast. Her children were nowhere to be seen."

Astuti was enjoying the story. A big smile connected the two sides of her headscarf.

"The Grand Lady accosted her husband. She shouted at him – Where are our children!? – but he didn't know. He was busy milling soya beans and rice. Unfortunately he had ground up his children together with the beans and rice."

Alfian pressed close to his mother.

"His carelessness annoyed the Grand Lady so she whacked the mortar stone he was using so hard its contents went flying. Soya beans and rice grains fell like heavy rain over the surrounding countryside mixed with the remains of the Grand Lady's children. Instantly everything turned fertile. She then went into her bedroom to calm down. She meditated there with such intensity that she vanished."

Astuti looked around.

"And this is where she vanished. Right here. *Alhamdulillah* – Allah be praised – people built a stupa here to mark the spot."

Java's distant past has left the island with a dazzling legacy of temple monuments. Many were sites of religious pilgrimage in pre-Islamic times, as the shrine of Nyai Agĕng Bagĕlèn probably was. Today high profile tourist attractions like the temple monuments of Borobudur and Prambanan are not especially important as living pilgrimage destinations, not unless you define secular tourism as a kind of pilgrimage. In effect they are profitable but mute exhibits in an island-wide museum.[1]

But Java also hosts *living* pilgrimage sites that are very far from fragile echoes of a pre-modern time. Their role in grass-roots religion is already immense, and today it is growing fast. (I'll consider the reasons for this in the final chapter.) The tombs of the famous Nine Saints – the *Wali Sångå* – are the pinnacle of a pilgrimage pyramid that embraces more than one hundred major holy places across Java and Madura. At least ten of them top one million visits a year. There are dozens of second tier sites that host at least half-a-million visitors a year, and scores of third tier sites

---

1 Candi Borobudur attracts tens of thousands of Buddhist pilgrims to the annual Waisak commemoration usually held in April, and Candi Prambanan hosts an annual Hindu ritual, Tawuran, that likewise draws big crowds of religiously motivated visitors. Apart from these events the two sites are important almost wholly as secular tourist attractions, nationalist symbols of Indonesia's cultural antiquity.

that manage to attract hundreds of thousands.

The focal point of most pilgrimage sites is a grave that houses the remains of a revered figure from the past. It usually takes the form of a stone ledger or wooden slab with an upright grave marker at each end. The markers are mostly plain, perhaps with a modest decoration or inscription. A few – like the headstone on the grave of Sharifah Ambami at the Aer Mata burial ground in Madura – are covered in beautifully carved floral ornamentation. Upright grave markers are usually wrapped respectfully in white, green or amber cambric, sometimes satin. More often than not the grave lies under a cube-shaped cloth or lace canopy, looking like an old-style four-poster bed. Some holy graves lie in the open air but most are housed in a small chamber called a *cungkup* that is often open at the sides. At major sites the *cungkup* stands like a small house surrounded by a tiled or carpeted floor inside a more spacious burial chamber, like a box within a box. Here pilgrims sit in ragged, circular ranks facing the *cungkup* and the sometimes invisible or mysteriously indistinct holy grave inside it.

Not all pilgrimage sites are gravesites. Some are built around a revered artefact (as the shrine of Nyai Agĕng Bagĕlèn is) or they may be a place where a concentration of power has "melted" the landscape, creating a cave, or a twisted tree or perhaps a mysterious emptiness. Some pilgrimage sites that look like graves are in fact traces (*patilasan*) or memorials that remind visitors of a significant event that happened there.

Pilgrims normally arrive in groups and their devotions can be varied. A leader will lead his party in recitations from the Qur'ān, including the powerful Throne Verse (verse 255 from the Surah Al-Baqarah) and the popular 36th Surah Ya Sin. The opening surah of the Qur'ān, Al-Fātiḥah, is always in the mix, often presented as a "gift" to the deceased or repeated several times as a kind of refrain. There may also be singing – sometimes quite raucous – of *ṣalawat* songs invoking Allah's blessing on the Prophet Muhammad. The group will fall into a chanted chorus of short phrases repeated over and over, especially "There is no god but Allah" (*La ilaha illallah*), called the *tahlil* chant in Indonesia. The leader of the group may say a prayer in Arabic, often mixed with Javanese or another Indonesian language. As his flock click their prayer beads, or read the prayers from small prayer books, or even follow the prayers on their mobile phones, he will plead for Allah's blessings on the Prophet Muhammad as well as on the other prophets and saints of Islam, including Java's local saints. He will ask Allah to forgive those who have gone ahead into the afterlife, to accept their deeds and imperfect piety, and give them a secure place at His side. He will plead for Allah's blessings on the pilgrim group, including safety for them on their journey home. The leader's sometimes lengthy prayer is accompanied by chorused cries of *"Amin!"* from the group.

At many holy tombs the standard litany is spiced with devotions of a decidedly non-standard kind, though permission to perform them varies wildly across Java and Madura. They include offerings of perfume, the scattering of flower petals on the holy grave, the burning of incense, and the giving of small gifts like cigarettes, food, tea, and cash. Some pilgrims expect a take-away reward for their devotions. They bring bottles of water to be charged with the power of the saint, they drink sanctified water from *"zamzam"* wells and fill bottles (sometimes jerry cans) with it, they scoop up flower petals that have absorbed the saint's power on the top of his grave, they rub their clothes or other possessions on the grave or adjacent parts of the tomb chamber, they waft incense smoke over their faces and breathe it in deeply.

Pilgrims regularly plead for personal favours (in Javanese: *ngalap bĕrkah*, to grab a blessing) or make a *nadhar* promise, vowing to repay Allah or a saint in some fashion if their plea is granted. Outside the tomb chamber they may take part in a ritual *slamĕtan* meal, or tear apart a mini-mountain of food in a *rĕbutan* ritual, or help to replace the power-charged cloth canopy that hangs over the tomb.

The history and management of a site is in the hands of a site custodian called a key-keeper (*juru kunci* or *kuncèn*). The key-keeper may function as a shaman-like intermediary, praying on behalf of the visitor or dispensing amulets charged with the kindly power of the saint. In some places, probably in most, there is a team of site custodians. At some the job is done by women. It is a prestigious office and usually a financially rewarding one.

For the crowds of foreign tourists who visit Indonesia, for business people, for most academics and researchers, even for many big-city Indonesians, the colourful, crowded pilgrimage sites of Java are little known and not always easy to see. With a few spectacular exceptions they are modest in the bricks-and-mortar sense, in fact positively self-effacing compared with monumental forebears like Borobudur and Prambanan. So they are protected from tourist industry hype that strives to whip up veneration of bigness – big monuments and big buildings. If they are monumental at all it is in the towering, sprawling edifices of their stories. Even these are half hidden in the esoteric garb of Java's regional languages.

The shrine of Nyai Agĕng Bagĕlèn represents much that is typical in Java's contemporary pilgrimage culture. Like many sites (but far from all) it is low profile. At the roadside a simple roofed gate and a small sign reading Bagĕlèn Burial Ground mark its otherwise easily missable entrance. But it is well known to local people, and by word of mouth it attracts visitors from far beyond its immediate surrounds. It is an enclave of stillness a short, but symbolically measureless, distance from the noisy highway that skirts the Menoreh Mountains to the north and gouges a traffic-choked scar across rice fields and coconut groves between Jogjakarta and Purworejo.

Most of Java's pilgrimage sites are similarly off the beaten track. Most don't appear on modern maps or make it into the pages of a Lonely Planet guidebook. They belong to an older geography. They form an array of landmarks inherited from the distant past that today are buried under the new geography of cities, highways, ports, railroads, factories, plantations, administrative boundaries and tourist attractions. But the old topography is still there. It is filled with spirit guardians, holy men and holy women, and Muslim missionary-saints all voyaging across a sea of stories. It is a world away from the new topography, which is mostly "empty" – more like a tradeable commodity than a living temple. The old places roost at the top of staircases on steep hillsides or lie in the darkness of caves or shelter in the few tiny scraps of forest still left on Java. They crouch behind high-profile mosques or under curving arbours of trees in quiet villages. They are in district-level towns – Blora, Tuban, Kediri, Demak, Tegal, Karawang, Sumedang, Banten Lama, Kudus, Magelang, Jombang, Mojoagung, Gresik – or in the cluttered old quarters of the island's major cities.

In their ritual cycles most sites obey a chronology that puts them out of sync with standard calendars and the working hours of businesses and offices. For certain purposes Java still sticks to its ancient five-day week, the *pasar*. When the five days of the *pasar* are partnered with the seven days of the universal seven-day week (called a *minggu*) it produces a cycle thirty-five days in length called a *lapan*. Certain *lapan* days, especially Friday Kliwon, Friday Lĕgi and Tuesday Kliwon are auspicious. The Islamic *hijri* year – a lunar year – is eleven days shorter than the standard Gregorian – or solar – year of 365 days, so annual occasions like the Islamic Fasting Month (Ramadhan), New Year's Day (the first of Muharram), the Feast of Sacrifice (Idul Adha) and the commemoration of a saint's death (*haul*) never have the same "standard" calendar date from one year to the next. *Lapan* days and *hijri* dates in combination with dates in the Gregorian calendar generate intricate cycles of wheels within wheels that give each pilgrimage site a unique signature of ritual events. Add to this the transformative chemistry of night when many sites awaken to reveal their most authentic selves, and you have a ritual timetable that hides itself from ready visibility.

Pilgrimage places are embedded deep in Java's oral culture. This means above all the culture of storytelling. Javanese speak of "the where-from and where-to of things" (*sangkan paraning dumadi*). This is what the stories of pilgrimage are all about. Holy places are libraries of history (the "where-from" of things) and sanctuaries of religious practice with its hope-filled narratives (the "where-to" of things). The stories are usually wildly unhistorical but also dramatic, wacky, poignant, funny, kitschy, uplifting, invariably fantastic yet often revelatory and profoundly true. Few of them are single-track narratives. Almost always they are complicated by variations, even contradictions. It is easy to get lost in the tangled deltas of pilgrimage narratives. Industrialised culture demands standardisation, and to some degree this book defers to that culture, hiding narrative variation behind the necessity to be economical.

Back at the shrine of Nyai Agĕng Bagĕlèn the custodian wound up his petition to the Grand Lady as the scarlet glow faded from his incense burner. My eyes had adjusted to the dark and I saw a stone stupa within arm's reach in front of me. It was like a jumbo-sized, squat, scuba diver's air bottle, black and about one and a half metres high by a metre in diameter. On top there was a low-sided, open, box-like impression, suggesting that at one time a pillar, or perhaps an obelisk or small steeple, might have fitted into it.

The custodian scooped up some flower petals from the foot of the stupa and wrapped them in a piece of banana leaf, fastening the package with toothpick-size pins of bamboo. He handed the package to me telling me it would give me safety on my trip home. In return I gave him a small amount of cash in an envelope. He slipped it unopened under the mat he was sitting on.

I crawled back under the curtain, swapping the warm shadow-world of the past for the harsh daylight of the present. It took time to make an exit from the porch. I had to greet about twenty smiling faces and shake twenty outstretched hands before I reached the yard and bent to put on my sandals. The crowd's courtesy was much more than the normal warmth of country people. They saw my presence as a tribute to the Grand Lady, proof that their respected matriarch had pulling power that reached far beyond Java into the semi-mythic lands of the great overseas.

The friendly visitors were all Muslims. As I walked down the shady path towards the highway I wondered how they reconciled their devotions at a stone stupa with their Islamic faith. Researchers struggling to trace the dynamics of religious change in modern Java seem to be unanimous in one thing: syncretic Javanised Islam is currently on the run, pushed hard by the forces of conservative, orthodox piety. In this "authentic" guise Islam is hostile to the veneration of any image or object that might tempt believers away from single-minded worship of the One God, Allah.

This book will test that perception. It is a perception that only holds water if one assumes that Java's unique religious heritage and Indonesia's pre-national history have died or are irrelevant to the present. In Bagelen, as elsewhere, they live. To illustrate, there is an old story that helps the people of Bagelen stay strong in Islam while honouring their semi-divine local ancestor.

In 1832 the Dutch rulers of Java appointed one of their Javanese allies Radèn Tuměnggung Cåkrånagårå the First as district governor of Purworejo, the region that embraces Bagělèn. One day as Cåkrånagårå was meditating in a mosque in Purworejo he fell asleep. His nodding head came to rest against the cylindrical stone block at the base of one of the mosque's wooden pillars. He dreamed that a woman of commanding and haughty appearance came to him instructing him to remove the stone block, take it to Bagělèn, and build a structure there to house it. It was to be, she said, a place of pilgrimage for her descendants.

It seems unlikely that the stupa in Nyai Agěng Bagělèn's shrine is in fact the stone plinth from a pillar in the mosque at Purworejo. There are nine similar but much smaller stupas in the garden outside the walls of the shrine. Most likely the story evolved as a means of incorporating a venerated pre-Islamic site and an ancient Buddhist matriarch into the world of Islam. Possibly the site was once a Buddhist sanctuary or small *vihara*. By redefining the stupa as an artefact from a mosque, Islam exerts a symbolic hold over the shrine, reaching out to embrace the crabby Grand Lady and making her one of its own.

In this respect the shrine is not unusual. Its fusion of holy ground, memorable story and religious devotions is almost normal in modern Java. It joins a hundred or more similar places, big and small, that form a sprawling inner archipelago across the island, even spilling into islands beyond Java. It is an archipelago that mirrors the island-laden geography of Indonesia. The countless atolls of pilgrimage are havens of refuge and respite, repositories of memory and boulders of resistance in the currents of modern change. They are also places that today are embedded solidly in the practices of everyday life for scores of millions of people. For these modern Indonesians saint veneration and local pilgrimage are central to their Islamic identity and the practice of their religion.

This book travels deep under the surface of Java to explore this world, largely unknown to outsiders. Here modernity, a globalised economy, Indonesian nationalism and Islamic orthodoxy have flooded an ancient civilisation – flooded it, but not drowned it. A hundred or more crowded pilgrimage sites rise from beneath the surface of modern Indonesia testifying to the survival of old Java.

In the following pages I will try to steer a course through this inner archipelago, riding on the rips and tides of faith, religious practice and pre-modern history that today still run strong under the choppy surface of Indonesia's modernity. Each landfall will reveal a different country and bring an invitation to explore a hinterland of stories. Each chapter will weave together place, story, people, devotional practices and my own bewildered experience of pilgrimage in Java.

Please join me.

# 1

# Drawing a line to Mecca

SUNAN KALIJÅGÅ AND THE CONTEST
FOR AUTHORITY IN JAVANESE ISLAM

"You know the confession of faith, the *Kalimah Shahādah*, don't you?"

"Yes, I do."

"In Arabic?"

"Yes."

"So why don't you say it? Why don't you just convert!"

It was a blunt demand, but friendly. Opposite me, staring into my face, sat Wahyudi from Medan in north Sumatra, and beside him his brother Mahmudi from Jogjakarta. Wahyudi's wife, clad in a black kaftan with a black *hijab* scarf drawn tightly around her face, sat behind them. She was listening intently but stayed silent, occasionally resting her chin on her husband's shoulder, looking at me like his thoughtful *alter ego*.

We were sitting on the steps in the front portico of the Grand Mosque in Demak, a small town about twenty-five kilometres east of Semarang in Central Java. Behind us the portico extended thirty metres left and right. From its gleaming marble floor four giant teak hurdles rose to support the dark ceiling. Heavy beams ran from hurdle to hurdle down its length, and between the hurdles hung several antique chandelier lamps with bulbous smoked glass shades on their many arms. At one end an enormous *bědhug* drum stood suspended in a teak frame. Its deep, resonant thumps would summon the faithful to prayer on special occasions. Behind the portico, through a row of glass-panelled doors, the high interior of the mosque proper was dominated by four massive cylindrical wooden pillars that supported the building's three-tiered pyramid shaped roof. Behind the mosque lay the tombs of the region's patriarchs, the revered rulers of Demak, Java's first independent Islamic state. A non-stop murmur of voices and chanting rose from the pilgrim crowds eddying through the complex.

When I politely declined to utter the confession of faith Wahyudi was amazed, as if I had refused a generous free offer in a department store. It was such an easy thing to do … just say in Arabic "I bear witness, there is no god but Allah and I bear witness Muhammad is His prophet." Could it be so hard to pronounce these simple words? Would anything bad happen to you? Islam is a light and easy garment to wear. Why not put it on?

I pondered my options. Given the location I figured it might be unwise to reveal I was an atheist.

"To properly utter the confession of faith," I said, "I must be sincere. I need *niat* – undistracted intent and sincere faith. But Allah has not given me *niat*. It would be dishonest and disrespectful to utter the confession of faith without *niat*. Don't you think?"

Wahyudi's answer surprised me.

"Not at all," he said. "To acquire *niat* you need to join the Islamic community, and you do that by saying the confession of faith. After you have joined up you can study the teachings of Islam and resolve your doubts. Only then can you acquire real conviction. But the first step is to join the community. Being a Muslim is like working in an office. In order to understand how the office works and to do your job well you need to join the office staff. That's where the confession of faith comes in. It's like a letter of appointment."

For Wahyudi, Islam was in the first instance the *ummah*, the Muslim community. What Muslims believe comes from the community and must be learned from the community little by little. The community was like a uniform. It would take time to become all that the uniform stood for. It was a view of religion at odds with an outlook that puts the epiphany of personal conversion first. Articles of faith were important, of course, but they had to be learned, and you couldn't learn them instantly from outside the community of faith. My mind leapt back to the early days of Islam's expansion. As the new religion swept across the Middle East and North Africa this is what conversion must have looked like. Sign up first, join us, we represent the truth and you will learn what that truth is if you come with us.

Half an hour earlier, I had noticed Wahyudi inside the Grand Mosque. With his wife and brother he had been walking gingerly around the four massive, dark-polished wooden pillars that support the high ceiling of the prayer chamber. He stopped at each pillar and placed his hand against it, but at the back pillar on the right he paused, leaned forward and pressed his forehead reverently against the wood as if performing an upright prostration. The pillar was the famous *såkå tatal* made centuries ago from planks and spars and off-cuts of timber that had been bound together to form a solid column. A board at the foot of the pillar announced who had made it: Sunan Kalijågå. Today he is Java's most beloved saint despite – or more likely, because of – his bandit pedigree.

Everyone knows the story of the *såkå tatal* pillar.

More than five hundred years ago, as Muslims began to set up mini states along the northern shores of Hindu-Buddhist Java, a cohort of religious teachers known as the *Wali Sångå* – the Nine Saints – decided to build a mosque in Demak. At the time Demak was a riverside trading settlement clipped from thick forest close to the northern coastline. Five centuries on, silt has pushed the coast some ten kilometres away from the modern town and the forests that once towered around it have long disappeared.

According to popular tradition the mosque was built in one night. Four of the Nine Saints were given the job of finding trunks of wood to make a quartet of pillars that would support the building's high, pyramid-shaped roof. Three of them – Sunan Gunung Jati, Sunan Bonang and Sunan Ampèl – each located a massive tree, cut it down and dragged it into Demak. But the fourth saint, Sunan Kalijågå, had been away meditating on the distant south coast and turned up late. He didn't have time to go hunting for a tree, so on the night of construction he contributed a pillar made from off-cuts of timber that littered the construction site. He glued them together and bound them with cords and iron hoops. It was just as strong as the other three pillars.

Today each of the four central pillars is labelled with the name of the saint responsible for it. In the quiet hours between the five *salat* prayer times, visitors slip into the airy ambience of the mosque and walk from pillar to pillar touching each of them. Invariably they linger reverently at Sunan Kalijågå's *såkå tatal*. From time to time flower offerings are placed at the foot of the pillar, much to the annoyance of mosque officials.

The interior of Demak's antique Grand Mosque.
The pillar on the right is the *såkå tatal* made by Sunan Kalijågå.

The Grand Mosque in Demak is one of the oldest in Java, possibly built some time in the 1470s. For many it is a model representing the house of Islam. The famous pillar is seen as a miracle sent down the ages by Sunan Kalijågå to enlighten the present. Like the *fascis* bundle of ancient Rome – rods of wood bound with leather straps – the *såkå tatal* pillar symbolises collective solidarity and authority. Strength, it says, lies in the bonds of unity and community. It tells Muslims to put aside doctrinal rigidity and find strength in their diversity. It says, as Pak Wahyudi did, that the common spirit of the *ummah* – the Islamic community in all its diversity – is the pillar that supports faith.

For a few the pillar is also an icon of modern nationalism. It mirrors the official motto of the Republic of Indonesia, *Bhinneka Tunggal Ika*, "In diversity there is unity". According to one author the *såkå tatal* is "a national treasure giving expression to national aspirations and the nation's spiritual essence." Part of that spiritual essence is the idea of a state across the islands of Southeast Asia "which provides protection for all ethnicities, where people are free to choose whatever religion, or profess whatever faith, they believe in".

Back in the 1980s strongman President Soeharto even spent state funds to renovate Demak's Grand Mosque. He attended the inauguration of the work where he proclaimed the official view of the Grand Mosque's role in modern Indonesia, paraphrased here by historian Nancy Florida.

> President Soeharto assured the assemblage that the restoration of the Mosque was neither a waste of money nor a luxury, but integral to the nation's development – in the largest sense of the word. Indeed the president saw the restoration as part of an effort to build up the nation's "spiritual capital" (*modal rohani*) into a source of working capital that would powerfully propel all aspects of national development.

The Nine Saints were among the earliest teachers of Islam in Java in the 1400s and 1500s. Their tombs dot the knobbly line of the north coast, from Cirebon on the border between Central Java and West Java, to Surabaya in the east. At each tomb souvenir sellers do a busy trade in pictures that depict the saints posing formally in a "team photo". History has not bequeathed us any contemporary likenesses of the nine, nor is it likely they ever met as a group. In fact their exact number and the details of their lives are indistinct in the haze of distant history. Some even doubt they existed at all. This is an unsettling claim for many Javanese who see the Nine Saints as cherished patriarchs, symbols of wisdom and gentle authority. But it is exactly for this reason the team photo is interesting. It is not historical but rather a modern imagining of sainthood projected on to the evidence-bereft screen of the past.

A souvenir portrait of Java's Nine Saints for sale at many pilgrimage sites. Back row left to right: Maulana Malik Ibrahim (often called Sunan Grĕsik) buried in Gresik; Sunan Ampèl, buried in the centre of Surabaya; Sunan Bonang, buried in Tuban; Sunan Giri, buried in Gresik. Front row, Sunan Kudus, buried in Kudus; Sunan Muriå, buried at Colo high on the slopes of Mount Muria; Sunan Kalijågå, buried in Kadilangu, Demak; Sunan Drajad, buried at Paciran between Tuban and Surabaya; and Sunan Gunung Jati, buried in Cirebon.

There is something matter-of-fact yet elusive about the faces in the team photo. Beturbanned (except for Sunan Kalijågå front centre) and bewhiskered, the images are clichéd but each has a stilted individuality. Headdress, beard, moustache and jacket are assembled in slightly different combinations of colour and style, like puppets in the cast of a shadow play. They are impassive but friendly. Their eyes stare with placid, unflappable conviction. They radiate authority without being threatening or overbearing.

There are two layers of authority, among many, that the picture spotlights. Viewed from one angle the saints line up like a town council or the executive board of a corporation. They embody the immense and very modern authority of management and bureaucracy. Viewed from another angle they line up like relatives at a family reunion. In this guise they embody the primal, comfortable, all-embracing authority of the extended family. Bureaucracy and family: there is nothing exclusively Javanese about these obsessions, but the Nine Saints are distinctively Javanese exemplars of the two institutions.

Most pilgrims at the tombs of the Nine Saints accept as fact that they met from time to time as a council to discuss missionary strategy and resolve issues in Islamic law or theology. Commonly the council is given a name: the Nine Saints Mission Council (*Majlis Dakwah Wali Sångå*). Tradition says that the Grand Mosque in Demak was the most frequently used venue for their meetings but the saintly committee is thought to have assembled in other places too. Adjacent to the tomb of Sheikh Abdul Muhyi at Pamijahan, south of Tasikmalaya in West Java, lies the Safarwadi Cave. Deep in its furnace-hot interior there are four natural chambers, the biggest of which is called the Grand Mosque. Pilgrims and local villagers believe the Nine Saints met there for prayers, travelling to the cave at warp speed through tunnels from their respective hometowns.

When I visited the tomb of another saint, Sheikh Jumadil Kubro in Semarang, the site custodian, Pak Afwan, described how the Mission Council was established and the first appointments made. Seated cross-legged on the floor and leaning studiously across his knee-high desk, he told me that Sheikh Jumadil Kubro came to Java from Turkey some time in the 1400s. After looking around, he returned to the Middle East and pleaded for an audience with the Ottoman ruler Sultan Mehmed the First. Islam in Java was in a terrible state, the sheikh reported. He suggested that the sultan summon a number of powerful and charismatic *ulama* clerics from the Middle East and North Africa to discuss how mission activities could best be developed in that far-flung outpost of Islam. The sultan agreed, the meeting took place, and an executive decision was taken. Nine learned *ulama* – each with his own portfolio of specialist expertise – would be appointed to teach Islam in Java.

Pak Afwan waved a small pamphlet across the table stirring a damp puff of movement in the still air.

"It's all written down here. They decided that the nine missionaries would be divided into three groups – three task forces, if you like. They also divided Java into three administrative divisions – marketing regions, if you like. One group of three would go to East Java, another group of three to Central Java and three would go to West Java. Their term of service would be one hundred years, and if any of them died or left the island before the end of that period, a meeting would be called to appoint a replacement. The nine *ulama* were selected, formally installed, and given the title "The Nine Saints".

I protested.

"Each of the Nine Saints lived at a different time over a period of about two hundred years. They couldn't possibly have met all at the same time."

Pak Afwan had a ready answer.

"As stipulated by the Ottoman sultan, the membership was fixed at nine but there was a regular turnover of appointees. Only one of the original appointees – Maulana Malik Ibrahim – was still around when the later, better known, cohort of Nine Saints took up their posts."

Today the process of conversion is unthinkable without the retrospective application of this management model, and it is even more unthinkable without the scaffolding of the traditional extended family. In most folk accounts of Java's conversion, Jumadil Kubro not only initiated the corporate management model, he also sired the line of teachers who implemented it. By most accounts, seven of the later generation of Nine Saints were directly related to one another through common descent from Jumadil Kubro, while the other two saints were grafted into Jumadil Kubro's line through marriage. So the conversion of Java was a family affair, as if the complex operation of preaching Islam could only be managed and have credibility within the powerful, closely integrated and trusted structure of an extended family.

Not a shred of uncontestable evidence can be produced to show that all the Nine Saints ever convened as a council or belonged to a single extended family. But bureaucracy and family are at the heart of modern Indonesian society. The ideas are so powerful that the history of Islam seems unimaginable without them. Despite its carefully drawn antique façade, the popular souvenir portrait is a glimpse of how Java is thinking today.

In the front centre of the Nine Saints team stands a figure dressed differently from his eight companions. This is Sunan Kalijågå. Unlike his fellow saints, who are always clad in the turbans and flowing robes of what is imagined to be the costume of Middle Eastern piety, Sunan Kalijågå wears traditional Javanese dress: a close-fitting batik headcloth (*blangkon*), a mandarin-collared jacket (*běskap, sorjan*) made of rough-spun black-and-brown *lurik* cloth, and a long batik sarong. This style of "traditional" men's dress probably developed in the nineteenth century, at least three hundred years after Sunan Kalijågå lived, so it too is a relatively modern reworking of tradition.

Today Kalijågå's life story is told over and over – in mosque sermons, in books and pamphlets, in television dramas, in history lessons at school, and in origin stories attached to the landscape and sacred tombs. He is a very portable culture hero who turns up in countless local tales while at the same time starring in his own over-arching epic. This super-story is an allegory in which Sunan Kalijågå embodies the transformation brought to Java by Islam. In his appearance, his accomplishments and in the events of his life he shows how Islam was "tamed" the Javanese way, in fact became putty in the hands of Java's Muslim converts.

The allegory begins around 1450 with the birth of Radèn Mas Said, son of the local lord of Tuban, a small but important emporium on Java's north coast. The lord was a Muslim who had been appointed vassal ruler of the part-Islamised town by the Hindu king of Måjåpait. His son grew up amid the luxuries of the local palace. Hidden deep in the DNA of the story there is a narrative gene, a fossil remnant of a previous age in the story's evolution. A thousand years of Buddhist presence in Java made the life of Prince Siddhartha – the future Buddha – part of Java's storytelling ambience. Prince Siddharta grew up cushioned by his father from the world beyond the comforts of the palace. Eventually when he ventured into that world and witnessed the reality of age, sickness and death, he decided to abandon his privileges and seek a deeper truth through study and austerities.

Radèn Mas Said also left the palace of his innocence. He seems to have had a falling out with his father when he discovered that the ordinary people of Tuban were starving while his father stockpiled food. He saw that the self-indulgence of his youth had been bought with the suffering of powerless fellow citizens. Outside the palace his first act was to raid his father's warehouse and distribute its food through the town. Then, hiding in a nearby forest, he helped himself to the goods of passing travellers and – like a Javanese Robin Hood – distributed the loot to the needy.

That at least is the story told by the direct descendants of Sunan Kalijågå. But its sheen of virtue is contradicted by other accounts (and there are many). According to a text titled *Suluk Linglung Sunan Kalijågå* (The Very Confused Sacred Song of Sunan Kalijågå) Radèn Mas Said unhinged himself completely from his former life and set off on a spree of violent crime. In keeping with Javanese custom (and to conceal himself from his father) he marked his new circumstances by giving himself a new name: Brandhal Lokåjåyå. *Brandhal* was the brazen marker of his profession – it means "gangster" or "bandit". He spent his days and nights gambling and taking opium. If he lost at dice he robbed and murdered to get more money. At night he broke into people's houses, killing the occupants and taking their possessions. He grabbed the wives of other men, and if a husband found out, Lokåjåyå put him to death without an instant of remorse.

One day in his forest retreat, he saw a lone figure approaching wearing fine white robes that shimmered in the sunlight. Lokåjåyå attacked. According to the *Suluk Linglung* (the basic story is incarnated and embellished many times over outside the covers of the *Suluk*) the wayfarer responded with a miracle. He multiplied himself into three extra men, each a replica of himself. Suddenly Lokåjåyå was surrounded by four identical white-robed figures. One of them felled him with a blow of his staff. He struggled to his feet and tried to run, but his way was blocked and he was again knocked to the ground. Half stunned he tried again to run, but in whichever direction he turned a whirling staff felled him. Lokåjåyå begged for mercy.

A key encounter in the folk history of Islam in Java.
Left, on the cover of a popular book, Brandhal Lokåjåyå
prepares to rob Sunan Bonang. Right, in a fresco on the waterfront
at Tuban, Lokåjåyå keeps guard over the holy staff of Islam while
a forest of pagan unbelief grows around him.

His opponent was the great saint Sunan Bonang who was wielding the staff of Islam. With his all-seeing eye he had noticed that Lokåjåyå was no bandit but a fellow saint ignorant of his sainthood.

"If you truly repent and submit to my will, I have a task for you," said Sunan Bonang.

"Spare my life and I will do whatever you command."

"Take this staff. Never let it go. Stay here and keep guard over it. Do not move."

Lokåjåyå sat down and planted the staff in the soil of Java. He took a firm grip on it and bowed his head in meditation. Sunan Bonang left. It was a year before he came back and in that time the tropical forest – symbol of native paganism – had grown over the meditating bandit. The saint peered into the tangle of trees but could see nothing. Concentrating his mind he set fire to the forest. As it burned away Lokåjåyå came into view bound in tree roots and somewhat singed. He was buried deep in contemplation of the divine and was still holding fast to the staff of Islam.

With a gentle *Assalam alaikum* (Peace be upon you) Sunan Bonang woke him. The former bandit emerged from his trance into spiritual maturity. To mark his elevated status Sunan Bonang gave him a new name, Sheikh Malåyå. The freshly minted sheikh was instructed to head west to Cirebon and there meditate on a riverbank for another year. Sheikh Malåyå set off, repeatedly stopping along the north coast road to teach the truth of Islam.

In Cirebon he established a riverside religious school that soon filled with students. Every night after prayers he would go to the riverbank and meditate. To ward off the beguiling but dangerous forgetfulness of sleep he would slip into the river and meditate for hours immersed to his neck in the cool current, an ascetic practice called *tåpå ngèli*, drifting away in meditation.

After a year he was again visited by Sunan Bonang who, impressed with his commitment, now ordained him a saint. He bestowed a new name on him: Sunan Kalijågå, "the saint who kept a vigil at the river".

Sunan Kalijågå embarked in earnest on his proselytising career. A sprawling metropolis of stories has sprung up around his exploits as a wandering teacher. Along the many avenues and lanes of this narrative city there is a common blueprint of story architecture and a distinctly Javanese style. Sunan Kalijågå adopted some artistic wizardry to help him spread the word. Among his many accomplishments – accomplishments that have grown in stature as his lifetime has receded into history – he was a puppeteer, a master of that most Javanese of arts, the shadow play (*wayang kulit*). In its

classical form, called *wayang purwå*, it draws most of its characters
and the general context for its stories from the Indian *Mahābhārata*
epic. It is astonishing that, in overwhelmingly Muslim Java, the
Hindu gods, heroes, villains, clowns and ogres of the shadow
theatre still cram the imagination. Although the popularity of the
classical shadow theatre is waning in the twenty-first century, its
characters, intricate iconography, symbolism and even its ethics
and philosophy remain core components of Javanese identity. The
Muslim saint Sunan Kalijågå is given the credit for this. Some even
claim he was the inventor of the heavily Hindu-tinted art.

Putting his puppeteering brilliance to work, Sunan Kalijågå
is said to have shown audiences the Islamic reality behind the
ancient Hindu stories, so persuading them to embrace the new
faith. Today, when connoisseurs of the shadow theatre speak of
this there is one example they often cite with a kind of excited
pleasure: the *kalimåsådå*. The term is pre-Islamic, probably a
Javanese transformation of the Sanskrit phrase *Kali-Mahaushadha*,
the magically potent medicine of the goddess Kali. In Old Javanese
literature the *kalimåsådå* becomes an all-powerful weapon in the
form of a book. In shadow plays too the *kalimåsådå* takes the form
of an esoteric book that no one can decipher. It confers immortality
on its owner, the king-hero Yudhistirå.

But for Yudhistirå worldly immortality is a burden. In one
play he makes an appearance in Islamic Demak and laments that,
because he is kept eternally alive by the incomprehensible words
of the *kalimåsådå*, he cannot join his family in the hereafter. A
Muslim holy man, thought by most to have been Sunan Kalijågå,
looks at the *kalimåsådå* and recognises it as the *Kalimah Shahādah*,
the Muslim confession of faith. The testimony consists of two
sentences in Arabic: *Ašhadu 'al lā ilāha illa l-Lāh. Wa 'ashadu*

*'anna muḥammadar rasūlu l-Lāh.* (I bear witness, there is no god beside Allah. And I bear witness, Muhammad is His emissary). When Yudhistirå utters these words he is at once released from the bonds of his eternal present and dies.

It is a brilliant piece of linguistic sleight-of-hand. The most powerful weapon in the *wayang* world turns out to be the Islamic confession of faith. As Yudhistirå – representing the survival of the pre-Islamic past – wanders like a ghost into the Islamic present, the power of the *Kalimah Shahādah* consigns him once and for all to the hereafter that he yearns for.

Muslims of today can go to Demak's Grand Mosque and see the grave of Yudhistirå for themselves. It is a visible clincher that confirms the truth of the story. It lies behind the mosque, lined up with the graves of Islam's fifteenth and sixteenth century pioneers, the contemporaries of Sunan Kalijågå. The grave is labelled "Darmokusumo", one of Yudhistirå's alternative names. Although plain in appearance it is about twice as long as a conventional grave. The stretched length of the grave signals the elevated status of its occupant.

Yudhistirå's grave is the resting place of an idea. Java's Hindu-Buddhist past has been banished to the hereafter by the power of Islam. This has de-fanged Hinduism and made it possible for the shadow theatre to live side-by-side with Islamic hegemony as comfortably as Buddhist Borobudur and Hindu Prambanan do, or, for that matter, the pyramids of Egypt and the ruins of Persepolis.

For many Javanese Sunan Kalijågå's life story is literally true, but for others it is an allegory rather than history. Sunan Kalijågå is an embodiment of Javanese Islam and his life story parallels the evolution of Islam in Java, with each stage marked by a name change. It begins with Islam's comfortable vassalage under Hindu-Buddhist rule (Radèn Mas Said) and proceeds through violence, pillage and war (Brandhal Lokâjâyâ) to peaceful proselytising (Sheikh Malâyâ) and finally to mass conversion and Islam's integration into the culture of Java (Sunan Kalijâgå). The saint's life also captures stages in the development of personal spirituality: from youthful innocence and self-indulgence, to outrage and rebellion, to the awakening of self-awareness and responsibility, and ultimately to the energy and peace unlocked by spiritual maturity.

The story goes that when the Nine Saints were building the Grand Mosque in Demak some time in the second half of the fifteenth century they couldn't agree on the orientation of the building. Muslims are required to pray five times a day towards Mecca, or more precisely, towards the box-like Ka'bah at the centre of the Sacred Mosque, the Masjid al-Haram, in Mecca. This direction is called the *qibla* (*kiblat* in Indonesian and Javanese).

The alignment of the *qibla* is no small matter. For most Muslims it has immense symbolic power. The Qur'ān makes this clear in Surah Al-Baqarah verses 143-144 in which Muslims are instructed to face toward the Sacred Mosque when they perform the ritual *ṣalat* prayer. Those who follow the Prophet are distinguished from those who have turned away from him by the direction they face. A misdirected *ṣalat* prayer, then, is not just an invalid prayer, it is a marker of unbelief.

But how could mosques be precisely aligned in fifteenth century Java halfway around the world from the ritual centre of Islam? The short answer is: they couldn't, at least not precisely. The astrolabe was widely known across the Islamic world and it may have been used. Or perhaps the solar method, called the *hisab rukyah*, was used. Twice a year, on May 28th at 12:18 and July 16th at 12:27 the sun is exactly overhead at the Ka'bah. It casts no shadow. But if you are at a distance from Mecca at the same moment the sun will cast a shadow. Java is eight thousand kilometres away and four hours ahead of Mecca in time. So in Demak at 4.18 pm on May 28th, or at 4.27 pm on July 16th, a line drawn along the shadow cast by an upright stick will point directly at Mecca.

I don't know of any evidence that the solar method was used in fifteenth century Java. Maybe early mosques were simply aligned in the general direction of the holy land to the west. In the case of Demak's Grand Mosque, legend has it the saints yanked the mosque this way and that in a grumpy but unsuccessful attempt to line it up with the Ka'bah. It was Sunan Kalijågå who solved the problem, putting the stamp of his authority on the alignment of the new building. The traditional history *Babad Tanah Jawi* (Clearing the Land of Java) and several other Javanese-language chronicles recount how he did it.

> After the evening prayer Sunan Kalijågå took up a position on the north side of the mosque. With his right hand he reached out to the Ka'bah, while with his left hand he grasped the peak of the mosque's roof. Then he concentrated. At once the Ka'bah appeared, looming over the mosque. Thus he brought the Demak mosque and the Ka'bah into alignment. This was immediately reported to Sunan Bonang who commanded all the saints to come at once to see for themselves. They came and saw that the *qibla* was now properly fixed. They were all greatly relieved.

Disputes about the accuracy of the *qibla* are not new in

Indonesia. The pushing and shoving among the Nine Saints was just the first round in a long tradition of argument over the issue. The first decade of the twenty-first century has produced a new challenge to the authority of Sunan Kalijågå's miraculous quick-fix. Burgeoning use of GPS technology, computers and Google Earth established that many mosques did not point accurately towards the Ka'bah. In fact some were so far off-target it was almost funny (to some). A line drawn west from certain mosques in Java led to Ethiopia, a Christian-majority country a thousand kilometres south of Mecca. For many of the faithful this was a shock. Centuries of pious prayer turned out to have been null and void. And suddenly the ritual soundness of current *ṣalat* devotions was dubious.

Indonesia's elite of conservative Muslim scholars scrambled to calm their congregations. Allah is all-forgiving, some said, and faithful Muslims need not be concerned that their prayers might be unacceptable. Then came a well-intentioned but bumbling official attempt to quell the unease. In January 2010 the government-sponsored Indonesian Council of Muslim Scholars (*Majelis Ulama Indonesia* or *MUI*) issued a *fatwa*, a formal religious ruling (Fatwa MUI no.3, 2010). It explained that if the Ka'bah was not visible, it was enough to simply face in its general direction. If Indonesia was east of Mecca then Mecca must be west of Indonesia and the *qibla*, then, was "in a westerly direction". The Director of Islamic Affairs in the Department of Religion explained that the Muslims of Indonesia had become confused because the country's incessant earthquakes were causing its tectonic plates to swivel, thus shifting mosques away from the direction of the *qibla*.

There was an almost audible gasp of disbelief across the country. Reactions ranged from anger to despair to howls of laughter. Didn't these learned clerics have a smartphone? Or a computer? Didn't they know what a tectonic plate was? Had they ever looked at a map of the world?

Most *fatwas* deal with issues in Islamic law but they are not legally binding, so many mosques simply ignored the new *fatwa*. They continued to face in the more precise north-west direction given by GPS apps and internet sites like *eQibla.com*. In a number of places there was confusion: people were facing in different directions as they assembled to perform the *ṣalat* prayer. Then, just months after the bungled *fatwa*, MUI back-pedalled and issued a new one (no.5, 2010). The *qibla* was now north-west again, with different areas of Indonesia free to determine a variation on this direction in accordance with their own geographical position.

On July 23rd 2010, a few weeks after the announcement of MUI's corrected *fatwa*, around 150 local Muslim leaders were summoned to the Grand Mosque in Demak and told that, thanks to the new *fatwa*, the *qibla* was to be shifted to the north-west along a line determined by experts. Instead of standing in *shaf* rows neatly facing the back wall and at right angles to the side walls of the mosque, worshippers would now stand in rows skewed to the right, half facing the right hand corner.

The arrangement offended local people. There was – as one newspaper delicately put it – "public disquiet". Eighteen months later, on January 12th 2012, a group of teachers and students from Islamic *pěsantrèn* schools around Demak entered the Grand Mosque. They forcibly rearranged the carpets and erased the *shaf* lines insisting on a return to the old *qibla*. Mosque staff tried to stop them and a "vigorous" debate followed, but eventually mosque executives caved in. The old *qibla* was restored.

When I visited the Grand Mosque in 2015 all signs of the new MUI-endorsed *qibla* had vanished and worshippers comfortably bowed in the direction gifted to them half a millennium ago by Sunan Kalijågå. It is worth adding that at the nearby Sunan Kalijågå Mosque, officials and local people ignored the two *fatwas* altogether and refused point-blank to change the *qibla* of their prayers. In fact they even refused to allow formal measurement of the *qibla* at their mosque on the grounds that "it could reduce the authority of Sunan Kalijågå, maybe even destroy that authority altogether".

The scientifically determined *qibla* (the one that lasted just eighteen months at the Demak mosque and didn't get a look-in at the nearby Kalijågå Mosque) is a product of science and technology and is therefore aligned with the attractions of modernity and the prosperity that modernity promises. It is also aligned with a rational, predictable and precise Islam, a variant of Islam that can embrace and welcome technology.

But this *qibla* has no indigenous stories to back it up and to that degree it lacks authority. Worse, the precisely calculated "scientific" *qibla* can be exploited by fundamentalist forces to exert narrow-minded moral and ritual pressure on Muslims, to cast them into a world where ritual precision and sharia conformity are all-important, and where cultural alignment tends to be towards the Middle East rather than towards the world of Javanese tradition.

The saint-determined *qibla* aligns Muslims with Javanese tradition, with the authority of saints, and with religious leaders who acknowledge that authority. It is couched in stories... not just any old story, but stories that are familiar, reassuring and fun, stories that are markers of strong community and traditions peopled by admired characters who mean a lot to those who tell the stories and listen to them.

To some degree the traditional *qibla* also expresses suspicion of modern technology and exasperation with modern government.

This scepticism was one prominent element that drove the group of students and teachers to occupy the Demak mosque, tear up its carpet and force a return to Sunan Kalijågå's *qibla*.

It was a Thursday evening when I left Demak's Grand Mosque. In the gloom of early twilight I hailed a motorcycle taxi and headed across town to the mausoleum of Sunan Kalijågå about two kilometres away. In Java a new day traditionally begins at sundown, not at midnight or dawn. So as night fell I crossed from Thursday into Friday, and at the same time went from Wagé into Kliwon in Java's ancient five-day week. The evening that marks the "dawn" of Friday Kliwon is an especially auspicious time. I knew Sunan Kalijågå's tomb would be crowded.

The motorbike drew up in front of a squat but massive red-brick gate topped by a dark, two-tiered, pyramid roof. A crush of people, their faces dappled in the glitter of fluorescent strip-lights and kerosene lamps, were shuffling over the gate's threshold into a covered, brightly lit shopping arcade. I breathed in the smoke-tinted aroma of fried food and grilled satay kebabs rolling over the tight-packed mass of pilgrim visitors. A hundred metres inside the gate, past scores of small shops and stalls, a squad of women in headscarves and young men wearing white skull-caps elbowed their way into the shuffling column. We were at the entrance to the mausoleum proper where footwear had to be removed. There were two options: buy a plastic supermarket bag from one of the ladies (you put your sandals in the bag and carried them with you) or hire a cardboard box from one of the young men who would keep your sandals in it until you came back.

I took the plastic bag option and jostled forward barefoot with sandals dangling from my arm. An open pavilion came into view where I was invited to sit at a low table, write my name in a guest book and make a donation. I gave Rp.50,000 (about US$4.00 ).

Next stop was the burial chamber itself. It has been renovated and rebuilt many times since the saint's death some time in the early 1500s, but it retains its traditional pyramid-shaped roof made of wooden shingles. The inner burial chamber is normally closed except for special guests and special occasions, but around it a verandah roof extends twenty metres outwards encircling the chamber and sheltering a spacious tiled floor dotted with tombstones. Hundreds of pilgrims were sitting among them in close-packed ranks.

Compressed inside a tide of people I inched forward, toe-length by toe-length, past a white box with a slot in the top. Seated beside it a small man was aggressively rapping on it with a wicker wand. Like others around me I tried to avert my eyes but he fixed a stern gaze on me and whacked the top of the box. I drew a bank note from my shirt pocket and inserted it in the slot.

A few metres on I scraped past what can only be described as a drinks bar. A crowd of women were reaching over one another with plastic cups and empty bottles in their outstretched hands. Using plastic bailers a small crew of men were scooping water from a rotund stone jar and splashing it into the cups and bottles. I found my face pressed against a sign. Drawing back, I took in its message: "Water jar bequeathed by Sunan Kalijågå". The sign explained that the water had been carried in buckets from the nearby river and was intended only for drinking and washing the face. Its stay in the holy water jar had consecrated it, but the sign still needed to allay the health fears of consumers. "This water has been purified in a settling tank and sterilised."

The crush of people fell away and I shoe-horned myself into a space against the back perimeter wall. I slid to the floor and took in the scene. A hubbub of prayer, singing and murmuring filled the air above a choppy sea of swaying heads. Almost everyone seemed to be in groups – families, parties of villagers, school classes – each cluster under the leadership of an older man. Young people were everywhere, even children, and there were as many women as men. Two women – one of them wearing a bizarre kaftan made from an American flag – nursed infant children who somehow were sleeping soundly through the clamour. Leaning against the back wall a trio of young men in black *pèci* fez-caps sat reading the Qur'ān, their lips moving silently, their fingers following the lines on the pages. A heavily built man in front of me kept bending forward and sighing loudly, each couplet of sighs followed by a subdued groan and a whispered "Allaaaah!"

I was sitting amid a family of pilgrims from Surabaya. One of them was an eleven-year-old boy introduced to me as Umar. He was wearing a snowy white, high collared, full length, Arab-style *thawb* tunic, an immaculately ironed formal black jacket and a white turban with a tail hanging down at the back. As his family bowed their heads towards the burial chamber and loudly intoned their prayers he kept glancing at me.

At last he leaned towards me and whispered:

"Can I practise my English with you?"

"Of course," I whispered back. "When you're through with your prayers, let's go out and find something to eat. I'm starving." I added an afterthought. "And bring your parents and your sisters, I bet they're hungry too."

Smiling to himself he turned towards the saint's burial chamber, lowered his head and in a loud, thin voice, broke into fluent Arabic, reciting the Surah Al-Fātiḥah, the first book of the holy Qur'ān.

Praise be to Allah the Lord of the Worlds,

The Compassionate, the Merciful,

Master of the Day of Judgement,

Only You do we worship, and only You do we implore to
help.

Lead us into the right path,

The path of those you have favoured

Not those who have incurred Your wrath or have gone
astray.

# 2

# "Thirsty? You can drink my piss!"

## Sunan Bonang on the edge of Islam's expansion

I was standing in the *alun-alun* square in the centre of Tuban on the north coast of Java. In the fifteenth century it had been one of the Muslim enclaves tolerated by the imperial authorities of Hindu-Buddhist Måjåpait. It was also the birthplace of Sunan Kalijågå.

I was looking at the towers and domes of the town's brand-new Grand Mosque. It stood on the west side of the square within sniffing distance of the rich and rank aroma of fish that rose from the waterfront. Between 2004 and 2006 the architecturally unique but modest colonial-era mosque that once stood on the site was rebuilt in a spectacular arabesque style. As I tilted my head to take it in, a middle-aged man sidled up to me. Without introductions, his eyes fixed on the mosque, he said thoughtfully in perfect English, "Disneyland has come to Tuban."

I could see what he meant. The new mosque has no less than six thin, pencil-pointed minarets each with its own colonnaded belfry-like chamber where a muezzin can look out over the town and make the call to prayer. The minarets overlook three gleaming, bright blue, slightly elongated domes decorated in a blocky pattern of yellow tiles. Two wings extend forward to the left and right of the main entrance, each topped with a dark blue, onion shaped dome. Throughout the mosque the polished marble floors reflect colonnades and doorways that are capped with ogee-pointed arches. The walls are covered in delicately drawn interlocking geometric motifs reminiscent of mosques in the Middle East and Iran. An internet site dedicated to the promotion of tourism in Tuban proudly likens the city's mosque to "a palace in the land of fables".

It was not *salat* prayer time but the mosque was busy. In the front courtyard a lively class of primary school children were being drilled by their *pèci*-wearing teacher in the recitation of the call to prayer. He uttered the first words of each line then conducted the children as they completed the line in a shrill, ragged chorus. Nearby, several parties of high school girls were busy taking selfies with squeals of laughter and sudden rushes to cluster around smartphones.

I walked left towards the southwest corner of the square. It was clogged with cars and pedicabs and scores of bobbing heads coming and going through an ochre-coloured roofed gate. Pushing among the pedicabs I made my way through the gate into a narrow roofed alley flanked by gaudy shops and stalls selling the knick-knacks of pilgrimage: Islamic-style clothes, prayer mats, religious books, dates and sweets, souvenirs, drinks. One hundred metres on, I turned right and stood before a low, whitewashed arched gate under a roof of wooden shingles. I had to stoop to get through it. I was now in a courtyard surrounded by open pavilions and a clutter of stalls selling perfume, clothes, food and plastic toys. The arabesque Grand Mosque was nearby, but I couldn't see it. I was deep in the world of traditional pilgrimage. Ahead, through several ancient, top-heavy roofed gates and walled courtyards filled with gravestones, lay the mausoleum of the sixteenth century saint

Sunan Bonang, one of the famous Nine Saints.

In 2011 a broad, peaked canopy was built over the mausoleum, more to protect pilgrims from the elements than to protect the mausoleum itself. Under it, the pyramid-shaped roof of the mausoleum slopes down to about one-and-a-half metres above ground level. Stooping under the eaves, pilgrims find a place to sit in a tiny area of tiled floor between the eaves and the inner burial chamber. The chamber's dark wooden walls stand on a low, white, brick-and-plaster platform decorated along its base with fretwork-carved stone panels.

Inside, the saint lies under a long, narrow ledger about half a metre high, seemingly made of stone layers. Along its length lie wooden trays for offerings of flower petals and banknotes. At each end of the ledger stands a headstone respectfully wrapped in white calico. A lace canopy hangs from a wooden frame above the grave, and on top of the frame copies of the Qur'ān, the Surah Ya Sin, and books of prayers and *dhikr* chants lie stacked. In the ceiling cavity massive, time-darkened teak beams support the wooden tiles of the roof.

Pilgrims sit in the narrow space between the tombstone and the wall, some with their eyes closed in prayer, some intoning *dhikr* chants, some swaying, some clicking prayer beads, and some taking in the sepulchral ambience with wide eyes. But most don't make it up the three steps into the cramped interior of the burial chamber. They have to be content with devotions in the outer area under the broad new roof. Even those who do make it inside are generally given just fifteen minutes to complete their devotions before they must make way for others.

Sunan Bonang's modest but quietly impressive mausoleum
with its two-tiered, pyramid-shaped *tajug* roof and low eaves as it
looked before 2011 when it disappeared under a broad, over-arching,
protective roof. An old and equally modest gate (below) marks the
entry point to the mortuary complex.

Sunan Bonang may have existed as a real person, though today a
dazzling aura of legend almost completely blots out what is factually
knowable about him. Probably he was born Makdum Ibrahim, the
son of Sunan Ampèl, an older member of the Nine Saints team. His

mother, so it is said, was Nyi Agĕng Manilǻ, the adopted daughter
of the Muslim regent of Tuban but also a descendant of Hindu-
Buddhist royalty from Måjåpait. Nothing certain is known about
his lifespan except that he was alive during the turmoil around
1500 that saw the evaporation of Hindu-Buddhist Måjåpait and
the rise of Demak, Java's first real Islamic state.

But were these the real facts of Sunan Bonang's life story? Did
he have a life story at all? According to Mohammad Lazim, a key-
keeper at the saint's tomb when I visited in 2003, Sunan Bonang
tried very deliberately to rub the facts of his life from the historical
record. He never married and had no descendants to tell his story.
(In ancient texts he is known as the *Ratu Wahdat*, the Celebate
Lord.) Seated among the shadows of the burial chamber Pak Lazim
told me that Sunan Bonang was the only one of the Nine Saints
who "did not have a history". In fact Sunan Ampèl strictly forbade
the writing down of his son's story.

Peering through the gloom at the dim whiteness of my exercise
book open on the floor in front of me I tried to write down what
the key-keeper was saying. He reached out and gripped my hand.
Dusty light from the tiny hatch-like door lit one half of his face.

"I had a guest here once," he said, "a journalist from Surabaya.
He tried to write down a biography of the saint, but his notes kept
disappearing. It was a sign that the saint did not want his history
written down."

He gently lifted the ballpoint pen from my fingers and stuck
it firmly in the top pocket of his shirt. I closed the exercise book
and leaned back against the dark solidity of the wall. Pak Lazim, I
sensed, was ready to talk. Off the record, as it were.

"Sunan Bonang was born in Bonang Village near Lasem,"
he said, ignoring the prohibition on telling the saint's story. "On

reaching adulthood he went to the land of the Tatars – western China – where he studied Islam. While there, he was known by the title Chin Bee. His full name was Nam Liang Song, which means 'worshipping the Lord God'."

My mind was racing. A distant era was speaking, but its voice was blurred and scarcely audible through the blanket of centuries. I could capture only a syllable here and there, and it didn't hang together. I remembered that Mongols had ruled China in the thirteenth and fourteenth centuries and had attempted a punitive, ultimately disastrous, invasion of Java in 1293. In the early 1400s the Javanese Sheikh Jumadil Kubro reputedly travelled to Ottoman Turkey. The town of Lasem had a prominent Chinese heritage with strong trade links to China. In the distant past Java also had connections with Central Asia. The saint Ibrahim Asmorokondi had come to Java from Samarkhand some time in the late 1300s. Given these connections, it was possible – just barely conceivable – that Sunan Bonang might indeed have studied in western China.

"After completing his studies in the Tatar lands," Pak Lazim went on, now speaking excitedly, "he came back and settled in Makassar where he spent ten years teaching Islam. He attracted a large following of students. Pining for his father in Surabaya, he set off across the Java Sea by *pĕrahu*. After nineteen days and nineteen nights he made landfall near Lasem where he had been born. He named the landing place Bonang and established a religious community there."

I had been there. The modern village of Bonang is on the coast about six kilometres north east of Lasem. It hosts several relics of Sunan Bonang, but the big attraction is the saint's Prostration Place (*pasujudan*) where he prayed and left evidence of his greatness pressed into stone.

Buses loaded with pilgrims pull in to a roadside parking area near the site. Alongside the buses eateries and small shops are festooned with plastic bags of salted fish, a local delicacy that pilgrims take home as a souvenir. A steep flight of steps leads about one hundred metres up a hillside. At the top, through a roofed gate, there is a spacious walled yard paved in stone. Two small, neatly kept buildings under tiled pyramid roofs dominate the yard. The first houses Sunan Bonang's Prostration Place and the second the tomb of a Champa princess. Each building has a verandah around it where pilgrims sleep and perform their devotions, including *ṣalat* prayers. There are places for ritual washing, simple bathrooms with toilets and a spacious rest hall open at the sides. The whole compound is meticulously maintained under the direction of a key-keeper and the local Sunan Bonang Foundation.

The Prostration Place consists of a single chamber about three by three metres in area. The entry door is usually locked and is opened for pilgrims by the key-keeper. The top and bottom halves of the door open separately. Usually only the bottom half is opened so visitors are compelled to stoop respectfully when they enter the chamber. The walls of the chamber are lined on the inside with white calico drapes. On the tiled floor there are four stones. The biggest is circular in shape, a little under a metre in diameter and flat on top. This is said to be where Sunan Bonang performed his *ṣalat* prayers. Beside it lies a smaller stone, also flat on top, with an impression in it shaped like the sole of a foot or shoe. Here the saint meditated yoga-style standing on one leg. Such was the weight of his spiritual authority that his foot left an imprint in the stone that can still be seen today.

Seated on the floor beside the stones the key-keeper leads pilgrims in prayer, punctuated by recitation of the Qur'ān's opening book, the Surah Al-Fātiḥah. On the verandah outside, visitors bend in *ṣalat* prayer, hoping that their proximity to the place where Sunan Bonang prayed will lend impetus to their own devotions.

About a kilometre from the Prostration Place, through village roads and lanes, lies what local people claim to be the true grave of Sunan Bonang rimmed by a solid, whitewashed wall. The grave is as minimalist as a grave can be – simply a square plot of open ground inside an iron pike fence. The saint lies – so the key-keeper says – under one of the mulberry bushes struggling to grow in the middle of the square. Pilgrims sit or stand beneath an open-sided shelter just outside the fence praying in the direction of the vacant space.

When I told Pak Lazim that I had visited Bonang Village and found only a footprint and an empty square of earth, he nodded.

"He has erased himself more completely than any other saint. And that is the greatness of his legacy. Like all saints, he left behind signs, but he was like a rich man who doesn't flaunt his wealth. By hiding his history he acquired extra charisma."

The secret Chinese history of Sunan Bonang lives a little-known life behind his better-known "official" (shall we say) biography told in scores of books and web sites. Officially, the young Makdum Ibrahim grew up in his father's *pĕsantrèn* school in Surabaya. Early in childhood he was already earmarked for a life of piety, good works and scholarship. As a young man he was sent by his father (together with a school friend Radèn Paku – later to become the saint of Giri) to study overseas. It is not clear how far they got. Some say they reached Mecca and spent time studying there. Others say the two young men got only as far as Melaka on the Malay Peninsula. The sultan of Melaka at the time regarded his city as "the true Mecca" (*Makkah* and *Melaka* sound similar) so they remained there and studied under Radèn Paku's father Maulana Iskak. Still other traditions say they reached Pasai in north Sumatra where they studied under the renowned Muslim scholar Sheikh Awwalul Islam, and a "scholar from Persia" possibly by the name of Sheikh Bari.

When Makdum Ibrahim returned to Surabaya his father ordered him to travel the length and breadth of Java until he found a grove of *kemuning* trees. For years he wandered, never sleeping or eating. One day a mysterious figure appeared to him. It was the Green One, the prophet Khiḍr who had once been a guide to Musa (Moses). Now Khiḍr became Makdum Ibrahim's guide, showing him the way to the *kemuning* grove in a place called Bonang. Here he settled and as his fame grew he became known as "the saint of Bonang". In time he became an influential member of the Nine Saints team, spreading Islam up and down the north coast of Java and playing a key role in the development of Demak.

There is a persistent tradition – sketched in the previous chapter – that Sunan Bonang was responsible for the miraculous transformation of Sunan Kalijågå from bandit to saint. There are also stories that he was an early commander of Demak's army, leading it across Java to the gates of Måjåpait. More than 400 years later, during Indonesia's war of independence (1945-1949), a unit of guerrilla fighters called themselves the Sunan Bonang Division in memory of the saint's warrior prowess.

Sunan Bonang may also have had a hand in the construction of Demak's Grand Mosque. It was in this mosque that at least some of the Muslim missionaries known collectively as the Nine Saints are said to have held meetings on strategy under the chairmanship of Sunan Bonang. Here too Java's best-known sufi saints, Sheikh Siti

Jenar and Prince Panggung, were tried for blasphemy and convicted. Both were charged with revealing cosmic truths that should (so the Nine Saints thought) be kept secret.

Sunan Bonang's hostility to sufi mystics was probably more political than theological. Like the Prophet Muhammad, he was a hands-on leader deeply knitted into the day-to-day fabric of social life. For him Islamic society was neither a remote utopia nor a swamp of compromise to be shunned by the religiously pure. Rather it was an arena in which Islam was called on to prove its viability as a practical way of life. Any hint that the mystical insights of Islam were incompatible with regular social order needed to be kept strictly under wraps, no matter how true they might be.

But like all Javanese Muslims of the time, he accepted that mystical practices were a viable path to knowledge of the divine. His challenge was to engineer a practical reconciliation between Java's powerful tradition of mystical monism and the dualistic doctrines of Islamic orthodoxy.

His efforts to do this are reported in a number of religious writings, the best known of them being the *Suluk Wujil* (The Sacred Song of Wujil) and a text known to scholars by the Dutch title *Het Boek van Bonang* but also by various other titles including *The Admonitions of Seh Bari*. In all likelihood Sunan Bonang was not himself the author of these texts, but their language and ideas are from the saint's time and they purport to describe something of what he thought and did.

A standout feature of these works is their preoccupation with paradoxes that in some cases are reminiscent of *koan* paradoxes in Zen Buddhism. Zen Buddhism uses paradoxes primarily to snap the mind out of conventional patterns of thought, but the writings attributed to Sunan Bonang use paradox to illustrate a mystical epistemology that directs the believer to knowledge of Allah.

Sunan Bonang seems to have thought that man and Allah are inseparable but not one and the same. Mystical thinkers in Java have expressed this idea through a variety of metaphors. One is that of the shadow play: God is the puppeteer and the puppets are humankind (and the screen is the earthly or cosmic backdrop). Puppet and puppeteer are separate yet have a kind of unity, since in a performance neither can exist without the other. There is also the metaphor of the mirror in which humankind is represented as the earthly image of God. Viewer and reflection are separate, but again, neither can exist without the other. So both metaphors permit duality to be preserved but acknowledge a kind of monism.

These are conventional images, but in the *Suluk Wujil* and the *Admonitions of Sèh Bari* they are given a radical subtlety. Because a totalistic or monistic view of the cosmos encompasses all things, even those that appear to be contradictory or irreconcilable, we can only really begin to understand cosmic totality by learning to accept contradictions and paradoxes.

The *Suluk Wujil* recounts how Sunan Bonang tried to teach this. One day he instructed two of his pupils – the dwarf Wujil and the servant girl Kèn Satpådå – to fetch a mirror and lean it against a tree. He told them to look into the mirror. Kèn Satpådå sat down cross-legged so she could be the same height as Wujil. The pair peered into the mirror.

"What do you see?" asked the saint.

"I see two images, me and Satpådå together," Wujil replied.

Sunan Bonang told Wujil to stand behind the mirror.

"Now, Satpådå, what do you see?"

"I see only my own image in the mirror. But Wujil has not

disappeared... I see him standing right there, behind the mirror."

With many variations (and, some would say, with many corruptions and misunderstandings) this image has taken its place among the key images in the iconography of Javanese mysticism. Existence and non-existence are illusory, just as the disappearance of Wujil's image in the "mirror" of existence is not to be taken as evidence of his non-existence.

Elsewhere in the *Suluk Wujil* the paradoxes multiply. Sunan Bonang teaches that existence manifests itself through four basic elements – earth, fire, air and water. Each embodies a contradiction or paradox. So, in the antiquity and fertility of the earth, age and youth are equally present. When you are young you do not see the old age that must emerge from you. When you are old you are still the same person you were when you were young, but where did your youth go? Age and youth are always within you, but like Wujil and Satpådå, they are not visible together in the "mirror" of perception. Similarly, in the element of fire we see both power and impotence. When fire rages, where is its inevitable dimming? And when the same fire dims, where did its bright raging force go? In air we see existence and non-existence. When the wind is blowing we can feel that air exists, but do we feel the stillness of its non-existence? And when the air is still where are the gusts that tell us it exists? As for water, it embodies both life and death. In the flow of life where is death? And in death where is life? Life evaporates into death as water evaporates into nothingness, and life returns just as rainwater materialises out of the same nothingness.

Sunan Bonang even sees contradiction in the Islamic confession of faith – the credo or *Shahādah* – which begins *La ilaha il-Allah* (There is no god but Allah). In the *Suluk Wujil,* as in many other mystical texts in Islam, the phrase is interpreted as embodying the ultimate contradiction. The first part (called a *nafi* or repudiation) says "there is no god", but this is immediately contradicted by the second part (called an *isbat* or assertion) "but Allah exists". Yet the two parts appear side by side as a unity expressing the core insight of Islam.

For most Javanese today, Sunan Bonang's mystical doctrines are little known and impossibly esoteric. The saint is now remembered mainly for converting unbelievers by spectacular displays of magic.

In this tradition is the famous story of Sakyakirti, a learned Brahmin priest. He scoffed when news of Sunan Bonang's reputation reached him in distant India. Packing up a library of books he set sail for Java determined to debate the upstart holy man and convert him to the Hindu faith. As his ship approached Tuban he addressed his followers.

"I am going to confront Sunan Bonang and debate matters of faith and knowledge with him. I swear to you that if he defeats me I will embrace Islam, and you will come with me into the new faith. But if I win, he will have to convert to Hinduism. If he refuses I will lop off his head!"

His followers shuddered, and as they did, wind began to whistle through the ship's rigging. Soon a gale was blowing from the west, pushing them quicker and quicker towards Tuban. The seas rose and a vast storm overtook the ship. Great waves poured into it, tearing it apart and sending it to the bottom of the Java Sea.

Sakyakirti survived and was cast ashore on the beach at Tuban. As he lifted his gaze and looked around he saw a man in a white robe standing before him. Sakyakirti called out to him.

"Friend, I am a Hindu priest. I have come from India to pit my knowledge against that of Sunan Bonang. But I think my journey has been wasted. I have lost all my books... they went to the bottom of the ocean with my ship."

The white-robed figure raised his staff, plunged it into the sand then lifted it up. Fresh water jetted from the hole he had made. Carried on the gush of water the Brahmin's library of thick books also spurted from the sand. They rolled over in the air and settled undamaged, dry and in neat piles in front of the dumbfounded visitor.

"Sir," said the priest, his voice trembling, "I see that you are the saint I have been looking for. I plead for your forgiveness and I gratefully embrace the faith of Islam."

There is a widespread perception that religious faith has the power to transform people in a radical, "magical" way, as the Javanese were transformed by the arrival of Islam. In popular story, if an individual has access to the truth of Islam, that truth manifests itself in invincible magic prowess. The story of Sakyakirti promises a debate that might have encompassed theology, law or mystical practice, but the debate was trumped by magic and a focus on Sunan Bonang's supernatural powers rather than his intellectual powers.

Similar stories about the saint are legion. For example, he is reputed to have invented the *bonang*, a small bronze kettle gong that today is a principal instrument in the Javanese *gamĕlan* or percussion orchestra. Sunan Bonang is said to have beaten a *bonang* gong to attract people to his mission gatherings and this is why he is known as Sunan Bonang. Other stories claim that the saint's gong could distinguish between good and evil. Its resonant peal uplifted the hearts of good people and inflicted paralysis on evil-doers. Once, when the saint was accosted by a gang of bandits, he struck his gong causing their chests and legs to tremble in consonance and their bodies to go limp. Sunan Bonang – the better-armed bandit – assured them of Allah's forgiveness for their criminal behaviour and they immediately converted to Islam.

The well-known traditional song *Tåmbå Ati* (Balm for the Heart) is also attributed to Sunan Bonang.

> *Tåmbå ati iku limå prěkarané*
>> There are five balms to soothe the heart
> *Kaping pisan måcå Quran lan maknané*
>> First, read the Qur'ān and digest its meaning
> *Kaping pindho sholat wěngi lakonånå*
>> Second, pray to God at night,
> *Kaping tělu wong kang solèh kumpulånå*
>> Third, keep company with pious people,
> *Kaping papat kudu wětěng ingkang luwé*
>> Fourth, get used to having an empty stomach,
> *Kaping limå dzikir wěngi ingkang suwé*
>> Fifth, remember God in *dhikr* chant through the night.
> *Salah sawijiné såpå biså ngělakoni*
>> If you can do even one of these,
> *Mugi-mugi Gusti Allah nyěmbadani*
>> Your wishes will be granted, God willing.

In recent times the song has acquired a jump-start of new life, even a cult-like following, in the exuberance of Indonesia's modern pop culture. In the first decade of the twenty-first century several singers and bands recorded successful versions of it. The best known is by Islamist singer Opick, but versions by the groups Kyai Kanjeng and Peterpan have also been hits. These transformations of Sunan Bonang's composition have appeared in a variety of trendy styles, including dangdut, Javanese kroncong and modern rock. The saint's Javanese lyrics have been translated into Indonesian and even into Arabic. At the time of writing, at least six video versions of *Tåmbå Ati* had been posted on YouTube. Most have the lyrics – in Javanese, Indonesian and Arabic – in karaoke-style subtitles along the bottom of the screen (type "tombo ati" into YouTube's search box to see a list of them).

There is another current of narrative that depicts Sunan Bonang in a very different light. In the notorious *Sĕrat Darmågandhul* (The Book of Darmågandhul) the saint is a cranky anti-hero on a mission to stamp out the ancient Hindu-Buddhist culture of the island's interior. He mounts an expedition to do this that turns into a disaster.

It is a compelling, eccentric and often humorous story, not least because Darmågandhul, the servant who lends his name to the book, is a scrotum – a wise and very inquisitive scrotum, but nevertheless a mere scrotum. We first meet him in an earlier book, the *Suluk Gatholoco* (The Sacred Song of Gatholoco) as companion of the hero Gatholoco. Gatholoco's appearance is unusual to say the least, especially for a character in a religious text. He is a walking, talking human penis.

> ... *warnané tan kaprah janmi*
>> ... he didn't look like an ordinary human being
> *Wandané apan bungkik*
>> He was small and bent over
> *Kulité basisik iku*
>> His skin was rough and scaly
> *Kalawan tanpå nètrå*
>> And he had no eyes
> *Tanpå irung tanpå kuping*
>> Nor a nose or ears

*Rĕmĕnané anèndrå sadinå-dinå*
　　He loved spending his days asleep
*Yèn ngĕlilir lajĕng monthah*
　　But when he woke up he was very demanding
*Tan kĕnå dèn arih-arih*
　　It was a real challenge to calm him down


Darmågandhul is his faithful sack-like servant (Darmågandhul means literally "he serves by dangling"). His appearance too is somewhat off-putting.

*Awon dĕdĕgé lir kébå*
　　He was like a sack and just as ugly
*Lĕmboné kĕpati-pati*
　　He hung down half-asleep
*Yèn nèndrå anglir wong pĕjah*
　　When he slept, he slept the sleep of the dead
*Nora duwé måtå kuping*
　　He had no eyes or ears
*Amung ing lambé iki*
　　Although he did have wrinkles like lips
*Nora duwé otot balung*
　　He had no muscles or bones
*Darmågandhul abélå*
　　Darmågandhul had been with (Gatholoco)
*Tapanirå awit alit*
　　Since childhood, keeping him company as he meditated
*Pan gumandhul angalong*
　　Hanging upside down like a fruit bat
*Waringin sungsang*
　　in an inverted banyan tree

The two texts – plus another closely related text, the *Babad Kadhiri* (The Chronicle of Kediri) – were written in the 1870s. All three are antagonistic to Middle Eastern Islam. They are not against Islam *per se* (though the *Babad Kadhiri* comes close) but they emphasise the pre-eminence of Javanese culture – especially Javanese mystical traditions – in the understanding and practice of Islam.

In the *Suluk Gatholoco* the penis-hero Gatholoco (who, by the way, is also an opium addict and gambler who drinks heavily, smells disgusting, dresses in rags and has an insolent manner) engages in a series of debates on religious matters with opponents who represent clean-living, Arab-style legalistic Islamic orthodoxy. He easily bests them, in fact he humiliates them. He ridicules the pretentiousness of their Middle Eastern dress, their faux-pious mannerisms and their claim to religious learning. But the debates are not really debates in the conventional, informational-logical-philosophical sense. They are more displays of Gatholoco's flair for wordplay spiced with spectacular exchanges of abuse. In fact Gatholoco is more the classic trickster-riddler of folklore than a philosopher or theologian. But despite his weird appearance he calls himself "The Perfect Man" and claims a place for himself "at the centre of the world".

Possibly the *Suluk Gatholoco* is a wry echo of Java's ancient tantric heritage. *Lingga* (phallus) veneration was widespread in pre-Islamic times. In Java, as in India, a lingga took the form of an erect pillar of stone, usually standing in the centre of a pedestal with a cleft in it called a *yoni*, which represented the vulva. The lingga was a symbolic assembly point for a multitude of deities and energies, including the supreme godhead Shiwa, local semi-divine monarchs, the revered ancestors, the ejaculatory and rejuvenating power of

Java's volcanoes, and (in conjunction with the *yoni* pedestal) the mystically charged, self-extinguishing ecstasy of sexual union.

Lingga veneration survived the arrival of Islam but it flowered into a complex array of speculations that fused Hindu-Buddhist tantra and yoga with Islamic sufism. When Islam arrived in the fifteenth and sixteenth centuries it came ready-packaged in a mystical doctrine that was widely welcomed across Java. Deriving ultimately from the thought of Arab sufi Ibn Arabi (1165 – 1240) and adapted to the Indonesian world by Sumatran mystics Hamzah Fansuri (died c.1590) and his pupil Syamsuddin Pasai (died 1630), this doctrine proposed that Allah and all of creation – including humankind – are of the same essence. Allah manifests himself in the world as an emanation that descends through seven stages, ultimately reaching humankind, the lowest and most material stage.

The parts of the human body – from the fontanel down to the genitalia – became metaphors for these descending stages of emanation. In time the metaphors themselves became a mystical "reality". The body was said to harbour symbolic abodes of the divine essence each with its own mystical meaning. The *Suluk Gatholoco* appears to settle on just three main bodily abodes rather than the seven, or twenty-eight, or even the infinite number that other variants of the doctrine propose. The divine essence saturates the body in different degrees of intensity, proceeding from the head (the *baitul makmur*) through the heart (the *baitul muharram*) to the genitalia (the *baitul mukaddas*). Here it is transmuted into the semen that generates new life. To further miniaturise the grandeur of the doctrine – moulding it to pre-Islamic belief in the power of the lingga – the penis itself is seen as a kind of mini human body with the *baitul makmur* in the glans, the *baitul muharram* in the shaft, and the *baitul mukaddas* in the scrotum.

Someone who becomes aware of his essential divinity becomes as perfect as that essence and is entitled to be called (or to call himself) a Perfect Man. But God's perfection is rarely evident in outward appearance, it is always an inward perfection. With his trademark arrogance Gatholoco calls himself "The Perfect Man" despite his outward ugliness. Here the Suluk seems to be recycling the pre-Islamic notion that power tends to distort its environment, like heat melting plastic. Those endowed with great spirituality may be ugly or deformed, in fact *should* be ugly or deformed, both physically and ethically. The greater the outward deformity and moral debauchery, the greater the inward perfection and the power that comes with it.

Gatholoco was labelled "a monster" by Philippus van Akkeren, the half-shocked, half-delighted scholar who, back in 1951, made Gatholoco the subject of his doctoral thesis. The mild-mannered Dutchman first went to Java in the 1930s as a Christian missionary. During the Second World War he was interned for three years in a Japanese concentration camp where he fought off hunger by immersing himself in study of the Javanese language. Thanks to his encounter with Java's eccentric vision of the human condition he lost his Christian faith. Later he ended up marooned in an Australian university, living comfortably but distracted by memories of Java that refused to dim as the shadow of old age crept over him. In his sixties he alarmed his students by leaping on to the top of desks in the lecture theatre and haranguing them on the evil of the Vietnam War, the barbarity of Westerners and the wonders of Javanese mysticism. In his Australian exile he was consoled only by his obsessive, and ultimately unfinished, study of the *Sĕrat Darmâgandhul*, a sequel to his previous study of the *Suluk Gatholoco*.

The *Sĕrat Darmågandhul* opens with a memorable vignette. The scrotum-servant Darmågandhul sits at the feet of his wise master and teacher Kalamwadi. In Javanese *kalam* is a literary word meaning "pen", but it is also a well-worn synonym for "penis". *Wadi* is the word for "secret", but it too suggests genitalia – the secret place of the human anatomy. So Kalamwadi's name is loaded with esoteric as well as sexual overtones. Apparently Kalamwadi is Gatholoco under a new, more prestigious-sounding name better suited to his status as a holy hermit. But he is also the repository of an underground history, one that – it is hinted – many in Javanese society would prefer to keep hidden.

Darmågandhul puts a question to Kalamwadi that has haunted the history of Java for five hundred years.

> *Dhuh sang dwijå kang yanjånå murti*
>> O twice-born teacher of great wisdom
> *mugi pukulun ywa pisan dukå*
>> please don't be angry
> *kawulå nyuwun pitakèn*
>> I would like to ask you
> *kang dados purwanipun*
>> what is the original reason
> *tiyang Jawi santun agami*
>> why the Javanese changed their religion,
> *nilar agami Budå*
>> abandonning the Budå religion
> *ngrasuk sarak Rasul*
>> and converting to the law of the Prophet?

Kalamwadi hesitates.

"It is risky to speak the truth about Java's history or blab the secrets of Java's kings. I could pay for it with my life!"

Darmågandhul tries to reassure him.

"True, in the old days that might have happened. But today our rulers are more open minded. They are tolerant of ordinary people. They put scientific knowledge ahead of subjective knowledge and personal interests."

In the late 1870s when the *Sěrat Darmågandhul* was written most of Java was under direct Dutch rule, and even in the four semi-independent Javanese princedoms of Ngayogyåkartå, Suråkartå, Mangkunagaran and Pakualaman, Dutch advisors – called Residents – kept a close eye on local affairs. The anonymous author of the *Sěrat Darmågandhul* seems to have thought that Dutch rule was more liberal than the old pre-colonial order, hence Darmågandhul's upbeat reassurances.

Kalamwadi is persuaded, but before he breaks his silence he first takes out some insurance. He invokes the protection of Allah with the pious phrase *Bismi-llāhi r-raḥmāni r-raḥīm* (In the name of Allah the most gracious and most merciful), after which he appeals for pardon to another authority, one much older than Islam.

"May the great ancestors of Java forgive me for daring to speak, for raising my voice to tell an ancient story that has long been hidden, a story that comes from memory, handed down by word of mouth, not recorded in any book."

Kalamwadi has good reason to seek the protection of a higher power. He is about to tell a story that will offend many Muslims. Java converted to Islam, he will say, not because Islam brought a higher truth to the island, but because King Bråwijåyå, the last king of Hindu-Buddhist Måjåpait, made the mistake of marrying a foreigner, a princess from Champa in Indochina who was a Muslim, and a very lustful one too.

"As he made love to her, forgetting himself in the throes of passion, she would whisper in his ear, telling him at great length about the glories of Islam and how much better the new religion was than the old Budå religion. Hearing what his wife had to say King Bråwijåyå's judgement became clouded. He didn't say anything, but quietly he began to change his thinking about Islam. Then, a while later, his wife's nephew came to pay a visit. His name was Sayyid Rahmat. He asked permission to settle in Ngampèlgadhing and teach the law and religion of His Honour The Prophet. The king agreed and that is exactly what Sayyid Rahmat did, telling the local people that Muhammad was God's prophet. More and more Muslim preachers began to arrive from overseas. They all sought an audience with the king, asking permission to establish settlements along the north coast. The king granted their requests, and before long they were everywhere. That's how the Javanese – in fact the entire land of Java – switched to the religion of the Arabs."

From Tuban the saintly Muslim missionary, Sunan Bonang, set off into the little-known interior intent on converting heathens. It was some time around the year 1500. Muslim merchants had long enjoyed a high-profile presence in Tuban, living under the protection of Hindu-Buddhist Måjåpait. But it was a different story inland where most people remained attached to the Budå religion. "Budå" doesn't mean just Buddhism. It is a catch-all term that also takes in Shivaite Hinduism plus a kaleidoscope of primal religions remnants of which have survived into the present.

The saint's plan was to head for Kediri, a semi-mythical,

jungle-shrouded town deep in the alien hills to the south. As Java shifted towards Islam in the late decades of the 1400s Kediri and its surrounds had remained a bastion of the Budå faith.

Centuries before Sunan Bonang's expedition, the interior had been ruled by the mysterious King Jåyåbåyå, an incarnation of the Hindu god Vishnu. When Jåyåbåyå died he left behind two of his senior ministers to protect and nurture his people. They became the guardian spirits, the *dhĕmit*, of Kediri. Tunggul Wulung presided over the looming cone of Mount Kelud, and Butå Locåyå guarded the paddy fields and rivers.

It was Butå Locåyå who waylaid Sunan Bonang as the saint neared Kediri. Their encounter has become famous in Java's archive of folklore. In the *Sĕrat Darmågandhul*, Kalamwadi describes what happened at some length. He can scarcely conceal his glee because, for Sunan Bonang, the meeting did not go well.

In the vicinity of the modern town of Kertosono, about seventy kilometres south of Tuban and thirty kilometres short of Kediri, the saint and his two followers came to the banks of the Brantas River. The Brantas rises in the hills near Malang about one hundred kilometres to the east. Initially it drains away towards the southern ocean, but as it approaches the coast it makes a right turn and snakes west. Then it turns back inland heading north towards Kediri. From there it goes further north and makes a generous curve east, ultimately unloading into the Java Sea through a ragged delta south of Surabaya. At the time of Sunan Bonang's journey the Brantas River seems to have been as much a religious frontier as a topographical one. Within its great arc lay the heartland of the Budå religion.

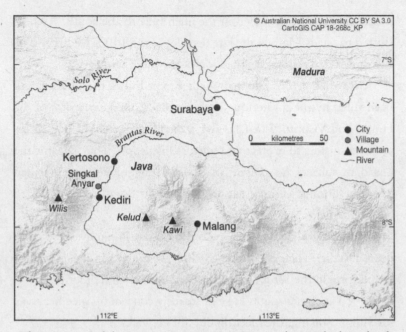

The great arc of the Brantas River in East Java enclosing the heartland of the Budå religion in the time of Sunan Bonang.

Sunan Bonang knew his reception on the other side of the river might be hostile. But buoyed by the truth of Islam he crossed anyway. He found himself in an eerie land beyond the certainties of his faith, a pagan land, a land that was soon to be erased from the present and consigned to a netherworld of memory in Java's collective mind.

As he penetrated into heathen territory he became thirsty. He commanded one of his young disciples to go into a village and ask for a drink. The village was deserted, only a teenage girl was to be seen sitting at a loom in one of the doorways. The young man stopped some distance away and called out softly and respectfully.

"Miss, would you be kind enough to give a thirsty traveller a drink of water?"

The girl looked him up and down. She took in his loose, snowy-white robe and his turban with its cloth tail hanging down behind.

"Thirsty, are you? You've just come from the river — doesn't it have enough water for you? Eh? Anyway, we don't have any drinking-water here. If you'd like to drink my piss, I've got plenty. It's good, clean, well-filtered piss and you're welcome to it!"

The shocked disciple beat a hasty retreat and reported what had happened to Sunan Bonang. Before he could check himself the saint let out an offended yell.

"Those people will never have water again!"

At that instant the Brantas River reared up and dived over its banks upstream. Driven by the saint's anger it crashed through the heathen countryside. Ricefields, gardens, villages and people were ripped up and drowned as the water sought a new channel. At the spot where Sunan Bonang was standing the current suddenly shrivelled to a trickle then disappeared altogether.

Having shifted the river eastward, Sunan Bonang was now on the west side again, outside the Budå frontier. He would have to make another crossing. But as he approached the new channel he found his path blocked by a figure standing under a tall tree. Flames licked about his body. He was radiating heat so intense that the saint's two disciples were overcome and collapsed on the road. Sunan Bonang's heat was no less intense and he too blazed with bright yellow fire. The two figures stood facing each other. Sunan Bonang spoke first. He had known at once who his challenger was.

"So, it's you Butå Locåyå. You're blocking my path. But no matter ... how are you? I hope you're in good health."

Butå Locåyå, like a modern immigration officer, was not to be soft-soaped.

"Where on earth are *you* from? You look downright weird. Your clothes don't fit … they're all baggy. That's not how Javanese people dress. You look like a praying mantis to me, not a Javanese."

Sunan Bonang kept his temper. He adopted the persona of an innocent tourist.

"I'm an Arab. My name is Sayyid Kramat and I come from Tuban. I'm on my way to Kediri to have a look at the ancient ruins there. I'd like to see the palace of His Majesty King Jåyåbåyå. Do you know where it is?"

"It's straight east from here in the village of Menang. But the palace has disappeared, the royal guesthouse has gone too, the women's quarters are no more, also the gardens. Everything was buried under ash during an eruption of Mount Kelud."

Butå Locåyå quickly exhausted his reserves of tourist small talk. He had an important question for the saint. Being a *dhĕmit* he lacked social graces and knew little about deference and respect. So he was blunt.

"You changed the course of the river and cursed the region with a shortage of water. Why? People don't deserve this. Only one person wronged you but many are now suffering. The punishment doesn't fit the crime. By what law did you do this? You were high-handed and thoughtless. You've plunged a lot of people into poverty. I should report you to the authorities."

"Feel free," said Sunan Bonang, keeping a grip on himself. "Go ahead and report me to the king of Måjåpait if you like. I'm not afraid of him."

Butå Locåyå almost spat his reply.

"That's no way for a person of rank to speak. You sound like a street hawker with a tray of tempeh on his head. You think you're untouchable, don't you? You flaunt your powers because you think you've got God Almighty – Hyang Agung – on your side and heavenly kith-and-kin all around you. You think you can get away with anything and never be in the wrong."

The guardian spirit was just warming up.

"Don't tell me you're like that other Arab – Ajisåkå – the one who came here a while back and crowned himself king of Mědhang. He was a pupil and disciple of Dajjal, the false messiah. He stayed around for just three years then took off back to where he came from. And he took all the wells and water sources with him. Ajisåkå was an Arab, you're an Arab, and you're just like him. You enjoy tormenting people. You take their water. You say you're a saint but actually you look like the false messiah to me, or the devil incarnate. A little girl makes fun of you and what happens? Instantly you lose your temper. You're a saint for goats, not people. If you were sent to minister to real people you'd show some generosity of spirit. You'd have a nobler mind. I may be a mere *dhěmit* living in the supernatural world, but at least I still have some respect for my human subjects and I do my best to take care of them. But you?"

Butå Locåyå got to the point.

"Put everything back the way it was, sir. Put the water back in the river and restore the ruined farmland. If you refuse to do this I will put a curse on all the Javanese who have converted to Islam. I'll kill them all. I'll go to Her Royal Highness Queen Angin-Angin who lives in the depths of the southern ocean. She'll give me the troops to do the job."

The guardian spirit's words struck deep and sharp into the saint's heart. He realised he had made a mistake. He had visited calamity on innocent people. His response was low-key. He pleaded for understanding. Sainthood was difficult. It came with certain occupational hazards. Speaking the language of power was one of them. Sometimes it got saints into trouble.

"Butå Locåyå, you need to remember I'm a holy saint. I cannot retract the words I have spoken. When a king speaks, his word is law and he cannot change it. It is the same with God's saints, like me. We cannot go back on what we have said. What is done is done."

A conciliatory note crept into his voice. He was prepared to offer his spirit adversary a compromise, or perhaps fob him off, with a promise that could only come true in the distant future.

"Locåyå, don't take it too much to heart. Look ... here's what I'll do. What I have decreed will be valid for just 400 years.[2] At the end of that time the Brantas River will move west again, back to its previous course."

Sunan Bonang and his (now revived) disciples hastened to the river. They sprang into the air and flew across it as nimbly as little children hop over a trickle of water. On the far bank they disappeared into the heart of Budå territory taking the message of Islam with them.

The gradual transition from the Budå religion to Islam swelled to a tipping point in the 1520s. Java's dam of religious inertia burst and a tsunami of Islam flooded over the old faith. Much was drowned, but not everything. Across Java an archipelago of places emerged – a kind of mnemonic geography – that kept memories of the Budå order alive. Old stories remained attached to old places. Post-advent places – especially, but far from wholly, Muslim grave sites – came

---

2   The *Babad Kadhiri* gives 500 years. The *Sěrat Darmågandhul* is equivocal. It says 400 years "coming up to" (*ndungkap*) 500. Calculating the terminating year of the period in terms of the modern Gregorian chronology is difficult, but some believe that in the early decades of the twenty-first century we are close to that point.

into existence each with its own origin story that was passed from generation to generation.

The Brantas River shifted course some time in the sixteenth century, possibly because of a volcanic eruption. It was an event tailor-made for story. Great power bends its environment, not just politically and socially, but topographically. When Sunan Bonang bent the course of the Brantas River he stamped the arrival of Islam's power on the landscape. Today Kertosono lies wedged between two arms of the river. On the eastern margin of town the main channel – Sunan Bonang's "new" channel – flows north, rising and falling with the seasons like a lazily pumping artery. Twelve kilometres to the west the old channel can still be seen cutting a slalom path through the rice fields, a withered remnant of what it once was. It lies on the land like a sign pointing to the past, a reminder that there was once a pre-Islamic order that has likewise withered. These mnemonic inscriptions on the landscape are there for all to see. They are vivid evidence that Islam has been, and still is, a power great enough to alter the landscape or re-name it. People may forget the coming of Islam in the distant past but the landscape remembers.

The names of places and everyday things may also trigger stories. By applying folk etymology (Javanese: *kiråtåbåså*), the components of a name are reinterpreted to suggest a hidden meaning that evokes memory of an event. Sunan Bonang and Butå Locåyå meet under a *sambi* tree (*schleicera oleosa*, also called *kesambi*, *kusambi* and *kosambi* in Indonesia). The flesh of the *sambi* berry can be used like tamarind to add tartness to cooking. Its nut is crushed to produce an oil, like macassar oil, that is used in the traditional process of making batik and to add lustre to hair. In the area around Kediri the *sambi* berry is called *cacil*, sometimes *kĕcacil*. According to the *Sĕrat Darmågandhul* the name came from Sunan Bonang. The saint picked up a *sambi* berry that had fallen from the tree where he and Butå Locåyå were arguing toe-to-toe.

"You see this *sambi* berry?" said the saint. "I'm giving it a new name. From now on it'll be known as a *cacil* berry. Why? Because under this tree you and I quarrelled like two little children (*bocah cilik*). The berry will have two uses. If you eat its flesh it will taste very sour and you'll pull a sour face. This will remind people of the sour expressions on our faces as we quarrelled. As for the nut, it will produce oil (*lĕngå*), and the oil will remind people that here a spirit creature (that's you) bulged his eyes in anger (*mlĕlĕng*) causing a mortal (that's me) to leave this place (*lungå*)."

The saint was not finished. Looking about him he saw a village.

"That village over there, to the north of where we're standing, I'm calling it Singkal which consists of the words *sĕngkĕl nĕmu akal* (we were saddened by our problems but we worked out a solution)."

Today the village of Singkal Anyar (New Singkal) stretches along the banks of the Brantas River about ten kilometres north of Kediri.

Still the saint was not finished. Deep inside Budå territory he came across a stone image of a giant ogress. Sunan Bonang lashed out, snapping off her massive right arm and punching a hole in her forehead.[3] Butå Locåyå, who had been stalking the saint at a safe distance, could not contain his indignation. He jumped out of hiding and confronted him.

---

3   The defaced statue – now called the Totok Kerot – can be seen today in its own mini park on Jalan Totok Kerot, about two kilometres north of Kediri's Simpang Gumul ceremonial arch (GPS coordinates: 7°47'52.23"S  112° 4'11.42"E). The *Sĕrat Darmågandhul* says Sunan Bonang chopped off the figure's right arm. In fact it is the left arm that has gone missing.

"Haven't you got anything better to do!? This statue has done no harm to anyone, and you've damaged it for no reason. Look at it ... you've ruined it! Why?"

"I defaced this statue," said Sunan Bonang quietly, "so people wouldn't pray to it, so they wouldn't give it offerings or burn incense here. If people bow down before idols they are infidels. They are lost souls, totally and completely."

"But the Javanese are well aware," said Butå Locåyå, "that statues are made of stone and nothing more. Stone idols have no power. We venerate them – we put offerings before them and burn incense – because we want spirits to come and live in the statues. We don't want spirits wandering around, living everywhere and anywhere in our trees and fields, because that's where we grow our food. So we give them a special place to live in statues like this ... and they like it there. They feed off the fragrance of our offerings, the smoke of incense refreshes them, and they stay away from mortals. If they have a home in a statue – especially if the statue is in a nice quiet spot under a big shady tree – they love it. They don't have to share their space with humans."

The guardian spirit turned sarcastic.

"But what about you Arabs!? You prostrate yourselves before the Ka'bah. That's a stone edifice too, isn't it? If it's wrong for us to venerate a stone statue, surely what you Arabs do is even worse!"

"The Ka'bah in Mecca was built by the prophet Ibrahim," replied Sunan Bonang, "and it's at the centre of the world. That's why it's made of stone, to mark its special status. For people who prostrate themselves before the Ka'bah, Allah will forgive all their sins."

"What!? How do you know your sins will be forgiven? Do you get a promissory note from God Almighty with a signature on it and a rubber stamp? Will it have a tax sticker?"

Butå Locåyå is furious. He launches into a tirade, making a pointed comparison between Arabia and Java.

"People here in Java fall for everything they hear about Arabia. But how many have actually been there to see for themselves whether it's true or not? They just accept at face value what they're told by homeless layabouts like you. That's why you've come to Java, isn't it? To peddle big talk and sell false news. But I know what Mecca is really like. It's dry and rocky, there's never enough water. People there hardly ever wash their arses after shitting. You can't get anything to grow. It's stinking hot and it scarcely ever rains. People of insight who are rational and can think for themselves say Mecca has been cursed by Allah. It is a desperate place, full of people who take the name of Allah in vain. Many of them sell their own people into slavery and sleep with their female slaves without marrying them. They treat the followers of other religions like animals. They forget that all people – irrespective of religion – are equally human, all are descendants of Adam. You, sir, should clear off out of here right now. You're a disgrace."

Although the *Sĕrat Darmågandhul* doesn't say so, we may imagine that at this moment Butå Locåyå's strident tone softens.

"Java, on the other hand, is a godly, prosperous country. Its climate is temperate, neither too cold nor too hot. There's plenty of water here, and everything you plant grows. The men are good-looking, the women are pretty. They are relaxed and measured when they speak. Everything you've said, sir, is the empty bluster of an ignoramus, someone who doesn't know what he's talking about, someone who believes in things that are not true. If you would like to know where the *real* centre of the world is, it is right here, where I'm sitting."

Butå Locåyå turns to the damaged statue.

"This statue was carved by His August Majesty King Jåyåbåyå. His magic powers were vastly greater than yours. He could see into the future ... can you do that? So clear off out of here right now. If you don't go I'll call my deputy, Tunggul Wulung of Mount Kelud. We'll give you a good shellacking, believe me. You won't get the better of us. And when we're through we'll take you up to the crater of Mount Kelud and toss you in. Then you'll really know what it's like to suffer."

After weathering more abuse from the agitated spirit, Sunan Bonang retreated, and with the crisis averted, Butå Locåyå disbanded his spirit army and went home to his comfortable cave.

Sunan Bonang, the villain of the *Sĕrat Darmågandhul*, is revered as a senior member of the Nine Saints cohort. At least four places claim the honour of hosting his tomb. The most favoured contender is the mausoleum in the centre of Tuban, the saint's hometown. Another is in the village of Bonang, near Lasem, Central Java, and another on the island of Bawean in the Java Sea, one hundred and twenty kilometres north of Tuban. A fourth spot in Kediri, less known than the other three, also puts up its hand.

The tomb in Tuban is one of the busiest pilgrimage sites in Indonesia, hosting at least a million visitors a year. Most do not make it to the saint's graveside. The burial chamber is simply too small. People sit in dense ranks on the tiled patio floor around the central chamber.

It was a moderately busy Saturday afternoon when I last went to the tomb of the saint without a history. At four o'clock I joined two hundred people sitting with bowed heads around the central burial chamber. Several quiet *tahlil* chants were echoing from different quarters of the floor, mixing gently with subdued chatter. In the front row a young man sat cradling his toddler son, swaying from side to side in rhythm with the chanting. Another young boy was carefully examining his brightly painted red fingernails. Two middle-aged village women in bright-red lace blouses and batik sarongs surreptitiously checked the SMS messages on their smartphones. By five o'clock the crowd had swelled to at least five hundred.

I paid my respects to the saint and backed out through the crush to the low eaves of the mausoleum. I bent double and manoeuvred my tall frame into the tombstone-filled outer yard. Peering from under the protective roof that arches over the ancient mausoleum I looked left across a perimeter wall. I could see the pointed towers and gleaming blue domes of Tuban's Grand Mosque floating above a canopy of trees.

The whitewashed brick and plaster wall between the new mosque and the five hundred year-old tomb of Sunan Bonang seems to mark a border just as definitively as the Brantas River once marked a border between the newly arrived brashness of Islam and the old order of the Budå religion. But in an ironic reversal, that older, more "Javanese" style is now partly embodied in the legendary figure of Sunan Bonang and his antique mausoleum.

Where once Butå Locåyå and Sunan Bonang stood on opposite sides of a river frontier, today the border has shifted. Sunan Bonang represents local, traditionalist religious faith and practice. A new border has jumped over him and now places him in the same territory as Butå Locåyå. The two have been thrown together – not allies exactly, but co-denizens of "tradition".

For some, Sunan Bonang's brand of traditional Islam, with its mysticism and magic and its obsession with holy places and the dead, has become the new heathen landscape. Across the border wall from the saint's tomb in Tuban stands the new, energetic, modern Islam, flaunting its high-rise domes and Middle Eastern minarets. The explosion in the number of pilgrims filing through Sunan Bonang's tomb is matched – possibly exceeded – by the surge of worshippers who now throng the shiny halls of the mosque. The forces of modernism, Islamic orthodoxy, and even *salafi* fundamentalism, are massing there.

"Tradition" is a suspect territory that is ripe for invasion, as the Budå lands were invaded five hundred years ago.

# 3

# Where the ancestor of Java's kings vanished into the sky

## JÅYÅBÅYÅ AND STRATEGIES
## IN THE DOMESTICATION OF ISLAM

In the *Sěrat Darmågandhul* Sunan Bonang – the intrepid trespasser in Java's heart of darkness – meets Butå Locåyå, the spirit guardian of the Budå lands. The saint is heading up the road to Kediri to visit the palace of King Jåyåbåyå, so he says.

Kediri is the first Javanese state to edge from the realm of legend into the half-light of history. King Jåyåbåyå is also an historical figure but wrapped in the exotic costumes of story and prophecy. Scarcely anything is known for sure about him or about Kediri, the mysterious realm that flourished amid the volcanoes, the tiger-haunted forests, and (at that time) the clear, fast-flowing rivers of the East Java hinterland. The very name Kediri is problematic: the state was also called Panjalu and Dåhå. It possibly came into existence in 1045 and seems to have collapsed in 1222 when it was overrun by the neighbouring state of Singåsari.

At the height of its power in the twelfth century Kediri hosted a brilliant flowering of court literature. Some of the poetic works from the period, as well as a small number of inscriptions, mention a king named Jaya Bhaya (the name means "triumphant over fear") who ruled from around 1135 to around 1159. According to the epic poem *Bharatayuddha Kakawin* (The Saga of the Bharata War) composed in Kediri around 1157 by court laureates Mpu Sĕdah and Mpu Panuluh, the great king presided over an era of prosperity and peace.

> The king and the god Vishnu are of one soul. Great claps of thunder are his generals in war. As if surrounded by rough, impenetrable ravines and canyons, he is difficult to approach. It is as if his greatness is clothed in the lush foliage of the forest. He is like a beautiful bathing place, or the unblemished beauty of a great poet's song.
>
> The world is beautiful and prosperous. Like jewels are the king's words to the humble and poor. Only virtue and right deeds are talked about now, not thieves or spies. Thieves have disappeared, and yet there are still people suffering pain, getting stabbed and getting tied up. But now these are lovers stabbed by sweet glances or tied up in tresses of unbound hair.
>
> Sudarcana the discus weapon lies idle, useless now to despatch great warriors on the field of battle. Now it is discus-like mirrors that get held up to cheeks to help ladies make themselves beautiful. The kris Nandaka is no longer used in battle. It has become the blades of eyebrows that stab the heart. And Pancajanya, the conch shell trumpet of the battlefield, now sounds only at twilight when ladies take up arms for the battle of love.
>
> So it is that now there is no resistance to King Jaya Bhaya the lord of Daha. He is a happy, light-hearted king. He enjoys himself by taking long walks in the mountains

and along the seashore. He is constantly composing beautiful songs and his people swoon away with delight at the sweetness of them. This then is how he is known to his people. They love him and the nymphs in heaven also sing his praises.

Today King Jåyåbåyå is probably the best-known royal figure in the historical imagination of the Javanese. He is popularly seen as the ancestor of all later kings. When the time came for him to die, he lifted himself from the face of the earth and vanished into the sky, a feat called *mukså* or "release".

The *Sĕrat Darmågandhul* does not tell us whether Sunan Bonang ever got to see Jåyåbåyå's palace. Tradition and old texts say it was at a place called Mamĕnang or Pamĕnang. The name survives in the modern village of Menang around eight kilometres from today's Kediri.

In 1860, more than three centuries after Sunan Bonang's sortie into Budå territory, a "discovery" was made in Menang. A villager by the name of Warsodikromo dreamed that King Jåyåbåyå had once sat enthroned in a place that was now a tangle of trees and bushes growing over a plot of boggy land. News of the dream spread among local people who set about looking for the spot. With the help of a psychic they located a scattering of hewn stones under an old *kemuning* tree on the edge of the village. People started coming to see what remained of the famous kingdom, pay their respects to the great king and petition him for help. Several attempts to reconstruct and renovate the site failed but its reputation as a place of sacred power grew.

After Indonesia's independence in 1945, a family-based

organisation called The Hondodento Foundation with links to the royal palace in Jogjakarta, set about raising money to rebuild the site. The project involved the construction of three main structures: a central sanctum marking the supposed site of Jåyåbåyå's disappearance, plus two small adjacent monuments symbolising respectively the king's abandoned clothes and his abandoned crown. Construction was completed in 1976. The small complex was named The Vanishing Place of His Majesty King Jåyåbåyå (*Pamuksan Sri Aji Jåyåbåyå*).

Today the central sanctum consists of a large concrete platform with tall contemporary-looking square columns around its perimeter. There are wide steps leading up to it and in the centre, open to the sky, stands a bulky, altar-like pedestal, evidently a stylised *lingga* and *yoni*. The pedestal is topped with a big concrete ball – like a huge eyeball – with a hole through it like the empty pupil of an eye. Its emptiness symbolises the king's miraculous absence and (so I was told) his powers of prophetic second-sight. On the floor in front of the structure stands an iron incense burner. The sanctum is shaded by tall, leafy trees. An open-sided pavilion for the reception of visitors stands nearby, as well as a utility block including toilets and a storeroom-office.

I first visited the Vanishing Place in May 1997 on the eve of the Javanese New Year's Day, the first of Surå. In the course of the afternoon and evening I felt, for the first time, the strange intensity that smoulders in ordinary events when place, time, history and people come together in a memorable way.

Surå (also called Muharram) is the first, and most hallowed, month in the Javanese calendar. The beginning of the year is a good time to set things right and ride forward on the momentum of good intentions and a clean slate. Javanese culture has something of an obsession with points of transition. They are magnets for the unexpected. Sometimes they are dangerous flashpoints. They must be negotiated carefully. Transitions – birth, puberty, marriage, transfers of office, death – must be set fast in the protective concrete of ceremony. In particular, the fragile bridge between one year and the next must be held steady with ritual scaffolding. Across the island many millions of people make their way to sacred sites, mostly holy graves, on the Javanese New Year's eve. Graves are markers of the transition from life to death. They represent the certainty of death as well as its uncertainty – the when and how of its coming.

The day was cloudy and humid. At around 2:00 pm I rolled from a minibus that had freighted me and a dozen others over the short distance from Kediri. At the Vanishing Place, under large trees and surrounded on three sides by grass-green paddy fields, the modest reception pavilion was already crowded with around a hundred people, mostly family groups. I found a scrap of tiled floor among the straw mats and slid into it.

The atmosphere was subdued. There was a vague tension in the air. As I introduced myself to my neighbours on the floor I uncovered the reason. In 1997 the Javanese New Year happened to coincide with the official campaign period for a general election. Possibly apprehensive about sponsoring any mass gathering during an election campaign, the Hondodento Foundation decided to postpone the main New Year's Day ceremony for three weeks until after the election. The decision was a topic of conversation and a cause of some disappointment as the crowd of pilgrims steadily grew through the afternoon.

Around 3:00 pm the site custodian Pak Sukarmen led a ceremonial *slamĕtan* meal in the pavilion. Food was brought in and placed on a low table. The custodian led prayers: first a long prayer in Javanese punctuated with chorused "*Inggih*" (Yes, Agreed) from the men and women sitting in a circle around the pavilion (the women sat behind the men except for those getting the food ready). The prayer concluded with a shorter segment gabbled in Arabic and greeted with repeated shouts of "*Amin!*" by those present. The food was put in hand-sized woven baskets and shared out. It consisted of rice mixed with a small quantity of noodles and cooked grated coconut, plus a small piece of chicken and a banana.

As people were finishing their food the weather suddenly changed. Wind ran over the paddy fields, rippling the water, twisting and shaking the long narrow blades of rice plants. Leaves in the surrounding trees began to quiver and bob. Flags and banners shook hard. The earlier stillness with its envelope of warmth and humidity evaporated. Within ten minutes, before the remains of the meal could be cleared away, a cowl of dark clouds had hidden the sky. Inside the pavilion I looked up and noticed light bulbs glowing in the gloom that was gathering under the roof tiles. Then, from the direction of Jåyåbåyå's sanctum, wind came pouring in like a jet of water through the open sides of the pavilion. Then rain, heavy, white, almost horizontal, scouring the broad steps of the sanctum and flattening foliage like waterweeds in a current. A deafening crack of lighting and an instant of brightness froze faces white and rigid. Half a tree came down not thirty metres away.

People sheltered as best they could, wrapping their belongings in their mats to keep them dry and trying to huddle at the rear edge of the pavilion, as far as possible from the sanctum that seemed to be the source of the storm. Most got wet. The floor was flooded.

The storm rolled away as suddenly as it had arrived. Brooms appeared to brush water from the tiles. Sodden mats lay stacked against the low back wall. Several people were wandering about looking dazed. One man who lived in Menang was staring at the tree. A large branch had partially splintered away from the trunk and hung down at a drunken angle. Its leaves lay fanned out and beaten flat on the wet earth. He told me he had never seen anything like it in all the years he had followed ceremonies at the site. The consensus from half a dozen people I spoke to was that Grandfather (*Éyang*) Jåyåbåyå had sent the storm as a sign of his displeasure at the postponement of the following day's New Year ceremony.

The afternoon sky cleared for an hour then dimmed to a hushed twilight. The crowd continued to swell. As night fell at least five thousand people – men, women and many children – crammed into the site. In the lanes of Menang Village a night fair materialised under kerosene pressure lamps, with stalls and roving hawkers selling fried food, garish plastic toys, multi-coloured balloons, second-hand clothes, confectionary and drinks. One house blazed with light as a screen was set up in its forecourt and *gamĕlan* instruments were laid out for an all-night shadow play performance.

I returned to my place in the reception pavilion. Between the pavilion and the shrine a dense mass of people inched forward. At the foot of the central sanctum they sank to their haunches, not daring to stand in the presence of the king. They made their way up the steps in an awkward squat-walk. In the centre of the shrine dazzling licks of orange flame leapt a metre above the incense burners, throwing a momentary glow over the intent, bowed faces of seated pilgrims.

Memory of the evening is still crystal-bright in my mind. I am one of eight or ten pilgrims sitting in semi-darkness crushed into a small circle on the tiled floor. I am talking to Retno who is sitting opposite me, her knees occasionally touching mine. She is forty-four years old, wearing a long loose batik skirt and a green blouse. She is somewhat worn for her age, but pretty and coquettish. She lightly slaps the arms of the men she is talking to. Unusually for an Indonesian woman, she is a very public and very heavy smoker.

Our circle bends inward to follow the conversation. More people are standing over us, packed tight and leaning forward, straining to hear what we are saying. Retno tells me she was married at the age of eighteen to a soldier in the Indonesian marines. Eight months after her wedding her husband was killed during Indonesia's 1975 invasion of East Timor. Since then Retno has lived off a war-widow's pension, putting several adopted children through school, as well as her own younger brothers and sisters. She has a house in nearby Kediri but she spends a lot of her time at Jåyåbåyå's Vanishing Place.

She fancies herself as a healer.

"I want to show you something," she says coyly and softly as if we are partners in a conspiracy. From her handbag she draws out a small cloth bundle. The crowd above us peer over our heads to see what is in her hand. I too lean forward to see what it is. She slowly opens the folds of cloth.

Lying in her hand, dark against the creamy cloth, is a small piece of wood, knobbled and gnarled, like part of a small branch. It is quite glossy, as if it has passed through many hands, perhaps over hundreds of years. A murmur, like a murmur of recognition, passes around the crowd.

But I am bewildered.

"Well, this is really interesting. Ahhh ... what's it for?"

Everyone leans forward to hear Retno's answer. There is pride in her face as she speaks.

"This is to help me regulate my menstruation."

None of the listeners seems surprised by this answer, but for me the conversation has swerved in a seriously unexpected direction. I'm groping for a response.

"I see. How fascinating. Where did you get it?"

"I got it after meditating at Sélomanglèng Cave ... you know, the ancient cave at Gunung Klotok Hill on the edge of Kediri."

Retno then tells us a story that feels like it has come out of a very distant place, transferred from woman to woman down countless generations.

"A thousand years ago," she says, "there was once a woman by the name of Déwi Kilisuci. She had a terrible problem – she did not menstruate naturally but every month bled through the pores of her skin. So she was shunned by society and couldn't find a husband. She went into the cave at Gunung Klotok and meditated there. Eventually the gods granted her wish and she was cured of her affliction."

Retno herself has no children. She cheerfully reports that her menstruation has always been irregular so she feels a special affinity with Déwi Kilisuci. Sometimes she communes with the legendary figure at Gunung Klotok and what she learns there she uses to help other women with menstrual problems.

The young man sitting beside her is Roy, aged twenty-seven. He was born and brought up in Kediri. He is unmarried. He has worked all over Indonesia in logging companies, and recently worked in Jakarta as a security guard at a Korean-owned shoe factory. Two weeks previously he happened to be working in a stifling hot part of the factory so he took off his jacket. For that he was fired by his Korean supervisor.

Roy is destitute. He says he made the journey by bus from

Jakarta to Jåyåbåyå's Vanishing Place for a total outlay of Rp.5,000 (about 45 US cents). He did this by carrying a name card he had received from a friend who was working as a manager for the Handoyo inter-city bus company. Impersonating his friend and flashing the name card as proof of his identity, he jumped from bus to bus in the Handoyo fleet down the length of Java. As he entered Kediri he saw his parents' house from the window of the bus. He saw his younger sister in the front yard. Roy says that he was too ashamed to get off the bus. He has nothing to give his parents or his sister.

As he tells his story Roy has tears in his eyes. He pauses with an embarrassed grin, but the tears run down his cheeks and drip from both ends of his ragged moustache. They splash on to his thin white t-shirt. On his chest, under a pair of clasped hands, a faded message reads "Spirit of Benevolence".

Roy sees life as a giant, slowly revolving wheel. At the moment he is at the bottom of the wheel's cycle of rotation. He has come to Jåyåbåyå's Vanishing Place to renew his commitment to patience and forbearance. He calls this *tawakkal* – an Arabic word – because, he says, he is a good Muslim. He plans to stay for three more days and nights. He feels hopeful that King Jåyåbåyå will send him an answer to his problems.

After the landslide conversion of Java from the Budå religion to Islam in the 1520s Islam reached an accommodation with the old order that allowed fragments of it to survive. One strategy was simply to redefine certain elements of Hindu-Buddhist culture as Islamic. In popular story King Jåyåbåyå was re-cast as a Muslim. Today he is almost universally regarded as a Nostradamus-like seer who authored the *Jångkå Jåyåbåyå* (the Prophecies of Jåyåbåyå, also often called the *Pralambang Jåyåbåyå*), a diverse body of traditions and texts with a series of cryptic, often bleak, prophesies at its core. They radiate the strong influence of Islam, which is unlikely to have been inherited from the Budå culture of the twelfth century. In fact the texts are all in modern Javanese, probably written as recently as the eighteenth and nineteenth centuries, so the king couldn't possibly have authored them.

Islamic though they are, the prophesies of Jåyåbåyå can still be seen as vehicles for the survival of Hindu-Buddhist authority. Their power to convince the true believers of today rests on memory of the supernaturally derived authority of the Hindu-Buddhist king who lends them his name. The Muslim authors of the *Jångkå Jåyåbåyå* texts must have been familiar with oral traditions relating to King Jåyåbåyå. Or perhaps they were inspired by pre-Islamic texts in which King Jåyåbåyå plays an epic role, in particular the Saga of the Bharata War.

Deep into the twentieth century King Jåyåbåyå remained a legitimating symbol. Before declaring Indonesia's independence in 1945, the first president of the new nation, Soekarno, is reported to have made three pilgrimage visits to the Vanishing Place of King Jåyåbåyå. According to an eyewitness his last visit was just days before the proclamation of independence on August 17th 1945.

"I have come here to ask King Jåyåbåyå for his royal blessing," Soekarno is said to have explained to his entourage. "I would like you all to help me."

He then remained silent at the site for seven minutes, after which he said: "It has been granted. Now we can go."

In the *Jångkå Jåyåbåyå* there are two iconic verses that have won a place in the gallery of proofs that King Jåyåbåyå could look into the future. Hidden in the verses, Soekarno makes a cameo appearance.

I have two predictions to make
About what will happen in the land of Java.
A yellow monarch will rule,
His soldiers will be very small
In fact his soldiers will be dwarfish in size.
They will come from the north-east
And the king's name will be King Jamus.
King Jamus will fall asleep
And will be overtaken by great turmoil.
He will stay only for the life span of a corn plant.

He will be replaced by Garudå Ngwånggå
Whose mother will be a Balinese princess.
He will rule in the land of Java,
With an army of demons and devils.
King Jamus will come again,
but will immediately have to withdraw.
The (new) king will establish his kingdom
Èru Cåkrå Èsmu Kingkin will be his name
And he will endure for one quarter of an age.

The first verse is interpreted as predicting the occupation of Indonesia by the Japanese during the Second World War. The occupation lasted three and a half years, this short period of time being expressed in the phrase "the life span of a corn plant". The second verse refers to the rise of independent Indonesia after the war. "Garuda" is seen as symbolising the Republic of Indonesia.

Indonesia's coat of arms takes the form of a garuda eagle with the symbols of the state philosophy of Pancasila emblazoned on a shield around its neck. Ngwånggå is taken to refer to President Soekarno. Ngwånggå is one of the alternative names of the shadow play hero more commonly known as Karnå after whom President Soekarno was named. Soekarno's mother came from Bali. The "army of devils and demons" refers to Indonesia's rag-tag guerrilla army that waged a fierce and successful struggle for the country's independence between 1945 and 1949. For true believers the clincher is in the last line. President Soekarno died in 1970, almost exactly 25 years, or "one quarter of an age" after declaring Indonesia's independence in 1945.

"King Jåyåbåyå had a Muslim teacher, you know," said Pak Idris, a mosque functionary at Kediri's ancient All-Saints Mosque (*Masjid Auliya'*). He was walking with me from Kediri's main street down a narrow side street past the mosque towards a large, newly built rest pavilion with a three-tiered roof.

I was sceptical. In the twelfth century Islam scarcely registered a presence in Java, and what little presence it had was confined to the distant north coast.

"True," said Pak Idris. "But he came up the Brantas River from the coast to sell perfume in Kediri."

"Perfume?"

"Yes, perfume and aromatic herbs."

He handed me a small, plain booklet.

"Take a look at this. It will tell you everything you need to know. It's been carefully researched."

Pak Idris left to busy himself with the sundown prayer in the mosque. I stretched out on the cool tiles of the rest pavilion and read the booklet. The perfume trader's name was Wasil Syamsuddin. He came to Java from Baghdad in the "Persian-Roman" region of the Middle East. He is said to have been tall and well built, and, like most Persians, he had long, wavy black hair. He had a way with words. He mixed well with people, spoke politely and was honest. Besides selling perfume and herbs he helped cure the sick. The people of Kediri thought his exotic Islamic prayers and chants were mantra charms that had healing power. He could also foretell the future and had a profound knowledge of Islamic mysticism.

When King Jåyåbåyå heard about Wasil Syamsuddin's exceptional character and powers he invited him to the palace to study and talk about life, politics, philosophy and mysticism. Because the king was blessed with a clear mind and an honest heart he was able to master his Muslim guest's knowledge, especially the "science" known as *ilmu ladzuni* or *ilmu isyaroh*. This had a big impact on him in later life.

In later times, the king, assisted by Wasil Syamsuddin, wrote a book containing prophecies about various events that were going to happen in Java. The people of Mataram, and groups who call themselves followers of Javanese sciences, call this book the *Jångkå Jåyåbåyå*, the prophecies of a king who was regarded as an incarnation of Vishnu by many in the Javanese population.

The *Kitab Musarar* (Book of Musarar) is one such collection of stories and prophecies allegedly written by King Jåyåbåyå, presumably with the assistance of Wasil Syamsuddin (it was in fact composed some time between 1749 and 1872). It is worth reading a little of it for the antique flavour of its storytelling, but also because it illustrates how metaphors – here the iron staff of religious authority and the wavy-bladed kris of Javanese identity and royal power – helped the new Islamic order to absorb the Budå order and adopt its authority. The *Kitab Musarar* tells of a priest-king from "Rome" (that is, the eastern Roman Empire, modern Turkey) by the name of Sultan Maolana Ngali Samsujen. His presence in Kediri comes to the attention of King Jåyåbåyå who invites the Muslim wise man to the palace. Despite their religious differences the two get on well. Thanks to this meeting Jåyåbåyå is destined to become a *de facto*, or honorary, Muslim.

When he arrived at the palace, Sultan Ngali Samsujen (i.e. Wasil Syamsuddin) was welcomed with great respect. Because the guest was a king and came from another nation it was proper that he be honoured. After everyone was formally seated, Sultan Ngali Samsujen spoke up:

"Hai Your Majesty King Jåyåbåyå, now is the right moment for me to tell you what the *Kitab Musarar* says about your future. You have just three more incarnations and then a division will occur, your kingdom will come to an end. Then another king will intercede."

His Majesty bowed respectfully before the Sultan.

"I know that already ... it has been decreed by the high god Batara."

His Majesty King Jåyåbåyå became a sincere student of the priest-sultan. Sultan Ngali Samsujen set forth all the content of the *Kitab Musarar*.

"And remember," he warned the king, "that your time is limited. You have just three incarnations left. In a future incarnation, Your Majesty will reside inside my iron walking stick. I will take it to the Ka'bah and leave it there (to absorb the authority of Islam). It will come into the possession of Imam Supingi who will hold it when he is giving sermons."

(*Imam* is a title carried by a Muslim religious leader, and Supingi is a Javanese corruption of Shafi'i, the founder of the Shafi'i school of Islamic law that today dominates in Indonesia.)

"This iron staff will be called Udharati. In the future a *maulana*, a descendant of the Prophet, will go to the land of Java and he will take the staff with him. It will be made into a kris and it will be honoured by the rulers of Java."

The priest-sultan then took his leave and vanished from where he had been sitting.

Today Sultan Ngali Samsujen, alias Wasil Syamsuddin the Muslim teacher, lies buried behind the All-Saints Mosque in the Setono Gedong complex in the densely packed centre of Kediri. According to a sign on the ancient *gapurå* gate leading into his grave, he bears the title Pangeran Mekkah, Prince of Mecca, or perhaps the prince *from* Mecca. The name "Wasil" is also a kind of title. It often appears after Syamsuddin's name: Ali Syamsuddin Al-Wasil, literally "Ali Syamsuddin the intercessor". *Wasil* comes from the Arabic term *wasīlah*, which is usually taken to mean "that by which one draws near to another, the means of approach". The idea of *wasīlah* is important in a religious context. It appears in the Qur'ān, for example, in Surah Al-Maidah verse 35.

Believers, be mindful of Allah. Seek to draw near to Him (*wasīlah*) and strive in His cause that you may prosper.

Wasil Syamsuddin, like most saintly figures at pilgrimage sites, is thought to be close to Allah. So if a pilgrim prays at his graveside he can access the saint as an intercessor or intermediary – a "means of approach" – who will make possible *tawassul* or a way of drawing near to Allah.

The site is very old, with stones, bricks and carved fragments that probably date from pre-Islamic times before the sixteenth century. The grave itself is housed in an airy *pĕndhåpå* pavilion about twenty by twenty metres square built in 2003. The high roof is supported by ranks of wooden pillars rising from marble plinths in a marble-tiled floor. The pillars are connected by horizontal beams and angled wooden braces that create a complex, but aesthetically attractive, criss-cross of rafters under the steeply angled roof of the building. The central well, directly above Wasil Syamsuddin's grave, is topped by a flat window that faces the sky some ten metres above the floor, admitting a pleasantly soft light into the chamber.

The saint's grave lies inside the remains of a cramped compound ringed by a low wall. Some parts of the wall still display ancient carved decoration. The grave and its two grave markers are swathed in apricot-pink satin. There are similarly coloured satin curtains around this central area, although they seem usually to be drawn aside to allow an unrestricted view of the inner area. Beside the saint's grave there are two much smaller graves holding, according to site custodian Pak Amir, the remains of two of Wasil Syamsuddin's pupils. Entry to the inner area is by way of an old, low, roofed gate. The inner area is surrounded by a stainless steel fence about four-by-four metres square. This in turn is ringed by a square newly-built brick wall about one and a half metres high in which another roofed gate stands that preserves some old stonework. This gate, like other remnants in the complex, has been somewhat crudely repaired with new bricks and stones, so the genuinely old and the relatively new – as if symbolising a central paradox of pilgrimage – are sometimes difficult to distinguish.

The tomb is promoted by the Kediri district government as a destination for "spiritual tourists" and it is popular.

> [Visitors] come to pray, recite the *tahlil* chant and read the Qur'ān. Some come simply out of curiosity. They may have various other reasons for visiting the site too. Some are seeking a divinely bestowed favour. Some may have a particular ambition or wish in mind, like setting up a new business or taking an examination. Others pray that they will meet their life partner, some pray for a steady and easy income and still others pray that their wife will allow them to take a second wife.

According to the key-keeper, there are never less than four busloads of visitors every day. In the lead-up to the fasting month of Ramadhan sometimes up to twelve buses a day arrive at the site, and the tomb is always busy during Ramadhan itself.

Over two nights I observed devotions around Wasil Syamsuddin's grave. On the auspicious eve of Friday Kliwon (a Thursday night) the site was crowded both inside the mausoleum and among the graves in the public cemetery outside. Many hundreds of people came and went during the night. I observed several visitors place plastic bottles of drinking water inside the stainless steel fence beside the saint's grave to be "charged" with the saint's power. One man even unscrewed the cap of his bottle, presumably to make it easier for the saint's power to enter. Surprisingly, there was a special area for women separated from the men's seating area by a low green cotton curtain. It was packed with a substantial crowd of women, possibly around a third of those in attendance. The majority of worshippers prayed silently, but some prayed aloud in Arabic, and some groups intoned the *tahlil* chant. The atmosphere was fervent but subdued and relaxed.

Around nine o'clock at Jåyåbåyå's Vanishing Place I left the pavilion and went a hundred metres into the neighbouring village. There, in the front portico of one of the houses, shadow puppets were lined up to the left and right of a brightly lit screen. Arrayed in front of it was a *gamělan* orchestra with at least twenty musicians. They were sitting cross-legged on the floor among upright gongs of varying sizes, horizontal gongs and bronze kettles, xylophone-like instruments using bronze and wooden keys, and drums. It was an exotic spectacle. But my eye was drawn to the middle of the ensemble where a man was sitting on the floor with a trombone between his knees. And beside him sat another musician with a brass trumpet, and beside him another with a European-style snare drum. Around the *gamělan*, with excited children already packing themselves into the spaces between the instruments, a dense crowd filled the front yard.

The puppeteer, dressed in a traditional rough-spun *lurik* jacket with a close-fitting *blangkon* headcloth, was seated cross-legged on the floor in front of the screen. He began the performance by rapping on a big box beside him with a small wooden handle-less gavel. I felt – as I always do at the beginning of a shadow play performance – a sudden rush of anticipation and a frisson passed over my skin. It is the unexpected modesty of the opening that always gets me. The *gamělan* started up quietly at first, almost hesitantly, with soft chimes and tinkling tied into a complex thread of melody from a two-stringed *rěbab* viol. The music began to swell. A row of female singers joined in, high and nasal, intoning their vocal line in the strange intervals of Java's five-note pentatonic scale. A dense writhing wall of music, instrumental and choral, rose up in front of the screen.

Then the music died away, and the puppeteer recited the standard opening of a classical shadow play. In formal, somewhat archaic language, he described the Javanese vision of utopia – the perfect state: beautiful, peaceful, prosperous, free of crime, ruled with justice by a firm but kind king.

As the puppeteer intoned the prelude I looked around at the audience. Most were ordinary villagers, hard-pressed by poverty, many no doubt living in conditions of environmental degradation and extreme population density, probably troubled by crime and injustice. They were listening entranced to the description of what (as they saw it) Java had once been. At this moment – amid the relentless and cruel struggle to earn a living, to simply survive – I felt the presence of an ancient civilisation, a civilisation with a written heritage that reaches back more than a thousand years. Today it is a wounded civilisation but it remains vibrant in the often squalid present.

The characters – spiky, brightly painted flat leather puppets – appeared pressed against the screen: the king, the princes, the ministers and generals of the kingdom. The king commanded his generals to take an army out to the borders of the realm and repel an invasion by greedy ogres from across the sea. On the screen the army set off – first the princes on their elephants, then the generals and knights on horses, then the rank and file of the troops. These took the form of big flat puppets cut out to look like platoons of soldiers, bristling with spears and lances.

Then, from the middle of the *gamĕlan* I heard a trumpet blast, and across the screen came a tank – a silhouette on a stick representing a big, armour-plated Sherman tank with a turret and gun. Jet fighters began to zoom by, then modern troops appeared to the accompaniment of the snare-drums: soldiers dressed in modern battle fatigues, wearing steel helmets, big boots and bulky back packs and carrying rifles (each a flat leather cut-out on the end of a stick, of course). Then, against a background of booming gongs and the clang of xylophones the trombone began to blare out in long sliding notes. On the screen a modern foreign tourist appeared, with a floppy hat, wearing a loud Hawaiian shirt, Bermuda shorts and wrap-round sunglasses, and with a camera, taking pictures of the passing parade. Java loves to laugh, and it seems Java can still laugh at itself and at the ogres from across the sea, the Europeans who have brought cosmic changes to their island, for better or for worse.

The friend I was with tugged at my arm.

"It's almost midnight," he whispered. "Come with us." I knew that the shadow play would continue for another four or five hours – right up until near dawn – so I left the bright lights and bright colours of the performance and followed my companion out of the village into the surrounding rice fields.

Five hundred metres away we came to an ancient bathing place called Tirto Kamandanu. It consisted of two brick and plaster bathing pools, one for men and one for women, inside a walled compound. Towering above the baths was a giant stone image of the Hindu god Vishnu, and backing this an equally massive image of the elephant-headed god Ganesha. Entry to the complex was through a large, Balinese-style, roofed gate.

In the late night gloom scores of men were waist-deep in the water of the men's pool, or squatting at the rim of the pool, washing their hair. Some were using soap or commercial shampoos, others were simply dipping their hands into the water and vigorously wetting their hair. Women were doing the same in the pool next door (although I didn't personally witness this). When I asked what was going on, one young man – blinking through the lather streaming down his face – replied that he had come to Jåyåbåyå's Vanishing Place and to the Tirto Kamandanu baths to renew his commitment to patience and what he called "trust in Allah". By ritually bathing and washing his hair on New Year's Eve he hoped to wash away the stains of the past year.

I surprised myself. I knelt at the pool's edge, cupped my hands in the water, and slowly splashed it over my hair. I stayed there for some time, kneeling and quiet, feeling the coolness on my neck and back, impervious to the subdued giggling and chatter around me.

I slipped away on my own and started to walk back towards the Vanishing Place. It was pitch black. The sky was starless. I was on an asphalt path but I couldn't see it beneath me. I had to feel for it with my feet. Left and right lay the gaping darkness of rice paddies. Ahead I saw a dim pulsing light. As I approached I came on the ghostly outline of a tree. In it, and across an adjacent paddy terrace filled with half-grown rice plants, thousands of fireflies were pumping out a fragile, spectral light. It was a massive crowd of tiny pin-points, winking on and off at one second intervals, in unison, flashing in total silence with clockwork synchronised precision. I stood scarcely able to breathe. For an instant something gripped me. In the darkness there were no boundaries and I felt connected to a force far, far beyond me.

I don't know how long the spectacle lasted, perhaps five minutes, but the moment of connection passed. I became aware of a tinny tinkling in the distance. It was the *gamělan* orchestra. I turned away from the fireflies and made my way towards it.

# 4

# Bandit saints of the borderlands

## KI BONCOLONO, THE LAW AND THE LAWLESS

At the tomb of the bandit saint Ki Agĕng Balak about twenty kilometres south-east of Solo in Central Java the saint is a menacing figure. He used to dress wholly in black, they say. He had a glowering face and a wide, thick, handlebar moustache. The moustache gives him away at once. It fits the stereotype of a Javanese rural bandit as snugly as an eye-patch and shoulder-parrot fit the storybook profile of a Caribbean pirate.

"He likes opium," said the elderly lady selling offerings in the vestibule. She was sitting at a low table behind a fragrant array of flowers and petals: red and white roses, curly yellow tendrils of *kĕnångå*, white pods of *kanthil*. They lay on trays in dense heaps like plumped up, brightly embroidered cushions. There were packets of clove-scented cigarettes too, even boxes of matches to help the saint light up.

She held up a tiny silver tube capped at one end like a mini tube of toothpaste. I took it between my thumb and forefinger.

"This is opium?"

"Yes, it is. Raw opium. Only five thousand rupiah."

There was history in the old lady's quavering voice. As early as the seventeenth century Dutch carpetbaggers were making good money importing opium – mostly from Bengal – and selling it in the islands of Southeast Asia. In the nineteenth century the Netherlands East Indies government took over management of the trade. While intoning pious warnings about the dangers of opium addiction they engineered a dramatic expansion of addiction by selling monopoly franchises – termed opium "farms" (*opiumpachten* or *opiumparceel*) – to retailers who were almost 100% Chinese. Around the turn of the twentieth century the franchise system was dropped and the government took the ultra-profitable business of drug dealing into its own respectable Calvinist hands. They expanded the territories where opium could be sold and appointed thousands of official opium dealers, mostly indigenous Indonesians. These set up points of sale, took over the operation of opium dens, encouraged women to get addicted as well as men, and sold user licenses to addicts. By the 1920s around 15% of Indies government revenue came from the opium addiction of its native subjects.

Maximising profit depended on enforcement of a dealer monopoly. This was hard to do. Unauthorised importation, possession and sale of opium was widespread, but even in small quantities it was illegal. It attracted fines, imprisonment or brutal physical punishment. In 1866 a total of 62,659 miscreants across the Indies were sentenced to whipping for minor violations of the law.[4] Many of the crimes related to unauthorised drug possession or dealing.

In Java minor infringements of the law, even offences against

4    Mayon Soetrisno's novelette *Nyai Adipati* issued in a single volume with the novelette *Nyai Wonokromo* (Jakarta: Progress, no date, probably around 2010) describes a late nineteenth century court case triggered by an indiscriminate whipping dealt out to twenty-one native staff in the household of a junior Dutch official after a picture of the Dutch queen goes missing from his house.

unwritten norms of polite behaviour, were dealt with in courts
of summary justice called the police roll (*politierol*). Until their
abolition in 1914 police roll assizes were the backbone of low-level
justice in the Indies. Usually convening sessions on the verandah of
his home or office, a petty Dutch official would hear a "report" on
each alleged offense prepared for him by his Javanese underlings.
Almost wholly dependant on the report he would declare a verdict
and, if necessary, pronounce sentence. There was little concern for
defence or rules of evidence, and there was no appeal against the
verdict or sentence.

Ki Agĕng Balak's beautifully kept grave,
and a tube of raw opium sold as an offering outside the entry door.

To make the system work a class of Javanese detectives,
informants and mediators evolved. Many of them worked on both
sides of the law. One of the many names for them was *kĕpĕtĕngan*,
"those who operate in darkness." James Rush, historian of Java's
nineteenth century opium culture, reports they were often ...

> ... appointed by headmen to protect villages from banditry
> and arson, and as detectives and "secret police" in the
> service of headmen, *priyayi* (Javanese bureaucrats) officials

and Dutch administrators. As such they often acted as *ketrangan* (court report) makers, specialists in producing airtight, and frequently false, solutions to criminal investigations ... [They] gathered in opium and gambling dens and consorted among fringe elements of Javanese society – dancing girls, prostitutes and pimps, traveling show folk, magicians and con men, fences and thieves, and the bands of bandits that preyed on the countryside.

In the vestibule of the saint's mausoleum I bought a tube of opium and put it among the flower offerings on my tray. Ibu Sidem, one of the site's three female key-keepers, took me to the door of the burial chamber. The room was tiled on the outside in peach pink. Beside the door a squat, black-tiled brick furnace sent a cream-painted chimney pipe through the ceiling. Ibu Sidem knelt before it and sat back on her heels. She took a lump of incense and placed it inside, poking at it with a pair of tongs. As it flared she intoned a prayer to the saint. It was a standard entreaty, beginning with a greeting in Arabic then switching to Javanese. She asked him to protect me from misfortune. She pleaded for his blessing on whatever endeavour I might undertake.

I pushed open the door and went into the burial chamber. The saint lived in homely comfort. The room was carpeted and air conditioned. In the coolness a grandfather clock chimed quietly against the back wall. Not far from the clock stood a decorative row of tall ceremonial umbrellas. A teapot and cups were laid out on a side table beside a bowl of bananas and scaly-skinned snake fruit. Soft brightness poured in from curtain-framed windows on three sides.

I sat down cross-legged beside the grave. Inside its box-like canopy of gold and green drapes I could see a low stack of solid wooden beams. I reached inside and scattered flower petals along the length of the beams. I placed the tube of opium on one of them, silently wishing Ki Agĕng Balak enjoyment of the treat and a quiet retirement.

His retirement has been anything but quiet. On ordinary days never fewer than ten visitors arrive at the tomb to pay their respects, but on Thursday nights hundreds of people turn up. The site is well known for its ritual meals. Pilgrims often make a *nadhar* contract with the saint. If their wishes are granted – and they usually are, I was told – they repay the saint by holding a ritual meal in his honour. If you are lucky enough to be at his tomb when a meal is on you will be invited to join in.

The tomb is at its busiest during Surå, also called Muharram, the first month of the Javanese-Islamic year. On the eve of the first of Surå – the Javanese New Year's Day – crowds jam the small complex and its surrounds. Numbers again swell in the last week of the month. The week climaxes with a ceremonial changing of the canopy on Sunday. In the days leading up to the ceremony there are entertainments – an all-night shadow play performance and girls in short skirts belting out Javanese *campursari* songs on a makeshift stage. There is a big thanksgiving feast too. Dozens of cows and goats are slaughtered, not to mention hundreds of squawking chickens. The food is cooked, spices and rice are added, and small, tasty servings are distributed free to the thousands who have turned up for the occasion.

The old cloth canopy that has shrouded the grave for the previous year is removed. After a year of proximity to the saint it has become infused with his special power and is highly prized.

The cloth is taken to the nearby Ranjing River and ritually washed before being cut into handkerchief-sized pieces. These are put up for sale to a jostling crowd of buyers.

The new canopy – usually donated by a beneficiary of the saint's largesse – is paraded through the narrow lanes of the village flanked by an exotic array of ceremonial umbrellas, spears, bowls of smoking incense and trays of flowers. But the real focus of attention is the *gunungan*. This is a cone-shaped mini-mountain of cooked rice liberally garnished with fruit and vegetables hoisted shoulder-high on a bamboo frame. As the procession approaches the saint's tomb a heaving mass of people fall on it, fighting for a fistful of its consecrated rice, even tearing apart the bamboo frame and carrying off its bits and pieces.[5] The mayhem subsides, the crowd disperses and the elderly move in. In 2004 I came two days late to the rite. But there were several skinny grey-haired men and women still squatting on the roadway picking up rice grains one by one.

"Sure the rice has been trampled," said a seventy-year-old farmer from Boyolali who had been at the site for two days, "but I know these grains can bring me good fortune. I will scatter them in my paddy fields. They will protect my crop from pests."

"They will protect my crop from pests."

Behind this simple statement lurks the shadow of Ki Agĕng Balak. According to anthropologist John Pemberton he was "a congenial, highly skilled thief, who stole from Dutch and Javanese of note residing in Solo in the 1930s and early 1940s and distributed

---

5    This kind of rite, called *rĕbutan* or *rayahan*, is widespread. The biggest is the annual Yaqawiyu rite, also called Apĕman, at the tomb of Ki Agĕng Gribig in Jatinom, Central Java. There is also an annual rĕbutan at the tomb of Jumadil Kubro in Troloyo, East Java, and the big Grĕbĕg rites in Jogjakarta and Solo revolve around rĕbutan events.

the loot to peasants". Like the *kěpětěngan* agents of former times he also helped those in trouble with the "pests" of law enforcement. Today, so I was told by a villager, people come to his tomb when they are caught up in a court case or are on the run from police. He is an underworld Mr Fix-it, running a kind of protection racket to save you from the shame and stress of a court appearance. At the very least he can get you a reduced sentence. But the tomb's shady reputation is a double-edged sword for those who seek refuge there. As the villager told me: "The tomb is well-known as a kind of hang-out for people with connections to the criminal underworld so naturally it's a magnet for the police. After a crime is committed the police often make a bee-line here to make arrests."

The police keep quite a close eye on the tomb. In 2004 the newspaper *Suara Merdeka* reported there had been an increase in the number of outsiders who had, in effect, taken up residence in the tomb complex. They were living well too. By joining in the thanksgiving meals conducted almost daily by grateful pilgrims they were eating better than the local villagers – at least so the locals claimed with sour smiles.

The people of Balakan – the surrounding village – were getting restless. Dozens of long-stay visitors were "problematic" and in trouble with the law, they thought. There was no evidence the visitors were anything but ordinary pilgrims, but the reputation of the site cast its shadow over them. Local officials and the police resolved to step up surveillance. They didn't want the tomb to look "messy", they said. They would check the credentials of the freeloaders and if there were any whose papers were not in order they would be sent packing.

But when I asked key-keeper Ibu Sidem about Ki Agěng Balak's criminal history she bristled.

"He was no bandit," she said with a touch of indignation. "He was a prince of Måjåpait." She was referring to the great Hindu-Buddhist kingdom that reached the zenith of its power in East Java in the middle years of the fourteenth century.

We were sitting in the outer gallery. Ibu Sidem settled in for a long talk. She adjusted her spectacles, smoothed her densely patterned dark-brown batik sarong over her knees and hitched up the purple cotton of her *kabayak* blouse to conceal her cleavage. As she unfurled her story a small audience of visitors crept up, one by one, to join us.

With mild-mannered patience she explained that Ki Agĕng Balak was originally known by the name Radèn Sujono. He was famous for his prowess as a healer and maker of weapons. A violent struggle developed between Måjåpait and the Sundanese people of West Java. The royal family of Måjåpait was convulsed by turmoil and Radèn Sujono fled west into Central Java. The king of Måjåpait ordered two of his retainers, Simbarjo and Simbarjoyo, to track him down and bring him home. They found him sunk deep in lonely meditation in a dense forest. Simbarjo and Simbarjoyo woke him and pleaded with him to return to Måjåpait. Only he, they told him, could calm the kingdom's turbulence.

Sujono refused, but undertook to settle the kingdom's problems from a distance. By intense meditation he had acquired several powerful magic charms, one of them called the *Aji Balak*. In Javanese the word *balak* means "to repel". Maybe it is also related to the word *bålå* meaning a calamity. By using the *Aji Balak* charm he was able to project his power into distant Måjåpait and the kingdom miraculously returned to order. Simbarjo and Simbarjoyo were impressed and decided to remain with him. When the three of them died they were buried together in the same grave. The jungle quickly reclaimed the spot and the location of the grave was forgotten.

The author with tomb key-keeper Ibu Sidem in 2013
as she tells the story of Radèn Sujono, fugitive
noble of Måjåpait who became Ki Agĕng Balak.

Some time later (no one knows exactly when) an old, poverty-stricken man by the name of Banggi went into the forest in search of food. As he dug desperately and fruitlessly in the earth for edible roots night fell, and from the darkness he heard a booming voice.

"Who are you, old man? It's late and here you are still scratching for something to eat! What a life! Why aren't you at home with your family? If you, your family and your descendants would like to live comfortably – if you would like to be well dressed, have full stomachs and live in good houses – I am prepared to help you. But you will have to help me too. You will have to look after me and my grave. And you must call me Ki Agĕng Balak!"

The old man accepted the offer and its implied contract

gratefully. He located the lost grave, cleared the undergrowth from it, and made offerings for the comfort of the saint. The saint kept his part of the bargain. Banggi's fortunes changed and he flourished. News of what had happened spread and outsiders arrived eager for a slice of the prosperity. A settlement called Balakan sprang up around the tomb. For his part Banggi took good care of the tomb and, when he died, passed responsibility for it to his descendants.

"Today the work is shared among six tomb custodians," Ibu Sidem concluded, "three men and three women. All of us are descendants of that old man who scratched for food in the darkness of the forest."

It was a comforting story that fitted neatly into a well-worn mould. It is common knowledge that when Måjåpait fell many of its nobles fled east to Bali, but what is less well known is that a good number fled westwards into Central Java, and even beyond. Some of them, like Radèn Sujono, found asylum deep in the forests that lapped in lagoons of dense vegetation around the island's volcanoes. In Javanese tradition forests are wild and forbidding places to be chopped down and cleared by the forces of order. The forest is fraught with fringe-dwellers: wild animals, ghosts, demons, crazy hermits and fugitives from the stern hand of central order. So when Sujono took refuge in the forest he joined a ragtag category of problematic beings living in badlands far from the centres of civilised society.

Today you can appeal to Ki Agĕng Balak when you need to repel a threat or calamity, especially one embodied in the courts and the police, the instruments of central order. From his hideout the saint sent help into the distant precinct of the Måjåpait court and this long-distance reach is what attracts pilgrims to his tomb today. I met some of them in the enclosed gallery around the tomb where a group of around forty were preparing to eat a thanksgiving meal. I sat down among them and was quietly handed a paper bowl. In it there was rice, shredded chilli peppers, a *gulai* curry of chicken and beef, and a big, crisp shrimp cracker.

The meal had been prepared by Ibu Sidem – it was one of her income-generating services. She also made a short speech in Javanese. She thanked Ki Agĕng Balak for the blessings he had bestowed on the guests. She politely thanked the guests too, wishing them good health and safety on their return journey.

We fell on the food. As I ate I learned the party came from Semarang, two hours away on the north coast. Ki Agĕng Balak had answered their prayers, they told me, enabling their leader to complete the building of a house. The simple but delicious meal disappeared in a few minutes. In a businesslike way, as if the terms of a commercial transaction had been met, the group cleared away the debris of the meal, slipped out to their bus and vanished behind a black puff of diesel smoke.

Their exodus revealed a trio of pilgrims – a young man with his sister and father – camped on plastic mats in one corner of the gallery. They had come the previous day from Jakarta. All three were pious practising Muslims, in fact the young man had just finished an undergraduate degree in Islamic law at the respected Hidayatullah State University of Islamic Studies. His sister, wearing a tightly wrapped *hijab* headscarf, had just finished a degree in economics at a minor Jakarta university. Months previously, before taking their final exams, they had come to Ki Agĕng Balak to ask for his help. Now they had come back, they told me, to express gratitude to the saint for their success. They planned to stay two nights. They would keep a thanksgiving vigil at his graveside through the coming night before returning to Jakarta the next day for their graduation ceremonies.

About a hundred kilometres directly north of Ki Agĕng Balak's tomb a knob of coastline protrudes like a bunion into the Java Sea. A thousand years ago it was an island but the emaciated channel of water that separated it from the mainland clogged up with silt, the water evaporated, and the island became welded fast to the Java coast. Today the scar of the channel is invisible at ground level but satellite images reveal the ancient strait that probably ran close to the modern inland cities of Pati and Kudus. At the centre of the knob stands the cone-like eminence of Mount Muria. According to legend, its once thickly forested slopes used to shelter the usual assortment of misfits. Among them were two bandits whose titles proclaimed their profession, Maling Kåpå and his younger brother Maling Gĕntiri. In Javanese *maling* means "thief who operates by night".

The two brothers lived on both sides of moral and legal respectability. Both were students of Sunan Ngĕrang, a great teacher of Islam in the Juwånå region of the north coast. Thanks to their Islamic learning and piety they had acquired potent magic powers, which they used to rob the rich. Being pious servants of religion, naturally they transferred the proceeds of their robberies to poor people and people in distress.

One day Sunan Ngĕrang held a thanksgiving gathering to celebrate the twentieth birthday of his daughter Roroyono. It was attended by guests from near and far. They included Sunan Muriå and Sunan Kudus, two of Sunan Ngĕrang's most promising pupils later to become members of the Nine Saints missionary cohort. There were other guests too, though their religious piety was far from flawless. These included Maling Kåpå and Maling Gĕntiri, and the boorish Pathak Warak. The latter was in line to become an *adipati*, a local despot. Pathak Warak means "rhino head", a name that evoked the rhino's aggressively lowered head and phallic horn embodying Pathak Warak's bullying lecherous character.

With this guest list the party was bound to be memorable. An "incident" occurred when Roroyono appeared carrying a tray of drinks. She was dazzling, a beauty beyond what any guest in the hall had ever seen. Her dark, well-oiled hair was coiled into a thick scroll held in place on the nape of her neck with ornamental gold pins. Her complexion glowed with *borèh* cream that lent it a bewitching greenish tinge. Her eyebrows were plucked into scimitar-like crescents above narrow lustrous eyes. Between her thin, lightly rouged lips her teeth had been attractively blackened. Her slim hips tapered into a tightly wound creamy batik wrap that reached to her ankles. As she walked her bare heels flashed voluptuous sexuality.

A momentary hush fell over the gathering. The pious students Sunan Muriå and Sunan Kudus were armed with the defences given them by their religious studies. Instantly they averted their eyes so the devil could not drag their gaze, and their thoughts, in the direction of sexual temptation. But Pathak Warak was not like them. He consumed Roroyono with the bulging eyes of a dance mask. He couldn't even blink.

As the girl approached him with the tray of drinks Pathak Warak spoke some "improper words" to her (the story I am summarising here does not tell us what those words were). Roroyono was flustered but she served him a drink. Rhino Head couldn't help himself. He reached out and groped parts of her body "that should not be touched". The girl had spirit. She became angry. She lifted the tray of drinks and dumped it over Pathak Warak. His clothes were left sodden. He half lifted his hand to slap her, but as hoots of laughter rolled around the hall he remembered that Roroyono was the daughter of his teacher. He swallowed his rage, but still he could not blink.

That night Pathak Warak stayed in Sunan Ngĕrang's house. Deep in the silent hours he left his bed and crept to Roroyono's room. Outside the door he whispered an *aji sirĕp*, a spell that puts its victim into a bewitched sleep. In perfect silence he shinned up to the roof, lifted some tiles and slid into the bedroom below. He lifted the sleeping girl, opened the window shutters and disappeared with her into the surrounding forest.

The following day Sunan Ngĕrang was distraught. He vowed that whoever could rescue his daughter would be well rewarded. If the rescuer was female he would adopt her as his daughter, and if male he would give him Roroyono's hand in marriage. Sunan Muriă took up the challenge. He appealed for help to Maling Kåpå and Maling Gĕntiri both of whom were citizens of his mountain domain and fellow students of Sunan Ngĕrang.

The two pious bandits agreed, urging Sunan Muriă to go back to his all-important duties as a teacher of Islam while they recovered the girl. They promised that, if they were successful, they would hand Roroyono to their "elder brother" to be his wife.

*Gancaring crită* (as Javanese storytellers say) ... to cut a long story short, Maling Kåpå and Maling Gĕntiri succeeded in recovering Roroyono. They returned her to her father who bestowed her on Sunan Muriă. The Sunan took his bride to his sanctuary on the slopes of Mount Muriă where the couple lived in blissful happiness. Maling Kåpå and Maling Gĕntiri were rewarded too. They got an allocation of land in the village of Buntar, which brought them great wealth.

At this point I should say *Sigĕg*, "End of story." But in the realm of storytelling, kidnapping a beautiful woman is a motif so delicious it demands repetition, especially if it comes with an improving moral lesson. So Roroyono was kidnapped a second time. Surprisingly though, the motif comes with a warning to men, and the warning is couched in Islamic terms. The story invites men to look critically at their macho male behaviour.

As Maling Kåpå and Maling Gĕntiri were escorting Roroyono back to her father after rescuing her they had been in a daze. They could not take their eyes off her loveliness. And now, in their comfortable premises at Buntar they squirmed with frustration. A respectable, law-abiding life was not for them. For one thing, they couldn't sleep. Roroyono's face seemed to float before them day and night. But she was married, and married moreover to their comrade in piety Sunan Muriå. So there was nothing they could do. Self-reproach struck deep into their hearts. Why had they been so quick to offer their friend a helping hand? They had done all the hard, dangerous work but it was Sunan Muriå who was enjoying the pleasures of marriage with the girl who should have been theirs. In one version of this story the author remarks:

> Here we see the wisdom of a religious education. That's why men have to keep a tight rein on their gaze. Men must do this to guard their honour, not to mention the chastity of their penises. If Maling Kåpå and Maling Gĕntiri had not kept staring at Roroyono's body they wouldn't have become ensnared by the devil who had set a trap for them in their greedy gaze.[6]

6  This echoes Surah 24 An-Nur (The Light) verse 30 in the Qur'ān which reads "Speak to men who believe and tell them to lower their gaze and guard their private parts. They will be purer if they do so."

The devil moved in and occupied the two men. They decided to snatch Roroyono from Sunan Muriå. They would make her their common wife. But when Maling Gĕntiri arrived at Mount Muriå he was ambushed by the Sunan's pupils. He fled upwards to the peak of the mountain where he perished in a fierce fight. Maling Kåpå was more cunning. He chose his moment and his *modus operandi* more carefully. He waited until Sunan Muriå was absent on a religious mission and sent Roroyono's guards into a deep sleep with his *aji sirĕp*. He grabbed his friend's wife and carried her off to a Buddhist sanctuary where he had once been a pupil. It was a protected sanctuary – an island in a river – headed by a Buddhist abbot.

But his triumph was short-lived. Sunan Muriå, being a good Muslim, made regular goodwill visits to the holy places of other faiths to "cement friendly relations". He decided to make a surprise visit to the sanctuary where Maling Kåpå had taken refuge. When he arrived he saw his wife lying on the ground bound hand and foot and the outraged abbot in fierce dispute with Maling Kåpå.

The abbot tried to untie Roroyono but Maling Kåpå defended his booty. He deployed his all-powerful Ultimate Magic Charm (*aji pamungkas*). The abbot retreated and Sunan Muriå stepped in. A fight broke out but it didn't last long. As Kåpå unleashed his charm the potent weapon bounced back off the super-invulnerable Sunan Muriå and hit the bandit. Karmic justice was done, it killed him instantly.

Sunan Muriå apologised to the Buddhist abbot. Fighting and death should not happen in a religious sanctuary, he said.

"No problem," said the abbot. "I now regret that I passed my knowledge on to him. He misused what he learned."

But he gently lifted the charred body. Maling Kåpå was, after all, his pupil and he deserved a respectful funeral.

That at least is one version of the Maling Kåpå and Maling Gĕntiri story, one among many. In modern Java the squalid deaths of the holy bandits do not seem to have harmed their reputation. In fact today, as *laissez-faire* capitalism gathers new momentum, they are heroes to many. Problematic heroes, sure, but heroes nevertheless. They patrol the borderlands between legal and illegal with all the confidence of modern business entrepreneurs. They even star in their own *kethoprak* stage melodramas.

In 2015 I visited a newly built shrine dedicated to Maling Gĕntiri about eight kilometres northeast of Blora in the borderlands between Central Java and East Java. Blora was once Java's premier source of quality teak for buildings, furniture and handicrafts. Surrounded by the remains of teak forests it is still known today by the nickname Teak Town (*Kota Kayu Jati*).

The shrine lies in a small copse of trees that also shelters a battered, weed-tangled public cemetery. The simple building consists of a deep, tiled verandah abutting a tiny, completely bare meditation cell. Beside the cell, through a door marked "Never Locked", a short, shallow flight of stairs leads down into the darkness of an enclosed crypt. There, using the flash on my camera, I was able to see a cube-like gauze canopy, black with soot from incense smoke. Under the canopy lay what looked like a tiled grave with the detritus of offerings littering its length. Melted incense drooled like grey candle wax down the side of the ledger, at one end stood a green plastic bucket crammed with flower offerings and banana-leaf packets, red joss sticks fanned out from the top of a brown ceramic jar, the acrid sting of scented smoke filled the air.

I sat for some time hoping that a caterpillar of light might help my eyes adjust and show me the whole room. But there was no window and no chink of light in the pitch blackness.

I returned to the verandah. As I sat listening to the quiet breathing of the trees a local farmer came splashing through the water of his nearby rice fields to welcome me and tell me a little about the shrine.

"It was funded and built by the local community with financial contributions from two members of the Blora legislature, Bapak Maulana Kusnanto and Ibu Ningsih. Bapak Kusnanto was a candidate for District Head (*Bupati*) of Blora at the last election."

"Did he get elected?"

"Not this time. But maybe he'll try again." He laughed. "And maybe next time Maling Gĕntiri will help him get into office."

"But Maling Gĕntiri was a thief and bandit who tried to abduct another man's wife!"

The farmer flaked some dry mud off his knees and nodded solemnly. He waved expansively over the rice fields beyond the trees.

"Around here Maling Gĕntiri is a hero. In fact we think he is our saviour, even the messianic Righteous King. True, he was a bandit but he came to his senses and changed his ways. He didn't die on Mount Muriå. He died here. Of old age."

In Java good-hearted thieves, thugs and bandits, plying their trade in the penumbra lands far from political authority, seem to occupy a permanent niche in the imagination, as they do in folklore all over the world. The Javanese word *rāt* (cognate with the Malay-Indonesian *darat*) means "the whole world" covering both land and people. For the holy brigand, contact with land and people

– the *rāt* – not only gives him life, but brings him *back* to life after the forces of authority have snuffed him out. The motif comes from deep in the distant hinterland of Javanese myth.

Let me grab a thread of this myth from the tangled back-stories of Javanese shadow plays. At the beginning of history the great god Wisnu (Vishnu) married the earth, Pĕrtiwi. The earth conceived and delivered a son, Sitijå, whose name means literally "born of the earth". Sitijå turned out to be tough and warlike with fangs and a lethal bite. His doting mother gave him a mighty magic charm, the Wijåyåkusumå flower that took the form of a dish fringed with sharp-pointed petals. The Wijåyåkusumå could bring back to life those who had died on the field of battle. Sitijå made good use of it. He stood up to the mighty King Bomånāråkåsurå (literally: "lord of the earth and the underworld") and killed him in combat. Then he revived his dead adversary and, like a python, swallowed his spirit and digested his powers, even (in some versions of the story) adopting his name and identity. As the story evolved so too the Wijåyåkusumå charm seems to have evolved into the Påncåsonå charm that draws on the regenerative power of the earth to reassemble the limbs of warriors that have been lopped off in battle. If the reassembled warrior touches the earth the Påncåsonå brings him back to life. So Sitijå (alias Bomånāråkåsurå) had the key to eternal vigour: simply reconnect with the *rāt* – the earth and its people.

Sitijå launched a war along the forest-filled frontier of Tunggårånå, the most remote of lands in the geography of the classical shadow theatre. There he met his end at the hands of Krĕsnå (Krishna) an incarnation of Sitijå's own father the god Wisnu. Krĕsnå used his discus-like *cåkrå* weapon to sheer off the head of his wayward son. As bits and pieces of body flew into the air one of Krĕsnå's generals caught Sitijå's torso on a latticework tray and prevented it from falling to earth. The Påncåsonå charm could not work its restorative magic and Sitijå perished for all eternity.

In the twenty-first century this ancient story still resonates with surprising force. It is a recognisable matrix behind tales of Ki Boncolono, a folk hero still honoured in the Kediri region of East Java. Ki Boncolono is a morally ambiguous but supernaturally powerful thief. For many local people he and Maling Gĕntiri are one and the same.

*Kediri Raya*, an internet site devoted to promoting tourism in Kediri, gives this version of the Boncolono story.

In former times, during the Dutch colonial occupation, the people of Kediri lived in destitution and oppression. The economy was dominated by the Dutch and they imposed unreasonable taxes. If these taxes were not paid the Dutch would seize people's crops. Just to eat, people had to go to the Dutch to buy food that they themselves had produced by their own hard work. This outraged Ki Boncolono. He was angered at the behaviour of the *mijneers*, the Dutch gentlemen, and was moved at the injustice inflicted on local people. Armed with supernatural powers and assisted by Tumĕnggung Mojoroto, Tumĕnggung Poncolono and his pupils – all of whom, needless to say, had magic powers – Ki Boncolono robbed the Dutch officials of their wealth. The proceeds of the robberies were distributed to poor people. Truly a noble thing to do. Instantly he acquired a fragrant reputation among the people ... he was feared, but at the same time admired, and the people always looked forward to his coming.

The Dutch were frustrated and angry. They did all they could to catch Boncolono, but their efforts always ended in failure. Whenever they managed to surround him, all Boncolono needed to do was press himself against a post, or a wall, or a tree, and he would disappear. Even if they shot him, killed him, or did whatever to him, Ki Boncolono would not die. As soon as his body hit the earth he would come to life again. The Dutch lost patience and decided to use the power of their money to deal with him. They announced a competition with a huge reward for whoever could catch or kill Boncolono. Several people knew there was a flaw in Boncolono's magic skills. They came to the Dutch *mijneers* and told them that they would have to cut Boncolono's head from his torso and bury the two parts of the body in places that were separated by a river.

And so, after plotting with local martial arts warriors, the Dutch put their plan into action. As has happened in other heroic tales, Boncolono was caught, and with the help of the martial arts fighters, he was put to death. Before he could come back to life his body was cut in two. The torso was buried on Kediri's Maskumambang Hill (*Bukit Maskumambang*), and Boncolono's head was buried under a banyan tree called the *Ringin Sirah* in the village of Banjaran. Maskumambang Hill is on the west side of the Brantas River, while Ringin Sirah is on the east side.

It was a Sunday morning when I made my way from the centre of Kediri to Maskumambang Hill on the western fringe of the city not far from the famous antiquity of Sélomanglèng Cave. As I strolled up the asphalt road towards the hill I found myself zigzagging through a confusion of parked cars and motorbikes. Clusters of thin young men in hoodies, and curvy girls in tight pants and high leather boots (many of them wearing prim *hijab* scarves) were overtaking me, all with robot-head motorbike helmets wedged under their arms. From behind clouds of dust and rows of fluttering banners came the howl of engines rising and falling like a squadron of chainsaws at work.

I had walked into a motocross meet. At the roadside entrance to Ki Boncolono's tomb stood a box-office tent decorated in garish advertisements for lubricating oil and cigarettes. There was no way to the shrine except through the tent. I explained I didn't need a ticket – I was heading for Ki Boncolono's hilltop shrine, not the Wirayudha Motocross slam. But the youthful staff had never heard of Ki Boncolono and didn't believe my story. An elderly foreigner trying to chisel free entry to a motocross event ... now that they *could* believe. So I had to pay up.

The scream of bikes slowly subsided as I levered myself up a narrow concrete staircase to a rounded ridge overlooking expanses of green hillside. At the summit, around 350 metres above the dusty humps of the race circuit, I came to the Āstånå Boncolono, the simple resting place of the holy bandit's headless remains. Breathing hard I pushed open a wooden gate and entered an open circular enclosure about fifteen metres in diameter. It had an outer perimeter wall one and a half metres high made of bricks and mortar, and immediately inside it an inner wall about one metre high made of old stones. The grave of Ki Boncolono lay aligned north-south together with the adjacent graves of Tumenggung Poncolono – supposedly the younger brother of Boncolono – and Tumenggung Mojoroto, the pioneer settler of the region. Each grave had a raised, rather battered concrete ledger called a *sĕkaran* (place of flower offerings) with upright spatulas of wood as grave markers at each end. Gnarled trees spread low branches over the tiny cemetery.

I was looking east over the perimeter wall at the shimmering centre of Kediri four kilometres away when a ragged male figure struggled to his feet from a shady spot between the inner and outer walls. He was wearing an olive-drab t-shirt two sizes too big for him and a locomotive engineer's peaked cap that rested on his ears. His dark trousers drew the eye down to his shoes – beautiful black pumps newly polished and gleaming in the dappled sunlight.

I introduced myself and we got talking. His name was Heri Suworo, the custodian of the site. He was a fourth generation descendant of the first custodian, he told me. He was at the site every day, rain or shine, busy or deserted, day and night.

"Ki Boncolono has two sides," he said, referring to the saint as if he were still alive. "On the one hand he is a thief ... that's his bad side. But he is also a giver of gifts and a reliever of poverty. So he is very human, pretty much like you and me, a mixture of good and not so good."

He crinkled the worn brown skin of his forehead.

"Visitors come up here with all sorts of requests. Sometimes their requests are impure and greedy, or simply self-serving. But as a Muslim it is not my business to interfere or pass judgement. And anyway, the saint's wife guards the gate at the entrance to the compound. She has been known to refuse entry to certain people if she sees that they come with impure hearts."

Pak Heri squinted at the blackened incense braziers and the debris of flower offerings at the foot of the saint's grave.

"From time to time people get signs from Grandfather (*Mbah*) Boncolono, even in broad daylight. For example, they might see a snake out of the corner of their eye. But they only get a sign if they pray to him without expectation of a favourable response."

I must have let slip a glance of scepticism because he added a stoic corollary.

"Indifference is important. But if it happens that your wishes *are* granted, or you unexpectedly get something from Mbah Boncolono that you didn't ask for, you *must* give something back as a freely given return gift."

He cited the example of Kediri's premier luxury dining address, the Bukit Bintang Restaurant. Located on a high point at the edge of town in lush gardens filled with gambolling monkeys, the restaurant had become a hit with Kediri's well-healed elite. Before starting construction the owner had come to Boncolono's grave for "consultations". He attributed the success of the business to the saint's patronage and – said Pak Heri – he had "given something back". The custodian wouldn't say what exactly had been given back but his shiny shoes seemed to offer a hint.

"The saint has given me a livelihood," he went on. "A couple of years ago I also got an unexpected gift from him. I found a small brass kris here. It appeared miraculously among the stones. I quickly carried it out of the burial ground in case it disappeared again and I stored it in a cupboard at home. I still have it. It has three waves in the blade and is decorated with an engraved image of the clown-god Sĕmar. It is inscribed with letters in Javanese script reading *pusåkå nåtå*, "royal heirloom"."

He directed a puzzled look into my eyes.

"Occasionally," he said, "it makes a noise in the cupboard."

I left Ki Boncolono's burial ground and manoeuvred down the long gangway of steps into the maelstrom of flags, dust and shrill engines at the foot of Maskumambang Hill. Pak Heri had given me an unexpected gift of information. In 2004, he told me, the site had been renovated. The 555 steps leading to the hilltop burial ground had been concreted, an iron handrail installed up its length, and a small formal gateway built at the roadside entrance. Beside the gateway a plaque had been erected. It commemorated the formal transfer of the site from "the extended Boncolono family and all his descendants" to the Kediri city government. It was signed by the current head of the Boncolono clan, Japto Soerjosoemarno (the name is sometimes spelled as it is pronounced: Yapto Suryosumarno).

"Pak Japto is a seventh generation descendant of Ki Boncolono," Pak Heri had told me with a pleased smile, "and it was Pak Japto who financed the renovation of the site."

Japto Soerjosoemarno has been prominent in the margins of Indonesia's violent modern history. A supporter and acolyte of military strongman President Soeharto (in power 1966 – 1998), in 1981 he became the leader of a semi-criminal paramilitary organisation called the Pancasila Youth (*Pemuda Pancasila*).

Pancasila was, and in principle still is, Indonesia's state philosophy, the foundation stone of the nation's constitution and laws. As the country approached independence at the end of the Second World War its leaders started thinking about a possible constitutional basis for the new state. There were three immediate options, none of them good. Like many ex-colonies Indonesia might have adopted the institutions of its former colonial masters, in this case a federal structure underpinned by Dutch constitutional models and laws. But fierce nationalism – or more accurately, anti-Dutch hatred – made this unthinkable. Equally unthinkable to Indonesia's non-Javanese majority was a constitution of Javanese origin based on the heritage of statecraft that had evolved in the great states of Java. These are summed up in the esoteric, *wayang-*

derived Hãstã Brãtã principles of leadership. An explicitly Islamic constitution was also problematic. In a country where some regions were populated almost wholly by Christians or Hindus an Islamic state was a recipe for disintegration, or at best instability. Even for Muslims an Islamic state was not an attractive proposition. In 1945 an attempt to make implementation of sharia law a constitutional obligation for Muslims was rejected.

So an anodyne solution was worked out. Five broad and inoffensive principles were formulated: belief in God, commitment to just and civilised humanity, the unity of Indonesia, Indonesian-style democracy, and commitment to social justice. An icon derived from indigenous symbolism was attached to each of the principles and they were given the name Pancasila, the Five Pillars. For a time Pancasila kept extremist ideology at bay, but by the late 1960s it had been appropriated by the Indonesian military, which policed interpretation of the five pillars to suit its authoritarian ideology and commercial interests.

The Pancasila Youth organisation was founded in 1959, initially as a mass movement dedicated to supporting Pancasila in the face of perceived attempts by leftist forces to weaken or destroy it. In the first half of the 1960s the organisation became known for its tough opposition to the Indonesian Communist Party. After President Soeharto's New Order government came to power in 1966 the Pancasila Youth acquired a well-deserved reputation for intimidation, violence and crime. Like the *kĕpĕtĕngan* of former times its members operated on both sides of the law, a delicate art described in a nutshell by American researcher Loren Ryter.

Various police commanders have periodically tried to bring in their most prominent leaders – Japto Soerjosoemarno and Yorrys Raweyai – on gambling, assault, or gun charges. Office managers who have been hit up for large contributions tend to regard them, to quote one colourful comment, as "bandits, rotten motherfuckers, gangsters, basically everything bad". Society broadly is "under the impression" that they are an organization of *preman* (street hoodlums) working as extortionists, debt-collectors, parking attendants, and nightclub security – when not outright violating the law. [...] Yet Pemuda Pancasila devotes considerable effort to correcting this impression. Pemuda Pancasila claims to be a principled, disciplined, and militant organisation of more than six million current members that vows to defend Pancasila and the 1945 Constitution, as it has done consistently since 1959. [...] It is the only youth organization brave enough to stand up for the youth of the informal sector. It "embraces" *preman* not for criminal purposes, but to raise their nationalist consciousness and return them to society.

Japto Soerjosoemarno (born 1949) took over national leadership of the Pancasila Youth in 1981 after spending much of the 1970s as a petty thug in the notorious Siliwangi street gang of Jakarta. He turned out to be an effective leader. In the course of the 1980s he struck out beyond Jakarta and developed a network of Pancasila Youth branches across the country. By the late 1990s Pancasila Youth claimed a membership of between four and ten million. Japto was rewarded with the task of providing personal security for members of the Soeharto family and their cronies. He was, then, both a gang member with a reputation for involvement in violent crime, *and* a high-profile associate of the nation's elite with a capacity to dispense patronage.

Today, despite having left the years of his youth far behind, Japto remains the movement's leader and most prominent spokesman. Pancasila Youth survived the 1998 removal of Indonesia's military order and the entrenchment of robust democratic institutions. Twenty years after the fall of Soeharto it still claims three million members. It remains the biggest paramilitary organisation in the country.

Japto presents himself as a defender of worker's interests against predatory, self-interested developers, contractors and investors. He is proud of the role he has played in providing employment and – through Pancasila Youth – a sense of belonging for street kids and young ex-convicts. He talks of the three years he spent studying conservation and game management. Apparently mimicking the traditional good-hearted bandit of the forest badlands, he says forests are Indonesia's lungs and must be defended against rich developers who think they own them. Forests are in fact the property of all Indonesians, he says, a resource and source of livelihood for countless ordinary people.

But, roving the border between Robin-Hood populism and criminal notoriety, he makes an eerie excuse for the profession of thievery in Indonesia's pillaged forests.

"In the management of forests, our nation's laws in effect instruct people how to become thieves. These laws actually create opportunities for business people to commit theft ... legal theft of course."

Like others in Pancasila Youth, Japto defends the organisation's reputation as a haven for *préman*, the Indonesian term for street thugs. He gives *préman* a romantic gloss.

"The term *préman* comes from the English *free man*. *Préman* are people who simply want to enjoy life on their own terms, that's all.[7] And if you claim that Pancasila Youth is a gang of *préman* thugs, well, I don't have a problem with that. Because people entrusted with the defence of the 1945 Constitution must have guts, they have to be *préman*. If they are not street-hardened *préman* where will they get their courage from? The Pancasila Youth have to be combat-ready. And as head of the organisation, that makes *me* the most *préman* of the *préman*, doesn't it."

There are many who would agree. Joshua Oppenheimer's Oscar-nominated documentary *The Act of Killing* (2012) unveils a chilling portrait of involvement by Pancasila Youth in death squads and the mass killing of leftists in 1965. With macabre enthusiasm, several now-ageing ex-killers re-enact their executions of leftists. As they do, they are sometimes decked out in bizarre, lollipop-coloured costumes, but mostly they are wearing the bright orange-and-black fatigues of Pancasila Youth. They used strangulation with wire, but they also slit throats, rammed sticks of wood up anuses or down throats, ran cars over their victims, chopped them up, or hanged them.

"It was as if we had permission to do it ..." says Anwar Congo, the depraved yet pathetic figure at the heart of the film, "and the fact is we were never brought to justice or punished for doing it."

Japto Soerjosoemarno, the self-proclaimed descendant of Ki Boncolono, makes several cameo appearances in *The Act of Killing*. Today he presides over an organisation that has left behind the murderous excesses of its past but still gets income from smuggling, gambling, extortion and general racketeering. (*The Act of Killing*

7   *Préman* is in fact derived from the Dutch term *vrij man* which originated in colonial times when it probably referred to non-attached men of working age, perhaps freed slaves. These "unregulated" men were a problematic category in colonial society, so the term for them acquired negative overtones that still shape its use hundreds of years later.

follows several Pancasila Youth heavies as they patrol a market in Medan, North Sumatra, extorting protection money from Chinese traders.)

In some of their official web sites the organisation is now moving warily and not very convincingly into the domain of honest introspection.

> There have been many twists and turns in the [...] history of the Pancasila Youth and these have shaped the reputation for toughness that the organisation now has. There is no denying that, in the eyes of the public, the Pancasila Youth movement is nothing like the sacred name that the organisation carries. In fact the Pancasila Youth are identified with the terms "young street criminals" and "lackies of the New Order". Today the Pancasila Youth are a frightening presence in the minds of the public, and this impression comes from the problematic behaviour of individuals within the organisation. [...] It is no secret that the Pancasila Youth have been backers of various criminal activities because it is from these criminal activities that the Pancasila Youth has been able to sustain its activities. The coffers of the Pancasila Youth have never been filled by what you might call "contributions by members".

In the same mould as legendary bandit-saints like Sunan Kalijågå (alias the bandit Brandhal Lokåjåyå) and Radèn Sujono (alias the opium addicted Ki Agĕng Balak), Japto also has aristocratic connections. His father was a noble of the Mangkunagaran royal house in Solo. Through him Japto has inherited a sonorous aristocratic title that he still prefixes to his name: *Kanjĕng Radèn*

*Mas Haryå*, abbreviated *KRMH*. This is trumped by the addition of *Haji*, a title that advertises his credentials as a pious Muslim who has made the pilgrimage to Mecca.

I took a motorcycle taxi from Maskumambang Hill, crossing the Brantas River into Brawijaya Street and beyond into Hayam Wuruk Street in the centre of Kediri. Bråwijåyå and Hayam Wuruk were kings of Hindu-Buddhist Måjåpait, commemorated, like several other pre-Islamic figures, in the street names of the ancient city. At the Sri Ratu shopping mall we wobbled head-on into a stampede of on-coming traffic and turned right into Joyoboyo Street. Along a high whitewashed wall we stopped at a wooden gate topped by a rough sign: "The Shrine of the Venerable Gentiri" (*Punden Ki Agĕng Gentiri*) and below it "Banyan of the Severed Head" (*Ringin Sirah*). An enormous padlock hung from the gate.

A big-nosed, pistol-packing Dutchman confronts Ki Boncolono in a
wayang-style relief on Kediri's gigantic Simpang Lima Gumul arch.

The air was thickening with the approach of nightfall. In the shadow of the wall traders were setting up tables and awnings for an evening carnival of streetside eating. None could tell me where I might find a key-keeper who could open the gate, but they all agreed, inside stood a tree that marked the burial place of Maling Gĕntiri's head, and all agreed that Maling Gĕntiri and Ki Boncolono were different names for the same person.

The proprietor of an eatery helped me drag one of his tables to the foot of the wall. I climbed on to it and stretching upwards was able to look over the wall into an empty plot of land. To my right stood the blank rear wall of the Sri Ratu shopping mall, and to my left, with the setting sun splintering among its branches, stood a lone banyan tree. A plaster and paling fence ringed the sinews of its trunk.

A small crowd had gathered beneath me to enjoy the spectacle of a foreigner standing unsteadily on a streetside table. As I returned to earth they offered me snippets of information about the tree and its famous severed head. A young woman waved a long-handled spoon at me and gave me a micro-lesson in history. She understood the metaphor of the head in a radical way. It was a momentary but revealing insight into a corner of popular memory that scholarly history and the official histories of school textbooks seldom acknowledge.

"When the Dutch chopped Boncolono's head from his body and planted the two parts on opposite sides of the Brantas River it was like they separated a leader – the head – from his followers, the body. And that's how they disabled the Indonesian people. They divided leaders from people so they could rule us and rob us."

On the eastern edge of Kediri about five kilometres from the Ringin Sirah stands an enormous ceremonial arch, the Crossroads

Monument of Gumul (*Monumen Simpang Lima Gumul*). Built in 2008 it imitates the Arc de Triomphe, though it is only about half the size of its French model. It has become one of Kediri's most popular tourist attractions. On its walls big relief panels celebrate an official version of the city's history and identity. One of the panels is a *wayang*-style vignette depicting Ki Boncolono confronting two big-nosed Dutch officials in nineteenth century dress, one of them holding pistols.

On a warm weekday morning, on my way out of Kediri, I stopped by the arch for a photograph. In the tiled plaza a schoolteacher wearing a neat flaxen-coloured *hijab* scarf over a crisply ironed, brown pantsuit was standing before a class of teenage girls. She pointed up at the Boncolono panel. I eavesdropped as she told her class the story of their city's ancestral bandit-saint. It was pretty much the same as the story on the *Kediri Raya* website. As she finished and prepared to move to the next panel her white-clad students raised their mobile phones to take selfies. As always I was drawn in as an exotic decoration. I looked over their shoulders as they clustered around the images on the screens of their phones. The laughing faces of Indonesia's future looked back, and behind them – pale and impassive – Ki Boncolono stood before the cartoonish lords of the colonial past. Beyond Ki Boncolono, unseen but present nevertheless, stood the orange-and-black clad figure of a street thug, the leader of a semi-criminal mass organisation and philanthropic father figure to young delinquents, Japto Soerjosoemarno.

# 5

# Dogs in the mosque

## PRINCE PANGGUNG AND ISLAMIC ATHEISM

Prince Panggung had just finished feeding his two dogs and was giving them a bath when the palace messenger arrived.

"I have been sent by your brother the sultan," the visitor called out. He stated his mission like a police officer delivering a summons. "In the name of the Law you are commanded to come to Demak and present yourself before His Majesty."

"I'll come at once," said the prince. "I imagine my brother has an important point of Law he wants to pass on to me."

Prince Panggung's dogs were sitting on their haunches beside him. Thoughtfully he stroked their newly washed fur.

"Messenger, would you mind carrying my dogs for me. They're feeling a bit unwell."

It was a request that put the royal messenger in a quandary. In Islam dogs are disgusting, polluting creatures, no better than swine.

"It would be better if you left your dogs here. It wouldn't look good if you brought them to a royal audience. They are unclean animals. Muslims must avoid contact with them."

Prince Panggung laughed.

"If my dogs stay behind, I stay behind too."

The messenger felt his throat fill with nausea but he picked up the dogs. It was his duty.

The prince's house was at Randu *Sångå* near Tegal, a good two hundred kilometres from the palace in Demak. As they travelled east along the north coast road to Demak the two dogs kept licking the messenger on the face. Inwardly he complained very loudly.

"These damned animals!" he said, gritting his teeth. It would have given him great pleasure to shoot them, but he didn't dare in front of their owner, the sultan's brother. So he gulped back his revulsion and took refuge in a knot of vindictive consolation. He knew what awaited Prince Panggung.

Sultan Trĕnggånå of Demak (ruled c.1521 – c.1546) was Prince Panggung's younger brother. He had received reports that the prince was becoming deeply immersed in contemplation of the Supreme Being and had lost interest in worldly things. His behaviour was becoming erratic. He no longer had concern for rules and regulations. He was ignoring the scriptures that contained the holy Law of Islam.

Worse, much worse, he had acquired two dogs, one black the other reddish. He called the black one Iman, "Religious Faith", and the red one Tokid, "The Oneness of God". Wherever the prince went his dogs went with him. They even went with him to Friday prayers in the mosque where they sat behind their master studiously memorising the Law of the Prophet with him.

This was outrageous behaviour. The Nine Saints – Java's paramount authority on religious matters – won an audience with the sultan to speak with him about his brother. Sunan Bonang was the first to raise his voice.

"Sire, what is your wish with regard to your brother Prince Panggung? His way of studying the Law comes into direct collision with social order. He is defiled by his two dogs, Religious Faith and The Oneness of God. He even brings the two animals into the mosque. If this goes on the Law will lose its authority. Strong measures are needed otherwise it will bring great ruin on society and do damage to the foundations of Islam in Demak."

All the other learned saints voiced their agreement, whereupon the sultan spoke.

"If this really is the case, what action do you recommend?"

Sunan Bonang answered: "He must be burned at the stake, of course." The other saints spoke up in unison saying: "Sunan Bonang's verdict is correct."

Since the sultan was the defender of the faith, and since it appeared that his brother was lost to the faith, the sultan spoke calmly to his chief minister: "Very well ... Minister, make ready a bonfire."

"Immediately, sire."

The sultan turned to the palace messenger. "Messenger, go at once to my brother Panggung and tell him that I, the earthly embodiment of holy Law, summon him."

Let me postpone for a moment my account of what happened when Prince Panggung arrived in Demak. I want to step back a little and take in the story's pre-history. It has origins in the life of Mansur Al-Hallaj, a Persian sufi executed for heresy in Baghdad, probably in 922. Across the Muslim world Al-Hallaj is the best remembered of all early sufi mystics. He taught that one must go far beyond conventional law and ritual to find Allah. He also claimed that he and Allah were one and the same. He is famous for repeatedly uttering the phrase *Ana l-Haqq*, "I am the Truth." Since *Al-Haqq* is one of the ninety-nine beautiful names of Allah this was taken to mean "I am Allah." As he aged he became increasingly radical and disorderly. He is said to have been drunk on the experience of union with the Supreme Being. Through his teachings, writings and personal example, he shared his sufi mysticism with ordinary people. This brought him to the attention of authorities in Baghdad who took the view that his anarchic mysticism – his religious "drunkenness" – was too esoteric for the masses to understand. It was a serious threat to social order.

Al-Hallaj was put on trial for heresy, imprisoned for eleven years, and eventually put to death by decree of the Caliph Al-Muqtadir. His execution was spectacularly gruesome and very prolonged. It is described in detail in many sources, including in the *Tadhkirat Al-Auliya'* (Memorial of the Saints) by the great Persian poet Farid Al-Din Attar (died c.1220-1230). Attar embellishes the horror of the execution with Hallaj's cryptic aphorisms as the renegade sufi loses his feet, hands, eyes, ears, nose, tongue and finally his head.

It was the time of the evening prayer when they cut off his head. Even as they were cutting it off Hallaj smiled. Then he gave up the ghost. A great cry went up from the people. Hallaj had carried the ball of destiny to touchdown on the field of resignation. From each one of his severed body parts came the declaration "I am the Truth." Next day they declared "This scandal will be even greater than while he was alive." So they burned his limbs. From his ashes came the cry "I am the Truth!"

The story rippled across the Islamic world, lapping into Java at its most distant edge where it generated several avatars. By far the best known is Sheikh Siti Jĕnar – Java's renegade saint of the red earth – who reputedly lived around the same time as the Nine Saints in the fifteenth and sixteenth centuries. Although Siti Jĕnar's existence is entirely anecdotal he remains influential in the twenty-first century. He is an assembly point for mystical ideas cultivated by a small army of writers who endlessly ransack his life for commentaries they disseminate in books, mass media articles and innumerable internet sites. Despite (or perhaps because of) his reputation as an anti-establishment radical with views hostile to Islamic orthodoxy, some of the books about him have been Indonesian best-sellers.

Like Mansur Al-Hallaj, Siti Jĕnar is alleged to have taught esoteric sufi doctrines. He claimed to be one and the same with the divine essence, uttering phrases like "I am indeed Allah" (*Iyå ingsun iki Allah*) and "I am the essence of the Highest Lord" (*Ingsun iki jatining Pangèran Mulyå*). He propagated a corpus of teachings known by the label "The unity of all things" (*waḥdatul wujūd*) that had evolved ultimately from the thought of Ibn Arabi (1165 – 1240). In this view Allah is limitless and thus encompasses all else that is in some way bounded, like the human mind for example. Although Allah is different from humankind (and all other manifestations of being), in His limitlessness Allah is also one with all other manifestations of being. When seekers see beyond the limitations that frame all that can be perceived they peek into divine limitlessness, and there they see the ultimate unity of all things.

Sheikh Siti Jĕnar is said to have opened a study centre that would introduce students to his vision of ultimate knowledge. But he placed no conditions on admission, nor did he lead students through stages of study. There was no study of sharia law, for example. This proved popular with his students who didn't have to perform the chore of *ṣalat* prayer five times a day. So his school was crowded and attendance at mosques plummeted. This upset the authorities of Java's nascent Islamic order.

The council of the Nine Saints did not dispute the substance of Siti Jěnar's teachings, but they were concerned that if ordinary people were initiated into this secret knowledge without preconditions and without careful indoctrination that encompassed devotional rituals and sharia law they might gain wisdom and fame but, as the respectable *Ensiklopedi Islam Indonesia* (Encyclopedia of Indonesian Islam) reports it, "they would also become total unbelievers".

It is worth pausing here to consider how extraordinary this view was. It was more than extreme, it was suicidally radical. It was a notch more radical than the teachings of Al-Hallaj himself. According to Javanese tradition the Nine Saints believed the deep heart of Islam must be fenced off from ordinary people because if the esoteric secret were known the knower would lose their faith and become a *kāfir*, an unbeliever. Unmistakeably this says that Islam has no substance at its core. Religion is purely outward, ritualistic, an array of symbols and practices, a cultural style, a social and political order. With their characteristic fondness for wordplay, Javanese sometimes call religion *agěman* (clothes, costume), a playful transformation of *agåmå* (religion).[8]

Fascination with Siti Jěnar has a long history. At the centre of current interest is a small book titled *Sěrat Sèh Siti Jěnar* (The Book of Sheikh Siti Jenar), possibly written in the 1880s by a certain Radèn Panji Nåtåråtå (known in later life as Radèn Såsråwijåyå)

8  The idea appears in a well-known phrase in the nineteenth century poem *Wédhåtåmå* by Prince Mangkunagårå the Fourth: *agåmå agěming aji*, "religion is the garb of the king" or "religion is the outward costume of inward nobility". The Javanese term for "to convert" is *ngrasuk*, literally "to get into" or "to put on" (the costume of religion).

who for a while was a local administrator in a district north of
Jogjakarta. Nåtåråtå extracted the *Sĕrat Sèh Siti Jĕnar* from a much
older text, the *Sĕrat Babad Dĕmak* (The Chronicle of Demak),
and "decorated" it with debates in which Siti Jĕnar bounces his
iconoclastic ideas off several, sometimes bewildered, interlocutors.

After introductory scene-setting, the *Sĕrat Sèh Siti Jĕnar* quickly
gets down to business.

[canto II verse 2] It is the essence of a human being (says
Siti Jĕnar) that a person is not created but comes into being
by himself. The great soul of existence becomes one with
him, and he becomes one with existence. The breath of
his life disappears into nothingness and his body dissolves
into the earth. [verse 3] Allah is created by humankind
through *dhikr* chant. Through *dhikr* we lose the sense that
essence and outward attributes are different. All becomes
One, and in that oneness we see The Divine. The power of
The All-Seeing Divine inhabits us. We are it, and it is us.
It is the movement of our lips as we chant that brings this
high essence into existence. [verse 4] In cosmic endlessness
there is no difference between "here" and "there". Human
existence is the only reality. The Lord of Pĕngging [with
whom Siti Jĕnar was conversing] plucked up his courage
and said: "The Allah that we bring into existence through
*dhikr* chant is just that … a form of words, something false,
in essence just a name."

According to Bratakesawa, an expert on Javanese mysticism
writing in the 1950s, the *Sĕrat Sèh Siti Jĕnar* was a basic handbook
for a religious movement called The Red Union (*Sarekat Abangan*)

"with thousands of followers" that flourished in the early decades of the twentieth century. The Red Union rejected the existence of Allah. They believed there was no life after death and holy scriptures were *"apus-apusan"*, full of lies to make it easy for some to rule others and oppress them. The Encyclopedia of Indonesian Islam claims that, around the same time, the Sheikh's teachings were also being manipulated by the Red Islamic Union (*Sarekat Islam Merah*) to support communist ideology. An anti-colonial communist rebellion in 1926-1927 was smashed by the Dutch authorities with heavy loss of life. With this failure, religious radicalism and its leftist political doppelganger went underground until after Indonesia's declaration of independence in 1945.

Four hundred years previously, another atheistic threat had received the same merciless treatment. The council of Nine Saints considered the case of Siti Jĕnar and decided that, like Al-Hallaj, he had to be put to death. There are many different accounts of how he died. According to several of them the renegade sufi was personally beheaded or stabbed to death by one or other of the Nine Saints. In some narratives, the saintly executioners are depicted as deceitful as well as cruel. After killing him they took his body away and interred it in an unknown place. The following day they produced a coffin that contained – so they said – the sheikh's body. When the coffin was opened for public display, inside lay the corpse of a scabby dog put there secretly by the Nine Saints. They told the spectators that, after his death, the sheikh had returned to his true form, proof that his teachings were heresy.

In another account – probably the most famous – the sheikh takes command of his own death. As his executioners close in on him ...

...Sheikh Siti Jenar had already set sail into the true life. Concentrating his mind, he closed fast the doors of breath and rolled up tight the essence of his being. Presently he set free the last of his breaths and simultaneously, like a flash of lightning, he untied the knot that held his life together. Nobody present realised what had happened, not his students nor the saintly visitors. In fact the saints had no inkling that it *might* happen. They approached him hoping to strike off his head, but Sheikh Siti Jenar had already gone to his end, making the choice he said he would make. He had passed through the gate of death with a smile, and was now in the afterworld, the world of true life, the place where at last he merged into the universal unity.

Javanese mysticism – usually called *kabatinan* or "innerness" and sometimes *olah kanoragan* "the discipline of non-bodyness" – has adopted the notion of *nafs* (self, psyche, ego, soul) from Middle Eastern sufism, but has refined it in Javanese terms. Somewhat like the old European humours, in Java there are four components of *nafs* (more commonly called *nafsu* in Java), two of them good and two bad. They are referred to by terms borrowed from Arabic. *Sufiah* (desire, wish) originates from water and is located in bone marrow. Its colour is yellow. *Sufiah* is the *nafsu* that brings about love, passion and keen involvement in social and personal affairs. *Mutmainah* (the outward-looking, egocentrifugal force) originates in the element of ether. Its colour is white. If it is developed and cultivated it gives rise to unselfishness and nurtures purity of mind. *Luamah* (the self-obsessed, egocentripetal force) originates in the element of earth and is located in the flesh. Its colour is black. Its nature is, among other things, evil, greedy, lazy and lustful. *Amarah* (energy, driving force) originates in the element of fire and is located in the blood. Its colour is red. In its nature, among other things, are anger and bullying insistence.

When Prince Panggung set out on the path to sufi knowledge he decided to purge himself of the *nafsu* that would weigh him down. Through long austerities he succeeded in evicting *luamah* and *amarah* from within himself. They became outwardly manifest in the form of two dogs, one black (representing *luamah*) and the other reddish (representing *amarah*). These "memories" of what he had once been became his constant companions. The names he gave them embodied two other ideas that he had also cast off: faith in the truths of religion (*iman*) and belief in the orthodox theology of Islam (*tauhid*, or in Javanese pronunciation, *tokid*).

In the audience hall of the palace at Demak Prince Panggung came before his younger brother, the Defender of the Faith. He raised his hand in polite salute. He also politely saluted the assembled Nine Saints. There was a murmur of consternation when they saw that he did not abase himself before the sultan and the assembly. But everyone sat down on the floor in proper order, and the two dogs also sat down next to the prince. In a calm and friendly tone the sultan spoke:

"Brother, you have done wrong. A verdict has been pronounced upon you according to the Law. Because your conduct is contrary to the teachings of the Law, you are to be burned at the stake."

Prince Panggung answered with a laugh.

"I am indeed guilty as charged. I have no desire to renounce what I have done. I will not resist God who has pronounced this verdict. I comply with His will and I do not seek to escape my punishment. A judgement made in accordance with the Law is also in accordance with divine will. The breach that you, my royal brother, blame me for committing is indeed a grave breach of the Law. But I must have committed it because it was God's will that I do so."

(Prince Panggung is here making a sarcastic reference to the view that because God is supposedly all-powerful, all things that happen must happen because He has willed them.)

With impeccable politeness the sultan invited his brother to immolate himself in the bonfire.

Prince Panggung grinned. He took off his two sandals and flung them into the flames. Then he whistled up his dogs, Religious Faith and Unity of God, and they galloped into the fire. For a time they enjoyed themselves playing, then Prince Panggung snapped his fingers and obediently they came back to him each carrying in its mouth one of his sandals. All who witnessed this were astonished and they said to themselves:

"The dogs were not even singed let alone burned. If the fire could not harm the dogs, there is even less chance it will harm Prince Panggung, you can rely on that!"

The Nine Saints looked sceptically at the sultan, so the sultan said to his brother:

"Now it's your turn. Into the fire with you. Don't just leave it to your dogs!"

"No worries little laddie," said Prince Panggung, addressing his younger brother somewhat cheekily.

When he reached the middle of the fire he jabbed his staff into the ground and, using it as a table, wrote a *suluk* in the middle of the flames.

When Prince Panggung finished writing the fire had gone out and he presented the finished work to the sultan. He then gave the sultan and the Nine Saints a cheery wave and disappeared, wandering off along the north coast with his dogs. In some versions of the story, the prince is consumed in the fire. The important point is he disappears, merging into the non-existence that is at the centre of his teachings.

Prince Panggung's composition, the *Suluk Malang Sumirang*, is a remarkable work. It belongs to a group of religious texts that deal with Islamic mysticism in its Javanese guise. Most *suluk* are poetic explications of Islamic orthodoxy, but some are eccentric or heterodox, and at least one – the *Suluk Malang Sumirang* – is bluntly hostile to orthodoxy. By orthodoxy I mean the mainstream of Islam that holds Allah and humankind to be wholly different. It requires Muslims to acknowledge the will of Allah as expressed in the Qur'ān and submit to it. Also important as models for godly behaviour are the *hadith* anecdotes that record what the Prophet Muhammad said and did (and did *not* do), rightly based laws, and the judgements of learned leaders of the *ummah*.

With no holds barred, the *Suluk Malang Sumirang* rejects anything and everything that is "orthodox". In particular (this is what it is especially famous for) it makes the startling assertion that perfect knowledge – *Islamic* perfection – is to be found in the faith and practices of infidels. In the *suluk* this is called *ujar kupur kapir*, the teachings of the unbelievers.

> *ananing aran tokidan*
>> But what is called the doctrine of the unity of God
> *lawan ujar kupur-kapir iku kaki*
>> and the teachings of the infidels, sir,
> *åjå masih rerasan*
>> don't keep going on and on about them.

*yèn tan wruhå ujar kupur-kapir*
> Because if someone doesn't know what the infidels
> actually say

*pasthi wong iku durung sampurnå*
> that person's knowledge is far from complete,

*maksih bakal pangawruhé*
> it is still raw.

*pan kupur-kapir iku*
> For what the infidels say

*iya iku sampurnå jati*
> in fact is the very essence of perfect truth

*pan wĕkas ing kasidan*
> indeed the highest perfection

*kupur-kapir iku*
> What the infidels say

*iyå sadat iyå salat*
> whether it concerns the confession of faith or *ṣalat* prayer,

*iyå idhep iyå urip iyå jati*
> also understanding and life and truth

*iku jatining salat*
> is the true essence of *ṣalat*.

The author of the *suluk* (supposedly Prince Panggung himself) makes a frontal assault on the rules and restrictions of religion and, indirectly, on the rules and restrictions of society that are governed by religion. He seems to categorise infidels as people who are living outside the pale, as it were, and therefore free of the narrow constraints of religious orthodoxy. In their freedom they are to be admired and imitated. Knowledge of the ultimate truth emerges from complete freedom. As soon as you call that knowledge "Islamic" (or put the label "Islam" on it) you are creating a boundary around it and thereby reducing it to something less than universal.

It is necessary to add, I think, that the author of the *Suluk Malang Sumirang* is probably not referring to infidel knowledge as being *literally* superior or more perfect, but rather is using *kupur-kapir* as a kind of metaphor for freedom from rules and restrictions. Nevertheless the assertion is provocative especially given that in the Qur'ān and elsewhere in Islamic religious writings, infidels are not exactly held up as models.

The *Suluk Malang Sumirang* is radical even in the terms of the mystical discourses of Java. Conventionally, mystical texts in Java have argued that esoteric knowledge is not to be revealed to the uninitiated or to the masses. It must be studied in a systematic manner within the context of sharia and conventional devotional practices. If esoteric knowledge is not studied in this systematic, "managed" way, it can explode out of control, bringing disaster on the practitioner, on society, and on Islam. Thus sharia and the conventional devotional practices of Islam are often described as the "garments" within which the mystic seeks mystical knowledge, sometimes also the essential first stage and foundation on which later stages of mystical enlightenment are built.

But the *Suluk Malang Sumirang* rails against those who scrupulously and unthinkingly observe sharia law, and it attacks conventional devotional practices like fasting and *ṣalat* prayer

Many people are totally clueless.
They talk and talk about how things should be said properly, they pray and fast,
keeping a careful count of their obligations, not deviating even a little,

and they think this is what makes a good Muslim,
ignorantly adding things up like rising yeast
until many practices become like fetishes.
When I was a small boy, I heard
you couldn't become a Muslim just by doing your prayers.
Where you lived didn't make you a Muslim,
you didn't become a Muslim by fasting,
you weren't a Muslim by the clothes you wear
and your headwear didn't make you a Muslim.
What I heard was ...
it is difficult to say what a Muslim is
but you are not a Muslim simply because you refuse
what is forbidden and choose what is permitted.
They spend their time avoiding sins, big and small.
They are careful not to speak the words of infidels.
These are people still immature in their knowledge.
They stick carefully to their schedule of prayers,
they are meticulous about fasting,
they don't want to get caught out doing anything wrong,
they are surrounded and constrained by rules and regulations.

The *Suluk* suggests that mystical knowledge is not exclusive or esoteric, at least, not ultimately. Nor is mystical knowledge dependent on the pedantic study of scripture.

Those who know the deepest truths threaten no danger
to the ordinary people who are their true disciples. [...]

In fact for those who know the real truth of things
the divine essence does not reside in the king

but is to be found among ordinary people.

People who don't know this

get carried away by their ruminations and knowledge.

They are weighed down by books and are under the spell of
   scripture.


Another up-front metaphor in the *Suluk* is drawn from popular
storytelling, in particular that of the shadow theatre. In Javanese
religious discourse, particularly relating to mysticism, there is a
long tradition of drawing on the shadow theatre for metaphors to
explain the relationship between humankind and The Divine, and
ultimately to make the point that The Divine is everywhere: within us
and all around us, except that we cannot see this truth. To illuminate
the point the *Suluk Malang Sumirang* takes the metaphor of Panji,
prince of Jĕnggålå, who went wandering disguised as a puppeteer.
He symbolises the all-pervading divine presence manipulating the
puppets of humankind like fragile shadows on the screen of life.


It is like Panji the figure in the shadow play story

who went out in secret, wandering day and night,

leaving the city of Gĕgĕlang,

travelling disguised as a puppeteer named Jaruman.

Keeping hidden his real origins,

no one knew who he really was.

When Panji performed a shadow play

people were misled by his outward appearance.

In truth they didn't know who he really was.

Everyone thought he really was a puppeteer.

They had no idea at all that he was a prince of Kĕling.

For those at a distance, they were too far away to see him

clearly.

For those who were up close to him he was no less
unapproachable.

For although he looked like Panji

people thought it was not him at all.

When Panji performed a shadow play

people's vision became blurred, they were deceived.

And that is the reality of perception and knowledge.

The *Suluk* is concerned not only to point out Allah's imminence
in ourselves and in the world, not only to assert that all existence
is a great unity, but ultimately to assert that the highest reality is
not Allah, but non-being. Only non-being is unitary and indivisible.
This truth places the *Suluk* decidedly outside the domain of Islam,
which is why, unashamedly and unreservedly, the author allies
himself with *ujar kufur-kafir*, the knowledge of the deniers and
infidels.

In a (futile) attempt to convey a sense of nothingness, the
author of the *Suluk* invests it with a quality, a sense, which he calls
*råså*, "taste" or "feel".

In emptiness there is Being,

in Being there is the true essence

that cannot be put into words.

It is a taste that cannot be felt on the lips,

it is not the delicious feel of that which is forbidden,

it is not a feeling that can be created,

it is not the pleasure that you get from laughing.

No ... it is not the taste that lies on the lips,

nor is it a feeling that you can feel.

My kind of taste is the taste that embraces
all kinds of taste
because it is a true taste, the *råså* that is felt in body and soul,
the most noble and mighty *råså*.

The *Suluk Malang Sumirang* has slapstick elements and the
sardonic Prince Panggung is himself almost a parody of a saint.
He is, like Mansur Al-Hallaj and Sheikh Siti Jěnar, perhaps also
like Gatholoco, a mad saint or a monstrous saint – a moral bandit
– whose enlightenment has carried him far beyond the rigidly
prescribed, humdrum certainties of religious respectability.

The time has now come to board a bus in Cirebon and head for
the town of Tegal on the coast about seventy kilometres to the east.
That is where Prince Panggung is buried, I had been told.

"But Prince Panggung disappeared didn't he?" I asked my
informant, Pak Hamdani, as we sipped guava juice in the lobby of
my comfortable, air-conditioned hotel in Cirebon.

"Like all saints, he left behind signs," said Pak Hamdani,
enjoying the thick, sugary, bright pink syrup. "The Javanese word
is *patilasan*, a trace. A trace can be just as potent as a grave with
a body in it. More often than not a *patilasan* is constructed to
replicate a grave and in the course of time people come to believe
that it houses holy remains."

The highway from Cirebon to Tegal was well-sealed, wide,
flat and well-maintained. But the bus was as uncomfortable
as I had expected it to be. It clung to a memory of earlier road
conditions as it bumped over imaginary potholes and hammered on
phantasmagoric stretches of gravel. I sat hunched on a rock-hard
seat, my chin chattering against my knees. My fellow passengers

were industrially packed into every cranny above and beside me, even below me (there was a five-year-old girl stretched out fast asleep on the floor under my seat). Eventually the middle-aged lady beside me – wearing a beautiful, lace-edged orange headscarf – couldn't contain her curiosity.

"You are going to Tegal?" she asked. She was incredulous. "Why?"

"I want to visit the tomb of Prince Panggung."

She understood at once.

"You mean *Mbah* (Grandpa) Panggung," she corrected me. "It's easy to find him. His tomb is on Jalan Kyai Haji Mukhlas a short distance north of the *alun-alun* town square. It's at the rear of the Panggung Mosque, and the mosque is just east of Pasar Pagi, one of the main markets in the centre of Tegal. Just take a pedicab."

In Java directions are often given according to points of the compass. As I struggled to imagine where north, south, east and west might be, she looked with slight distaste at my sandals and shabby safari jacket. I sensed she felt sorry for me. Perhaps she thought I was visiting the tomb to ask Mbah Panggung for financial support. She reached into her plastic carry-bag and offered me a tetra-pack of guava juice. I gulped it down gratefully.

"Actually, you don't need to go by pedicab," she said, full of concern. "You'll probably get ripped off. You can walk to the tomb from the *alun-alun*. It's only about a kilometre."

She was right. A ten-minute walk from the *alun-alun* brought me to the biggish Panggung Mosque on Jalan Mukhlas. I turned into an alley beside the mosque and headed for the last house on the right facing the mosque's verandah. This was the home of the key-keeper, Bapak Fodli.

One of the pleasures of pilgrimage in Java is the discovery

that each site has its own identity, sometimes aggressively asserted and occasionally wacky. The tomb of Mbah Panggung was no exception. The experience began with the loquacious and very hospitable Bapak Fodli who claimed to be a fifth generation descendant of Mbah Panggung, a claim that could hardly be true if Mbah Panggung lived in the sixteenth century. Aged around fifty and sporting a neatly trimmed moustache, he was wearing a black *pèci* fez-cap, a red and black checked sarong and a batik shirt beautifully decorated in dense black vine-like lines on a cream background. He was an embodiment of the stereotypical simple but natty key-keeper.

Over a glass of sweet black coffee and a heap of freshly fried manioc chips he confirmed that the two dogs, Religious Faith and The Unity of God, were buried there together with their master. But he added an item of information I hadn't heard before: Mbah Panggung's five favourite shadow puppets were also buried there.

The busiest times at the tomb, he told me, are any Friday but especially Friday Kliwon. This means that from Thursday at around four o'clock in the afternoon through the evening into the early hours of Friday morning a regular stream of visitors stop by his whitewashed plaster-veneer front room before heading to the tomb to pay their respects. The tomb is one that should be visited before a pilgrim leaves to visit the tombs of the Nine Saints, he said. Visitor numbers are irregular, but there are never less than a dozen people a day. Sometimes there may be more than one hundred.

"Most visitors are local people but some come from distant places. Mostly they come with problems relating to making a living or family. All of them come away with a solution."

Pak Fodli was enjoying his work, crunching enthusiastically on the manioc chips.

"Even President Soekarno came here once," he said. Noticing my sceptical look he added "But it was before he became president. He visited the tomb to *ngěblěng diri*."

"*Ngěblěng diri*? What's that?"

"It means you shut yourself in a room – in this case the tomb chamber – and meditate in darkness."

"Most people," he said, "come with a strong wish for a favour – a *niat* – and if that *niat* is granted by the saint they will come to the tomb again to give thanks. This is called *kaul*. The tradition at the site is to express thanks in any of three main ways ..."

He held up three fingers and bent each finger down as he itemised the options.

"You can repay the saint by helping the poor, or you can whitewash a local prayer-house or mosque, and the third option is to cover any nearby grave with a fresh cotton canopy."

It was about 4:30 in the afternoon. As we sat talking two pilgrims appeared at the door. One was a young man aged about twenty-two, his companion a woman aged about eighteen. Following proper procedure the couple had come first to the key-keeper's house to state what their *niat* was. The young man said he wanted a job as a truck driver.

After leisurely pleasantries (where are you from? how did you get here? do you have any children? are you staying overnight or going straight back home?) garnished with the normal outbreaks of laughter, Pak Fodli asked me if I would like to come with the couple to the tomb. I hope my nod was not too eager.

"Right," he said, standing up. "Let's go to the island."

I wasn't sure I had heard correctly. The island? We walked out and turned right past the verandah of the mosque and headed away from the street. As we walked Pak Fodli explained that in the distant past the tomb had been on a small island close to the shoreline. Or perhaps it was a hump rising from a coastal swamp. Over time the shoreline had crept north enveloping the island, and later still the town of Tegal had grown up around it. Today, the tomb of Mbah Panggung is at least a kilometre from the sea, but like a tiny blip of information from five hundred years ago, it is still called "the island". It was a reminder that if the geological history of Java's north coast could be speeded up the coastline would seem to writhe. Fat with silt from the rice fields of the interior it would billow out into the shallow waters of the Java Sea.

About one hundred metres from the mosque we came to Mbah Panggung's tomb. It consisted of a square brick-walled enclosure under lush but straggling trees in the middle of an extensive, not very neat, public cemetery. In the centre there was another walled enclosure with the burial chamber standing in the middle of it. It was an unprepossessing structure not in any way traditional in form. In fact its roof was just a flat, sloping sheet of corrugated iron. The wooden-walled room underneath housed Mbah Panggung's grave. There was an upright headstone at each end. Between them lay a long brown ledger-stone worn smooth and shiny in places. Beside it, set into the tiled floor were two short headstones without a connecting ledger. These marked the grave of what Pak Fodli called the saint's "adjutant".

Outside the burial chamber, inside the inner wall of the yard but beyond the left and right ends of the building, there were two small graves. Both were very plain as befits the resting places of two dogs. Iman's was on the left and Tokid's was on the right.

Pak Fodli led the way into the burial chamber followed by the young couple and me. We sat down cross-legged on the floor beside Mbah Panggung's grave, Pak Fodli a little in front of the rest of us.

From battered rucksacks the couple produced a plastic bottle of drinking water, some water in a plastic bag, a sachet of monosodium glutamate, a packet of salt, a can of Axe spray deodorant and a bottle of body lotion. These were lined up on the floor close to the grave near the headstone.

The key-keeper then intoned a fairly lengthy (about ten minutes) prayer in a mixture of Arabic and Javanese. It included reverential addresses to Mbah Panggung and Sunan Kalijågå and culminated in a gift of Al-Fātiḥah. The two visitors looked on, from time to time closing their eyes, turning their palms upwards and loudly uttering "Amin". At the conclusion of the prayer Pak Fodli handed the couple some flower petals taken from the top of the grave wrapped in a banana leaf. They also got a small block of incense. The key-keeper told them to place the flowers at the four corners of their house and to do this on their wěton day. The wěton occurs once in every 35-day lapan cycle. It is a kind of monthly birthday, commemorating the day in the lapan cycle on which you were born.

Pak Fodli picked up the bottles, packets and cans and helped his guests pack them into their rucksacks. By their proximity to the grave they had been charged with Mbah Panggung's power. Like medicine, that power was tangible, portable and transferrable. Drop by drop it would suffuse the couple's meals, drinking water and bath water. "Essence of Saint" would be rubbed on the skin to boost their confidence and bring good luck in the search for work.

As they backed out of the burial chamber the couple slipped some banknotes into Pak Fodli's hand. I could see it wasn't much, but equally I sensed that it was as much as the couple could afford and as much as Pak Fodli expected.

As I exited the burial chamber I noticed five more small graves in the yard outside, all simple and all alike, three to the left of the chamber door, and two to the right.

"They are the graves of Mbah Panggung's shadow puppets," said Pak Fodli, gesturing vaguely towards them. "Let's have some coffee and I'll tell you about them."

Back at the house we slurped more strong, sweet, black coffee as new pilgrim arrivals waited patiently on the front porch. I tried to quiz Pak Fodli on the puppets. I knew that Prince Panggung had a special connection with the city of Cirebon. Cirebon had made the saint its own by toning down his credentials as a fearsome heretic and attributing inoffensive puppeteering skills to him. According to the *Babad Cirĕbon* – the traditional court chronicle of Cirebon – Prince Panggung was the son of Sunan Kalijågå, "the saint of Kalijågå" a village formerly beyond the city boundaries but now in the suburbs of Cirebon. In this tributary of the Panggung story, Prince Panggung inherited his father's skills in the performing arts. The very name Panggung means "stage" or "platform", and gives us the Javanese term *manggung ringgit*, "to perform a shadow play". As word of his skills spread the prince became a well-known puppeteer at the court of Demak, performing with such power that he could be seen at the village of Bonang one hundred kilometres away. Everyone everywhere could hear his voice clearly, so it is said. In Cirebon today, he is respected as the ancestral muse and patron of local performing arts, especially the shadow theatre and Cirebonese genres of dance.

The five puppets buried at Panggung's tomb were the five Pandåwå brothers, icons of the classical shadow play and warrior heroes of the epic Bharatayuddha war. They star in stories with roots deep in the heart of Java's Hindu past.

"To the left of the door as you exit," said Pak Fodli, lining up five cigarettes on his coffee table to represent the graves, "lies the eldest brother Puntådéwå, beside him Åntåsénå, then Arjunå. The two graves to the right of the gate belong to the twins Nakulå and Sadéwå."[9] Popular tradition claims that the shadow theatre in its modern form was invented by Sunan Kalijågå, or rather, he "adapted" it so that it projected an accommodation between pre-Islamic Javanese arts and the tenets of Islam. At Mbah Panggung's tomb the five Pandåwå brothers had been claimed for Islam. They embodied this accommodation.

The Five Pandåwå brothers. From left to right: Puntådéwå, Åntåsénå, Arjunå, Nakulå, Sadéwå.

"You see, each of the Pandåwå heroes symbolises one of the five *rukun Islam,* the five religious obligations of a Muslim," Pak Fodli explained. "The personality and reputation of each puppet expresses the essence of the counterpart religious obligation. So

9   Each of three older characters has many alternative names: Puntådéwå is also known as Yudistirå and Darmåkusumå; Åntåsénå is also known as Wrĕkodårå and Bimå, and Arjunå is also known as Janåkå and Pĕrmadi.

Puntådéwå, the leader and moral touchstone of the five Pandawas, represents the spirit of *Shahādah*, which is the testimony that there is no god but Allah and Muhammad is his prophet. Åntåsénå, the strong vigorous second brother, represents the spirit of *ṣalat*, the five-times-a-day prayer that is the pillar of religion, just as Åntåsénå is the firm pillar of the five Pandawas. Then we have Arjunå, the ascetic meditator who represents the spirit of the annual Fast. In the famous story *Arjunå Wiwåhå* (The Marriage of Arjuna) he sits deep in meditation, resisting the appetites of the flesh just as good Muslims must resist the blandishments of hunger, thirst and sex during the Fast."

Pak Fodli pushed three cigarettes to one side.

"We can group the first three *rukun* together because we can't avoid them. They are the essential, obligatory components of the Five Obligations."

He turned to the two remaining cigarettes.

"Nakulå and Sadéwå represent the remaining two of the Five Obligations: the giving of alms and the pilgrimage to the holy land. These so-called obligations are not one hundred percent compulsory. You do them only if you can *afford* to do them. That's why the two lesser obligations are represented by Nakulå and Sadéwå, the two youngest, and therefore lesser, members of the five Pandawas."

"And the dogs?"

Pak Fodli glanced at the lengthening queue of pilgrims on his front porch.

"The two dogs are like a barometer," he said. "They measure the degree or height of your mystical knowledge. People stay at the tomb overnight. If their mystical knowledge is mature and advanced, Religious Faith and The Unity of God may appear to them in human guise during the night. But if their mystical knowledge is immature, the dogs will appear to them in dog form, one black one white."

I had a notebook full of questions, but Pak Fodli excused himself. The crowd of visitors on his front porch had spilled into the alley. They were patient, but night was falling ...

Back in my hotel room I reviewed the recording I had made of the key-keeper's long, meandering narrative. He had spoken rapidly, even passionately, in Indonesian liberally mixed with Javanese. The information had flooded past me before I could absorb more than a small part of it. So I replayed his account of Prince Panggung's execution. His kindly voice, interrupted from time to time by slurping sounds as he lifted a glass of coffee to his lips, delivered an interesting variant to the story.

"In former times, if a Muslim got licked by a dog, he would have to slice off the part of the body that got licked. That was in the bad old days before Islamic law arrived. Now we have a rule that if you get licked by a dog all you have to do is wash the spot seven times, once with soap and then rinse it six times.

Now, it came to the attention of the king in those days that there was a man who was claiming to be a saint, and that he slept with his dogs. So what was the punishment for this according Islamic law? After a time he was summoned by the king. The king said, "You claim to be a Muslim, but you sleep and eat with your dogs." In the end Mbah Panggung was sentenced by the king to be burned. After all, someone who merely got licked by a dog would have to slice the stain off, so someone who slept and ate with dogs deserved a worse punishment: to be burned.

So it was announced that all the sub-district administrators would have to come and find out what would happen to Abdurrakhman (that was Prince Panggung's original name). So Abdurrakhman was summoned and burned. They made a bonfire, but Abdurrakhman threw his sandals into the fire ... whoosh... the white dog, Iman, went into the fire and was told to get the sandal. It emerged with the sandal: not one hair on its body was singed. Then the dog in the grave on the left, Tokid, emerged too from the fire and was not burned at all.

The king was angry. "I'm not punishing your dogs, I'm punishing you! Get in there!" Panggung went into the fire. He emerged again. He was not burned at all, but when he came out he was carrying a book. This happened in Pajang in the region of Demak, or maybe it was in the lands of Radèn Fatah. Anyway ... he came out of the fire unscathed, not burned at all and carrying a book. The book was a book for the propagation of religion, that is, it was a *wayang* book, a book about the shadow theatre. You know, *wayang* as a science used by the saints to spread Islam."

I heard myself asking: "Was that book the *Suluk Malang Sumirang*?"

Pak Fodli sounded uncertain.

"I don't know for sure," he said. "But in any case the book is now lost. It used to be kept here at Mbah Panggung's tomb, but some years ago there was a fire, and the book together with the whole tomb was destroyed."

I recalled that more than a hundred years ago when Dutch philologist and student of Islam D.A. Rinkes visited Prince Panggung's tomb, he reported that the key-keeper of the time told him the *Suluk* had been destroyed in a fire at the tomb some fifty years before. Pak Fodli's recollection, then, may have been a faint echo of something that happened in the mid nineteenth century.

Fire as a test of truth and purifying agent is as conventional a symbol in Java as it is in most cultures. In the Indian *Rāmāyaṇa* epic – as popular in Java as it is in India – the heroine Sintå is kidnapped and held captive by the ogre Dåsåmukå. After she is rescued, her husband Råmå suspects that her loyalty and purity have been compromised. She proves they are unsullied by volunteering to step into a fire and emerging from it unscathed. In the Qur'ān – the most authoritative of all texts – the prophet Ibrahim (Abraham) is accused by idolaters of smashing their idols. As a punishment he is thrown into a fire. But God says "Let the fire be cool" and he emerges from the flames unscathed (Al-Qur'ān Surah 21, verses 68-69).

The multi-resonant symbol of the bonfire in the Panggung story casts a flickering light of irony over the saint's "punishment". Here it is Islam that is being purified but it is atheistic mysticism that emerges from the test unscathed and healthy.

Today, however, the tomb of Prince Panggung is anything but a hotspot of mystical radicalism, still less of atheism. Stories and practices at the tomb have knocked the sharp edges off the saint's extremism. Today the eccentric heretic is addressed as *Mbah* (Grandpa) as if he was a member of the family or an affectionately honoured ancestor. He is a patron of the arts, an admired, even inspiring muse-like figure especially to connoisseurs of the shadow theatre. The shadow puppets at the tomb are metaphors for orthodox, regular religious practices – the components of the Five Obligations.

Pak Fodli claimed that after Mbah Panggung survived the bonfire the Nine Saints were so impressed they appointed him their commander-in-chief and secretary, and he is seen in this reassuringly familiar bureaucratic guise today. When local people are preparing to visit the tombs of the Nine Saints, they should first check in with their secretary at his tomb in Tegal, said Pak Fodli, just as in a previous age, if they wanted to meet with any of the Nine Saints they would have to first make an appointment with their secretary Prince Panggung. Even the dogs have been tamed. They are no longer real quarrelling, licking dogs, but have been reduced to "barometers" for measuring progress in mystical exercises.

It is hard to avoid the conclusion that Mbah Panggung's tomb functions to help manage a wild narrative and a wilder ideology. The management process even has an architectural dimension. Today the saint does not wander the north coast with his dogs but is walled up in a burial chamber within an enclosure under a heavy tombstone. And like all today's saints, he too has his "secretary" – the key-keeper or site custodian – a bureaucrat functionary who regulates access to his power.

To top it off, the *Suluk Malang Sumirang* has, in effect, "disappeared". In the narrative at the tomb, Prince Panggung's radical mystical text has become Grandpa Panggung's innocuous book on the shadow theatre that can be used to help spread religion. A measure of its new, unthreatening character is that, unlike the *Suluk Malang Sumirang* that proved its credentials by being composed in fire and surviving fire, the "book about *wayang*" was destroyed in a fire at the tomb site.

# 6

# "We plead for your grace, O prophet of Medina, O saints of Tarim!"

## MBAH PRIOK AND THE RESILIENCE OF SACRED SPACE

At seven o'clock on the morning of April 14th 2010 a convoy of buses, vans and personnel-carrying trucks, sardine-packed with almost 3,000 well-padded, helmeted police carrying truncheons and perspex shields, descended on the Jakarta International Container Terminal in the waterfront Koja area of north Jakarta. They came with two bright-yellow shovel-arm excavators, two jet-black water cannon trucks and a good supply of tear gas canisters. They were on a beautification mission.

The target of their artistry was the holy tomb of Habib Muhammad Hasan Al-Haddad, better known as Mbah Priok. At the time, the tomb was a ramshackle oasis in the heart of the busy terminal. The Jakarta International Container Terminal was easily the biggest in Indonesia, covering around one hundred hectares. Twenty-four hours a day a pall of clanging and rumbling hung over the vast complex. Caravans of trucks criss-crossed its jagged dunes of containers, cranes hoisted huge boxes between their spider legs, motorbikes buzzed up and down narrow iron canyons. An estimated 70% of Indonesia's burgeoning import and export trade flowed around Mbah Priok's resting place.

The purpose of the police operation was to secure the 4.5-hectare tomb so that most of it could be flattened and used to stack shipping containers. The operation was carefully planned. Commanders of the taskforce knew there might be resistance from the local community but they had the law on their side. In any case, they thought, deployment of overwhelming force would guarantee success.

They were wrong. By the end of the day three police officers lay dead, more than seventy police and hundreds of local people had been injured, eighty vehicles had been torched or wrecked and a good number of office buildings in the terminal were left with sightless windows and fire-blackened walls. Tens of thousands of vehicles lay in stagnant tentacles along the freeways and streets of Jakarta's northern quarter. Operations at the terminal seized up and for many days could not be untangled. Billions of rupiah in losses were recorded.

In short, the operation was a disaster.

As the police advanced down Jalan Dobo – the access road to the tomb – violence was already in the air. A noisy crowd of young men had set up makeshift barriers of wood and burning tyres at the entrance to the tomb's parking lot and had armed themselves with stones and crude weapons. The police used their excavators to smash the barriers and a perimeter guard post. Fighting broke out. A police phalanx edged across the parking lot towards the entrance of the tomb under a hail of stones. Before they could reach it the defenders counter-attacked. Molotov cocktails flared amongst the police and simultaneously the red-faced defenders were upon them with knives, sticks, sickles and bamboo pikes. The police fell back into Jalan Dobo. Both sides were shocked. For a short time there was a lull, but it was a lull that, by mid morning, had incubated a new explosion of anger.

Ambulances shuttled back and forth between the wild ebb and flow of the riot and the nearby Koja Public Hospital. Victims of the violence started to fill the hospital's wards. At the emergency in-patients unit a queue of bloodstained police jostled with bloodstained protesters. For one of them it was too late. Ahmad Tajudin, a police officer, was dead on arrival. Judin, as he was known, lived nearby in the densely populated neighbourhood where he had been renovating a small house in readiness for his wedding. Ironically he had been a regular visitor to Mbah Priok's tomb. He had last bowed his head before the holy grave just two weeks before his commanders ordered him to join the security escort assembled for its demolition.

He had fallen on his face in the yard before the arched entrance to the tomb, his skin shredded with stab wounds. As he was dragged away his blood left a tapering black smear in the dust. According to newspaper reports he died from loss of blood as his friends rushed him down Jalan Dobo towards the hospital. In his last moments he breathed a brief message.

"I'm sorry. I was just doing my job. I didn't want to destroy the tomb. I thought we were going to demolish something else."

Around late morning a big crowd of youths belonging to the radically conservative Islamic Defenders Front (*Front Pembela Islam* or *FPI*) filtered out of the surrounding slums and joined the defenders at the tomb. Dressed in the Front's trademark white shirts with white fez-caps and turbans, some with checked scarves wrapped around their necks, they brought an edge of extremist aggression to the tomb's defence. Tear gas and water cannon seemed only to enrage them. They took over Jalan Dobo and split the police, forcing some south towards the city amid burning trucks and cars, and hounding others north into the labyrinth of the terminal. Around four hundred police squeezed through the container stacks and stumbled out onto the dockside where they cowered at the water's edge. A flotilla of small boats was mobilised to evacuate them by sea.

Mid afternoon President Susilo Bambang Yudhoyono intervened. He issued an eight-point road map for resolution of the confrontation, including an instruction to observe a *status quo* on demolitions within the tomb precinct. Around four o'clock the fighting eased. Police commanders ordered the total withdrawal of all units. Defenders roamed the terminal mopping up police stragglers. The pungent stink of burning rubber rolled away from charred vehicles and piles of debris littering the streets.

Talks got under way involving Habib Ali Al-Haddad representing Mbah Priok's family and its supporters, Habib Salim Alatas a senior leader of the Islamic Defenders Front, Prijanto the Deputy Governor of the Special Region of the Capital, and the north Jakarta police commander. The following day, as local people dismantled wrecked cars and combed the debris for saleable scrap, the Governor himself made a belated visit to the scene. He spent fifteen minutes in conciliatory prayer before the holy grave together with Habib Ali and Habib Salim.

Mbah Priok's tomb had survived the riot and remained in the hands of the saint's descendants backed by their thousands of supporters. The instigators of the attack had not known that beyond the tomb's dusty parking lot, through the tall whitewashed arch of its outer gateway, across a partly roofed concrete courtyard, through another small archway and inside a spacious but unprepossessing burial chamber, lay a story that modelled a world they scarcely recognised.

There are many sides to the dispute over Mbah Priok's tomb, but essentially it was the power of this story that confounded the tomb's enemies.

The story of Mbah Priok is not spectacular or of epic length. But its short span is heavy with motifs that give it resonance far beyond what the business executives, politicians, bureaucrats and police commanders of Jakarta were capable of imagining. It was easy for them to dismiss it as a wacky folk tale. For some – if they knew about it at all – the story was *kampungan*, daffy hillbilly stuff. It was easy to mock its bizarre events and motifs, as some openly did. For others it violated the norms of Islamic orthodoxy. It was idolatrous.

The story has many variations. Mbah Priok's *manaqib*, or official biography, was authored by Muhammad bin Ahmad Al-Haddad, a member of Mbah Priok's family, and published in a small book sold at the tomb. In this account the saint was born in 1727 in Ulu Palembang, literally "upstream from Palembang" on the Musi River in south Sumatra. He was of Hadrami Arab descent with an impeccably Hadrami name, Hasan Al-Haddad, and a pedigree reaching back to the Prophet Muhammad. As a child he studied Islam under his father and grandfather. When he reached adulthood his family despatched him to the Hadramaut valley in south-eastern Yemen to connect with his Arab roots and further his religious studies. He stayed there several years before returning to Sumatra.

Hasan Al-Haddad resolved to dedicate his life to the teaching of Islam beyond his Sumatran homeland. In 1756, aged 29, he set sail for Java in a *pĕrahu*, a traditional sailing boat. He went with a relative, Ali Al-Haddad (possibly his brother, though the biography doesn't say exactly who he was) plus three trusted companions of strong faith. Their plan was to teach Islam and make pilgrimages to several holy places in Java, including the tomb of the Hadrami Arab saint Husein Alaydrus at Luar Batang in Batavia (today's Jakarta), Sunan Gunung Jati in Cirebon and Sunan Ampèl in Surabaya.

They had scarcely lost sight of land when a Dutch gunboat spotted them and gave chase, opening fire with cannons and rifles. But the *pĕrahu* was under divine protection and not a single shell or bullet struck it. Eventually the Dutch called off their attack. After two months at sea and several stops along the way they were approaching the island of Java when they were struck by a squall with violent waves and heavy rain. To stay afloat they had to jettison everything on the boat, keeping only a few litres of raw rice and a big iron cooking pot called a *priuk*.

The storm passed but Hasan and his companions now faced starvation. They began to prise off the planks of the ship to fuel a fire under their cooking pot. They broke an oar in two and burned part of its handle. When they ran out of rice Hasan removed his Middle Eastern robe and stuffed it into the cooking pot. He then prayed to Allah for help, and when he lifted the lid from the pot the robe had become fragrant cooked rice.

A few days later another storm blew up even bigger than the first. A gigantic wave roared over the *pĕrahu* and threw its passengers into the sea. The three trusted companions of strong faith drowned, but Hasan Al-Haddad was able to swim back to the boat now drifting overturned on the heaving water. Astride the keel Hasan and Ali managed to perform their *ṣalat* prayers.

After ten days Hasan weakened and died. Ali remained clinging to the boat with his brother's body, also with the cooking pot and the broken oar. A pod of dolphins appeared and escorted the boat to landfall near the harbour of Batavia. There Hasan Al-Haddad's remains were buried and the grave marked with the broken oar standing at its head and a plank of wood from the boat planted at the foot. The latter took root and grew into a *tanjung* tree.

The *priuk* cooking pot was placed next to the grave. After a time it began to move, little by little, of its own accord. Eventually it reached the sea and disappeared under the water. Today, some people say that every three or four years the cooking pot comes to the surface. It is, they say, as big as a house.

Some twenty-three years later – so, around 1780 – the Dutch authorities decided to extend Batavia's port eastwards towards the site of Hasan Al-Haddad's grave. The construction process was disrupted by mysterious events that took the lives of hundreds of workers and their Dutch overseers. Precisely what these events were is not detailed in the biography, but (so the story goes) the colonial authorities were forced to halt construction. They reviewed the project using what the document cryptically calls "a telescopic viewing from the other side" (*pengekeran dari seberang*). Perhaps the phrase signifies no more than use of a theodolite or telescope to survey the site from another angle or look at it from across the bay. But conceivably it may mean that the Dutch took a peep at the site using supernatural powers of perception. In any case, they were astounded to see a grave and, sitting atop it, a man in a white robe clicking his prayer beads.

The colonial administrators summoned their Indonesian foremen to ask them what was going on. Everyone agreed that the only way to find out was to bring in a "person of knowledge", a psychic who might know how to communicate with the white-robed figure. They located a pious Muslim who could do this and commissioned him to prepare a report. It revealed that the figure had two polite requests. "First, if the Dutch government insists on building a port at this spot, please move me away. And second, before you move me, please contact my younger brother, Zein Al-Haddad, who lives in Ulu Palembang."

The authorities at once sent a ship to Ulu Palembang, collected Zein Al-Haddad, and brought him back to Batavia. The young man confirmed that the grave was indeed that of Hasan Al-Haddad, his long lost elder brother. The family had heard nothing from him since he left years before to preach Islam in Java. Zein Al-Haddad remained in Batavia about two weeks "to take in the situation". He monitored the move of his brother's grave to a plot of unoccupied land on Jalan Dobo, Koja, where the grave remains to this day.

Everyone who witnessed the move agreed that despite years in the ground the shroud around the body was unsullied. The body itself was also still intact. All its physical attributes were still perfect and it gave off a sweet perfume. As they moved the pristine body its eyelids quivered as if Hasan Al-Haddad was still alive.

The story of Mbah Priok is a modern confection authored no earlier than the 1990s. So it is worth asking why it has struck such a loud chord of appreciation in the slums and traffic-clogged streets of Jakarta's harbour precinct, and insinuated its way into the villages of Java far beyond Jakarta.

The story is unique but its conventions are instantly recognisable to those brought up in the ambience of Java's folk literature. It runs on well-oiled wheels of symbol and motif along avenues of structure that connect it with narrative networks (students of literature would call them intertexts and metatexts) that run deep into the age-old heart of Java's cultures. It is the discovery of these familiar connections that makes the story believable and powerful, pleasurable too.

Let me illustrate. Indonesia is an archipelago nation. Few symbols are more universal in its literature than the sea. The sea is often represented as a repository of supernatural power, including the power of Islam. Take, for example, the story of the Muslim saint Sunan Giri who probably lived in the late 1400s. Tradition relates that, as a newborn baby, he was put in a casket and set adrift on the sea by his mother. (The motif is probably taken from the Middle Eastern story of Musa or Moses whose mother set him adrift among the rushes of the Nile). Currents bore the future saint into the Java Sea where he was picked up by a trading vessel belonging to a rich Muslim businesswoman. She recognised the saintly attributes of the child and adopted him, raising him to become a renowned teacher of Islam and ultimately the ruler of Giri near Surabaya, one of Java's earliest Islamic polities. She gave him the name Jåkå Samudrå, literally "the young man from the sea".

Another example. The greatest of Java's saints, Sunan Kalijågå, acquired part of his mystique through an encounter with the prophet Khiḍr on the shores of the Java Sea. Khiḍr appears in the Qur'ān in Surah 18 (Al-Kahf) verses 65-82 in which he meets with the prophet Musa. The meeting appears to have taken place at or near "the junction of two seas" and the two undertake a sea voyage during which Khiḍr performs several enigmatic acts that – it turns out – reveal his prophetic powers and moral integrity. Musa pleads with Khiḍr to be accepted as a follower and taught "something of the higher truth that you have been taught". In the counterpart Javanese story Sunan Kalijågå is led by Khiḍr into an ocean-like ambience where he pleads with Khiḍr to be initiated into the higher mysteries of Islam. Khiḍr grants the wish and initiates Sunan Kalijågå into the advanced knowledge of sufism focussing on the symbolic meaning of colours. What ultimately predominates in the Javanese narrative is the impact of the sea as a force that symbolically erases the old order and gives birth to the new.

So when Hasan Al-Haddad's body was brought ashore at Tanjung Priok in Batavia, and buried at a place called Pondok Dayung, he brought with him the transformative power of the sea as represented in a host of popular stories. For the people of north Jakarta whose livelihoods depend on maritime commerce, a saint from the sea who erases old despairs and gives birth to hope is exactly what they were looking for.

The story of Mbah Priok takes three other symbols already familiar to the people of north Jakarta, erases their old meanings and reshapes them to fit its own purposes. The place name Tanjung Priok was probably attached to the locality in pre-Islamic times. The name derives from the Malay terms *tanjung* meaning "a cape or promontory, a point of land jutting into the sea" and *priok* or *priuk* "a big cooking pot". So it describes a jutting curve of coastline shaped like the curve of a cooking pot. But in the Javanese language *tanjung* is a species of tree with white, perfumed flowers. It is this meaning that Mbah Priok's story adopts. In the saint's story the *priok* becomes literally a cooking pot rather than a pot-shaped curve of coastline. The earthy image of a cooking pot – one that in the *manaqib* story miraculously produces food – is attractive to the mostly impoverished people of the north Jakarta. And as the story tells it, the saint's pot disappeared into the fecund depths of Jakarta's harbour to emerge every three or four years as big as a house.

A souvenir sticker displaying the three main motifs in the saint's story:
a *priuk* cooking pot, an oar with a broken handle, and a *tanjung* tree
ornamented with fragrant white blossoms. Tanjung perfume
is sold at the tomb as an air freshener.

Pondok Dayung – where Mbah Priok was first buried –
probably means "place to go rowing", a seaside spot where the
people of Batavia once went out in boats to enjoy the coolness of
sea air. But again Mbah Priok's story adopts only the literal meaning
of *dayung*, "oar" which becomes part of the saint's grave, like an
upright grave marker.

In short, the creation of north Jakarta's place names is now
attributed by many to Mbah Priok and the names are engraved on
the landscape as reminders of the saint's life and legacy. The three
key icons – *tanjung* tree, *priok* pot and *dayung* oar – are also etched
in full colour on the walls of the saint's tomb complex, stamped on
all its publications, and even sold as a take-away sticker.

It was a convergence of three formidable forces that brought
excavators and their police escort to the gateway of Mbah Priok's

tomb in 2010. First there was the hubris of well-financed, aggressive, globalised commerce. Then there was government, jealous of its status and powers, backed by coercive bureaucracy and police. And last, there was the indignation of a self-righteous but insecure and easily offended Islamic establishment.

For decades the Jakarta International Container Terminal had been managed by a state-owned public company called Pelabuhan Indonesia II, usually shortened to Pelindo II. The name means "Indonesian Ports". In 1999 the Jakarta government fully privatised the company making it a limited liability corporation. The prefix *PT* (an abbreviation of *perseroan terbatas*, "limited liability") was attached to its name. PT Pelindo II launched a search for capital to fund an ambitious program of renewal. The Singapore-based port management company Grosbeak bought fifty-one percent of its shares. Grosbeak was a subsidiary of Hutchinson Port Holdings, a Hong Kong based company that in turn was a subsidiary of what is probably the world's leading port management conglomerate, Hutchinson Whampoa Ltd, later to be known as Hutchinson Holdings. In the course of a later reorganisation Grosbeak was gulped down and digested by Hutchinson Port Holdings, but at the time of the riot it was still the majority shareholder in the terminal business.

Hutchinson Port Holdings alias Grosbeak placed several members of its senior management in key positions within PT Pelindo II. Then, with its hand inside its Indonesian puppet, it sought to assert ownership over the valuable pocket of land occupied by Mbah Priok's tomb. They were making a new attempt to accomplish something that had been tried before without success. In 1969 and 1972 the Dobo Public Cemetery where Hasan Al-Haddad was buried had been officially earmarked for development as part of

Jakarta's port facilities. In 1987 and again in 1996 the Minister of Internal Affairs authorised the National Lands Authority to issue legally enforceable deeds to Pelindo II permitting the company to occupy and develop the site.

The first step was the exhumation of remains, which got under way in 1996. Over the next two years the Public Cemeteries Office shifted around 28,000 graves from the Dobo cemetery to the Budhidarma Public Cemetery in Semper, south of Koja. The job was completed in August 1997 with the transfer of Hasan Al-Haddad's remains and those of another eleven members of his family. Early in 1998 the Public Cemeteries Office formally reported that the Dobo cemetery was now clear, empty and ready for development, and this had happened without objections from the family of Hasan Al-Haddad.

But history intervened. On May 20th 1998 President Soeharto was forced from office amid widespread rioting and the economic turbulence of the Asian Financial Crisis. Indonesia crumbled into economic chaos. With the fall of the New Order regime the nation stood on the edge of disintegration with its economy badly wounded and its political system discredited. The old certainties dissolved, and with them the old fear of authority. The Haddad family seized their chance to make a come-back on the land they had unwillingly vacated.

In 1999 the Public Relations and Legal Affairs Bureau of the Ministry for State Owned Enterprises reported that "some reconstruction has taken place on the Dobo cemetery site" and shortly thereafter "a house has been built". Newly emboldened, in 2002 the Al-Haddad family brought a civil action against PT Pelindo II in the state court of North Jakarta seeking recognition of their ownership. They argued that two documents from colonial times – a deed of ownership dated 1916, and a land tax document – proved that the tomb's custodians held rights to the land, and those rights had never been revoked or given up. When the burial ground was cleared, they said, they had not protested through fear of reprisals from the Soeharto government. In any case, they added, the remains of Hasan Al-Haddad had never been removed. Only the headstones had been taken away.

Pelindo II counter-argued that the site had been government land, in fact a public cemetery, in Dutch colonial times and rights over it were therefore transferred to the Indonesian state at independence. Between 1969 and 1985 a series of ministerial directives confirmed that the land was state-owned and was part of the tract earmarked for the port of Tanjung Priok. In 1987 the Minister of Internal Affairs issued a formal certificate ceding "Management Rights" – in effect a kind of ownership – to Pelindo II, and in 1996 this was backed up with a "Permission to Occupy and Develop" certificate.

The court ruled in favour of PT Pelindo II. The Haddad family did not appeal and they stayed put at the tomb. Without bothering with official permits they continued rebuilding the site as a pilgrimage destination. As construction progressed the fame of the site grew and pilgrim numbers swelled.

The question of ownership floated in limbo until 2008 when the Jakarta International Container Terminal embarked on a number of expansion projects. The holy tomb was like "an enemy in their armpit" (as one observer put it to me, but not too loudly).[10] Its presence not only offended against good business practice by

10   The Javanese saying *mungsuh munggwing cangklakan* "an enemy in your armpit" is roughly equivalent to the English phrase "a fifth column" or perhaps "a wolf in sheep's clothing" describing someone intimately close to you who is, in fact, your enemy.

obstructing efficient land use, but its increasing clientele of pilgrims and its program of religious devotions kept disrupting the flow of goods and traffic in and out of the terminal. Container trucks tangled with busloads of pilgrims on Jalan Dobo and the road was regularly closed to accommodate the overflow of devotees during the tomb's weekly *pengajian* prayer and study sessions, not to mention during the massive annual commemoration of the saint's death.

Hoping for decisive action PT Pelindo turned to the second of Mbah Priok's adversaries, the government. At first nothing happened. When the north Jakarta court handed down its decision in 2002, Indonesia was just three years into a momentous transformation. President Abdurrahman Wahid had managed to put the genie of military tyranny back in the bottle of civilian authority. But it was a transformation that could not be implemented everywhere instantaneously. Many in the Jakarta government had lived with Soeharto's thirty-two years of military rule and they knew that military authority dies hard. They were caught in a vice of competing interests. On the one hand they were driven by the necessity to ensure Indonesia's import-export trade operated at maximum efficiency and the interests of investors were prioritised. Naturally they were also hoping to enjoy a personally invigorating splash of money from the revitalised port. On the other hand they wanted to honour the new necessity to be tolerant and humane, to respect the rule of law in the spirit of the post-Soeharto reforms. They were reluctant to call in troops or police in case they discovered that the genie of uniformed violence was not as bottled up as they thought.

Above all they did not want a repetition of the so-called Tanjung Priok Incident, a massacre that had come to symbolise all that was arbitrary, intolerant and violent about the old government. On the evening of September 12th 1984 several thousand people marched out of the Koja slums protesting against a government policy proposing that every organisation – including religious organisations – adopt a uniform ideological starting point (called the *azas tunggal* in Indonesian) which would be defined by the New Order government.

The protesters, all Muslims from nearby mosques and prayer rooms, also had a more particular grievance. They demanded the release of four men who had been arrested for their part in a dispute with military-connected "security" functionaries. The dispute had escalated from an initially trivial incident into a quarrel charged with (viewed from the government side) anti-government dissent, even subversion, and (viewed by local people) defilement of a place of worship and an insulting attitude to religion. Locals were especially offended by the behaviour of two functionaries who had barged into a prayer room without removing their footwear and desecrated it by using drain water to clean anti-government posters off its walls. When people protested a quarrel broke out. Over two days the bad blood curdled into scuffles and the burning of a motorbike, and the four local men were detained on suspicion of committing "political crimes". Clerics from a nearby mosque joined the dispute and it was their rhetoric that triggered the protest march.

When protesters spilled into the streets of Tanjung Priok government troops were waiting. They opened fire, killing twenty-four protesters and – by official accounts – wounding scores more. Unofficial reports put the death toll at more than one hundred. The government claimed the mob had been "armed with homemade weapons" and troops had no choice but to open fire in self-defence.

More than two decades later, when the case of Mbah Priok came up, the Jakarta authorities had not forgotten the Tanjung Priok Incident. Struggling to change their authoritarian stripes, they were spooked by fear of what might happen if they trampled too crudely over religious sensibilities. Nor had local people forgotten the government's contempt for their lives and their places of worship. In Indonesia's new atmosphere of openness, with nascent respect for human rights, they were prepared to risk defiance.

Prodded by business interests, the Jakarta government eventually decided to enforce the court's ruling almost eight years after it had been handed down. In January 2010 they issued an eviction notice to the custodians of the tomb. The notice was ignored. A month later they issued an ultimatum: vacate the site within one week. This too was ignored. The deadline passed and the implied threat came to nothing. But a month later the government found a rationale for moving on the tomb. It was going to be "beautified" they said, a process that would involve some unavoidable demolition work.

The guardian angels of this initiative were the Civil Service Police Units (*Satuan Polisi Pamong Praja*) universally known by their shortened name Satpol PP. They made up most of the task force that attacked the tomb. The Satpol PP are somewhat different from regular police. They are special units attached to local administrations. They are charged with local peacekeeping duties and with the enforcement of local ordinances. The Satpol PP also have a reputation for poor training, poor discipline and corruption.

In the fallout from the riot the Satpol PP were condemned for their aggression and knee-jerk violence. They were, said the Chair of Jakarta's legislature, "like brutal street thugs". But others suspected the Satpol PP were being scapegoated for orders issued by an unknown figure higher up the command tree. Indonesia's

National Commission for Human Rights undertook to find out who this person was and whether there had been any bribery involved in efforts to "free up" the disputed holy site. If there had been bribery, this would be referred to the Commission's wonderfully named Taskforce for the Elimination of Legal Mafia (*Satuan Tugas Pemberantasan Mafia Hukum*).

The mediation talks that followed were chaired by Jakarta's deputy governor Prijanto. They involved Habib Alwi Al-Haddad representing the custodians of the tomb and descendants of Mbah Priok, plus a local parliamentarian and long-time enemy of authoritarian violence A.M. Fatwa, also the head of Indonesia's Council of Muslim Scholars, Ma'ruf Amin, and the director of PT Pelindo II at the time R.J. Lino. The parties agreed that the tomb should remain exactly where it was, parts of it would be renovated (at company or government expense), and a new access road to the tomb would be built that would free container traffic from entanglement with pilgrims.

Mbah Priok's family had out-manoeuvred their business and government adversaries and had won a decisive victory. But now they had some religious challengers to face.

Ma'ruf Amin's appearance at the talks signalled a sudden interest in Mbah Priok by top-level members of Indonesia's Islamic establishment. Ma'ruf Amin was (and remains) a leading conservative cleric. Besides heading the government-backed Indonesian Council of Muslim Scholars he had been a long-time senior executive and advisor in the huge traditionalist religious organisation Nahdlatul Ulama. In 2018 he was chosen by President Joko Widodo as his running-mate – the prospective Vice-President of Indonesia – in the presidential election of 2019.

Many in this powerful, newly devout elite were hostile to saint veneration and local pilgrimage. They thought the practice was a blot on the scripture-based purity of Islam, and worse, it was downright idolatrous. It seduced its practitioners into the most unforgiveable of sins, the worship of something beside the one God, Allah. It was also a laughable and shameful reminder of Indonesia's backward past, scarcely worth the attention of scripturally savvy, educated modern Muslims.

But the violence of the riot and the Koja community's fierce attachment to their holy tomb, not to mention the involvement of the fanatical Islamic Defenders Front, shocked the Council of Muslim Scholars. It dawned on them that something more than pious dismay was called for. They decided to dig out some facts. The council commissioned a study of the Mbah Priok case by a team of respected sociologists and religious scholars. Titled *Kasus "Mbah Priok"* (The "Mbah Priok" Case) it was published four months after the riot. The study unfolds with the compelling momentum of a cold case being dragged into the hard light of forensic scrutiny. It reveals a netherworld of fantasy and fabricated claims that call into question the dates in the saint's official *manaqib*, the sanctity of the tomb, and – not least – the motivations of the tomb's pious custodians.

The team discovered there was no credible record of a Hasan Al-Haddad travelling from Palembang to Java in the eighteenth century. Using family-tree records compiled by the Rabithah Alawiyah – an organisation of Arab Indonesians established in 1928 – and recollections by respected scholar Alwi Shihab whose family is connected by marriage with the Al-Haddad family, plus interviews with Haddad family members in Palembang, the report concluded that a certain Hasan Al-Haddad had indeed been born into the Hadrami Arab community of Palembang, but in 1874, not 1727 as claimed in his biography. In 1927, aged about 63, he set out on a voyage to Java to visit the famous holy grave of the Hadrami Arab saint Habib Husein Alaydrus at Luar Batang, not far from Koja in north Jakarta, but he died at sea before arriving. So, although events in the official *manaqib* roughly correspond with events in the research team's carefully documented account, in the *manaqib* Hasan Al-Haddad is given the authority of antiquity with the dates of his birth and death pushed back about 150 years into the more distant eighteenth century. (Hasan Al-Haddad's modern title *Mbah*, Grandfather, also confers the authority of age on him even though, according to the official *manaqib*, he died childless at the age of twenty-seven.)

There was more. The team examined maps of Batavia from 1883 and 1918 that pinpoint the city's sacred sites. There was no sign of Mbah Priok's tomb in them. Around the same time the Dutch scholar L.W.C. van den Berg was investigating the Hadrami Arabs of the Dutch East Indies and he too made no mention of a holy tomb dedicated to "Mbah Priok". Cemetery records show that after his death at sea in 1927 Hasan Al-Haddad was buried at a spot called Pondok Dayung on the waterfront about two kilometres west of the Koja container terminal. Shortly after, when Dutch authorities expanded Batavia's port facilities, the remains were shifted to the public cemetery on Jalan Dobo. Even at that time there was no hint Hasan Al-Haddad's grave had become a holy place. There was, the research team concluded bluntly, no documentary substance at all to the claim that Mbah Priok's tomb was a sacred place more than two centuries old. It was a fiction.

This was bad enough, but with the authority of scripturalist orthodoxy at stake it was a jolt to learn that, at Mbah Priok's exuberantly crowded tomb, right under the noses of the Council of Islamic Scholars, *bid'ah* practices were flourishing. *Bid'ah* means "innovation" but theologically subversive innovation. Since Islam is already perfect, innovations threaten to diminish that perfection. At worst *bid'ah* might seduce Muslims into idolatry, the most unforgiveable of all sins. Despite the report's veneer of detachment its authors were aghast. "If these practices are not straightened out," they said, "we fear they will plunge pilgrims into the grievous error of apostasy."

The report details the tomb's offences at some length. By way of illustration it focuses on several "deviations" from sharia orthodoxy in a homily (called a *siraman rohani*, literally "a spiritual sprinkling") delivered by Habib Ali Zainal Abidin Alaydrus in July 2010, about three months after the attempted demolition of the tomb. The most serious is the claim that Mbah Priok is a saint and a pioneer disseminator of Islam in Jakarta. The report points out that at the age of 27, he had no special credentials as a learned cleric, and even the saint's official *manaqib* acknowledges he died at sea before reaching the island of Java. But in the homily Mbah Priok is cloaked in the attributes of a messiah. Some believers think he will "greet us in the afterlife when we die" and even reappear in this world to "drink coffee and eat with us". Such is his holiness that devotees were advised they should honour him by wearing only pure white clothes in the tomb precinct and walk backwards when leaving the tomb in order to avoid turning their backs on the saint.

Habib Ali, so the report claimed, represented Mbah Priok's tomb as more holy and sacred than any mosque or prayer room, in fact more holy than the Ka'bah itself. The "holy water" available at the tomb, he said, was just as holy and spiritually invigorating as the holy Zamzam water at the Sacred Mosque in Mecca. These assertions were consistent with efforts to cloak the tomb in an aura of sanctity that would give it status equal to, or greater than, that of the great centre of Islam in Mecca. (A banner that appeared at Mbak Priok's tomb shortly after the attempted demolition read: "Verily Allah the Most High has sanctified the Ka'bah and glorified it. If it should happen that a commoner tries to bring down the Ka'bah, demolishing it stone by stone and setting fire to it, his fault will be greater than that of someone who scorns or belittles any of the saints of Allah the Most High." Evidently the tomb was now being invested with the hallowed character of the Ka'bah, the focal point of Islam in Mecca.) The Prophet Muhammad too was summoned up. In tones of incredulity *Kasus "Mbah Priok"* reported

> Before a *pengajian* session gets under way, and later as people rise to their feet during the reading of the Prophet's life story, fireworks are normally detonated. They see fireworks as essential to the teaching of Islam. They believe that the Prophet is present among them during the reading of his life story and the fireworks are let off to welcome him.

According to one eyewitness account recorded in the report "… Habib Ali Zainal Abidin Alaydrus prayed that anyone who didn't accept these beliefs about Mbah Priok and the tomb – whether learned and pious clerics or anyone else – would hopefully encounter misfortune, meet a quick death, and go to hell." The researchers were horrified that after uttering these words he piously recited the Al-Fātiḥah, the opening book of the Holy Qur'ān. All this was totally contrary to the teachings of Islam, they said, not to mention the exemplary model given by God's Prophet who had always been considerate and compassionate, and was never given to bringing down curses on people.

Night was falling with its usual tropical swiftness when I visited the tomb of Mbah Priok in October 2015, five years after the abortive attempt to demolish it. Spotlights were beaming crystal brilliance over the sooty darkness that had started to fill the container terminal's crevices and gulches. Outside, in the dingy streets of north Jakarta the usual dense lines of traffic groped forward packing the air with pale blue exhaust fumes. High above the gridlock a couple of empty flyover roads curved up from the middle of the container terminal and slanted away on spindly columns to fuse with an unfinished raised expressway. The flyovers were a response – a very expensive response – to the failed demolition of the tomb. When finished they would take container trucks far above the choked arteries of ground-level traffic. Their entry and exit points were deep in the terminal's heart not far from Mbah Priok's tomb.

I headed down the wide, special access road that had once carried container trucks and was now reserved exclusively for pilgrim traffic to and from the tomb. It was a Thursday evening, and as happens every Thursday evening, the tomb would be hosting a *pengajian* session (they called it a *majlis takdzir*), a package of *ṣalawat* music, prayers, *dhikr* chanting, scripture readings and homilies culminating in a late-night visit to the saint's tomb. There would be food too.

By traditional reckoning "Friday" begins at sundown on Thursday. On the night I visited, Friday was locking cogs – as it does every thirty-five days – with Kliwon, one of the days in the five-day *pasar* week. Friday Kliwon is an auspicious day, a day on which prayers are more likely to be heard and wishes granted. I arrived at sundown as arrangements were being made to accommodate the bigger than normal crowds that the coincidence of days would bring. Wide sheets of plastic were being unrolled in the courtyard before the entrance to the tomb complex. Already visitors were staking their claim to spaces where family groups would sit. Left and right of the entrance big screens had been set up to relay proceedings by closed circuit television from the inner hall where the *pengajian* would take place.

Pilgrims pay their respects around Mbah Priok's
newly renovated burial chamber. [©Iwan Amir]

Picking my way through clusters of pilgrims I turned left in front of the entrance gate and went through a side door into the adjacent home of Habib Ali Zaenal Abidin bin Abdurrahman Alaydrus – Habib Ali for short – one of the two habibs in charge of the tomb. I slipped off my sandals and sank to the floor in his high-roofed, spacious reception verandah. To the left a row of green slatted doors led into the interior of the house. Spare spaces on the wall above and between the doors were covered in a pastiche of framed portraits, calendars, genealogical tables and fragments of text in Arabic and Roman script. On the carpeted floor stood kettles of tea and long ranks of fat jars apparently kept permanently packed with nuts and nibbles for the habib's many guests.

It was a bad time to drop in. At six o'clock in the evening Habib Ali was somewhere in the interior of the house performing the *maghrib* sundown prayer, and after the prayer he would be heading for the neighbouring hall to spend the next hours leading the *pengajian* session. But despite this tight schedule, after a few minutes the front door flew open and the habib – who claims direct descent from Mbah Priok – strode into the verandah. He was a tall handsome man aged in his thirties with a moustache, a neatly trimmed goatee beard and traces of Middle Eastern ancestry in his features. He was wearing a full length, white, Arab-style *thawb* tunic and an embroidered white fez cap. *Ṣalawat* songs were already booming from loudspeakers, a prelude to the elaborate *pengajian* program that he was about to lead, but he grasped my hand warmly and leaned towards me, shouting into my ear over the music that he was personally preparing some fried rice for me.

He disappeared back into the house and a few minutes later one of his assistants deposited a big dish of orange-brown fried rice in front of me with a glass of plain tea. I dug into the spicy, slightly salty mixture. I was hungry and the food was delicious. But as I ate, more food kept appearing. There was Jakarta-style stir-fried vegetables, and Jakarta-style rice cooked in coconut milk. There was *lalab* – fresh raw greens including cucumber, spinach and lettuce – plus a dish of salted dried fish and aromatic *petai* beans. I sat surrounded by plates. This was hospitality gone far beyond what my appetite could handle.

Habib Ali made a second appearance, grinning broadly at my predicament. He was now wearing his devotional vestments: a long green and white robe, a stole scarf around his neck and a tight fitting Arab turban on his head. He wished me an Indonesian *bon appetit* (*selamat makan*) though I couldn't hear his words over the din of the *ṣalawat* songs. Then, gathering his robes around him, he stepped through a door on the right into the main hall where hundreds of pilgrims were seated on the floor waiting for him to take his place on a platform at the far end, grip a microphone, and lead them through the *pengajian* program.

Having eaten as much as I could, and leaving most of the banquet untouched, I wobbled to my feet and headed for Mbah Priok's tomb. I had to make my way down an aisle under the exposed ceiling beams of the still unfinished main hall. There were many hundreds of people in the hall. A fence along the aisle separated women from men. At the far end Habib Ali was intoning pious greetings in Arabic. These placed Mbah Priok high in a hierarchy of sanctity that included the Prophet Muhammad, the saints of Islam and the beloved holy men of Islam. It also recognised him as "lord" (*shahib*) of Jakarta's harbour precinct.

*Assalamu'alaika yaa nuurullah*
   Peace be upon you, O light of God
*Assalamu'alaika yaa rasuulullah*
   Peace be upon you, O messenger of God
*Assalamu'alaika yaa nabiyullah*
   Peace be upon you, O prophet of God
*Assalamu'alaika yaa auliya'allah*
   Peace be upon you, O saints of God
*Assalamu'alaika yaa habiiballah*

Peace be upon you, O beloved paragons of God
*Assalamu'alaikum yaa shohibul*
Peace be upon you, O lord
*wilayah wal maqom keramat*
of the territory and holy tomb of
*Tanjung Priok, al-imam al-'arif billah*
Tanjung Priok, leader and knower of God
*al-habiib Hasan bin Muhammad*
Habib Hasan bin Muhammad
*Al-Haddad.*
Al-Haddad.

The greetings closed with solemn recitation of the Al-Fātiḥah with chorused accompaniment from the hall.

Habib Ali then moved on to a recitation of the *Ratib Al-Haddad*, the Holy Litany of Al-Haddad, a selection of short prayers and extracts from the Qur'ān interspersed with repeated recitals of Al-Fātiḥah and exhortations to piety in poetic Arabic. It was composed by Mbah Priok's ancestor, the saintly Hadrami author Abdullah ibn Alawi al-Haddad (1634 – 1720). As unobtrusively as possible (not easy when you have to walk alone down the middle of a crowded hall) I hurried towards a narrow arched gate in a whitewashed wall at the far end, and through it into the spacious area that hosts the saint's tomb.

Before me stood Mbah Priok's burial chamber. It had been newly and attractively re-built. Its white walls, with fluted square columns at each corner, reached up to the high ceiling. Six tall dark varnished windows and a slatted double door were ranged along each wall. Through the windows visitors could see Mbah Priok's grave, a two-metre tall rectangular box with a peaked roof clad in dark drapery. The spaces above, below and between the windows were filled with portraits and framed slabs of text. In pride of place was the saint's genealogy tracing his descent from the Prophet Muhammad. There were also portraits of Haddad family members as well as Mbah Priok himself.

An enlarged photograph of Mbah Priok's grave was also prominent. It showed a vertical bar of bright light lying across its cloth canopy. According to an adjacent information panel the light had appeared at seven o'clock on the morning of the attempted attack on the tomb. Its miraculous appearance broadcast a message: "Let us all be on guard to secure Tanjung Priok, and Jakarta in particular."

I sat crossed-legged with my head bowed on the broad tiled platform around the burial chamber (the chamber's interior is opened only on special occasions). A party of around forty pilgrims – half of them women – silently materialised around me. They came from Magelang in Central Java and were on a commercial pilgrimage tour. Each was wearing a wind-breaker jacket with the words *Ziaroh Auliya* – Pilgrimage to the Saints – embroidered across the back, and under it their three destinations: Pandeglang, Banten Lama and Jakarta. Their leader, dressed in white, addressed them quietly in formal Javanese. He told them the *manaqib* story of Mbah Priok more or less as it appears in the booklet sold at the entrance to the complex. Then he turned, faced the tomb, greeted the saint *Assalamalaikum,* and presented him with a gift – a fervently felt, beautiful rendition of Al- Fātiḥah.

The gift was repeated several times, like a refrain, during the sequence of prayers and incantations that followed. The pilgrims remained about twenty minutes at the tomb before winding up in business-like fashion, taking some quick, hushed photographs on their mobile phones, then exiting to join the *pengajian* in the main hall.

As I left the tomb area I merged with a crowd jostling around a small waterfall that tumbled past some fat *priuk* jars down an artificially assembled stone wall into a small pool. Along the front edge of the pool there was a row of spigots with plastic cups attached to them. A notice in Indonesian on the adjacent wall read: "Sheikh Sayyid Mbah Priuk's blessed holy water. Feel free to drink it and take it home. It's FREE." Pilgrims were pushing plastic bottles under the torrent, or stood sipping from cups filled at one of the spigots. I also took a sip.

"It tastes different, doesn't it?" said a plump, bespectacled, middle class-looking woman about forty years old. She was dressed in a trendy apricot and lilac batik blouse and brown slacks, her head loosely enclosed in an attractive cream-yellow *hijab* scarf. Her pink-rimmed glasses matched her modestly rouged lips. She slipped two plastic bottles of holy water into a huge, expensive-looking handbag slung over her shoulder.

"For my son," she whispered. "He's doing a university entrance interview next week."

As I headed back through the main hall towards the exit I squatted for a moment to talk to a group of smiling women. The cacophony of the *pengajian* was hammering the air around us but they seemed impervious to it. Using their fingers they were delicately lifting food from plates on their laps. The dish was *nasi kebuli*, spicy rice cooked in goat meat broth mixed with coconut milk and topped with a sprinkling of raisins. It was served with a chunk of goat meat and slices of fresh cucumber and tomato.

*Nasi kebuli* is a dish of Middle Eastern origin. It is a special favourite of Arabs from the Hadramaut Valley of south-eastern Yemen. The Haddad family trace their origins back to the town of Tarim, an ancient centre of pious learning in the Hadramaut Valley. They are especially proud of their ancestor, the blind Sufi cleric and renowned author Imam Abdullah ibn Alawi al-Haddad who lived his entire life in Tarim and who lends his name to the Al-Haddad mosque in the centre of the town. His *Ratib Al-Haddad* is a core item in the weekly *pengajian* at Mbah Priok's tomb and is reproduced with an Indonesian translation in a booklet sold at the door of the tomb complex.

An esoteric *wafaq* talisman that invites the faithful to seek
the blessing of the Haddad family's forebears in Tarim, Yemen.

The current generation of the Haddad family emphasise their connections with their forebears in Tarim and with the Hadrami diaspora in Indonesia. Reminders of Hadrami culture are everywhere in the complex. They include icons and fragments of text that recall Tarim. One icon is available as a talisman – called a *wafaq* or *ruqyat* in Arabic, and usually an *isim* in Indonesian – that pilgrims can buy and take home. It is a sticker in the form of a large circle with the Arabic letter /ḥa/ standing for Haddad at its centre. Around the letter are the numbers 1030 and 110, cabalistic references to Ahmad Al-Habshi and Abu Bakr bin Salim, two famed holy men of fifteenth century Tarim whose descendants have been closely allied with the Haddad clan. The talisman is a gesture of benediction for the revered ancestors of Mbah Priok, for the saint himself, and for current members of the Haddad clan. At the left and right margins are the pious exclamations *Ya Razzaqu* "O provider of sustenance" and *Ya Fattahu*, "O opener of the way." At the top and bottom of the talisman two cryptic phrases appear: *Daarkaah yaa ahlal madinah* and *yaa Tariim wa ahlahaa*, "We plead for your grace O prophet of Medina, and yours O saints of Tarim".

As the saint's stature grows, so too does the stature of Hadrami culture with its veneration of the Haddad family and its sufi-tinged dialect of Islam. Stress on the Hadrami connection seems also designed to protect Mbah Priok's tomb and the Haddad family from future threats. Devotional practices at the tomb are given authority, even protected, by the tomb's veneer of Arab piety. Reputedly the town of Tarim has the highest concentration of *sayyid* – descendants of the Prophet – anywhere in the world and is the resting place of literally thousands of saints. Devotional practices in the town are tolerant of sufism and local pilgrimage. The town has resisted the strictures of Wahhabism that are hostile to saint veneration and dominate in neighbouring Saudi Arabia.

In Java, religious fundamentalists are combatting saint veneration and local pilgrimage by encouraging Java's famously syncretic Muslims to adopt the devotional "purity" of Arabian Islam exemplified in the Wahhabi austerity of Saudi Arabia. But Mbah Priok's tomb turns the veneration for all things Arab to its advantage. It emphasises its Hadrami Arab character, and under this umbrella sanctions heterodox practices that are popular with the ordinary people who crowd the tomb.

So for the moment government, business and the Islamic establishment have to live with Mbah Priok. They don't have much choice. Holy ground, sainthood with an Arab face, and the power of a story embedded in age-old storytelling conventions have conspired to win a decisive victory over the most powerful institutions in modern Indonesia.

# 7

# The guardian of the mountain and his advertising contract

## Mbah Maridjan

### AND NOSTALGIA FOR AN OLDER ORDER

The Fire Mountain Merapi at dawn seen from the centre of Jogjakarta. Behind it looms the cone of its twin, the Ash Mountain Merbabu.

If the day is fine you can look north from the centre of Jogjakarta and see the silhouette of Mount Merapi – sometimes razor sharp, sometimes blurred – rising into the warm air about thirty kilometres away. Over the last five centuries Merapi has erupted on average every six or seven years. Whenever haze around the mountain clears, which is most mornings during the dry season, a banner of smoke can be seen streaming off the summit.

Beside a narrow stretch of road not far below the summit a polished tablet about a metre high sits chiselled into rough rock amid ragged grass. Its gold letters list the names of thirty-nine local people who died a quick but terrible death in a storm of gas and white-hot dust that rolled down from Merapi's crater on October 26th, 2010.[11] At the head of the list stands the name Mbah Maridjan, a celebrity known to many millions of Indonesians. He remains as famous today as he was at the time of his death.

Mbah Maridjan died in the scorched ruins of his house. In the weeks before his death Merapi had grown restless. The government of Jogjakarta listened nervously to warnings from monitoring stations on the slopes of the mountain. The message was unmistakable, an eruption was imminent. People on the upper slopes should move at once to evacuation centres in Jogjakarta, said the local government. But Maridjan refused.

Four years previously, during a similar emergency, he had also refused to budge, even resisting pleas from the Sultan of Jogjakarta himself. And Merapi had simmered down. Local people were convinced Maridjan knew the mountain better than the volcanologists who had been shouting at them to get out while the going was good. But in 2010 the volcanologists and the government got it right. Maridjan was unearthed hunched on the floor of his kitchen (some say his bathroom), little more than a human cinder buried under ash.

For twenty-five years he had been the guardian of the mountain, a traditional office bestowed by the royal palace of Jogjakarta. Maridjan inherited the office from his father and his appointment was confirmed in a royal charter issued by Sultan Haměngkubuwånå

---

11 Across all the slopes of Mount Merapi the death toll from the eruption that day totalled more than three hundred.

the Ninth in 1982. The job came with a courtly title, Mas Panèwu, and a sonorous official name, Suraksohargo, literally "good guardian of the mountain". He was a very ordinary villager who, to his genuine surprise, became a national celebrity. For decades before the eruption that killed him millions of Indonesians turned to him as an exemplar of old-style steadiness. He was unassuming but aware and vigilant, loyal to duty, connected to the past but also warily at home in the modern world.

Several cryptic sentences are inscribed above the names of the dead on the memorial tablet. They try to be culturally inclusive. They marry the new authority of "Indonesia" with the age-old authority of "Java" as Maridjan himself had tried to do. The top two sentences are in the national language, Bahasa Indonesia. Layered beneath them come two more sentences, both of them in Javanese. Indonesia and Java live in an uneasy marriage. The two sources of cultural and political authority come from very different quarters of Indonesia's cultural compass.

THIS MONUMENT REMINDS EVERY ONE OF US THAT WE MUST LOVE THE ENVIRONMENT. IF WE DO NOT, NATURE WILL VENT ITS ANGER ON US.

EMBELLISH THE BEAUTY OF THE WORLD.

HAPPY ARE THEY THAT TURN A BLIND EYE, BUT HAPPIER STILL ARE THEY WHO REMAIN AWARE AND KEEP THEIR GUARD UP.

The top two sentences hint at the anxiety Indonesians breathe every day in the air of public rhetoric. Natural disasters loom large in the nation's geology. They loom even larger in history and in the national psyche. Whenever disaster strikes, moral panic strikes too like a Pavlovian reflex. Allah speaks through natural phenomena and His voice is stern. As the Qur'ān says: "We send signs only to frighten you [i.e. to scare you away from evil]." (Surah 17 Al Isra' verse 59)

The most spectacular example of this in recent times was the clamour of sermonising triggered by the earthquake and tsunami in Aceh at the northern tip of Sumatra in December 2004. At least 170,000 souls (many more by some estimates) were wolfed down in the devastation. Instantly the Qur'ān was scoured for parallels that would give survivors – and the entire Indonesian nation – a moral heads-up and affirm the authority of religion. Many pointed out that Allah spoke in two idioms: the verses of the Qur'ān, called *ayat qauliyah*, and through natural phenomena. In fact natural phenomena, it was said, are also "verses" called *ayat kauniyah*. They reveal divine will and power as Quranic verses do.

Over and over, morally instructive parallels were drawn between the Aceh calamity and legendary events in Middle Eastern history. The Qur'ān tells, for example, how certain arrogant people in the prosperous kingdom of 'Ad (thought to have been in southern Arabia) rejected the admonitions of Allah's prophet Salih and challenged him to demonstrate his powers. He obliged with an earthquake that left them sprawled dead in the ruins of their homes (Surah 7 Al-A'raf, verses 77 and 78).

The tsunami too was foreshadowed in the story of Nuh (Noah) and the great flood.

Do you wonder that a reminder from your Lord has come
to you at the hands of a man (Nuh) from your own people
to warn you, and to induce you to fear Allah so that mercy

may be shown to you? However, they denounced him, so We delivered him, and those in the ark, and drowned those that denied Our revelations. For they were indeed a blind people. (Al-Qur'ān Surah 7 Al-A'raf, verses 63 – 64)

For twenty years before the tsunami a secessionist rebellion had gripped Aceh. Again and again efforts to negotiate a settlement failed. But within eight months of the disaster the rebel Free Aceh Movement (*Gerakan Aceh Merdeka* or *GAM*) and Indonesia's central government had hammered out an agreement. It gave Aceh broad-ranging autonomy while preserving the territorial and constitutional integrity of the Republic. The huge death toll was not decisive in the peace process, but most observers agree it concentrated the minds of hard-liners on both sides. At the negotiating table it was a quiet but insistent *kauniyah* presence. On Merapi's memorial tablet, the phrase "nature will vent its anger on us" echoes the warning of Aceh's tsunami.

The two Javanese sentences are well-known but cryptic clichés. "Embellish the beauty of the world" (*Amĕmayu ayuning bawånå*) is a saying usually taken to mean that the far-sighted, cultured individual strives to add value to the natural beauties of Java by "decorating" the lives of those who live there. The sentence beneath it is even better known, probably as familiar to Javanese people as "To be or not to be ..." is familiar to speakers of English. It comes from a poem titled *Kålåtidhå* (A Time of Darkness) by nineteenth century court poet Radèn Ngabei Rånggåwarsitå (1802 – 1873). In the poem's most famous stanza Rånggåwarsitå looks aghast at the colonial "age of madness" (as he sees it) that is gripping nineteenth century Java.

*aměnangi jaman édan*
> Living in the age of madness

*éwuh åyå ing pambudi*
> we are confused, where do we turn?

*mèlu édan nora tahan*
> To join in the madness would be unbearable,

*yèn tan mèlu nglakoni*
> and yet if we don't join in

*boyå kěduman mélik*
> we miss out on the necessities of life

*kalirěn wěkasanipun*
> and we end up hungry and destitute.

*ndilalah kěrså Allah*
> Well, it happens to be God's will

*běgjå-běgjané kang lali*
> happy are they that turn a blind eye (and join in the madness),

*luwih běgjå*
> but happier still

*kang éling lawan waspådå*
> are they who remain aware (of the madness) and keep their guard up.

However much we recoil from the mad world around us, says the poet, we have little choice but to live in it as it is. But we must never forget our better selves. Drawing on the squint-eyed wariness of Java's peasantry and the aloofness of patrician mystics, the poet takes the path of suspicion and detachment, participating but never forgetting himself in the midst of the madness.

The cruel challenge of trying to live a spiritually aware life in modern times strikes a loud chord in modern Java. What does the paradox of detached involvement look like?

Mbah Maridjan was one model.

In February 2007 I met Mbah Maridjan – then around eighty years old – at his home in Kinahrejo on the upper slopes of Mount Merapi. At the time there was no public transport to his village, so I hired a taxi in Jogjakarta. We crept north out of the city weaving through crowds of motorcycles and mini-buses. The road was a narrow ramp that sloped arrow-straight up to the mountain resort town of Kaliurang. Five kilometres short of Kaliurang we found a sign reading "Merapi Golf" with an arrow pointing east. We made a ninety-degree turn right and twisted around a horizontal contour line across the slope of the mountain for about two kilometres before turning left and resuming our upward climb. We skirted the Golf Course, a bizarre intrusion of an alien sports ritual among the silt-filled gashes of the mountain's upper waterways. The road was steep and took us through a sequence of poor but exotically named villages: Gondang, Pangkurejo, Kalikuning, Pelemsari and finally, at the top extremity of the road, to Kinahrejo, a tiny hamlet flattened against the mountainside amid steeply angled fields of manioc, maize and fodder-grass.

Mbah Maridjan wasn't at home when I walked into his compound about ten o'clock in the morning, but his wife invited me to wait in their simple sitting room. The house was far from spacious. The walls and corners of the sitting room were crammed with colourful oddments of costume and ceremonial umbrellas. A pair of shiny black shoes lay in one corner. On the whitewashed wooden planks of the wall, paintings and photo images of Jogjakarta's ten sultans stared with stiff authority.

When Maridjan arrived half an hour later he was wearing loose black cotton shorts and a grimy t-shirt. A pair of rimless glasses sat awry on his face. His feet were smeared with dry mud. He had been, he said, with a note of genuine apology, at work in his garden. He disappeared into the interior of the house and came back five minutes later wearing crumpled long trousers, a short-sleeved shirt and a black fez-cap. He was a small wiry man with greying hair and a round face crinkled with what looked like the lines of a permanent small smile. His bare feet had been given a quick rinse in my honour.

The conversation began with a stumbling exchange of greetings and pleasantries. He explained that the name of the village, Kinahrejo, came from the words *kinā* meaning "quinine" and *rĕjå* meaning "prosperous". In Dutch times an attempt had been made to grow quinine there, but it didn't last long and bequeathed only an ironic name for the impoverished hamlet. But as soon as he established that I spoke Javanese he apologised for his poor Indonesian and broke into Javanese more rapid and more richly fledged than I could fully take in. Maridjan lived in a world that was outwardly part of a new state called Indonesia, but inwardly it still ran on the age-old rhythms of Javanese culture. Nevertheless, a sentence dropped here and there gave me the impression his Indonesian was perfectly serviceable. He chose Javanese more as a statement of cultural, or perhaps courtly, preference than as a communicative necessity.

Maridjan told me two histories of Mount Merapi, both of them rooted in Java's tradition of storytelling and theatre. The first he described as a "*dhalang's* history". A *dhalang* is a traditional puppeteer, the multi-skilled storyteller and manipulator of cut-out leather shadow puppets that skitter across the screen in night-long shadow dramas. This first history told of a time before Java had been peopled. It was a tilted world, full of valleys and crevasses. To flatten it out and keep it steady the great god Bathårå Guru (also known as Siwå) consulted with the demi-god Narådå and instructed another god, Bathårå Bayu, to lift up a Himalayan mountain and shift it to Java, crumble it over the landscape, and fill in the island's crevasses and steep-sided valleys. But the plan didn't work out. A mountain was indeed lifted from the Himalayas and carried to Java but it was broken into just four bits. The fragments were dumped in the middle of the island to form a quartet of mountains: Merapi, Merbabu, Sumbing and Sundoro. Java got weighed down in the middle, sure, but its surface was no less choppy than before. Maridjan's crazy-angled fields bore witness to the survival of the island's primordial geography.

The second history, he said, was a *"kethoprak* history". *Kethoprak* is a genre of traditional stage theatre. The stories are mostly reconstructions of events in the turbulent century between the fall of Hindu-Buddhist Måjåpait in the last decades of the 1400s (probably given its *coup-de-grace* in 1527) and the rise of Muslim Mataram in the 1580s. According to Maridjan, the first ruler of Mataram, Panĕmbahan Sénåpati, appointed a trusted retainer, who also happened to be a giant ogre, to be guardian of Merapi, conferring on him the name Panĕmbahan Sapu Jagat. A contract was worked out whereby Sapu Jagat agreed to guard the mountain provided Sénåpati and his successors paid him an annual tribute of cast-off clothes and royal regalia.

Jogjakarta still pays this tribute in annual mirror-image ceremonies known as Labuhan. The rite is held simultaneously high on the slopes of Merapi and among the breaking waves of the southern ocean at a holy site called Parangkusumo. Parangkusumo is the southern extremity of an ancient axis that runs from the summit of Mount Merapi, through Jogjakarta at its mid point, down to the sea.

Maridjan confirmed that he managed the Merapi arm of the high-profile gift-giving rite, a task he had inherited from his father and ultimately (he added with a self-deprecating laugh) from the ogre guardian Panĕmbahan Sapu Jagat. But the guardian of the mountain was eager to emphasise his credentials as an orthodox Muslim. He ushered me out the front door and led me up a nearby hillside. Overlooking Kinahrejo Village a small mosque had been beautifully renovated and painted in soft peach-pink. Its tiled, pyramid shaped, two-tiered roof sloped down to a neat verandah across the width of the building. The outer walls and verandah floor were sealed with gleaming ceramic tiles in attractive brown and pink. Although he did not tell me so, I heard elsewhere that Maridjan himself had donated most of the money for the reconstruction of the mosque. Glancing at me with pride he kicked off his sandals and led me through the dark varnished front door into the bare interior. An aroma of fresh paint sweetened the air and a signboard leaned against one of the walls. It gave the name of the mosque: *Al-Amin*, "trustworthy, honourable, honest". It was as much a tribute to the mosque's benefactor as an exhortation to devotional piety.

For Mbah Maridjan the Labuhan ceremony was Islamic through and through. Islam requires Muslims to believe in *jinn* – spirit entities – and to respect them if they are Muslims (which the spirits of Merapi are). Islam also requires Muslims to honour their parents and elders. The spirit guardians of the mountain are deceased elders – ancestors – so it is proper and irreproachably Islamic, to honour them. The Labuhan rite is a colourful, self-confident act of Islamic piety practised Javanese style.

*Labuh* means "to cast something into the sea, a river or into a crater as a token of homage". By extension it also means "to serve someone" even (in the context of everyday life) "to devote oneself to a task". Both ritual and service meanings lie behind the Labuhan rite.

Preparations for the Labuhan get under way at Kinahrejo several months before the date of the rite. The guardian of the mountain, his assistant and all their helpers clean up and repair the path that leads up to the venue of the rite on the upper slopes of the mountain just below a kind of high-altitude frontier called the *kĕndhit*. The *kĕndhit* is an imaginary cummerbund that girdles the mountain at the boundary between the cloud-wrapped scree of the summit and the forested slopes below. Several days before the Labuhan, palace functionaries visit the guardian to inform him exactly when the rite will take place. Some time later the guardian goes down to the palace to report that all is ready. The palace makes a modest payment to him to help defray costs. At the same time, around the home of the guardian the villagers of Kinahrejo are busy erecting stalls and shelters where they will sell food and drinks to visitors. They also spring-clean and spruce up their houses to accommodate guests who are going to come from all over.

The *Labuhan Merapi* rite begins with a delivery of cast-off royal regalia from the Jogjakarta palace to the local sub-district office at Cangkringan on the slopes of the mountain below Kinahrejo. They usually consist of complete sets of traditional clothes – male and female – long batik loin cloths, sarongs in various patterns, women's waist sashes, men's batik head cloths, even bolts of plain cloth. There are nail clippings and locks of the sultan's hair, flower offerings, incense, betel leaf, perfumed oil and a variety of food offerings including a big cone of cooked rice decorated with fruits, vegetables, hard-boiled eggs and chilli peppers, plus spice-loaded *klobot* cigarettes, perfumed oil, and a small amount of cash. The offerings are carried in a sizable wooden box.

Meanwhile, on the same day, at precisely six o'clock in the morning, the guardian and his assistant set off from Kinahrejo for the two-hour walk down the mountainside to Cangkringan where they will take delivery of the palace offerings. Both are dressed in traditional Javanese dress: a long batik sarong, a Mao-style *sorjan* jacket and a close-fitting *blangkon* batik head cloth. They walk under golden umbrellas.

At the same time, back in Kinahrejo the ladies are busy preparing food offerings in the kitchen of the guardian's house. They cook two roast chickens, a whole chicken boiled in coconut milk, rice balls and cones of rice, coconut-flavoured spicy vegetables, various items of food from the market, fried nibbles, mixed vegetables, meat-filled steamed rice rolls, shrimp crackers and much more. Before they get to work they place flower offerings around the kitchen – on shelves and racks, in sinks and tubs, and on the braziers used to cook the Labuhan offerings. The flowers keep the resident *dhanyang* spirits happy and ensure nothing goes wrong with the cooking. The foods have to be as tasty as they can be, and the notoriously grouchy *dhanyang* must be kept from tampering with the cooking process.

Shortly after midday the guardian accompanied by his assistant and a cluster of local officials return from Cangkringan to Kinahrejo with the box of regalia and offerings, this time making the up-hill journey by car. Already hundreds of spectators are milling through Kinahrejo, and more will arrive in the course of the afternoon and evening.

The regalia and offerings are respectfully accommodated overnight in the guardian's house. Prayers and traditional entertainments fill the evening. Exactly at the hour of midnight the Labuhan ceremony gets under way attended by a squad of costumed courtiers from the Jogjakarta palace accompanied by district and sub-district officials and other special guests. To begin, the leader of the rite – the guardian of the mountain – recites mantra prayers and burns incense alone in the kitchen, surrounded by aromatic food offerings. The food is then borne into the sitting room where it is prayed over by all in attendance. The prayers are led by a *modin*, a mosque official, who also burns incense before intoning his prayers in Arabic and Javanese. The modin mentions that the Sultan of Jogjakarta gives the offerings to the ancestors who reside in the mountain as a gesture of love, respect and thanksgiving. He prays that the Sultan and his family, the nation of Indonesia, its leaders and the Indonesian people be forever granted long life, peace and good health, and be protected from catastrophe and natural disasters. The rite ends with a *slamĕtan,* the ritual consumption of the food offerings that have been set out on dry-grass mats. The room is jam-packed and hot despite the chill of the air outside. The meal is only for those wearing full traditional Javanese dress. Those in everyday "western" clothes are allowed to follow proceedings from the rear, sitting behind those dressed more properly in Javanese style, or if space is limited (as it always is) they can follow proceedings in the frigid air outdoors.

The following day at six o'clock in the morning, in temperatures close to zero, the wooden box crammed with offerings of palace regalia is lifted and – in the shade of golden umbrellas – is carried by palace functionaries in a winding procession up the mountainside to a spot just below the *kendhit* frontier where the Labuhan ceremony will be held. Local elders and palace functionaries march in front under golden umbrellas. They are wearing traditional dress: men in batik sarongs, *sorjan* jackets made of pin-stripe *lurik* cloth, and tightly fitting *blangkon* headcloths; women in colourful *sĕmĕkan* bodices – many bare-shouldered – and ankle-length batik sarongs so tightly wound around their hips, buttocks and thighs that they are compelled to move their legs mainly from the knees down, walking with small, mincing steps. At the rear of the procession come hundreds of ordinary people wearing thick jackets to keep out the cold, some looking out from under baseball caps, beanies or woolly head-scarves.

A slow walk of about two hours brings the procession to a boulder known as the *pĕlabuhan*, the place where the offerings are delivered. Here the party sits crossed-legged facing the summit and to the accompaniment of invocations in high Javanese, with their palms pressed together above their faces in the *sĕmbah* gesture, they deliver the offerings to the spirit denizens of the mountain. The guardian burns incense and prays as he proffers the offerings to Panĕmbahan Sapu Jagat. After this the senior members of the procession eat the food offerings together. The offerings of traditional clothes and cloths are then distributed to certain people who have reserved them long in advance. Most of those in attendance are public figures – local district heads, police officers, prosecuting attorneys, and others. As they receive the powerful gifts they hand back to the guardian gifts of money in gratitude for his services and to help him defray the costs of the ceremony. The ritual offerings are carefully stored away by their new owners as powerful objects that will boost their authority, give wings to their careers, and also help keep at bay black magic, hostile spells and disaster.

Supernaturally bestowed favours are not wholly monopolised

by the rich and powerful. On the edge of the rite – as one observer records – crowds of people are hoping for some trickle-down.

> In Mbok Pujana's eatery I came across Ibu Petrus and her son who was a student at Gadjah Mada University. They were members of a party that had come in ten minibuses from a *kampung* neighbourhood of Jogjakarta. Their ambition was to attend the *slamĕtan* ritual in the hope that they would be blessed by the Sultan and the ancestors of Merapi with safety and good fortune. I also met Ibu Ngasiyah, dressed in the proper attire of a Muslim woman with a *hijab* headscarf. She had come with her husband, from their home in Bantul, south of Jogjakarta, about forty kilometres from Kinahrejo. They had brought gifts of rice and sugar for the guardian, but they also hoped that their attendance would bring them *bĕrkah*, good fortune and blessings.

For the most part, the whole apparatus of the Indonesian state – including the palace of Jogjakarta and its sultan – feels impossibly distant to the people of Merapi's tilted world. But there is another realm – a "virtual" realm – that even today many feel is closer to them than the organs of the state and its officials. In many ways this virtual realm resembles what they know of real government. It has departments, officials and a bureaucratic structure that both resembles that of the real world, and at the same time embodies an ironic, even critical, vision of that real world.

Different communities on the slopes of the mountain nurture varying visions of their virtual government. Its headquarters lie under the crater of the mountain. According to Elizabeth Prasetyo and Heri Dono in their book *The White Banyan*, Maridjan once saw this place in a dream and was able to describe it.

> I saw a path leading up to the crater and there was a green door there leading into the side of the mountain. The interior of the crater was full of chairs beautifully arranged, but the door itself was shut. When I reached the crater I was told that I was not permitted to sit on any of the chairs. Instead I was given a carpet and a cushion. The door into the crater opened but there were guards at the door sitting on chairs at a table, and on the table there was a book. [...] And up there I seemed to see a great *alun-alun* square with ranks of soldiers marching across it, and with crowds of people in it who – as it seemed to me – were waiting to attend an audience. My father was still alive at the time and he burned incense for the sustenance of hungry soldiers.

The dream resurrects accounts of an ancient tri-partite alliance between the spirit queen of the southern ocean, the spirit guardian of Mount Merapi, and the rulers of the now vanished state of Mataram and its successors. The alliance negotiates an accommodation between Islam on the one hand, and on the other the primal faiths of Java including Hinduism and Buddhism. The story goes that the founder of Mataram, Panĕmbahan Sénåpati (ruled c.1582 - 1603), had a faithful retainer, Ki Juru Taman. Despite advancing years Ki Juru Taman (the name means literally "gardener") worked hard maintaining the gardens around the Mataram palace in Kartå near modern Jogjakarta. According to one version of the story, when his lord asked him whether he had any ambition to enjoy his twilight years free from the demands of palace duties, the gardener replied:

"Your mercy, my Lord. The only happiness I have is to serve you. And all I ask is that you permit me to serve you until death takes me. For me, the greatest grace I could wish for is Your Highness's matchless favour."

One day a mysterious bright light drew Panĕmbahan Sénåpati south to the shores of the southern ocean. There he meditated with such intensity that the waves were stilled and the spirit queen of the south, Nyai Rårå Kidul, was compelled to emerge from the water. Dazzled by her beauty the young lord pleaded with her to help him achieve his ambition to become a great king. She promised to send her supernatural energy to reinforce his troops, but there was a condition. In battle he must never deploy them with their backs to the southern ocean.

"If you can meet this condition, rest assured I will send my best troops to supernaturally enter into each of your men."

There was another condition.

"Your Highness must be prepared to become my husband."

The young prince had fallen in love with Nyai Rårå Kidul at first sight, but she was a were-spirit with a body that was half fish. She saw his hesitation.

"You and I are indeed different. Totally different. You are an ordinary mortal, I am not. But I can change that. We can be the same. You can be my husband, just as mortal women have mortal husbands. It's not difficult."

She raised her hands as if in entreaty and an egg appeared in her palms.

"Eat this egg raw and you will become like me: powerful, invulnerable, immortal."

Still the prince hesitated. He looked closely at the egg. In some versions of the story it is called the Egg of the World, or the Egg of Existence (*Ĕndhog Jagad*). But as far as the prince could see it was an ordinary hen's egg. Nevertheless a strange feeling came upon him. The allure of the queen collided with fear of the sacrifice he must make of his mortality and his newly acquired Islamic faith.

The queen was cunning. She saw his doubts and reassured him.

"You don't need to eat it right now. Take it home. Eat it when the moment is right, when you feel you have what it takes to truly reach for your ambitions."

Sénåpati tore himself from the company of the alluring queen and started back towards his palace. But on the way he had an encounter that changed his view of the tempting egg. At a lonely place in the forest he met the saint Sunan Kalijågå, the embodiment of all that Javanese Islam stands for. Dressed entirely in black, with a penetrating gaze that radiated authority, the saint knew at once that Sénåpati had been consorting with the spirit queen of pagan Java.

Luckily Sunan Kalijågå was no enemy of Java's ancient culture. He did not command the prince to relinquish the egg. Rather he gently chided him.

"Do you know what will happen if you eat that egg? You will become a spirit creature like the queen of the southern ocean. Like her, you will be invulnerable and supernaturally powerful. You will achieve all your aspirations for worldly power. You will live forever, or at least until existence ceases. You will marry the queen and she will be at your side eternally. But you will live in the depths of the ocean and you will no longer be human. Is that what you want?"

A chill gripped Sénåpati. He felt his skin creep. Was that the future promised by Java's pre-Islamic culture?

"However, there is a way ..." the saint mused. He didn't say exactly what the way was. In oracular fashion he hinted that the egg might be "given to someone who would be a more appropriate recipient, someone not far from you, someone who is totally devoted to the service of Mataram".

The great saint politely took his leave and vanished, but Sénåpati now knew whom to approach. When he reached the palace he summoned his elderly, loyal gardener. He was less than subtle.

"Uncle," he said, using "uncle" as a familiar but respectful term of address for any older man, "do you have what it takes to lift your level of devotion to me?"

"Of course, Your Highness." (There was scarcely any other answer he could give.) "Whatever your wish, it is my command."

"Break open this egg and eat it raw."

The gardener did so and instantly morphed into a giant. The transformation was so sudden that Sénåpati and his adviser took a startled step backwards. The gardener now dwarfed the betel trees in the palace garden. Even seated cross-legged he towered above his royal overlords. Panĕmbahan Sénåpati explained to him that, in his new guise, he would be immortal and would have the honour of serving Mataram for ever. His task would be to stand guard over Mount Merapi.

"Whenever you see signs that the mountain is about to erupt, it will be your task to calm it. If it does erupt you must try to channel the lava, sand, stones and anything else it throws out so that it does not cause havoc in the lands of Mataram, or worse, destroy the kingdom."

Although bewildered at his sudden change of form, Ki Juru Taman felt a great honour had been conferred on him and he left immediately to take up his new post. More than four hundred years later he is still at his post, though today he is more commonly known by the name Éyang Merapi or Panĕmbahan Sapu Jagat, also Kyai Sapu Jagat.

The loyal, hard-working gardener Ki Juru Taman transformed into an obedient giant after eating the egg of Java's primordial pagan power. [Illustration by Har in Harnaeni]

*Sapu Jagat* means "he who sweeps the world". The ex-gardener – now Supreme Spirit of the mountain – has the power not just to protect and warn, but also to sweep the world clean of evil and insurrection by allowing eruptions of Java's ancient energy to take place. It is also his job to guard and contain that power, to ensure it doesn't trouble the new order of Islam that extends from the foothills of the mountain to the distant extremities of the island.

A company of spirit officials is on hand to do Sapu Jagat's bidding, though their names and duties vary across the communities of the mountainside. For some, the key figures to be venerated are Ĕmpu Råmå and Ĕmpu Pĕrmadi, ironsmiths whose forge flares into eruption from time to time. The lanky, long-nosed Kyai Pètruk is in charge of the spirit troops of the realm. He is one of the most beloved of Merapi's denizens, especially on the north and east slopes. He often appears in dreams to warn people of impending eruptions. Among other officials are Åntåbogå who commands the spirit troops around the base of the mountain. He ensures that the mountain remains upright and on an even keel, that it does not collapse flat on to the surface of the island. Mégantårå rides a flying horse and regulates the mountain's weather while Kyai Sapuangin has responsibility for the winds that swirl around the mountain.

The female deity Nyai Gadhung Mlathi wears a tight-fitting shoulderless *kĕmbĕn* blouse and an equally tight-fitting batik sarong. Young and bewitching, she is (so I've been told) a regular guest in the dreams of local men. She keeps an eye on the villages of the mountain and ensures that vegetation and crops grow lush and green. Other names too have survived into the present: Kyai Grinjing Wĕsi and Kyai Grinjing Kawat are adjutants of Kyai Sapu Jagat. Then there is Kyai Branjangwĕsi, Kyai Kricikwĕsi, Kyai Bråmågĕdali, Kyai Wola-wali and Radèn Ringin Anom. Perhaps it is this exotic company of military officers, bureaucrats and courtiers who are responsible for the *lampor* phenomenon. Even today there are people who swear they have heard the chilling jingle of horses' trappings and the shouts of their riders as spirit officials and troops travel the invisible highway between the summit of Merapi and the realm of the spirit queen of the southern ocean.

Mbah Maridjan was inducted into modern commerce through the weird world of mountaineering. He told me of his astonishment when he discovered that, for some people, climbing Mount Merapi was a kind of sport. The mountain was a physical obstacle, a secular challenge rather than a sacred place. Even more astonishing, climbers were prepared to fork out good money for local guidance as they played the game of mountain bagging. Maridjan supplied information about the best route to take, about safety precautions and evacuation procedures, and the weather conditions climbers could expect. He told them Merapi was supernaturally charged and dangerous, especially above the *kĕndhit* frontier. Climbers would always face their biggest challenges up there, he said. The slopes were unpredictable. At any moment boulders might come tumbling down from the crater and deadly gas could hiss forth. Fierce winds filled with shards of sand that rasp the skin off, or are loaded with sharp gusts of rain, can hit without warning. The frigid air can turn suddenly searing hot. Climbers might find themselves coughing through corrosive sulphur fumes or choked by the smell of gas.

He gave climbers the same advice that centuries of tradition had bequeathed to him. Above the *kĕndhit* boundary the mountain is at its most unpredictable. To safely negotiate the frontier they had to pay the mountain, its palace and its guardians proper respect. Those who ignored local custom – who failed to show the necessary respect – would feel the terror of these warnings. For some climbers, especially foreigners, Maridjan's advice was a dollop of exotic, memorable topping added to the confection of their mountaineering adventure.

He discovered another astonishing fact: fame is a saleable commodity. If you become a celebrity, just being yourself is a commercial asset. You don't need to do much. You are a natural resource that can be excavated and sold (using the heavy lifting equipment of the mass media, of course).

From the mid 1990s and into the first decade of the new millennium Maridjan acquired a media profile that made him a familiar figure far beyond the geographical and social territories of Merapi and Jogjakarta. His fame coincided with a period of turbulent transition in Indonesia. No country was harder hit by the Asian Financial Crisis of 1997-1998. Unemployment, prices and corruption all soared. In 1998 the authoritarian certainties of the New Order came to an abrupt end with President Soeharto's resignation. A new constitution and democratic reforms let loose the unpredictable forces of multi-party democracy, followed by extreme decentralisation and radical media freedoms. In 1999 East Timor seceded. In 2000 vicious communal violence broke out in Maluku and Sulawesi, and the Aceh rebellion seemed more intractable than ever. The project of a united, prospering Indonesia seemed suddenly to go rotten. In the circumstances it was inevitable that the normality of tradition – or a modern reconstruction of tradition – would make a comeback.

Maridjan had become known for his simplicity, dedication to duty, loyalty to the sultan and his willingness to work for very modest rewards. He was the ritual master of Merapi's *kěndhit* frontier, a place of transition. In a time of unpredictable and dangerous economic and political transition Maridjan's steady stewardship of the unpredictable and dangerous mountain was a reassuring model. His respect for tradition was one way of barricading people from the wrath of eruptions, whether natural or political-social.

In 2006 Maridjan signed an advertising contract with the Sido Muncul pharmaceuticals company. Sido Muncul specialises in herbal tonics and medicines known generically as *jamu*, sold mostly in small sachets. One of its most popular products was a tonic known as *Kuku Bima* (Bima's Thumbnail) made from ginseng and other traditional medicinal herbs plus ground-up extract of sea horse. Bima (also called Wrěkodårå and Åntåsénå) is the second of the five Pandåwå brothers, heroes of the classical Javanese shadow play. He is an icon of bluff masculinity, with a huge, half-naked muscle-bound body, rich black facial hair, and a warrior temperament. He cultivates enormous thumbnails like talons that he uses to rip open opponents in combat. His thumbnail is also a symbol of male virility. Bima pushes it between his index finger and middle finger in a not-very-subtle simulation of sexual intercourse. The Kuku Bima tonic was said to be good for men's sexual potency, promising improved sperm quality, improved erections and improved longevity in love-making.

In 2004 Sido Muncul rejigged the product. Ginseng was retained as a major ingredient but the other raw herbs were abandoned to be replaced with processed taurine, vitamin extracts, raw honey and caffeine. The new product still rode on the momentum of its old brand name but it was no longer primarily a pick-me-up for sexually insecure men. Rather it became an energy drink – available in four fruit flavours – targeting active men and women.

The advertising campaign was built around television commercials highlighting the drink's invigorating properties for sportsmen and women. In 2006 Maridjan joined two other national celebrities – champion boxer Chris John and actress-author Rieke Diah Pitaloka – to film a series of television commercials on the slopes of Merapi. The commercials show the volcano in eruption with a long cloud of hot ash billowing down its slopes. Maridjan stands looking defiant while Chris John bounds up the mountainside across quaking ash-covered terrain. The two shadow-box and later shake hands against the background of the mountain. Maridjan shouts the new slogan of Kuku Bima, "Roså! Roså!", Javanese for "Strong! Strong!"

Rieke appears with a group of children. She points at Chris John and Maridjan:

"They put their bodies on the line," she tells the children, "and Kuku Bima is the drink of men who put their bodies on the line."

At the age of seventy-nine Maridjan had become an icon of virile, defiant, risk-taking energy. His face would appear on the redesigned packaging of the new drink together with the catchword that was now to define him: "Roså!"

The campaign was an immense success. A little more than a year later, Sido Muncul had sold over a billion sachets of the new Kuku Bima. The drink grabbed more than 10% of Indonesia's very competitive sports supplement market, generating income for Sido Muncul estimated to be more than two trillion rupiah (about one and a half billion US dollars). By July 2008 the company was claiming sales of 200 million sachets a month, and the product was accounting for 65% of its income.

Maridjan's face was everywhere. He began to enjoy modest prosperity. He renovated his house, but not extravagantly. He bought a car and began to travel. He maintained his ultra-simple life-style and – so the villagers of Kinahrejo told me – was generous with his money. The renovation of the village mosque was only one of the local projects that benefited from Maridjan's new-found wealth.

Five years after the guardian's death, I again visited Kinahrejo. Demoralisation lay like a grimy blanket over the village. The little that remained of Maridjan's house had become a shabby tourist attraction. It was a confusion of grey rubble: broken slabs of concrete, the frames of several windows and doors leering at crazy angles, the melted and fused debris of a kitchen – smashed crockery and twisted pots. A burned out car had turned brown with rust. Beside it stood the skeletons of two motorcycles. In a small storeroom the instruments of a *gamĕlan* orchestra had survived more or less intact, but now lay dust-covered and silent. Across the sandy yard opposite the wreckage of the house stood a simple souvenir stall operated by Maridjan's daughter. Tourists lined up to buy Maridjan t-shirts, souvenir photographs, videos of the eruption, rolling-pin foot massagers, prayer beads, bags of peanuts, packets of *krupuk* crackers, and psychedelic-coloured sweet drinks. What had once been Maridjan's pride and joy – the nearby pink mosque – was so badly damaged in the eruption it had been demolished. In its place stood a shack with bamboo-weave walls. Hope had labelled it *Masjid Al-Amin*.

Maridjan's grave is in the village of Srunen, a little over two kilometres as the crow flies from Kinahrejo. Between his house and his final resting place lies a deep gash of rocks, sand and intermittent cascades of water. At most times it is impassable to vehicles. On the pillion seat of an *ojek* motorbike I headed down the mountainside to a crossing point where the bike was able to weave and jump among rocks and spin its wheels through sand to the other side of the gash. It was a rough crossing. I felt slightly sick as we headed back up the steep ascent to Srunen. From Mbah Maridjan's compound it was a total distance of around fifteen kilometres to the small parking area and shaded reception desk at his final resting place.

I slumped gratefully onto a bamboo bench under a roof of corrugated iron and picked up the site's guest book. The roughly scrawled entries told me that over the preceding days there had been a steady stream of visitors from all parts of Java as well as from Palembang (south Sumatra), Medan (north Sumatra), Pontianak (west Kalimantan), Tenggarong (east Kalimantan), Banjarmasin (south Kalimantan), even from Malaysia and East Timor. A short walk from the reception area brought me to Srunen's public cemetery where, in the upper left corner, surrounded by wild grass and spindly, new-growth trees, a tiny walled compound had been built. Though a crudely arched gateway lay the grave of Mbah Maridjan. It was a dark stone ledger about half a metre high with twin headstones, decorative engraving along its sides, and the occupant's name inscribed on white marble at one end. Flower petals were heaped down the length of the grave and on the ground at one end lay a small slab of stone for burning incense.

I sat in the quiet coolness and paid my respects. In my mind's eye I recalled my two meetings with the guardian and I thanked him for his hospitality.

As I slowly picked my way back along the gravel track to the reception shelter, dreading the misery of the motorbike ride back to Kinahrejo, I was joined by Debora and Febby, two thirtyish women from Jakarta both wearing pastel green cotton slacks and red t-shirts. They worked "in retail" they told me, managing a branch of Indomart, the nationwide chain of mini supermarkets. I had seen them earlier carefully spreading flower petals along the guardian's grave.

"Mbah Maridjan was truly a saint," Debora said, her forehead crinkled in an earnest frown. "He was an incarnation of Sunan Gĕsĕng."

Suddenly I was listening closely. I had twice been to Sunan Gĕsĕng's tomb in the village of Tirto not far from Magelang, one of several tombs that claimed to host his remains. He was the famous "singed saint".

"Mbah Maridjan was dug up from under a layer of ash," Debora went on. "They found him kneeling with his forehead pressed against the kitchen floor, facing Mecca."

The ribbon of Sunan Gĕsĕng's story was unrolling like sub-titles across the bottom of my mind.

Centuries before, a certain Cåkråjåyå – a Hindu – had come under the spell of the charismatic saint Sunan Kalijågå. Cåkråjåyå earned a precarious living as a palm sap tapper, collecting *arèn* sap or coconut nectar to make sugar. As he worked he would sing a short ditty.

*Lontang-lantung, wong dèrès buntuté bumbung*
Dingling-dangling, palm tappers have a bamboo tube
hanging down like a tail

One day as he was working and singing, Sunan Kalijågå happened to pass by. The saint complimented Cåkråjåyå on his voice and song, but offered him another "better" song.

*Lakilah lakilĕlah, mukamadarrasulĕlah*

This is a garbled variant of the Islamic confession of faith uttered in Arabic:

*La 'ilaha 'illà l-Lāh, Muḥammadur rasūlu l-Lāh*
There is no god but Allah, and Muhammad is His emissary.

Cåkråjåyå liked the song and agreed to replace his old one with the saint's new one. He resumed work singing the new song. He didn't understand the words but by singing them he had unwittingly become a Muslim. He was delighted to see that the sweet sap now flowed much more abundantly. He poured the sap into a bamboo mould and let it dry. When he broke open the mould he was astonished to see that the sap had turned to gold.

He realised Sunan Kalijågå was no ordinary person. He pleaded with the saint to accept him as a disciple. Kalijågå put him to the test. He left for Mecca to pray, commanding Cåkråjåyå to take care of a bamboo staff – a symbol of Islam – and not to move until he came back. After some time Kalijågå returned to find that a thick forest of bamboo and grass had grown up at the spot and Cåkråjåyå could not be located. The saint ordered that the forest be set alight. After it had burned away Cåkråjåyå was seen hunched over and scorched amid the ashes. Kalijågå commanded him to rise, praising him for his fortitude and obedience. He conferred the status of "saint" on him and gave him the name Sunan Gěsěng (in Javanese *gěsěng* means "scorched, singed, burnt").[12]

We had reached the reception shelter. Pak Karyono, one of the custodians of the site, was sitting on the bamboo bench with one knee hugged against his chest puffing on a clove-scented cigarette. He confirmed Debora's conjecture, Maridjan was a modern scorched saint. Like Sunan Gěsěng, he was humble, poor, loyal and strong in faith. His death while prostrate facing Mecca had given him impeccable credentials as a Muslim.

Karyono looked intently at the smouldering end of his cigarette. He had a surprising piece of information and he produced it hesitantly.

"Actually," he said, "we don't know exactly where Mbah Maridjan is. He has disappeared."

Debora and Febby stared.

---

12  I need not remind the reader, I hope, that the story of Sunan Gěsěng almost exactly replicates the story of Sunan Kalijågå himself as summarised in Chapter One. The motifs of the two stories rise from deep in the folk history of Javanese Islam.

"You mean ... he's not here?"

"Well, yes he's here, but we don't know exactly where."

Karyono explained that, as prescribed by Islamic law, Maridjan had been buried as quickly as possible after his death.

"The burial was very hurried," he said, "because the mountain was still erupting. People were scared. And just two days after the burial, Merapi dumped a great cloud of ash on Srunen. We all evacuated downhill. When we came back the cemetery had disappeared. A shroud of hot dust lay where it used to be. When the dust cooled we looked for Maridjan's grave, but we couldn't find it. The wooden marker had been blown away, there was no mound of earth that we could see."

"So what about the stone grave we have just visited?" said Febby looking bewildered.

"That's only a guess. It's roughly where Maridjan is."

Pak Karyono sucked on his cigarette.

"Actually, Maridjan has returned to Merapi."

He pointed at the slope of the mountain.

"He's somewhere in there."

# 8

# How to be a queen in Madura

## PRINCE JIMAT:
### A GAY SAINT, PUSHY WOMEN AND ISLAM

Ludrug is a genre of popular theatre born in the port city of Surabaya in the early decades of the twentieth century. Most ludrug plays are satirical, funny, usually rude domestic melodramas. They are half improvised but each performance is knitted together using well-tested templates of plot and character. There are musical elements too: dance, *gamělan* or other kinds of orchestral accompaniment, and mini-sermons sung at the audience in the blunt idiom of East Java.

In ludrug, female roles are usually played by men.[13] Ludrug's transvestite actors take a lot of trouble to represent women accurately. Men in the audience – women too – are often astounded they cannot see the man inside the female character on stage. Knowing that the demure and fabulously pretty young woman, or the yelling middle-aged harridan, or the doting mother of a wayward son, is in fact a man carries the audience into the fraught terrain of gender construction and sexual orientation. On stage, men fall in love with women who are really men, or to put it

---

13  All-male actors used to be the rigid rule in *ludrug*, and mostly it still is, but recently female actors have started to appear in some plays.

another way, men fall in love with men who are indistinguishable from women. Heterosexual men in the audience who are attracted to the transvestite men on stage are protected from guilt or anti-gay prejudice by the comic power of the play. The audience can also see the theatrical stereotyping of women as exactly that: male-manipulated sexist stereotyping. Female characters, being in fact male, acquire a freedom to say and do things that might not be possible if they were played by women. Sometimes the mask drops for an instant (intentionally) and the "woman" reveals her inner masculinity: her voice suddenly dives an octave, she utters a men-only word, she scratches her crotch, she paws a male character or aggressively snuggles up to him. The subversion of "normality" and the exploration of dissonances in the social construction of gender – what men and women have in common and what divides them – these are at the heart of ludrug. And like an eminence overlooking every performance looms the elephant in the room, patriarchal Islam with its generally strict delineation of gender roles and its generally strict segregation of the sexes.

Ludrug has roots deep in the culture of Madura, the island that stretches out long and flat off the north coast of East Java. At its western end Madura nudges into the busy port of Surabaya where it discharges Madurese migrants into the city. In the east it frays into small islands flung across the shallow warmth of the Java Sea. History has locked Madura and Java into a sibling-like embrace but the two cultures are very different. Unlike Java with its rowdy diversity, Madura is relatively homogenous. Its language and arts are very distinct. Its people are energetic and mobile. Some say they are human embodiments of the rough sea salt that used to be their island's main export. They are also strong and conservative Muslims.

Ludrug (called *loddrok* in Madurese) probably developed out of Madurese performance arts brewed up with *kěthoprak* and other genres of Javanese theatre in the cultural cauldron of Surabaya. In the classical performance arts of Java – the opera-like *wayang wong* for example – it is normal for certain male characters to be played by females. The truly masculine man has strongly feminine traits. The great hero Arjunå – invincible on the battlefield and irresistible to women – is normally danced by a young woman. But in Madurese performance arts the opposite applies: behind the attractively feminine woman lies the toughness of a man.

It is true the women of Madura have a reputation for male-style toughness, but they also enjoy pop fame for their sexual skills. The Madurese themselves have a saying: "Outside Madura you sweeten your coffee by stirring it with a spoon, but in Madura it is the cup that does the stirring and the coffee is much sweeter." Madurese society shows signs that it evolved from a prehistoric matriarchy. Even today, in an age of Islamic patriarchy, the preferred marriage is matrilocal: the husband moves into his wife's extended household and comes under the authority of the wife's parents, at least for a time. If the wife happens to be the youngest sibling in her family this is an almost universal arrangement. Women are able to initiate divorce too, and often do. They can even base their case for divorce on the sexual inadequacies of the husband.

At the same time patriarchal Islam, speaking through the ranks of powerful religious scholars, ensures that public power, especially political authority, remains solidly vested in men. Since the coming of Islam in the early 1500s it has never been possible for a woman to formally occupy the apex of political power in Madura, whether as local king, *bupati* or even village head. But, as in the institution of marriage, Islam did not entirely displace the old order and women continued to wield a certain amount informal political power. Narratives have evolved that make it possible for the pre-Islamic matriarchy to survive like a seam of salt under the heavy layers of post-conversion patriarchy. The blended symbolism of the two narrative streams remains embedded in the origin stories of certain sacred sites, especially at Madura's prestigious royal burial grounds. Here the ancient aura of the place has protected the matriarchal components of its stories.

At the eastern end of Madura, orbiting at the outermost edge of Java's cultural solar system, lies Sumenep, the dusty capital of what was once the island's most powerful state. Just outside town, like a tiny satellite, lies the Asta Tinggi royal burial ground with its sacred tombs asleep on a high hill. In these depths of cultural space distance coincides with history. Asta Tinggi's stories take visitors into the surreal, ludrug-like world of Madura's distant past, with pushy women, gay men, son-less rulers and murder.

In October 2015 I boarded a bus in Surabaya's Bungurasih terminal hoping to survive the four or five hours of jolting travel to Sumenep. I found a seat right behind the driver's. Beneath me a diesel engine shuddered quietly. The bus would leave when it was full.

Hawkers shuffled up and down the aisle dropping samples of their merchandise into passengers' laps, patiently picking them up a few minutes later. A packet of men's socks fell across my knees followed by a white Muslim *taqiyah* cap and a small sachet of peanuts. I ignored them, and after a few moments they disappeared. A cling-wrapped meal on a black plastic tray slid on to my lap: rice, fried chicken, a lump of yellow tofu and a bright red blob of chilli sauce. A minute later it was snatched back to be replaced by a string of white prayer beads, a coiled up leather belt and a small stack of primary school textbooks. A shabby duo of buskers plunked at their ukuleles and sang songs of lost love under a TV screen at the front of the bus. I groped in my pocket for change to drop into the styrene cup they waved in front of each passenger.

Donald Duck, Mickey Mouse and Minnie Mouse marched in a frozen procession across the top of the front window, each glowing translucent in the sunlight. In this bus at least, Donald, Mickey and Minnie had converted to Islam. The strip was wreathed in a verse from the Qur'ān in Arabic script: *Sabbiḥi asma rabbika al-'a'lā,* "Glorify the Name of your Lord Most High." (Surah 87 Al-A'la, verse 1) New passengers jostled up the entry steps, shoving lumpy shopping bags in front of them, their small laughs announcing their embarrassment. A set of pink nail clippers, a small bunch of cling-wrapped grapes and a newspaper materialised on my knees.

Beside me a teenage girl was looking apprehensively out the window. She tugged at her pastel green headscarf and checked the knot on the cloth-wrapped box riding on her knees. She was too shy to talk much but she was on her own and seemed to be quite pleased to find herself sitting beside a harmless, elderly foreigner. Eventually I learned she was from Probolinggo, a small town on the north coast of Java half way between Surabaya and the sharp southward bend of coastline that leads to Bali. She was travelling to Pamekasan for a short stay with relatives. Pamekasan is about seventy kilometres as the crow flies across the inland sea that separates Madura from Java. Like most people in Probolinggo the girl was an ethnic Madurese. Her family in Probolinggo, she said, could still tell the story of her family's migration to the Java mainland three centuries ago.

The driver-side door flew open and the driver violently hoisted himself into his seat slamming the door behind him. He pulled a towel tight around his neck, threw a packet of clove-scented cigarettes on to the dashboard and rattled the gear stick with a grease-stained hand. A bag of batter-coated fried bananas, some sheets of stickers with Quranic verses on them, and a packet of discount singlets were quickly removed from my lap as hawkers raced to vacate the bus. We were on our way.

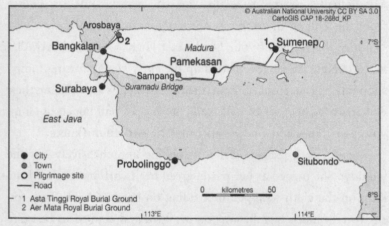

The island of Madura at the eastern end of Java
showing the dead-end location of Sumenep.

The trip began with one and a half hours of manoeuvring along city tollways and through the cluttered streets of Surabaya's harbour precinct. It was a relief to break out into a tree-lined avenue leading to the Suramadu Bridge. Opened in 2009 its five-kilometre span lifts vehicles across the Madura Strait from the traffic-crazed hubbub of Surabaya into the stillness of Madura's ancient landscape.

The Suramadu Bridge has brought Surabaya's brash mix of squalor and glass-clad modernity as far as Bangkalan in west Madura. Beyond Bangkalan Madura opens into a landscape of dusty fields and seaside mud flats, whitewashed mosques, spiky wooden fishing boats and cattle markets. As the bus cruised east the island dried out. We were travelling back in time accompanied by the incessant yodelling of the bus's two-tone horn. Through their mobile phones passengers stayed connected with the world they were leaving. There was even a dirt-crusted USB power point beside the driver where they could recharge their phones.

A sharp squabble broke out between the Javanese conductor and a Madurese passenger who refused to pay the full fare. The conductor threatened to throw the passenger off. "Pull over!" he shouted to the driver. The Madurese, they say, are short-tempered but the shabby client paid up and sank into sour silence. Three hours into the trip my teenage companion jumped from the bus in the almost empty terminal at Pamekasan. She was greeted with kisses and hugs by a line of women in orange, red and yellow kaftans matched up with yellow, red and orange headscarfs. We drove on. Trees grew sparse and spindly. Salt pans appeared with small hills of mud-flecked sea salt baking in them.

I had been sweating in my seat more than four hours when we arrived at the outskirts of Sumenep. I clambered out into a small mob of shouting *bécak* pedicab drivers. The mid afternoon air was hot in my face as my *bécak* laboured through the placid traffic of Sumenep's main thoroughfare. Scraggy trees flanked the street with glimpses of rice fields behind motorbike showrooms and banners over the footpath advertising cigarettes and instant noodles. We turned into the Wijaya I Hotel, Sumenep's premiere hotel, where I secured a VIP room. Its Formica-topped table was scarred with at least a dozen black welts from cigarette butts that had burned out along its edge over many years. The room had no soap, no towel, no toilet paper and no hot water. But for Rp.135,000 a night, about ten US dollars, it was a good deal and I was glad to move in.

In the remote past a number of small fiefdoms scratched an existence around Madura's scarce water sources. The modern history of the island began with its conquest by the forces of Mataram, a state centred deep in the interior of Central Java. From the late years of the 1500s the rulers of Mataram unrolled their empire northwards, picking off Java's coastal states one by one and relentlessly pressing in on their toughest enemy, the rich port city of Surabaya. In 1624 Madura fell after a bloody campaign and the following year Surabaya succumbed. Madura's mini-states were welded into a single vassal territory with a new capital at Sampang, about a third of the way along the island.

But the island's unity lasted scarcely more than half a century. In 1680, in the wake of a rebellion by the Madurese prince Trunåjåyå, the eastern half broke away from the west. While remaining a nominal tributary of Mataram the splinter was snapped up by the Dutch East India Company.

The men who occupied high office in Madura had to be satisfactorily heterosexual so they could father male heirs and thereby uphold the integrity of succession and the masculine authority of monarchist culture. But what do you do when a ruler fails to produce a male heir, whether by bad luck or because he is secretly gay? It was a challenge that appeared not once but four times in east Madura in the seventeenth and eighteenth centuries. And when it happened it was the women of the Madurese aristocracy who came to the rescue. Their solutions, including murder, made them kingmakers but at the same time reconfirmed their subordinate status in the ruling order. It was the old paradox and a universal one: they were instruments of their own oppression.

The Dutch were careful to keep their hands off palace politics, at least in the early decades of their presence in Madura. It was just as well. Within a few years of Sumenep's re-emergence as a distinct state there was a crisis over succession. When the first regent of the re-constituted Sumenep, Tumĕnggung Yudånagårå, died in 1684 he left behind four daughters but no son. According to Madurese custom, in the absence of a male successor the daughter of a deceased king could be the custodian and conduit of his power but she couldn't formally ascend the throne herself. Each of Yudånagårå's four daughters had married, and each of their husbands was eager to grab the gift of kingship that his wife could now pass to him.

One of the pretenders was Pangèran Panji Pulangjiwå. He had been born a minor aristocrat but had the good luck to attract the eye of Radèn Ayu Artak (also often written Arta), the oldest of the four princesses. Their marriage put Pulangjiwå first in line for a shot at the throne but his accession was far from a sure thing.

In 1685 a senior merchant in the Dutch East India Company, Jeremias Van Vliet, was instructed by company executives in Batavia to impose order along the restive north coast of Java's eastern half. He was given a force of 190 militiamen and a mandate to take firm action. Van Vliet summoned Sumenep's four contending brothers-in-law to a meeting in Surabaya in March, 1685. Pulangjiwå was blunt: the whole of East Madura was his, he said. He was the husband of Yudånagårå's eldest daughter and had been endorsed by Yudånagårå's chief minister. Van Vliet managed to persuade him (or so he thought) to share power with his brothers-in-law – at least until Mataram and the Dutch East India Company had considered the succession issue. But Pulangjiwå had no intention of sharing power.

In July Van Vliet convened another meeting, also in Surabaya, this time for all the local regents of north-coast Java and Madura. Pulangjiwå hurried across from Sumenep but his brothers-in-law failed to turn up. Seizing the moment he insinuated himself into the good graces of Van Vliet. When the Dutchman set off for the palace of the ruler of Mataram in Kartåsurå, Central Java, Pulangjiwå together with a company of men-at-arms from Sumenep was at his side hoping to get the supreme ruler of Java – the Susuhunan – to endorse him as regent of East Madura.

The difficult journey to Kartåsurå did not end well. Van Vliet and Pulangjiwå joined up with a column of Dutch troops whose commander, Captain Francois Tack, had been ordered to Kartåsurå to collect some debts and try to stop Java's incessant fighting. But Mataram's capital was in turmoil. On arrival Captain Tack found himself surrounded in the town square by hostile Balinese mercenaries. There, on February 8th 1686, he met a gruesome death skewered on their pikes and krisses. Around seventy-five of his men also died. Van Vliet and Pulangjiwå barely escaped with their lives. Pulangjiwå's hopes of a formal confirmation of his authority in East Madura were left in disarray. Dispensing with the formality of recognition by the central authority of Mataram he returned home with his troops and imposed his authority over Sumenep by force of arms with the backing of his new Dutch mentors.

From our vantage point in the present Pulangjiwå is an indistinct figure, but Dutch records have left us with a momentary close-up of the ambitious, persistent and pragmatic prince. In July 1685, during Van Vliet's second meeting in Surabaya, Pulangjiwå had an outwardly friendly but no doubt inwardly tense encounter with Cåkråningrat II, ruler of West Madura and a senior figure in the court of Mataram. Cåkråningrat had ruled the whole island before it was chopped in two five years earlier. Now he wanted to reassert his birthright in the east. Very likely his meeting with Pulangjiwå, under the calculating eyes of merchant-soldier Van Vliet, was an opportunity for the older man to assess the mettle of his much younger adversary.

In a scene described in Dutch records as "touching" the regents of west and east Madura had a friendly chat. There is no portrait of the meeting but from pictures of other similar meetings it is possible to reconstruct the scene. Pulangjiwå sat cross-legged on the floor before his elderly rival who was sitting on a bench. Both men were wearing dark, high-collared jackets with a dense line of buttons and embroidered piping down the front. The jackets lapped over batik sarongs with their characteristic diagonal rows of intricate patterning. The handle of a wavy-bladed kris protruded from their waist sashes. Batik headcloths fitted tightly over their heads, each with a knob-like bag at the nape of the neck to hold their locks of long hair. The hairy-faced Van Vliet and his adjutants were probably wearing high-collared, red military jackets with gold epaulettes. A long sabre would have been hanging down the length of their white trousers. The two Madurese nobles were probably barefoot, although they might have been wearing lightweight indoor slippers. Van Vliet would have been wearing tough leather boots.

Dutch records tell us that Pulangjiwå raised his hands and pressed his palms together in a gesture of respect for Cåkråningrat. For his part, Cåkråningrat shed tears and insisted the younger man rise and sit beside him. With bowed head Pulangjiwå listened intently to Cåkråningrat's fatherly advice, solemnly swearing to maintain amicable relations with him. But the friendliness was all sham. Less than a year later the pair were at each other's throats and Pulangjiwå was pleading with his friends in the Dutch East India Company to help him make war on Cåkråningrat.

Pangèran Panji Pulangjiwå died in 1702 (it is not known when his wife Radèn Ayu Artak died). Like his father-in-law before him, Pulangjiwå also failed to sire a son. But he did produce a formidable daughter, Radèn Ayu Gambrèk, known to posterity by her royal styling Radèn Ayu Cåkrånagårå. Like her mother, Gambrèk had scouted around and chosen a minor aristocrat, in this instance a cousin, as her husband. Prince Råmå, as he was originally called, adopted his wife's name and was installed as Cåkrånagårå the First, ruler of Sumenep.

For reasons I have not been able to uncover Radèn Ayu Cåkrånagårå divorced her consort in 1705 and he died shortly after. In the light of later events it is possible he was murdered by his ex-wife. His main legacy, and an important one, was a baby son, Prince Jimat. The Radèn Ayu, Jimat's mother, now turned to another cousin, Radèn Sudĕrmå, whom she married thereby conferring on him the office of regent. But Sudĕrmå didn't last long either. Apparently he deluded himself into thinking he could rule without listening to his wife. In 1707, fed up with her husband's independent-mindedness, the Radèn Ayu joined in a plot to have him murdered. Probably he was poisoned although details of the plot are not known for sure. Radèn Ayu Cåkrånagårå was not, and never could be, the properly recognised regent of Sumenep. But she now ruled in her own right while ostensibly acting as guardian for her son Prince Jimat until he could come of age and ascend the throne.

Radèn Ayu Cåkrånagårå died in 1711 but the young Prince Jimat had to wait until 1721 before he inherited full authority over Sumenep. Aged around twenty he won the endorsement of Sumenep's mentors and protectors, the Dutch East India Company, adopting the official title of Cåkrånagårå the Second. He proved to be an energetic ruler. He had learned how to butter up the Dutch and was adept at tiptoeing around his rival in West Madura. The once all-powerful Central Javanese state of Mataram was collapsing on itself and no longer threatened the remote edges of its old empire. Jimat embarked on a campaign to expand Sumenep's sphere of influence into the Javanese mainland. War had depopulated the far eastern salient of Java and Jimat filled it with Madurese colonists, mostly ex-soldiers. He incorporated the north coast of East Java into the Madurese culture sphere where much of it remains to this day. At the height of his reign, when summoned by Dutch authorities to a meeting in Semarang, "he came with a fleet of thirty vessels, and all his subjects seemed to be in great awe of him".

Today memories of Prince Jimat's prowess as a soldier and the glory he brought to Sumenep remain bright, its glamour maintained with the generous polish of legend. But few people are aware – at least not publicly – that he was brazenly gay. In 1732 Dutch authorities received a letter from Prince Cåkråningrat the Fourth, ruler of West Madura, accusing his rival in the east of being homosexual. "He used to have a certain Bagus Pringa as his lover," wrote Cåkråningrat, "followed by Bagus Surono; if certain men are handsome he recruits them and uses them as his husbands." Cåkråningrat knew enough about his Dutch overlords to sense he might be able to turn their Protestant prudery to his strategic advantage. Laying it on thick he claimed that Jimat's behaviour "was a serious offence against custom, and brought diseases, crop failures, and the ruin of cities and villages in its train." The stiff-necked businessmen of the Dutch East India Company were probably shocked but to their credit they took no action.

When Prince Jimat died in 1737 he had never married and never fathered any children. Again Sumenep faced a succession crisis and again the women of the ruling family stepped up to play their role as kingmakers. One of Jimat's sisters had a son who was shoe-horned into the job with the title Cåkrånagårå the Third. Incredibly, when he was deposed in 1751 he too had no male successor. This time another of Jimat's sisters stepped in. She proved to be as formidable as her ancestor Radèn Ayu Cåkrånagårå had been fifty years before. Her name was Radèn Ayu Tirtånagårå, and for four years she ruled Sumenep as "protector" – in effect queen but without formal inauguration.

The story goes that Radèn Ayu Tirtånagårå had a series of vivid dreams in which she saw and fell in love with her future husband, the man who would become the next regent of Sumenep. Following directions given to her in the dreams she rode out into the countryside in a golden carriage and found him with a sickle in his hand gathering grass for fodder. His name was Muhammad Saod and he was already married with two children. This did not deter Radèn Ayu Tirtånagårå. She commanded him to return with her to the palace where she married him, and by marrying him made him regent. Like previous "regents by marriage" Saod adopted his wife's name, being known officially as Tuměnggung Tirtånagårå.

I had a restless night in my hot room at the Wijaya I Hotel. At 3:30 in the morning I was blasted out of bed by an hour of high-decibel *dhikr* chants and *ṣalawat* songs hammering on the doors and windows of the neighbourhood from loudspeakers at the local mosque. As far as I could tell the neighbourhood slept sweetly through the half-musical cacophony, but being unused to it, I couldn't. Nevertheless, as my head cleared and I relaxed into the rhythms of the incantations, I felt – as I always do – a powerful affection for the aural ambience of Islam. It is a very

public, very melodic ambience, as comforting and as beautiful (yes
... beautiful, even when wrenched out of shape by screeching pre-
dawn loudspeakers) as Islamic architecture, dress, food, etiquette,
calligraphy and decoration.

I dined alone in the breakfast room, thoughtfully enjoying the
chilli-fired heat of the fried rice (topped with a fried egg, of course)
and the almost chewable sweetness of the tepid brown tea that came
with it. Around eight o'clock I was standing at the front entrance
of the hotel gently shaking the big toe of a *bécak* driver asleep on
the front seat of his pedicab. He brought me to the foot of a steep
incline about two kilometres from the centre of town. From there
it was a short but physically demanding walk up a steep hill to the
gate of the Asta Tinggi burial ground. Outside the entrance three
large buses and a dozen mini-buses were already jammed against
lines of dishevelled streetside cubicles selling drinks, crumpled
packets of snacks and fresh fruit.

Roughly square in shape with high perimeter walls about one
hundred metres in length Asta Tinggi is divided by internal walls
into four quarters. The two rear quarters are filled with a choppy sea
of tombstones that lap against the mausoleums of Sumenep's rulers.
In the rear left compound (the north-west quarter) there are three
simple but airy burial pavilions, somewhat battered and built in a
plain traditional style with wide verandahs, tiled *joglo* roofs and low
eaves. They are lined inside with elaborately carved wooden panels,
some of them brightly painted. Here, among relatives, spouses and
dwarf courtiers lie Sumenep's most revered early rulers: Prince Panji
Pulangjiwå, Prince Jimat and Bindårå Saod.

The morning sun was already baking the walkways of the
complex. Leaving my shoes at an inner gate I hobbled bare-foot
over a blistering belt of tiles to the modest, open-sided pavilion that

was the site office. At nine o'clock in the morning it was crammed with visitors. I squeezed into a clear spot on the steps, crouched and peered over ranks of multi-coloured veiled heads and black fez-caps into the interior of the office.

"Pak George!" a voice called from the front of the crowd. A portly figure jumped to his feet and blinked back at me through thick round glasses under his fez-cap. It was Pak Achmad Muriadi, a guide from Surabaya who specialised in "spiritual tourism". I had met him a year earlier during a visit to the Rahmat Mosque in Surabaya reputedly built by the saintly schoolmaster Sunan Ampèl in the fifteenth century. Together we had visited the nearby tomb of Mbah Karimah, Sunan Ampèl's mother-in-law.

A narrow path instantly opened in the crowd and I stumbled through it to the front. Assuming I was a Christian (I didn't correct him), Pak Muriadi positioned me before his flock and proudly introduced me as an "enlightened" Christian. This was greeted with loud laughter. Mobile phones appeared and for five minutes religious duties were abandoned as I posed for a score of photos in a vortex of chatter and more laughter. Eventually order was restored and I sank to the floor to listen to site custodian Pak Zainal Ilyas introduce his long-deceased holy charges to the party of visitors.

Pak Zainal was wearing a dark batik *blangkon* head cloth, a collarless white t-shirt and neatly pressed black trousers. He pointed at a diagram on the wall slashed with big green arrows that showed the correct route for visitation to the site's tombs. His finger hovered for a moment over the mausoleum of Prince Panji Pulangjiwå, the opportunistic, belligerent, ruthless successor to Sumenep's founding ruler.

"Prince Panji Pulangjiwå was the most pious of all the figures buried here," he deadpanned. "His piety conferred special powers on him. He died and was buried before Asta Tinggi existed. But he vanished from his original grave and later, when the Asta Tinggi burial ground was built in the mid 1700s, he miraculously reappeared in his present mausoleum."

The custodian had dropped into a style of storytelling kept alive at countless pilgrimage sites. The power of the site impresses its exemplary piety on the saint's life. Royal tombs like Asta Tinggi are not places where the sins and shortcomings of rulers can be spotlighted, or even mentioned. In Javanese there is a saying (well-known also in Madura): *Mikul dhuwur mĕndhĕm jĕro*, literally "Carry high, bury deep." These days the saying is taken to describe a child's filial duty to uphold and embellish the good name of their parents and "bury" their shortcomings. In the feudal past it described the obligation of nobles, courtiers and subjects to glorify their ruler and carefully ignore or cover up his faults. The stories of kings that circulate at their tombs can be as shiny as the best blurbs of a modern public relations agency. And when, occasionally, stories do veer away from the template of moral improvement they often sport a cheeky grin and occasionally, at least in Madura, a dark complexion too.

An armada of stories from the wider world of Islam has discharged its cargo of motifs and symbols into the emporium of Madurese history. Tales of holy men who can be in two places at once (a feat known as bilocation) or who can travel great distances at miraculous speed, decorate folk traditions all over the world and fill the annals of every religion. Islam is rich in such stories. An example is the prophet Khiḍr, a popular and powerful figure in all parts of the Islamic world including Indonesia. He is not subject to the mundane restrictions of normal humans but can appear in more than one place at the same time. The prophet Muhammad travelled from Mecca to Jerusalem in one night on the back of a great flying steed, the *bouraq*. In their biographies Pulangjiwå and his royal companions also advertise these motifs.

Pak Zainal Ilyas drew a deep breath.

"Once, when Prince Panji Pulangjiwå was waging war, the news spread among his troops that he had been killed. With heavy hearts they abandoned the battlefield and headed back to the palace. But when they arrived they found their prince already there as large as life and entirely unharmed. This was just one of Pulangjiwå's amazing feats."

The custodian glanced again at the site map, pointing to the second stop on Asta Tinggi's sequence of devotional stations.

"Prince Jimat was also impeccably devout," he said. Echoing the contents of Asta Tinggi's small guidebook, which he probably had a hand in writing, he summed up the prince's claim to piety.

"People used to say that Prince Jimat's real name was Ahmad, an Arab name. Maybe this is true, but today he is known by the Madurese name Jimat. He was a genuinely truthful man, carrying out the commands of Allah, upholding Allah's way and the way of the Prophet. He immersed himself in the remembrance of Allah and became a master of *dhikr* chanting. Because he was so devoted to *dhikr* – spending long hours reverently praising the greatness of Allah – people gave him the Madurese nickname *jimĕt*, which means "sitting motionless". And that's how he came to be called Prince Jimat. But others say he got the name because he was an expert maker of *azimat*, magic religious charms. Actually these explanations of his name are in effect pretty much the same, because *dhikr* chanting and the making of *azimat* charms are both equally valid acts of worship."

Pak Zainal turned to the mausoleum of Muhammad Saod, the

third figure in Asta Tinggi's trio of saints. Saod, he reminded us, was the son of a peasant farmer.

"Despite his humble origins he had the special powers of a holy man even before he was born. One day while his mother was at prayer his father returned home from the fields and knocked at the front door. Muhammad Saod, who was still in his mother's womb, heard the knock and called out:

"Mother is doing her prayers, father!"

Later the infant's father asked who had called out to him.

"It was the baby in my womb," his wife answered. "Ask him yourself."

But before he could say anything the infant had already answered from inside his mother's belly.

"It was me who answered your call, father, because mother was performing her prayers and could not be interrupted."

The custodian added that Muhammad Saod's name came not from the Arabic *saud* meaning "happy, fortunate, blessed" but from the Madurese word *saut* meaning "to answer" as the baby had answered from within its mother's womb.[14]

Surrounded by fellow pilgrims I left the Asta Tinggi site office and headed for the three burial chambers in the north-west quarter of the complex. I was especially interested in the mausoleum of the famously expansionist, famously pious, and not-so-famously gay Prince Jimat. For several months a moral panic had been rippling through Indonesia. Several senior ministers in the Indonesian government saw social ruin in the rising public profile of the

---

14   The story of a precociously pious baby speaking from its mother's womb is well-known across the Islamic world. In all likelihood the story was attached to accounts of Muhammad Saod's life many years after his death to more fully domesticate Islam in Madurese culture.

country's small but ancient community of lesbians, gays, bisexuals and transvestites. According to Defence Minister Ryamizard Ryacudu, the LBGT community were waging a scary war because "we don't know who our enemies are".

"In a war against a foreign country," he thundered, "it's easy to identify the enemy and mount a defence. But with LGBT we can't see whom we're up against, and suddenly we've been brainwashed. If someone dropped a nuclear bomb on Jakarta, the city would be destroyed but Semarang wouldn't be affected. But modern war is different, it is fought in the mind. And that's the danger [of LGBT], it destroys everything everywhere."

It was a droll echo of Prince Câkrâningrat's warning three hundred years earlier that Prince Jimat's gay behaviour would bring "diseases, crop failures, and the ruin of cities and villages". In January 2015 the Indonesian Council of Muslim Scholars (*MUI*) issued a *fatwa* declaring homosexuality to be "unnatural" and "a curable disorder". Orientation towards the same sex and homosexual acts should be punished, in certain circumstances by death, they said. By the time of my visit to Asta Tinggi the ripple was morphing into a tsunami.

I ducked under the low front eave of Prince Jimat's modest mausoleum. Inside I found an airy chamber about twenty metres square lined at the rear with richly carved wooden panels. On a glossy-tiled platform under the dark beams of a *joglo* roof stood a row of three tall cream-coloured stone ledgers between two smaller graves left and right. (The two small graves house the remains of Jimat's favourite dwarf courtiers.) The headstones were wrapped in amber cambric. Around them, like the pillars of a four-poster bed, stood a wooden frame for the cube-like lace drapes that covered the graves. The drapes had been lifted to allow visitors direct access to the saint and the grace radiating from the stones.

I did a quick count. Forty-five people belonging to at least three different parties were sitting shoulder-to-shoulder around the main row of three graves. A subdued potpourri of voices crowded the warm air of the mausoleum.

I joined a group of around twenty visitors from Jember in the interior of East Java. Most were women. At least six children were sitting solemnly among them. Many of the women, and some of the children, had well-thumbed Arabic prayer books open in front of them. Two of them were reading verses from their mobile phones. They were clustered behind a stern-faced young man wearing a white *pèci* fez-cap who led the group in their devotions. He began with a brooding but beautiful recitation of the Throne Verse, verse 255 from Al-Baqarah, the second surah of the Qur'ān. The women mumbled along with him, the children contributed a shrill counterpoint. None could tarnish the simple grandeur of the words.

> *Allahu la ilaha illa huwa Al -Haiyul-Qaiyum*
> Allah! There is no god but He, the Living, the Everlasting.
> *La ta'khudhuhu sinatun wa la nawm*
> He is never drowsy nor ever falls asleep.
> *lahu ma fi as-samawati wa ma fil-'ard*
> What is in the heavens and on earth is His alone.
> *Man dhal-ladhi yashfa'u 'indahu illa bi-idhnihi*
> Who shall intercede with him except with His permission?
> *Ya'lamu ma bayna aydihim wa ma khalfahum*
> He knows what the future holds for them and what
> is behind them.
> *wa la yuhituna bi shai'in min 'ilmihi illa bima sha'a*

And they know nothing of his knowledge except
what He wills.

*Wasi'a kursiyuhus-samawati wal ard*

His throne encompasses the heavens and the earth,

*wa la ya'uduhu hifdhuhuma*

and their preservation does not burden him.

*wa Hu wal 'Aliyul-Azheem*

He is the Most High, the Exalted.

The group leader then prayed for the repose of the Nine Saints
of Java mentioning each by name. He paid his respects to Prince
Jimat, calling him a *waliullah*, God's saint, foremost among the
saints of Madura. There followed a plea to Allah to be generous
with the necessities of life, to raise the status of their children and
help them grow into faithful Muslims. He asked that Allah bless the
party with divine protection especially on the return trip to Jember.
Each step in the prayer was punctuated with recitation of the first
book of the Qur'ān, the short Al-Fātiḥah, which was repeated like
a refrain at least five times. The lengthy string of prayers wound up
with a throbbing *tahlil* recitation *Lā 'ilāha 'illā-llāh* (There is no
god but Allah) repeated twenty or thirty times.

It was an hour before the burial chamber emptied. As they left
many of the women stepped up to Prince Jimat's grave and reverently
laid their hands on it. Some scooped up a few flower petals from
the tray that lay along the top of the ledger stone and stowed them
carefully in their handbags. For a few minutes there was silence
in the chamber, interrupted only by the swish of the caretaker's
straw broom as he swept aside the petals and scraps of cellophane
littering the floor. He turned to a small, open-topped wooden box
overflowing with banknotes and cleared it of its contents.

I introduced myself and we got talking. He had his own stories about the prince.

"Prince Jimat crossed over to Java and personally helped clear the forest for settlement by his Madurese subjects. That's why we get so many visitors from over there. They are descendants of the first settlers and they revere the prince as the founder of their communities."

A babble of voices signalled the approach of a new crowd so I hurried to put a particular question to the caretaker. I was a bit nervous about asking it. Going into a pilgrimage site and suggesting that the Muslim saint buried there was gay ... well, it could be tricky. So I tried to be delicate.

"According to a letter preserved in Dutch archives Prince Jimat preferred men to women. That's why he never married and had no offspring. Do you think that's true?"

I had expected him to be defensive or offended, maybe angry. But not at all. A broad smile spread across his weather-beaten face.

"Yes, that's true," he said. "He *was* (a split-second pause) ... strange. But despite that he was a *wali* – a friend of Allah – and a *habib* – a loved-one of Allah."

Later I put the same question to site custodian Pak Zainal Ilyas and got a completely different answer. He explained that Prince Jimat's reputation as a homosexual (he used the term homosexual, which I hadn't dared to use) was lies and slander concocted by the prince's enemies to sabotage his great power.

"It's not possible Prince Jimat was a homosexual," he said fixing me with a horror-struck glare. "His power, even in death, lifts him far above that. Why, birds fall out of the sky stone dead when they fly over his tomb."

I was sitting in a hire-car speeding back west towards Surabaya. Beside me the driver, Pak Kadar, laid one hand lightly on the steering wheel and with the other pressed a mobile phone to his ear. In loud voluble Madurese (I didn't understand a word of it) he was arguing non-stop with a succession of callers. From time to time he lifted his hand from the steering wheel to stab the air as he shouted. He steadied the steering wheel with his knee, expertly finding a way through the shoals of motorbikes swimming along the road.

A few kilometres beyond Pamekasan the phone ran out of power. Pak Kadar wanted to turn back and recharge it in Pamekasan, but I said no. I threatened to leave the car and catch a bus. I'm in a hurry, I told him, not wholly truthfully. Fearing the shame of abandonment by a foreign guest he drove on in tense silence. A dazzling white arabesque mosque came into view and Pak Kadar's face lit up. He pushed his *pèci* to a rakish angle on the back of his head.

"I have to do my prayers," he said. It was indeed *luhur*, time for the midday *salat* prayer.

I sipped tea in a roadside eatery while Pak Kadar disappeared into the mosque. It was half an hour before he came back smiling broadly. As he revved the car and swivelled it on to the highway, already he was jabbing at the keyboard of his newly recharged phone.

I turned my thoughts to the enigma of Madura. Pak Kadar's bristling moustache and aggressive shouting was a perfect accompaniment to my confused ruminations. Matriarchy and patriarchy, Madura and Java, gay and straight, Islam and pre-Islam, masculinity and femininity, tradition and modernity: these were hopelessly crude binaries. And anyway, they simply didn't work in Madura. But I wasn't about to give up. I was heading for a spot near Arosbaya about fifteen kilometres from the city of Bangkalan at the western end of the island. Maybe there, in the Mother's Tears royal burial ground, I would find a clue that would rid me of my bewilderment.

In 1624 a massive Mataram army, probably around 50,000 men, crossed to Madura and attacked Surabaya's ally Arosbaya. The savagery of the battle is still remembered. Mataram losses are said to have reached six thousand and their commander lost his life. Today the Madurese speak proudly of their resistance, and especially of the role their women played. One story goes that when some badly wounded Madurese soldiers retreated from the battlefield they were executed by their womenfolk. "They were cowards," said the women of Arosbaya. "They had wounds on their backs, so they must have been running from the enemy!"

A survivor from the devastated remnants of Arosbaya's royal line found favour with the tyrant of Mataram, Sultan Agung. Probably without irony the sultan bestowed a new royal name on him, Cåkråningrat (Mandala of the World), giving him nominal authority over the whole of Madura and a new palace at Sampang, about a third of the way along the island's south coast. But today Cåkråningrat's consort, Sharifah Ambami, is better remembered than her husband. She has become an icon of Madurese womanhood, carrying the title Mother Queen (*Rato Ebu*) of Madura. Madurese women – and women from across the strait in Java – flock to pay their respects to her at the Mother's Tears (*Aer Mata*) royal burial ground.

The burial ground lies in the village of Buduran. (Half-hidden in the name of the village there is an echo of the name

"Buddha" hinting that the site may have been sacred to Buddhists in pre-Islamic times.) It takes the form of a long walled compound oriented roughly north–south. It sits on a low, windy escarpment above coastal flats and a thin sinuous river. From the roofed entry gate at the southern end there are four rectangular enclosures rising in shallow steps one behind the other. The first is an open cemetery area. After traversing it I passed into a reception area through a massive, very old stone gate topped by a weighty stone roof. In an open pavilion on the left I was politely greeted by the site key-keeper who was sitting cross-legged on a woven mat behind a shin-high desk. Here visitors take off their shoes, get information about the site, and, if necessary, have a member of the site-staff escort them around. As at Asta Tinggi here too my bare feet stuttered over scorching-hot tiles before I found relief under two large, airy and elegantly simple *joglo* roofs set on solid wooden pillars open along the sides. The two pavilions sheltered scores of graves belonging to the Cåkråningrat royal family.

An air of cool reverence fills the two chambers. No visitor can browse the graves without being astonished at the splendour of their carved stonework. An extraordinary artistic tradition is on display: the whole complex is a profusion of headstones and bas-relief panels chiselled with baroque density in sandstone and marble. In keeping with the Islamic injunction against pictorial representation of people or animals, the designs are wholly floral or abstract.

In the centre of the uppermost section, on a raised floor at the rear, lies the tomb of Sharifah Ambami. Its two upright grave-markers and the ledger stone between them are wrapped in white calico. A long narrow wooden tray for petal offerings lies along the top of it. An ace-of-spades shaped sandstone panel engraved with intricately beautiful depictions of flowers and trees overlooks the grave.[15]

The story of Sharifah Ambami is well known. During her husband's long absences at the court of Mataram she became lonely and turned to meditation for consolation. She prayed long and hard, pleading with Allah for her descendants to be granted royal authority over Madura for seven generations into the future. Her prayers were rewarded when the figure of the Prophet Khiḍr appeared to her. In Islamic tradition Khiḍr is the mysterious bearer of favours to those who are true to the faith, and the queen took his appearance as a sign that her wish had been granted.

But when she told her husband what had happened he became angry. Just seven generations? She should have asked that the royal house be granted the right to rule in perpetuity, he said. Caught between her own measured plea and her husband's insistence on eternal entitlement, Sharifah Ambami retreated to the holy place known as Aer Mata in the hills near Arosbaya. There she returned to contemplation with renewed intensity. Feeling the sting of her husband's anger, she could not contain her grief. As she meditated tears streamed from her eyes. In time she reached the ultimate level of mystical perfection and vanished into the divine presence leaving behind a pool of tears.

The story of the queen's tears rides on the back of a much older folk tale that also explains the origins of the site's springs. In distant times, it goes, long before Islam came to Madura, there was no spring at Aer Mata, only forest. In the earth under one

---

15  When I visited the Aer Mata burial ground in October 2015 Sharifah Ambami's grave had been caged behind a protective fence of iron pickets draped with lace curtains. This obscured most of the beautiful carving on the grave's head panel.

of the biggest trees in the forest lived a good-hearted spirit who owned a fine *gamĕlan* ensemble. Young lovers would come to the tree bringing offerings of fragrant flowers and saffron rice. If the offerings were pleasing to the spirit, the *gamĕlan* would rise slowly and majestically from under the earth and produce ravishing music played by invisible musicians. But if the spirit disapproved of the match the *gamĕlan* would remain beneath the earth.

One day a young couple came and placed offerings beneath the tree. They watched in wonder as the *gamĕlan* emerged, but the instruments remained silent. The lovers' offerings and their betrothal, it seemed, had been rejected. Bewildered and frightened they began to weep. Their tears flooded over the *gamĕlan* inundating its gongs, kettles and cymbals. When the orchestra sank back beneath the earth, two instruments remained behind filled with salt tears. These became the two brackish springs of Aer Mata.

This ancient story is not so well known today. It appears to have been "drowned", like its spectral *gamĕlan*, under the newer story of Sharifah Ambami's Islamic piety. The motif of the pool of tears is all that remains in the new version. It would be easy to say that Islam and the imperatives of aristocratic culture appropriated and ultimately erased the beautiful but pagan older story. I would prefer to argue that Islam, embodied in the figure of the queen, generated an incarnation of the story in which Islamic elements figure prominently, but a pre-Islamic element has a place as well, and is even given an acceptable (in Islamic terms) context in which to be preserved and passed on.

There are several stories about the origins of West Madura and its conversion to Islam. The best known is preserved in a body of local histories collectively called the *Babad Madura*. According to this account, a certain Aryå Ménak Sĕnåyå, a descendant of the king of Hindu-Buddhist Måjåpait, stole the clothes of a celestial nymph, Pĕri Tunjung Wulan, as she bathed in a pool near Sampang. (The same motif appears elsewhere in Indonesia, most notably in the Javanese story of Jåkå Tarub and Nawang Wulan, the mythic ancestors of the Mataram royal line.) Aryå Ménak Sĕnåyå married the nymph, and a descendant of the couple, Kyai Dĕmung, installed himself as regent at Kota Anyar, also called Palakaran, on the north coast of West Madura.

Kyai Demung's son and successor, Prince Pragalbå, extended his authority over much of Madura. Through the thickets of semi-legendary variation that have grown up around the story, it is possible to guess that the Hindu-Buddhist Pragalbå probably lived in the early decades of the 1500s. In Madurese tradition he came to be known as "the lord who nodded" (Pangèran Onggu'). His nod was a less-than-resounding endorsement of Islam. The story behind it gives us a blurred glimpse of that distant moment when Madura began to turn away from Hinduism-Buddhism towards the Islam that is so strongly stamped on the island today.

When Pragalbå's son Pratanu heard about the new religion he summoned his senior commander Ĕmpu Bagĕnå and instructed him to go to Dĕmak to find out about it. (In other versions of the story, Pratanu himself went to Dĕmak.) Bagĕnå did so, studying under one of the Nine Saints, Sunan Kudus, and converting to Islam. After several years he returned to Madura and reported to Pratanu. Pratanu was angry that his underling had impertinently preceded him into the new faith, but he too converted. Madurese tradition gives a precise date for this key event: 1528. But Pratanu's father Pragalbå, still ruler of Palakaran, remained obdurately Hindu. It was only as he lay on his deathbed, stricken with illness and unable to speak, that he indicated his acceptance of the new faith with a feeble nod of the head. Such stories, myth-ridden and often contradictory, suggest that West Madura's conversion to Islam may have been a bottom-up process (unlike the top-down process of mainland Java) with the aristocracy clinging as long as it could to the Hindu-Buddhist trappings of power.

Tradition says that Pratanu succeeded his father in 1531. He built a new palace for himself at Arosbaya and stayed on the throne, so it is said, until 1592. Although Pratanu was a Muslim and presided over the creation of the Muslim community in West Madura, his authority was still drawn, at least in part, from the pre-Islamic magic of the Madurese landscape. He appears to have identified himself with the ancient sacred place in the hills near Arosbaya that today is called Aer Mata, and he came to be known to posterity as the Lord of the High Ground (Panĕmbahan Lĕmah Dhuwur).

Arosbaya was erased as a centre of temporal power but the "high ground" remained and was not forgotten. Sharifah Ambami, who eventually came to occupy the high ground, was originally a Muslim outsider. With the swapping of gender roles that seems so characteristic of Madura, she represents the values and heritage of Islam whereas her husband stands for the island's pagan, female-oriented indigenous heritage. She was heir to an impeccable Islamic pedigree that reached out into the wider world of Islam and stretched back, by some accounts, to the Prophet himself. According to the key-keeper at Aer Mata, Sharifah Ambami was a fifth generation (others say third generation) descendant of Sunan Giri, the great "saint of the mountain" who, around the year 1500, was leader of the Muslim community in Gresik on the Javanese mainland.

Sharifah Ambami's husband, Cåkråningrat the First, on the other hand, came from a line that traced its descent to a celestial nymph and oriented itself around the local high ground of Aer Mata. Twin genealogical lines are recognised in Javanese historiography as "right-hand" (Islamic), and "left-hand" (Hindu-Buddhist) lines of descent. Through her children Sharifah Ambami fused the two lines. She also predicted that the Cåkråningrat family would rule for a further seven generations. Jabbing at a genealogical chart, the key-keeper at Aer Mata explained that the Cåkråningrat line in West Madura died out in 1882 after exactly seven generations. True, there were nine successors to Cåkråningrat the First, but two of them were brothers of their predecessors in office and thus of the same generation. This, said the key-keeper, is proof beyond dispute that Sharifah Ambami was, and is, close to Allah.

About halfway along the western wall of the Aer Mata burial ground an unobtrusive gate leads from the compound to a steep staircase that drops down past a tiny mosque clinging to the face of the escarpment. At the foot of the staircase the path turns right and after thirty metres reaches a small square building. This houses the spring of fresh water that people believe still brims with the tears of Sharifah Ambami.

In the Aer Mata site office, and in the main *pĕndhåpå* pavilions, the water is on sale for Rp.5,000 a bottle (about 40 cents US). It is labelled "water from the tomb of a mother's tears". Besides having the tonic and curative properties normally attributed to holy water at countless pilgrimage sites, this particular bottle of brackish tears makes female power, Madurese tradition and Islamic piety a tasty, drinkable cocktail.

I bought a bottle for myself and another for Pak Kadar. He was delighted with the gift and immediately took a swig from the bottle. As he gunned the car away from Aer Mata towards Bangkalan I was pleased with the water's effect. His driving had definitely become more circumspect.

Night was falling and Pak Kadar crinkled his eyes each time the headlights of approaching cars lit up the windscreen. He was careful to turn *off* his headlights as other cars approached. They turned off their headlights too. As we hurtled towards on-coming vehicles a delicate conversation – like Morse code – started up, each vehicle flashing its headlights momentarily then dousing them. I pinched my eyelids together and braced for impact. But each time, Pak Kadar leaned forward, peered through the front windscreen and lifted his foot from the accelerator. The two vehicles brushed past each other in total darkness. After passing he turned on the headlights again, lighting up the empty highway and accelerating into the blurred dimness ahead.

I was reassured. I was in safe hands. Nevertheless, as the next car approached, I prayed (to whom?) that his phone would not ring.

It was around eight o'clock in the evening when we arrived at the Ningrat Hotel in Bangkalan. In colonial times it had been the spacious home of a plantation officer. Today the house has been beautifully renovated in Madurese style, with cool open corridors, ornately carved doors and high ceilings decorated with traditional Madurese motifs. Standing among the gold-painted posts of the hotel's *pĕndhåpå* vestibule, Pak Kadar shook hands with a neatly uniformed security guard. They were old friends.

"We were in Qatar together," he told me.

"Qatar? What were you doing in Qatar?"

To my astonishment he answered in English. It was halting but passable English laced with a Pakistani-Indian accent. Until that moment he had given no hint he spoke English or had travelled overseas.

"I working at Qatar. Five year. With my friend here. We making big buildings."

He pointed at his modest but brand-new Toyota Avanza.

"This car from my money at Qatar."

Pak Kadar had to return that night to Sumenep. A local family had booked him to take them to a wedding in Surabaya. He had already been eight hours on the road with me and still had around eight hours of overnight driving ahead of him.

As we parted I mentioned that I was hoping to see a ludrug play in Surabaya.

"Have you ever been to a ludrug performance?" I asked him.

"Been to a performance!? Before I went to Qatar I was a member of a ludrug troupe! I was on stage almost every night."

Again I was stunned.

"What role did you play?"

He drew himself up to his full height, snatched the *pèci* from his head, puffed out his chest and wiggled his bottom. He pushed his lips into a trumpet-like pout.

"Usually I played the role of the nagging wife," he said in a grating but uncannily accurate female falsetto.

Suddenly he seemed to deflate himself. The *pèci* reappeared bashed flat on his head, his moustache drooped and his voice fell to a nasal whine.

"But sometimes I played the hen-pecked husband."

The small crowd of onlookers fell about laughing.

## Postscript

In February 2016 the Indonesian Broadcasting Commission (*Komisi Penyiaran Indonesia* or *KPI*) issued a directive to all radio and TV broadcasters requiring them to more strictly police programs that "portray men acting like women". The Commission is a government-funded but independent body that provides oversight of public broadcasting, supposedly without interference by business or the state. It is also tasked to deal even-handedly with public complaints about broadcasting.

The Commission claimed it was responding to complaints from the public. The directive told the chief executives of broadcasting enterprises that men were no longer allowed to appear in female dress, wear female style make-up, talk like females, or use female body-language (including walking, sitting and gesturing like females). They were not to promote or suggest approval of female life-styles for men. Men were not allowed to greet one another in a fashion more appropriate to females, nor were they allowed to use the special vocabulary and idioms commonly used by effeminate men.

The Commission said effeminate behaviour and language "showed disrespect for norms of etiquette and decency and disregard for the protection of children and young people".

News of the directive spread across Indonesia's social media where most users appeared to support it. But not all. Connoisseurs of ludrug and a number of other traditional arts like gĕmblak and reog in which men take female roles protested that the directive was an attack on the indigenous arts of Java and Madura. These were arts that had never caused problems in the past and were popular with the public.

As one exasperated Facebook user put it:

"Does the culture we have inherited from our forebears have to be extinguished just because of LGBT? No way. That doesn't make sense. But no matter ... let the dogs bark. The camel-train will continue on its way."

# 9

# Where money comes from

When Marsinah looked through the keyhole into her husband's room she saw two black dogs copulating. The meek and obedient woman she had once been vanished. She snatched an iron bar. The heavy rail curved above her head and smashed into the door. She stepped through the splintered gash and swung the bar at one of the dogs. Blood spurted across her face. The second dog yelped and jumped from the room. In a frenzy, Marsinah smashed the bar down again and again into the pile of hair and meat on the floor. Chips of bone sprang from the ribcage, a mangled jaw spat fragments of tongue, the pupil of a crushed eye looked back over the jerking body.

Marsinah lowered the bar, panting. Slowly the wreckage of skin and dark blood began to curdle. The dog dissolved, and in its place the naked corpse of her husband appeared, still recognisable but bloodied and lifeless.

Three days later Marsinah dreamed she was walking along a road cobbled with human skulls. One of them addressed her. It was the skull of her husband. Beside him lay the skulls of three children. He confirmed he had made a contract with the spirit queen of

Mount Måndhålikå to supply her with their children. In return she would be his lover and make him rich. And when the time came, he would join her in the infinite abundance of the spirit realm.

In summary, this is the climax of a novel in Javanese, *Préwangan Gunung Måndhålikå* (The Spirit Helper of Mount Måndhålikå, 1981) by Dyaning Wiratmoko. The Mount Måndhålikå of the story is fictional, but the name resounds with supernatural overtones. It echoes the name of a small island off the north coast of the Muria salient in Central Java opposite the seaside remains of a Portuguese fort. The island of Mandalika is said to be the abode of a white were-crocodile with a special liking for white-skinned victims (i.e. Europeans).

Through a ghostly veil of allegory and folk motifs the novel is a study in the sociology and psychology of money. It tells the story of Juwahir, a Javanese Faust. He works hard and fulfils his religious obligations, but unrelenting work and strict piety cannot extract him from the torment of poverty. He is humiliated beyond what he can bear by the suffering of his wife and five small children. He is bewildered by the experience of living destitute in a world overflowing with plenty. Wealth is mysterious. He sees others enjoying it, it is close-by, occasionally he can touch it. He is doing everything right, but somehow material security lies beyond his reach.

Juwahir consults a local villager who had once been poor but now, mysteriously and without apparent effort, has become super rich. Other villagers suspect he got his money with the assistance of a spirit helper. The newly wealthy villager tells Juwahir if he really wants to be rich he must go to Mount Måndhålikå and meditate there for three nights.

Without telling his wife, Juwahir sneaks off to the mountain and climbs to the summit. There he finds a grave where he settles down, head bowed, to meditate. After two nights a beautiful woman appears to him. She is the spirit queen of Mount Måndhålikå. She agrees to help him get rich but there is a price to pay. In the first place, after his death he must himself become a spirit citizen of the mountain. Second, he must provide "offerings" in exchange for her assistance. The queen makes it clear what these offerings must be by inviting Juwahir to look into a well. In the water at the bottom he sees a terrible vision of his youngest child, an infant daughter, her eyes bulging, tongue hanging out, face swollen and black. He sees a similar image of his fourth child, then his third. Unable to bear the sight he draws away. The beautiful queen asks him if he has seen all and whether he will feel regret. Juwahir shakes his head – there will be no turning back and no regrets.

The spirit queen reveals the final condition of their contract. Every night before the *pasar* day of Wagé, Juwahir will receive a visit from her and must make love with her. At that moment he is dazzled by the queen's beauty and intoxicated by her perfume. They grip each other in passionate sexual intercourse. Afterwards Juwahir falls asleep and does not see his partner leave in the form of a big, black, glossy dog.

Juwahir returns home and at once his fortunes change. Suddenly he is rich. Within two months he is building himself a new house. In it he has a special room where he spends every night before Wagé alone. On these nights a black dog appears, magically enters the room and stays the night with him. In Juwahir's eyes his guest is not a dog but the beautiful queen of Måndhålikå.

As Juwahir becomes richer tragedy stalks his family. First his infant daughter is run down on the highway. She lies with her eyes bulging, tongue hanging out, face swollen and black, exactly as she appeared when Juwahir saw her image in the well. Then his fourth child, also a girl, falls ill with fever. She raves, pleading with her father not to let her head get planted at Mount Måndhålikå. She too dies. Three months after Jawahir's visit to the mountain grave his third child, this time a son, falls from a tree and dies. After each death Juwahir wraps a length of banana trunk in a shroud and passes it off to family and neighbours as the dead child. And each time the queen of Måndhålikå appears in canine form to claim her payment. Juwahir hands his dead child to the dog, who disappears with the body in its jaws.

The people of the village grow suspicious of him. More and more he is ostracised, even by his close neighbours. Juwahir and Marsinah become uneasy. Juwahir finds no peace or happiness in his newfound wealth but rather anxiety and the feeling that a host of unseen eyes are watching him. Marsinah starts to suspect her husband. Having already lost three children she fears the others may follow and that she herself may be fated to die as an offering.

Then she sees the dogs in her husband's room ...

A menagerie of shapeshifting creatures prowl the cages of Java's story genres; not just were-dogs but were-pigs, were-tigers, were-cats, were-apes, were-crocodiles, were-bats, were-snakes, were-fish, even creepy were-chickens. Mass circulation magazines in Indonesian – *Liberty*, *Posmo*, *Misteri* – and their satellite internet sites, not to mention smaller circulation magazines in Javanese like *Panjebar Semangat*, *Jaya Baya* and *Djaka Lodang*, run features in every issue with titles like "Rescuing the victims sacrificed for wealth", "The money-spinning shadow puppet at Mbah Soka's shrine", "Nyai Puspo's magic way to wealth" and "My child was eaten by a were-snake". Like the vampires and were-wolves of Euro-American culture, the *kitsune* fox-ghosts of Japan, and the many other shapeshifters of folklore across the world, Java's shapeshifters are comfortably at home in the twenty-first century. They are as much staples of popular narrative today as they were two hundred years ago when Europeans first noticed them. The resilience of were-wolves and vampires in Europe and America may have something to do with primal fears about sex, violence, infectious diseases and science, but in Java shapeshifter stories are about money (mostly).

Dutch scholars first came across were-creatures in the nineteenth century as they waded into the shallows of Javanese literature. They were astonished to hear about a scaly, sexually voracious, snake-like creature – looking something like Jabba the Hutt of *Star Wars* fame – who could assume human female form and make you rich. She was called a *blorong*, said the prolific researcher G.W.J. Drewes in 1929.

She lives on the renowned south coast of Java. [...] People conceive of the *blorong* as having a fishlike form, like a sort of mermaid, whose tail is covered with scales of gold. Others attribute to her a human head and still others think she has several limbs. She bestows her wealth on a man, who, after he has enjoyed it for a time, then becomes her property. He becomes part of her house the entirety of which is constructed from the remains of her victims. The doors and walls are made of human remains, as are the roof, the fences and even the pedestals of the watertanks. A man will come across her place of residence suddenly and unexpectedly. He is given instructions to return home on a certain date to prepare a sleeping chamber to receive Nyai

Blorong as his bride. The goddess of money appears to him as a beautiful woman, but with a snake-like tail which she coils around her victim. For several hours he must endure the constriction of her tail, but eventually his strange bride goes and leaves behind her a house full of money.

The coins littering the house, said Drewes with scrupulous solemnity, are the gold scales shaken loose from the blorong's skin during the turbulence of love-making.

In the rice-roots society of Java cash is relatively new. There have always been coins in Java but they were the currency of royalty, wealthy traders and the religious elite. For ordinary people the norm was subsistence, barter, payment in kind and payment in corvée labour. In the peasant economy the growing of food, the building of a house, the making of tools and valuable ornaments – in short, material wealth – was created in a very immediate way before people's own eyes, either through the exercise of their own energy and skills or through participation in collective work involving the members of their close-knit community. There was nothing invisible about the creation of prosperity, what little there was of it.

But with the arrival of the nineteenth century and the global marketing of Java's agricultural plenty, cash began to move from the distant periphery of the peasant world towards its centre. Having subjugated the island's heartland during the Java War, the Dutch consolidated their domination of local underlings by paying them in cash and dismantling the old bottom-up system of payment by land appanages, corvée labour and tribute in kind. Even then, payment in cash only went down to the level just above the village head. Well into the twentieth century the island's thousands of village heads continued to be paid with allocations of land (called *lungguh* or *bĕngkok*) worked on their behalf by landless villagers. Below the village head, cash was still little known.

For Java's peasantry it was "natural" and unproblematic for aristocrats and foreigners to be wealthy, but when cash began to flood into the peasant economy it brought with it a new phenomenon – wealthy people who were not aristocrats or foreigners. The commoner *nouveau riche* possessed far more than they could possibly have made with their own hands. Where did it come from? In the old world view it could only be attributed to invisible agents – powerful creatures with access to the infinite wealth of the supernatural. Thus were the half-human creatures which had always existed in Javanese tradition resurrected and given a money-spinning role.

Stories of Java's shapeshifting money-spinners usually make a bluntly negative moral judgement about modern commerce and those who succumb to it. Behind their captivating human veneer, cashed-up shapeshifters are sub-human: malignant, ugly, ruthless, terrifying and ultimately deadly. People who enter into a commercial contract with them must abandon their humanity and become animals, like them. The alliance with money generates the repugnant image of sexual copulation between human and animal.

Shapeshifter stories also broadcast a negative view of individual will and action. By contracting and maintaining an alliance with a were-creature the human protagonist is driven by individualistic desire. He (it is usually a male) acts in secrecy, as Juwahir did, without consulting family or community. His solitary will is depicted as dangerous because when it takes hold it compels him to act self-destructively and "forget", doing things he knows must bring calamity on himself and his family. The Javanese have a proverbial saying often quoted today: *mèlik nggèndhong lali*, desire for possessions carries forgetfulness with it. Showing the destructive consequences of putting individual will and interests first, shapeshifter narratives stress the moral superiority – in fact the pragmatic necessity – of community cohesion, communal will and collective interests.

*Préwangan Gunung Måndhålikå* closes with a vision of hell. Juwahir and his three children have become cobblestones in the spirit realm of Måndhålikå. The novel also opens with a vision of hell. The hopeless agony of Juwahir's poverty is a hell on earth. In shapeshifter stories the anti-hero is caught between two hells. There is a desperate poignancy about his commitment to getting relief from the agony of poverty, however temporary that relief may be and however high the price. He takes the initiative to get out of one hell through a transaction he knows will ultimately consign him and his family to the other hell.

Juwahir met his captivating shapeshifter partner at a grave, a doorway into the infinite wealth of the supernatural. If he had been in another story, at a different grave, he might have turned to another genus of money-spinning business partners, the toddler-demon known as a *tuyul* (Javanese spelling, *thuyul*). That is what the fictional Sukoharto did in a typical *tuyul* story published in the Indonesian-language magazine *Misteri*. Sukoharto means literally "loves money".

Sukoharto's heart was pounding. He peered warily into the gloom. Everything was silent. Suddenly his eyes widened. There they were, emerging from the darkness, eight of them, jostling one another as they came towards him.

They were all different. Some of them had heads much bigger than their torsos. They looked top-heavy and seemed to have trouble staying upright. Others had weird-looking pin-heads on the top of fat little bodies. Others again were skinny and bony as if they had never eaten.

And their faces were all different too. Some of them were horribly wizened. Others had cute, chubby faces. But they all had one thing in common – they were quite small, probably about the size of a *golèk* puppet. Yet small though they were, from the hard lines on their faces Sukoharto could see they were not children.

*Tuyuls* are indeed "adult" but they behave like children. In the folklore of Java they are representations of the real people we all know whose tunnel-vision pursuit of money has left them emotionally stunted, with all the me-centred immaturity of an infant. They like to play games. They can be temperamental and easily distracted or upset. They are demanding and cause havoc in a household if they become frustrated. They like flashy objects, especially coins. If you have adopted a *tuyul* it can go out and gather money for you, secretly getting into people's houses, even rifling their safes and cash boxes. A *tuyul* can make you very rich, very quickly.

But if you own a *tuyul* there is a downside. They charge the same steep price for their services that were-creatures do. Owners must pay for their good fortune with the health, even the lives, of their family. Like shapeshifter stories, *tuyul* stories make a damning moral judgement about the economic order that weighs so crushingly on Java's poor. It is an implied judgement to be sure, but it is one that is crystal clear. By showing the destructive consequences of placing individual will and interests above all else, *tuyul* narratives also stress the moral superiority and pragmatic necessity of community cohesion, communal will and collective interests.

Despite the moral warning advertised loud and clear in *tuyul* stories many Javanese have an affectionate fascination with the deceptively cute little creatures. In fact you can visit supernaturally charged places and order one for yourself. I have been to one of these places, a tall *kětos* tree in the village of Bero about ten kilometres east of Klaten in Central Java. I didn't get my own *tuyul*, but I met real people who earn a modest living from the tree.

With a dense, complex crown of foliage the *kětos* tree stands about twelve metres high. It is in the middle of a square enclosure about eight by eight metres in area, bounded by a low wall and surrounded by village houses. There is a roofed doorway in the wall with a low upper edge that forces you to stoop respectfully as you pass through it. Inside, at the foot of the gnarled trunk, a small cone of fused, blackened ash marks the spot where countless incense fires have sent their powerfully scented smoke into the foliage above. Around the cone, in a mosaic of red and white petals, lie the scattered remains of flower offerings.

According to local villagers the tree is inhabited by Kyai Bândhå and his wife Nyai Bândhå, two "presences" who can help you solve your problems, especially problems earning a living. In Javanese *bândhå* means "wealth" or "worldly goods". (The term is an ancient borrowing from Sanskrit and is related to the English terms "bond" and "band".) The couple are often referred to collectively as Mbah or Éyang Bândhå (Grandfather/Grandmother Bândhå). Kyai and Nyai Bândhå don't have a describable form. They are "too fine" the villagers told me. Local tradition links the couple with the twelfth century ruler of Kediri, King Jåyåbåyå, popularly thought to be the ancestor of all later Javanese monarchs. As we saw in Chapter Three, King Jåyåbåyå did not die but vanished into the sky from a spot in the present-day village of Menang near Kediri. When he disappeared, Kyai and Nyai Båndhå, who were among his retainers (in some versions of the story, his grandchildren), fled west to Klaten. There they fasted and meditated with such intensity that they too vanished. A *kětos* tree grew at the spot, and eight hundred years later it remains their dwelling place.

The tree is sacred to the surrounding community. The spirit descendants of Kyai and Nyai Båndhå are thought to live in the houses of the village giving protection to the families they live among. If the tree is abused – for example if its branches are cut off for kitchen fuel – it will bring illness to the person responsible. And anyway, the wood from the tree will not burn. Nor does the tree fruit prolifically and its seeds cannot be used for propagation.

Bero's *kětos* tree is patronised mostly by small traders and local citizens. Often people come from a distance: Surabaya, Jakarta, Banten, Semarang and Solo, even from Sulawesi, Kalimantan and Papua, occasionally even from overseas, especially from Malaysia. Visitors to the site believe that Kyai and Nyai Båndhå can help them live more comfortably, get promoted at work and recover from illness. The couple can also help them guard against theft, so valuables will be safe wherever they are left.

The night before Friday Kliwon is the best time to petition Kyai and Nyai Båndhå, so I was told. Apart from this there are no special days – people can come at any time. Visitors may hold a communal meal with prayers under the tree, especially if Kyai and Nyai Båndhå have granted them a wish or favour. The foods prepared for the meal are carefully prescribed by custom. The two spirits eat well. On the menu there is rice cooked in coconut milk with salt, a whole chicken boiled until dry in a herby broth, a selection of vegetables and meats, two hands of *råjå* bananas (the two hands coming from opposite sides of the banana stalk), rice balls, and a selection of fruits, cakes and sweets bought in the market.

On the night before Friday Kliwon villagers give food to the spirit descendants, or "grandchildren", of Kyai and Nyai Båndhå who live with them. They do this in their own homes. Whatever is given to the grandchildren must be given in sets of two: two glasses of tea, two cigarettes, two sets of flower offerings. But the grandchildren must not be given rice.

And the *kĕtos* tree – so it is whispered – is the capital of a *tuyul* nation. Here, those who know the correct procedure can acquire their very own *tuyul*.

In 1985 Bero was the reluctant host to a gathering that has passed into journalistic legend. For a few days Kyai and Nyai Båndhå and their kingdom of *tuyuls* blinked in the spotlight of national fame. A well-known psychic and historian, Amen Budiman, organised a national seminar in Semarang on the "Non-Physical Realm". The seminar was to climax with an excursion to the *kĕtos* tree in Bero. According to Amen Budiman, the idea of visiting the tree came to him after reading an old manuscript in Javanese titled How to Acquire a Money-Spinning Creature at Bero (*Tåtåcårå pados pasugihan dhatĕng Bĕro*).[16] He wanted to make an on-the-spot verification of the manuscript's claim that *tuyuls* lived there.

---

16   I have not been able to track down any information about this text.

"Who says the tuyuls are in Klaten!" A newspaper cartoon published
during the *tour de tuyul* fiasco suggests that, beyond Klaten, Indonesia
has plenty of kleptomaniacs who are *tuyuls* in human guise.
[*Kompas* 29 October 1985, p.4]

Indonesia's mass media seized on the excursion with a kind
of gleeful ferocity. They dubbed it the *tour de tuyul*. Mocking the
backwardness of villagers is a national pastime but this time there
was ambivalence in newspaper reports. Their mockery came mixed
with cautious curiosity.

On the morning of Sunday, 27 October 1985, a crowd of
several thousand people descended on the normally sleepy village.
Local officials were far from pleased. The fiasco that followed was
reported in delighted detail by newspapers, local and national.
Welded together and summarised, their accounts went something
like this.

Thousands of visitors to the *kĕtos* tree in the village of
Bero, which is reputedly the site of a kingdom of *tuyuls*,
were dispersed by local officials yesterday and had to

return home disappointed. Members of the *tour de tuyul* group from Semarang were stopped by local officials from entering the courtyard adjacent to the sacred tree.

A number of officials said that they had taken this action because the tour group had not informed them they were coming and had not sought permission from local officials to make a visit. Consequently, when the group arrived it was instructed to go straight to the Palar village hall, about three hundred metres from the tree. This instruction was also given to the dozens of reporters, including a team from the state television station TVRI, who had turned up hoping to cover the event.

The crowd of visitors included people from Semarang, Jakarta, Madiun, Surabaya, Kudus, Pekalongan, Tegal, Aceh, Cirebon and other places, not to mention people from the village itself and its surrounding areas. Old and young, men and women, and even small children, were jammed into the area around the tree close to the houses of the village.

The normally quiet village was jumping with noise and activity. Villagers were quick to take advantage of the crowd. They set up parking areas, charging Rp.100 for each bicycle and Rp.200 for motorbikes.

In a hasty effort to calm the excitement, village officials produced a loudspeaker. From the vicinity of the *kĕtos* tree they broadcast an announcement, given in Javanese and Indonesian.

"Ladies and gentlemen," said an official with the loudspeaker, "Please return to your homes. There are no *tuyuls* here."

They tried to shoo people into the village hall, but most of the crowd managed to stay put near the walled tree waiting for the arrival of the *tour de tuyul* group.

The funny thing is, many local people had no idea why so many visitors had suddenly descended on their village. Those who did know joined the crowd in the hope of catching a glimpse of a *tuyul*. Some local people whispered their conviction that the *kĕtos* tree was indeed a holy and haunted place. Every Thursday night, especially on the night before Friday Kliwon, there were usually people there beneath the tree meditating or fasting, and asking for favours with the help of the tree's custodian. A lot of people came from Surabaya, Jakarta, Semarang, Solo and elsewhere. If their requests were granted they would hold a *slamĕtan*, a ritual thanksgiving meal. A number of villagers said that the wall around the tree, with its doorway, had been built by a grateful pilgrim whose wishes had been granted.

Everywhere people were making jokes about *tuyuls*. Whenever a pretty girl went by, or a small child with a shaved head, they would say "Ah, here we are – a *tuyul*!" They were even calling one of the more avaricious of the village officials "the *tuyul*". Some of the local school children admitted that they got called "*Tuyul*" at school, which upset them.

In the midst of the noise and turmoil there were moments of tension, for example when officials tried to push back the crowd and send them packing back home, and again when they frisked some of the reporters from Jakarta in an effort to find out more about the visiting para-psychologists.

Meanwhile, at the village hall, civilian and military officials were waiting. A police officer from Klaten yelled into the dense mass of people telling them to disperse. "As a police officer," he said, trying to sound menacing, "I will not hesitate to use police methods. I am ordering those of you who have no business here to remove yourselves from this place now. I repeat, get out right now!"

No one moved. They were waiting for Amen Budiman, who was scheduled to arrive a little later. When he did arrive he was hustled into a special closed room to be questioned by local officials and police officers.

When he emerged, Amen Budiman announced that the excursion was off.

"Our visit here was for the purpose of research in anthropology and para-psychology only," he said. "All we wanted to do was make some scientific observations. It's not our fault that thousands of people have turned up as well."

Amen went on to say that people seemed to be particularly interested in *tuyuls*, despite the fact that the seminar had discussed a much wider range of matters to do with the non-physical realm. *Tuyuls* were only one of the species of spirit creatures that had been discussed. "Our focus was not just on *tuyuls*," he said. "But if people want to focus on *tuyuls*, that's entirely up to them."

When I visited Bero seventeen years after the infamous *tour de tuyul* I found village officials still defensive about it. It was difficult to get local people, even the custodians of the *kĕtos* tree, to discuss the tree's reputation. The village was not to be represented as an embarrassing pocket of superstition standing like a stray cow in the headlights of Indonesia's joyride into modernity. But the usual mixed messages were on display too. Visitors to the tree are welcome, even foreigners, people told me. They bring an income to the village. In fact rules have been put in place that oblige serious petitioners to return to the tree again and again. As one of the site custodians, the elderly Ibu Kardikem, told me, if people want to get their own *tuyul* or spirit helper (*prewangan*) they have to come back on seven successive Fridays bringing food offerings and spending money on each occasion.

"You have to spend money to make money," she said matter-of-factly. "These days, if you want a *tuyul*, it will cost you six million rupiah (around $500 US at the time of my visit). This also covers the obligatory thanksgiving meal and other overheads. Pay up front and we'll send you your *tuyul* immediately. No more to pay."

But Ibu Kardikem hedged her pitch with a warning.

"A *tuyul* and its new boss don't always get on. Like small children, *tuyuls* can be difficult and unpredictable. Far from enriching the owner a *tuyul* may cause havoc in the family, especially if the owner and the *tuyul* have incompatible fields of energy."

The Javanese phrase *ngalap berkah* means "to grab a blessing". It describes what people do (or hope to do) when they go to a holy site and plead for a financial favour. But the practice upsets many Muslims. They believe the purpose of religious devotions is to praise Allah, or simply obey His laws and commandments, or, for a few, to seek mystical connection with Him. To approach Allah or His saints with the intention of enriching yourself is seen, at best, as irrational and backward. At worst it is idolatrous, a violation of divine law and an offense against Islam. Some look on the practice with horror.

Hostility to *ngalap bĕrkah* is voiced in its most extreme form by fundamentalist Muslims, especially those influenced by Wahhabism, the austere variant of Sunni Islam that is the state religion of Saudi Arabia. The founder of Wahhabism, Muhammad ibn Abd al-Wahhab (1703-1792), led a movement in Arabia to cleanse Islam of the cultural and ritual accretions that, in his view, had contaminated it over the centuries since the time of the Prophet and the early generations of Muslims.

In essence Wahhabism is an insistence on the purity and primacy of *tauhid*. Tauhid means affirming Allah's indivisible oneness and solitary uniqueness. (By extension, tauhid is also the general term for Islamic theology, theology being basically the study of Allah and Allah's presence in the world.) Any place, object or action that compromises the absolute integrity of tauhid is idolatrous. Muhammad Wahhab and his followers nursed a special hostility to holy graves and saint veneration. For them the practice of seeking help from any supernatural source other than Allah, or using the dead as intermediaries to access the godhead, or going to graves in search of spiritual merit or a favour, or hoping for emotional and psychological succour, all these beliefs and practices were idolatrous, contemptible, the most serious of evils and an insult to Allah.

The early Wahhabis set about destroying graves and other sacred places across Arabia, including the graves and homes of key figures in the early history of Islam. Some spots were rebuilt when Arabia fell under Turkish rule in the nineteenth century but a good number were levelled for a second time when the Wahhabist Kingdom of Saudi Arabia was established in 1932. As Wahhabi influence rippled across the world, energised with Saudi oil money, sacred sites in distant places came under threat. In Malaysia, a once lively culture of local pilgrimage disappeared and the sites themselves have largely been erased. The desecration of holy places is rare in Indonesia, but it does happen. In 1985 a number of stupas on the Buddhist temple-monument of Borobudur in Central Java were damaged in an Islamist attack that foreshadowed the Taliban's destruction of the Buddha statues at Bamiyan in Afghanistan. Amrozi Nurhasyim and his brothers, responsible for the Bali bombings of 2002 that killed 202 people, are reputed to have vandalised gravesites in the Lamongan area of East Java after adopting fundamentalist *salafi* practices in Afghanistan. In 2013 the tomb of the eccentric but saintly Prince Prawiropurbo (died 1933) in Jogjakarta was desecrated by around thirty young men whose identity remains unknown. Besides smashing parts of the tomb and burial chamber the attackers painted the words *"syirik"* (idolatrous) and *"haram"* (forbidden) across the interior of the burial chamber.

But there are Javanese Muslims who defend the practice of *ngalap bĕrkah*. They keep a low profile, preferring quiet practice to loud words. I once heard their counter-view expressed with unusual passion during a visit to Langsé Cave just east of Parangtritis on the Indian Ocean coast south of Jogjakarta. To reach the cave I had to climb down a sheer cliff about 150 metres high. It was a white-knuckle descent. Flattened against rocky outcrops, clinging to roots, ropes and a few lengths of rickety bamboo ladder, I took one and a half hours to inch down. At each step I looked down past my scrabbling feet to the sea frothing on rocks below. Halfway down, sweat-sodden and trembling from exhaustion, I vomited. But I made it to the bottom.

Under the ragged, dripping rocks of Langsé Cave I met Pak Abdullah, a pilgrim who was about to enter the cave with the cave custodian. He invited me to join him. We climbed from the mouth of the cave down a rough stairway into an ankle-deep pond of muddy water that led into some narrow passages. The custodian was carrying a single candle. Twenty-five metres inside the cave he stopped and set the candle down on a rock. From somewhere in the gloom he produced a plastic hose and poured a spate of water over Pak Abdullah's face and into his mouth. Langsé Cave is best known as a place for meetings with Ratu Kidul, the spirit queen of the southern ocean, but on this occasion the pair prayed to Éyang (Grandfather) Langsé, the spirit guardian of the cave. Pak Abdullah had a special request: he was hoping to lay his hands on enough money to pay his daughter's tuition fees at an office management school.

Later, sitting cross-legged on the bottom lip of the cave entrance, just metres from the turmoil of water bursting on the rocks beneath, I asked him whether, according to Islam, it was idolatrous to be harassing Allah or Allah's saints for financial favours.

"Harassing?"

He lit a clove-scented cigarette and considered his answer. Suddenly he broke into Arabic.

"*Kallaa inna l'insaana la yathghaa 'an rra'aahu 'staghnaa.*"

Seeing my blank look he translated.

"The Qur'ān says: Man puffs himself up with arrogance because he thinks he can do everything himself."[17] As if in illustration he released a long puff of scented smoke that was instantly whipped away by the sea wind.

---

17   Qur'ān Surah 96, Al-'Alaq (The Clot), verses 5-6.

"But all things come from Allah," he went on, "and the truly devout Muslim must acknowledge this. Not to acknowledge it — to claim that the good things of life come from your own efforts and not from Allah — *that* is idolatrous. *That* is giving yourself god-like powers. So it is only proper that the devout Muslim ask Allah or one of Allah's saints for whatever it is that he or she wants. It would be arrogant and idolatrous *not* to do so!"

"But here, in this cave," I said, "you are praying to a guardian spirit Éyang Langsé, not to Allah or a saint. How does *that* work?"

His voice was hoarse above the roar of the waves but he spoke with vehemence.

"Allah has always connected with humankind through intermediaries. The process is called *tawassul* ... okay!? God's prophets, even local guardians, have been *wasilah* – spokesmen and intermediaries – connecting people with the divine. Even Muhammad received the holy words of Allah through a spirit intermediary, the angel Jibril."

Abdullah's passion reminded me that for many Javanese Muslims religious ritual is decidedly transactional. Devotions at sacred places are like commercial practices—the pilgrim enters into a contractual relationship with the supernatural, with a saint or with Allah.

In Islam, the supreme transaction involving a believer's person and possessions is the one in which Allah purchases the believer's soul, person and goods in exchange for eternal bliss. The Qur'ān assures believers that Allah will abide by His promises — His contractual undertakings. This is made clear, for example, in Surah 61, As-Saff, verses 10–12.

O you who believe, let Me inform you of a trade that will

save you from painful punishment. Believe in Allah and His messenger and devote your money and your lives to the cause of Allah. This is the best deal for you, if you only knew it. [If you do this] He will then forgive you your sins and admit you to gardens beneath which rivers flow, and to beautiful mansions in gardens of eternity. That is indeed the supreme triumph.

In Java, devotions at pilgrimage sites are often seen as contracts or transactions. Even the giving of donations is not an unselfish act but one that buys social status and divine merit for the giver. *Nadhar* contracts are common. A *nadhar* contract is one in which the pilgrim makes a vow to do something—support a charity, hold a thanksgiving meal, make a donation to a pilgrimage site—that is conditional upon divine fulfilment of a request. In other words, commercial transactions are metaphors for devotional transactions. Quranic commentaries often recognise this. Take, for example, this commentary on the word 'commerce' or 'trade' (*tijarat*) as it occurs in Surah 35, Fathir, verse 29.

[The verse presents] a metaphor from commerce. [The believer] must deny himself the use of some of what God has provided, as a merchant puts aside some of his wealth to invest as capital. Only the Godly man's commerce will never fail or fluctuate; because Allah guarantees him the return, and even adds something to the return out of His own bounty.

So when pilgrims pay cash for services at a sacred site or make donations it is an embodiment of the transactional process that is at the heart of devotions. It is not an intrusion, diminution or corruption of devotion, but rather an integral part of it — a material manifestation of the interaction between devotee and Allah. As Pak Abdullah reminded me at Langsé Cave, asking Allah or His saints for money is irreproachably *Islami*.

Wonosari, high on the slopes of Mount Kawi in East Java, is one of the most remarkable holy places in Indonesia, though you won't find it on a map. It calls itself a village but it is more like a small, busy town. Its cobbled main street is too narrow and too sharply raked to take cars. A flight of steps clambers up into the bottom end of the street through a solid arched gate labelled in Java's *hånåcaråkå* script "Mount Kawi Mausoleum" (*Pasaréyan Gunung Kawi*). A steep walk of about one kilometre leads through two more roofed gates, the last surmounted with a chronogram (also in *hånåcāråkå* script) reading *Aruming kusumå pinudyèng jagat*, "The fragrance of flowers (i.e. noble heroes) is praised throughout the world." This corresponds to 1871, the year the site was established. Beyond lies a hall housing the tombs of Éyang Jugo together with his adopted son and disciple Iman Sujono. The two saints are Java's most famous supernatural sources of money.

As I write this I have before me a biography of Éyang Jugo published around 1954 by a Chinese-Indonesian, Im Yang Tju. It is the oldest account of the saint I have been able to find. Between its bright red front cover and the austere advertisements for cigarettes and car parts at its rear it serves up a smorgasbord of tapas-sized tales about the saint. Im represents him as a mysterious healer who emerged periodically and unexpectedly from the jungles of nineteenth century Java. After staying around for a while dispensing cures for human and livestock ailments, he would disappear as mysteriously as he came. The mini-stories are speckled with glimpses of life in the nineteenth century: a cholera epidemic, a famine, forests full of wild animals, punishment for Chinese who cut off their pigtails, European-built telegraph lines and railroads fissioning across the countryside like cracks in the glaze of fine porcelain ...

Éyang Jugo had big ears, a big stomach, a big laugh and a gentle, tolerant outlook. "His eyes were like moonbeams," says Im Yang Tju. "Whomever he looked at would get a strange feeling, like a baby gazed at by its mother." He got his name from the village of Jugo, about twenty-five kilometres from Wonosari, where eventually he took up residence some time between 1850 and 1860. Initially he lived in a dilapidated cow yard. Later a house was built for him that has become a tourist attraction and a valuable source of income for the village.

Im invests the name "Jugo" with meaning far weightier than a mere label for a village. He explains that *sajugå* is a Javanese term meaning "single" or "one", so the name "Jugo" captures the saint's Hindu-Buddhist monism. Éyang Jugo once proclaimed the essence of this monism, affirming not only the ultimate unity of all things but also (given that all things are One) the ultimate futility of making hierarchical and moral distinctions, even species distinctions.

Everything in this world – mountains, rocks, trees, all that moves and all that is unmoving – everything is One (*sajugå*). Deer, wild cats and wild cattle, all creatures that have wings and all that crawl, the wild and the tame, all are One. The learned and the ignorant, lord and servant, you and me, in reality we are all One.

It was a rare outburst. The saint didn't talk much and refused to be a teacher. He was a model and example, he said, nothing more. But he attracted disciples, among them Radèn Mas Iman Sujono, a fugitive aristocrat from the Kasunanan Palace in Suråkartå who had been an officer in the army of rebel Prince Dipånagårå during the Java War. After Dipånagårå's defeat remnants of his army dispersed into the mountains and villages of Central and East Java. Iman Sujono came to Jugo Village after years of wandering. His arrival was as mysterious and as supernaturally destined to happen as Éyang Jugo's had been.

Éyang Jugo's disciples attributed a philosophy to him, which they called The Way of the Three Holies (*Dharma Trisanta*). The Three Holies were Truth, Compassion and Steadfastness. At a glance this scarcely amounts to a "philosophy" but Im Yang Tju is at pains to stress that living by The Three Holies is complicated. It demands mental rigour and ruthless self-awareness.

> The essence of The Three Holies is truth, but the pursuit of truth can lead to tunnel-vision and self-righteousness. This is a danger that must be checked with compassion, but compassion too brings dangers. When the pursuit of truth is coupled with compassion it can become wishy-washy and melt away. So you need steadfastness to ensure the persistence of your commitment to truth in the face of obstacles and even death. Cultivating and balancing all three of the holies is not easy but it can be accomplished through intense meditation.

Seven years before his death Éyang Jugo instructed his followers to climb the slopes of nearby Mount Kawi and prepare a burial site for him. When he judged his time had come he gave up eating and set off on foot for the mountain taking frequent rests along the way. When he reached the grave in today's Wonosari he lowered himself into the open gap, sat down cross-legged, and calmly breathed his last. According to Im Yang Tju this happened in 1879, but other accounts give 1871. His adopted son and chief disciple, Iman Sujono, inherited an instantly thriving pilgrimage site and became its chief key-keeper. When he too died a few years later he was buried side-by-side with his beloved master. Today they are known by Hokkien Chinese titles: First Great Teacher (*Thay Lo Su*) and Second Great Teacher (*Djie Lo Su*). In the generations since Iman Sujono's death, his descendants have continued to hold the office of key-keeper.

From the outset the mausoleum at Mount Kawi with its folksy Chinese-Buddhist ambience attracted pilgrims eager for easy money. Probably there were several components of symbolism that, when assembled, formed a money-spinning turbine. In the first place Éyang Jugo looked and acted like a *budai*, the fat, pot-bellied, laughing Buddha of Chinese folklore. The laughing Buddha is identified with contentment and prosperity. Like the *budai*, Éyang Jugo lived in poverty during his visitations but he was a bearer of wealth and a harbinger of good times. His unassuming presence is said to have transformed the village of Jugo. He cured sickness with holy water and radiated fertility into gardens and rice fields. Jugo Village became an idyll, with "beautiful surroundings, paddy fields filled with water, white *kunthul* herons flying this way and that, and the pleasant knocking of wooden bells at the necks of water buffaloes as they munched on the plentiful grass." He even suppressed the ruinous eruptions of nearby Mount Kělud.

The *budai*-like Éyang Jugo attracted Chinese devotees. Their stories of miraculous cures and commercial success became famous and attracted more devotees. Many Chinese pilgrims believed – and still believe – that Éyang Jugo came to Java from China. But some doubted this, so with characteristic reluctance the saint explained that the enormous distance between Java and China was an illusion.

"Think carefully, my children. If you stand facing north, where are you?"

"We are in the south looking north, of course."

"Without moving, turn around and face south. Now, where are you?"

"We are in the north looking south, of course."

"See? You can be in the north and in the south at the same time and in the same place."

With these simple trick questions he erased the illusion of distance and difference. More Chinese devotees turned up, some of them already rich, others about to become rich. The reputation of Mount Kawi as a centre indifferent to religious and ethnic boundaries, even boundaries of wealth, snowballed.

Around 1930 a businessman from nearby Malang, Ong Hok Liong, set up a cigarette factory in the city. Like many Chinese entrepreneurs Ong regularly visited Mount Kawi to petition Éyang Jugo and Iman Sujono for business success. During one visit around 1954 he dreamed he saw some *ubi talĕs*, a kind of starchy edible taro tuber. When he asked the key-keeper what the dream meant he was told it was a whisper from Éyang Jugo instructing him change the name of his factory from the plodding Strootjes Fabriek Ong Hok Liong to the resonantly earthy Bentoel, a local term for *ubi talĕs*. The change of name galvanised sales. Soon Bentoel was one of Indonesia's leading tobacco brands. It catered especially for the country's unique obsession with aromatic clove-flavoured *krètèk* cigarettes. In a country where most men were (and still are) addicted to smoking, this brought Ong Hok Liong immense wealth. When he died in 1967 he was a multi millionaire and Bentoel had grown into Indonesia's second biggest indigenous cigarette enterprise. The company was listed on the Jakarta stock exchange in 1987 and in 2009 a majority of its shares were bought by the international conglomerate British American Tobacco.[18]

Ong's spectacular success was Mount Kawi's success. If stories are to be believed (and who can doubt them?) many other successes have followed, each adding to the site's momentum. In the minds of its many visitors Mount Kawi is a money mountain.

Sixty years on from the publication of Im Yang Tju's book, Islam is now stamping its growing authority on the story of Éyang Jugo. The saint has been drawn into the popular history of Islam's dissemination in Java. As often as not, he is now represented as a preacher from the same mould that produced the Nine Saints. Relief panels on two of the roofed gates depict him as a tall Arab-looking figure wearing a turban and long white Middle Eastern robe. He has an Arab-sounding name too: Kyai Zakaria the Second.

Indonesian nationalism has also muscled in on the saints. Both Kyai Zakaria and Iman Sujono are given origins – embellished with official-looking genealogies – in the prestigious royal palaces of Central Java, which, for a time at least, were centres of resistance to colonial power. Both saints are represented as officers in the army of Prince Dipånagårå, leader of the anti-Dutch rebellion of

---

18   In 2016 Bentoel International Investama employed around 7,000 people and claimed a 6% share of Indonesia's huge tobacco market. Recently Bentoel has been adversely affected by competition, a downturn in the popularity of smoking and staff unrest.

1825 – 1830 that today is seen as a proto-nationalist movement. Dipånagårå embodied messianic Islam entwined with resistance to foreign domination. According to popular myth (totally unsupported by scholarly history) he escaped from capture by the Dutch in 1830 and set up several units of clandestine supporters, one of which was led by Kyai Zakaria alias Éyang Jugo. The prince himself secretly visited Mount Kawi to meet with Kyai Zakaria and organise renewed resistance which included unrest in parts of Central Java in the years after 1830. It is this amalgam of Islam and nationalism that is now pouring into the mould of sainthood at Mount Kawi. It is summed up in the site's printed guidebook.

> Two charismatic figures are buried in one grave at this mausoleum, namely His Grace Kyai Zakaria the Second, and Radèn Mas Iman Sujono. They came from the palaces of nineteenth century Mataram. The former was descended from the rulers of Kartåsurå in the eighteenth century, and the latter was a descendant of Jogjakarta's rulers in the same period.
>
> In their lifetime both were renowned for their charisma and exemplary character, although as human beings they were not, of course, free from human failings. Both were famous religious figures and preachers of Islam. They were also leaders and models who were close to ordinary people, especially the people of East Java. They were respected for their patriotism, especially as loyal followers of Prince Dipånagårå in his war against the Dutch colonialists between 1825 and 1830.

The booklet makes a point of stressing the Islamic credentials of Kyai Zakaria and Iman Sujono. Paying respects to them is (stressed with capital letters in the guidebook) acceptable – even recommended – according to Islamic law.

> Being true warriors the two gentlemen refused to submit to the Dutch Company after the war, so they travelled to other parts of Java. There they changed the direction of their struggle. They set about fighting for national unity and strove to educate people in agriculture, uprightness of character and proper behaviour based on religious idealism, *tauhid*, devotion to God and living by the sharia rules of religion.
>
> So it is clear that anyone who makes a pilgrimage to the graves of the two saints is NOT DOING WRONG. As pious followers of Islam we undertake this pilgrimage in order to beseech God to have mercy on the souls of the two saints. This is permitted by religion.

The increasingly explicit Islamic profile of the two saints has not eroded the diversity and tolerance of Mount Kawi. If anything it has enhanced it. Chinese-style buildings continue to be built or renovated beside mosques, an Islamic *pěsantrèn* school and other Islamic religious buildings. The pilgrim clientele continues to be diverse in ethnicity, religious faith and place of origin. According to the site guidebook an increasing number of foreigners are visiting Mount Kawi, including pilgrims from Singapore, Malaysia, China, Taiwan, India, the United States, the United Kingdom, Hong Kong, Japan, Australia, Canada, Suriname, the Netherlands, Germany, Zanzibar and various countries in the Middle East.

Mount Kawi's reputation as a source of wealth continues to sit comfortably on the multi-coloured cushions of its diversity. In the last quarter of the twentieth century it even produced a new icon of commercial success vastly richer than Ong Hok Liong. His name was Liem Sioe Liong (1916 – 2012), also known by his Indonesian name Sudono Salim. Liem was an archetypal *cukong*, a Chinese sleeping partner in enterprises fronted by indigenous Indonesians. He was a long-time business associate and close confidant of President Soeharto. Under Soeharto's patronage Liem became the richest man in Indonesia and one of the richest in Asia. In 1996, a year before the Asian Financial Crisis put a brake on his operations, Liem's companies were turning over an estimated $US 22 billion a year. His Bank Central Asia had become Indonesia's biggest private bank, his Indocement factories were Indonesia's biggest producer of cement, the Bogasari flour mill in Jakarta was the world's biggest flour mill, and his Indofood corporation had overtaken Nissin of Japan as the world's leading manufacturer of instant noodles. Working closely with the Soeharto government he also obtained a monopoly on the import of cloves, an essential ingredient in Indonesia's beloved *krètèk* cigarettes.

For years Liem was a regular pilgrim to Mount Kawi, making the three-hour drive from Surabaya four or five times a year. According to Liem's biographers Richard Borsuk and Nancy Chng, he always consulted "the fortune-tellers" there before making substantial business commitments.

Liem must have had many prayers answered as he donated heavily for upkeep of the area, paying for road improvements and building a dormitory for worshippers. He also donated towards construction of a Goddess of Mercy (Kwan Im) statue in the area.

Besides paying his respects to Éyang Jugo and Iman Sujono, Liem was also a devotee of *jiamsi*, a Chinese technique of divination popular at Mount Kawi. The inaugurations of his factories were all calculated to the minute using the time and date of his birth according to the Chinese calendar. His divine consultations even reached the more mundane levels, such as whether the timing was right for his banks to obtain a foreign exchange licence.

Today there are several *jiamsi* shrines in Wonosari, some of them built in octagonal form and painted bright red with Chinese style roofs. And right beside one brash-looking, brand-new Chinese temple in the main street stands the big Iman Sujono Grand Mosque, built – so everyone in Wonosari proudly told me, confirmed by the site custodian – with funds donated by Liem Sioe Liong, a non-Muslim.

It was the day before the First of Surå, the Javanese New Year's Day, when I last visited Wonosari. In the late afternoon I slipped through a side door into the hall that hosts the twin tombs. The hall was modestly spacious, about fifteen metres in width and about twenty metres long. A plain claret-red carpet covered the floor. Above, half-pyramid alcoves were recessed into the dark wood of the ceiling. Bunches of hanging lights cast bright illumination through the room. Four big grandfather clocks stood along one wall facing four others on the opposite wall. Several tall ceremonial umbrellas – dark green with gold edging – stood furled at intervals around the room. The walls were lined with dark wainscoting and several carved, varnished posts supported parts of the ceiling. Two fences of stainless steel piping, about half the length of the room, partitioned off channels along the left and right walls that led to doors at the inner end marked *Jalan Keluar* (Way Out). Between the doors a pleated, beige-coloured curtain stretched across the hall above a step-high platform like a proscenium stage. Behind it lay the graves of the two saints. A heady perfume of tuberose and sweet incense filled the air.

I crept into a slot between two young, smooth-faced Chinese women squatting against the wall. A *slamĕtan* meal was in progress. *Slamĕtan* means "that which brings you peace and safety" or perhaps more accurately "that which rescues you from disruption and danger". In a clear space in the centre of the hall a key-keeper was sitting cross-legged facing the hidden graves with a pile of papers on his lap. He was dressed in formal Javanese style. A close-fitting *blangkon* batik head cloth covered his hair and he was wearing a black, double-breasted jacket over a dark brown batik sarong. Seated in packed ranks around him was a large crowd of mostly Chinese Indonesian men and women with a good minority of Muslims among them identifiable by their *pèci* caps and *hijab* headscarves. Each had a food-laden cardboard box in front of them. Not used to sitting on the floor, some of the Chinese were squirming in discomfort. The key-keeper lifted his sheaf of papers and in a rapid monotone read out messages from petitioners addressed to Éyang Jugo and Iman Sujono.

"From Robert Wijaya of Pekalongan, I ask for good health and a clear run in life, and I ask that my business affairs run smoothly and I make good profits. From Jensen Chen in Mojokerto, I ask for good health and a clear run in my affairs, and may my business thrive. From Budi Tantowi in Blitar, I ask for good health and a clear run in my affairs, with lots of profits, and may I find a wife very soon ..."

The messages continued in quick succession for around half an hour, over a hundred of them. When the last sheet of paper had dropped to the floor the key-keeper launched into a long Islamic prayer of supplication and thanks addressed to the two saints. It began in formal high Javanese then shifted to Arabic punctuated with chorused calls of "Amiiiin" from the assembly. As the prayer finished everyone gathered up their boxes of food and, with business-like speed, vacated the hall. Within minutes the room was empty and the site staff were slamming doors. As I left I managed a quick question for the key-keeper who was standing beside the exit door.

"I would like to pay my respects to the saints. When will the hall open again?"

"At eight o'clock tonight," he said abruptly, pushing the door shut behind me.

Outside, the sun had set. In the shadows scores of people were already queuing before the entrance waiting for the later session. I headed down the steps away from the shrine into the glittering lights below. Thousands of people were browsing the small rickety stalls that packed both sides of the pedestrian street. To the left a long strip of tables were loaded with heaps of flowers, mostly red and white roses but also fragrant, curly kĕnångå petals and tiny white lotus-like kanthil pods. They were on sale in plastic pans ready to be taken up to the burial chamber for ritual scattering on the twin graves. Two curvy girls in bright gold chiffon dresses and black tights stood in my way holding out sample packets of Djarum 76 Gold Filter krètèk cigarettes. Of course I politely accepted and was rewarded with dazzling smiles and requests for a souvenir selfie. A bit further on, several stalls were bristling with young green déwandaru trees already potted for easy removal to apartment balconies and middle-class front yards. The tree is believed to have miraculous powers. If a *déwandaru* leaf inadvertently falls on you it will bring you riches.

A belt of small eateries and souvenir stalls stretched along the opposite side of the street. Under their diamond-bright lights they were piled high with woven wicker handicrafts, carved stone figurines, ceramic vases and pots, opal stones and opal rings, antique coins, tiny *wayang* figures and wooden amulets. Further down customers were sitting on benches sipping drinks before counters stacked with glistening lumps of fried chicken, piles of apples and hardboiled eggs, quarries of dirt-crusted *bentul* taro tubers, cones of crackers and nuts, and steaming heaps of roasted and boiled corn cobs. Ranks of bottled drinks stood in psychedelic uniforms with other more anonymous drinks lying bloated among them in plastic bags. All were tumbled under thick bunches of bananas and grapes dangling from above among sachet strips of coffee and medicines.

It was tempting to browse, but I had an appointment with Bapak Nanang Yuwono Hadi Projo, the head custodian of the Gunung Kawi complex. Pak Nanang was a seventh generation descendant of Iman Sujono through one of the saint's two wives, Nyi Juwul (died 1890). His genealogy appears in several publications and looks reliable. Down a side alley, past the clanging din of a shadow play, I was ushered into his front room and invited to take a seat on the floor. Pak Nanang was aged in his forties with a neat but already greying moustache. He was wearing a black *pèci* fez-cap, a dark grey jacket over a black shirt, and a jet-black, full-length sarong. He spoke with pride about the ethnic diversity and religious tolerance of Mount Kawi.

"It comes back to family," he said. "Most of the Chinese who come here think Éyang Jugo is their ancestor. And we, the Javanese

Muslims of Wonosari, most of us are descended from Iman Sujono. Iman Sujono was the adopted son of Éyang Jugo. So here Chinese and Javanese belong to the same family."

He tapped the ash off his *krètèk* cigarette into a souvenir ashtray on the floor and invited me to help myself to some locally made cheese-flavoured pastry balls.

"It's also more pragmatically profitable to be a family member. After all, if you honour Éyang Jugo and Iman Sujono as family members – your personal ancestors – they can't treat you second-class, can they? But if you approach them as mere predecessors and nothing more, they may give your requests lower priority."

Recalling my conversation with Pak Abdullah at Langsé Cave I asked Pak Nanang whether it was properly Islamic to petition saints for financial help. He gave me a lengthy and very considered answer.

"Putting requests direct to Allah is problematic. It involves many twists and turns. Allah is a source of infinite power, too overwhelming for us to approach. If we Muslims put our requests direct to Allah, it will not work. It is unthinkable that Allah will grant them, truly that is not possible. When the prophet Muhammad received the first revelation – even though it came to him by way of the angel Jibril – he fell ill from the impact. So for this reason Allah's gifts are channelled through middle parties, through our ancestors, through the saints or by way of the prophets or the angels. When we ask for things it is they who filter God's communications otherwise we would be overwhelmed."

I was sorry to leave Pak Nanang's company. He had been hospitable, patient with my often ignorant questions, and respectfully thoughtful in his answers. But the Javanese-Islamic New Year's Eve was also one of the busiest nights of the year at Mount Kawi and he had much to do. I feared I might outwear my welcome so after half an hour and the obligatory group photo I took my leave and returned to the main street. Opposite the key-keeper's house a Chinese dragon dance was shattering the air with drums and cymbals. Watched by hundreds of excited people, acrobats were teetering along raised bamboo poles between dragons prancing, ducking and undulating around them. At the edge of the crowd light was spilling from the doorway of a *jiamsi* shrine. Inside, a press of people – I would say about a quarter of them were Muslims – were shaking bamboo cups filled with thin stalks of bamboo inscribed with Chinese writing. When one stalk fell to the floor it was grabbed and taken to a counter where a bored-looking functionary read it and swapped it for a slip of coloured paper bearing enigmatic aphorisms in Indonesian.

Shortly before eight o'clock I was back at the mausoleum entrance and the crowd had grown. Many were standing or squatting on the steps or in the tiled forecourt. Some were sitting on mats under holy *déwandaru* trees. Others were lying asleep under batik cloths and piles of blankets along the walls. I settled down to wait. Beside me, also waiting in the rapidly cooling air, sat a Chinese-Indonesian businessman, Handoyo aged 28, his wife (aged about 24), his younger brother (20) and a male friend (30).

Handoyo is from Singaraja on the north coast of Bali where he owns and runs a grocery store. Since 2010 he has visited Mount Kawi at least once every year (although he missed a year in 2013). He makes this annual pilgrimage to express his thanks to Éyang Jugo for the success he has had in business and for the good fortune he has enjoyed in his marriage.

He cites two examples of the blessings that Éyang Jugo can bestow. Some years previously his younger brother suffered an attack of chicken pox and couldn't shake it off. After coming to Gunung Kawi and petitioning the saint, he says, his brother made a quick recovery. Handoyo points to his grinning, healthy younger brother as visible proof of the saint's powers. He also has a friend who wanted to open a pharmacy in Singaraja. After several years trying to get a permit and failing, his friend came with him to Gunung Kawi where the two of them paid their respects to Éyang Jugo and conveyed their wishes to him. After this his friend got the permit he needed and his pharmacy is now thriving. So he too now joins Handoyo on his annual visit. Together, says Handoyo, putting his arm around his friend's shoulders, they express their thanks to the saint and make gifts of money to the custodians of the sanctuary.

A few minutes short of 10 pm the doors of the hall snapped open. The crowd jumped to its feet and flooded in dragging their possessions with them. Within seconds a churning mass had packed the floor. Beside the stage a site functionary wearing black trousers and a black shirt with a megaphone at his mouth commanded everyone to sit down. The crowd sank to a squat, some were kneeling. A hush settled over the hundreds of heads.

I looked around. Most of the eager faces were young men and young women in roughly equal numbers. A few were middle-aged, but hardly anyone (besides me) was old. Almost everyone was carrying a pan of flower offerings. Some had plastic bottles of water. Behind me a teenage girl and her father were each hugging a six-pack of Red Bull energy drink.

Half an hour passed. Suddenly, without warning, the stage curtains were yanked aside. A cloud of incense smoke billowed into the hall and the scrummage of people pressed forward on their knees. Somewhere behind me a small child began to wail but was at once hushed by the kisses of her mother.

A barking staccato of instructions came from the megaphone.

"Don't stand! Don't push from behind! Leave through the side exits! No talking among yourselves!"

At the front of the hall, on the slightly raised platform stage, the two graves lay side by side scarcely visible under a jumble of food, flowers and bottles of water. Between them incense burners were puffing dense clouds of smoke into the close air. Left and right of the stage hung two big white-faced kitchen clocks. Above the graves, pressed against the wings of the stage, were two round dishes of Arabic calligraphy – "Muhammad" on the left and "Allah" on the right.

Two site custodians were hunched in front of the graves hard at work. As smoke swirled around them they grabbed pans of flowers from the front row of devotees, scattered them around the graves and turned to a big pile of what looked, from a distance, like Indian samosa pastries. These turned out to be packets of flowers and incense wrapped in brown paper that were given to each devotee in exchange for flower offerings. On their knees in the front row of the human wall, some were praying with their heads bowed and hands clasped, coughing into the incense smoke. Others had their hands raised in supplication. Others handed their bottles of water to the custodians to be passed through the smoke. A Chinese woman, about thirty years old, handed a big open leather handbag to a custodian who swept it through the current of smoke and returned it. Another handed over a wallet, another a mobile phone. A *peci*-wearing Muslim stood up half-crouching, removed his chic-looking blazer jacket and handed it to a custodian who opened it out and allowed its silk-lined interior to float momentarily above an incense brazier. As the owner shrugged himself back into the jacket he pressed some bank notes into the custodian's hand.

Stepping over kneeling devotees I stumbled out through a side door clutching my brown-paper packet of flower petals. In a side room a site functionary was sitting at a knee-high desk sorting piles of hand-written petitions and wads of bank notes. Along a wall, platters of freshly cooked food were queued up on the floor waiting their turn to be charged with the power of the saints. Outside, off the porch area, people were milling around two big stone jars beneath a sign reading *Drinking Water,* and underneath it *Water Jar Bequeathed by Éyang Jugo (Kyai Zakaria II).*

Everywhere money was changing hands.


As people emerged from the side exit they turned sharp left and performed a half-circumambulation of the building. At the rear men and women paused and faced the blank back wall with the holy graves hidden just metres inside. Some dropped to their knees and clasped their hands in Christian-style prayer. Others looked up, opened their palms and lifted their arms. Some lit incense sticks and pushed them into cracks in the stonework of the wall. Many simply stood silent with their heads bowed.

It was close to midnight. I completed the short walk and looked down the outside length of the hall towards the entry gate and beyond it into the main street of Wonosari. In the previous hour a heavy mist had drifted off the mountain and was filling the alleys of the village. The air had turned frigid. The tiled streets were glistening. Lights were muffled behind clammy haloes. The crowds had thinned and people were hurrying instead of sauntering. It felt spooky. I shivered.

Somewhere a hidden loudspeaker was sending the current top-of-the-charts pop song into the hardening chill of night. Its soft beat and the baby-voice of the female vocalist – the voice of Indonesia's modern pop culture – echoed with only the tenderest hint of irony along the quietening streets of the holy village.

> *Tuhan t'lah pertemukanku dengan dia*
>> God has brought me to him
> *Dia yang kuimpikan*
>> He, the one I have dreamed of
> *Tolong buat dia merasa aku*
>> Please make him feel that I
> *Slalu ingin dengannya.*
>> Want always to be with him.

# 10

# In the forests of the future

## Èrucåkrå, the coming Muslim messiah

He was about thirty years old, clean-shaven and neatly dressed in a purple-and-green checked sarong, a white t-shirt and a black *pèci* cap. He talked softly, gesturing with both arms, but I found it hard to concentrate on what he was saying. I was distracted by the stump of his right arm. Severed below the elbow it poked the air like the jagged point of a broken drill, a deformed twin following the rise and fall of his good arm.

We were sitting in the burial chamber of the saint Sunan Pojok in Blora, Central Java. According to a booklet that sketches the official history of the site, Sunan Pojok started out as an officer in the army of Mataram in the time of Sultan Agung (reigned 1613 – 1646). In 1619 Mataram forces overwhelmed the north-coast trading town of Tuban and Sultan Agung appointed Sunan Pojok – known then as Suråbahu – as his vassal regent. The booklet claims Suråbahu held the office for forty-two years, long past the death of his Mataram overlord. He is said to have been a brutal and successful commander. He managed to defeat a detachment of Netherlands East Indies Company militia in an engagement that supposedly (but very doubtfully) took place on 20 November 1626.

Suråbahu became a saint by having the luck to die while passing through a teak forest near Blora. His prowess in war, the spooky ambience of the forest and the remoteness of the site drew devotees to his grave in the tree-hooded village of Pojok. Here the normal process of mythmaking kicked in, promoting him to the rank of saint. Later his grave was shifted to its present location just off the *alun-alun* square in the centre of Blora. The name Pojok – the power-charged place of his passing – came with him.

The man before me had suffered blinding pain. I could see the record of it in his wary, dark-ringed eyes. It was stamped in plaited scars across the flesh of his arm. He told me his story but he found it difficult to speak. From time to time his voice quavered and he stopped to sip water from a plastic bottle.

For years he had worked as a lumberjack in the forests of Kalimantan. He made good money. He was an experienced and respected professional who worked hard and valued safety. But he longed to return to his Javanese home and three years previously he had made it back to Blora. It was difficult to find work. One day he was offered a job felling trees in a teak plantation. He would be well paid but the work was to be done at night, no questions asked. It was – he knew at once – theft, but theft without much risk. Local villagers were partners, a local politician got a cut, the police had been paid off. What could go wrong?

On the first night they pushed deep into the forest in an old truck. They identified a tree and cut into its iron-hard base with a chain saw. Within half an hour the tree had come down and the crew set about trimming the trunk and cutting it into transportable logs. As the saw bit into a branch, without warning the chain snapped. The metal whip tore off the forester's lower arm and killed his work mate instantly. They had no medical expertise and no first aid equipment. The work party became disoriented in the darkness. It took hours of agony to escape back to town. Without modern medical treatment or painkillers the arm healed slowly and not neatly. Now he had no future, he could not work, he had no money.

"I am being put to the test," he whispered. "I should not have gone into the forest that night."

He had felt the sting of death but not its release. He now saw the forest as a living thing with its own stumps and its own pain, like his. He cupped his left hand around the ragged end of his arm and glanced up at a big plaque on the wall above Sunan Pojok's grave. In beautiful Arabic lettering – flowing gold on a green background – it proclaimed lines from the Qur'ān's forty-first book, the Surah Fussilat, verses 30-32:

> Those who say "Our Lord is Allah" and stand firm in that conviction, the angels will descend on them saying: "Do not fear or grieve, but receive glad tidings of the paradise you have been promised! We angels have been your friends in the life of this world and remain so in the hereafter. In paradise you shall have all that your heart desires, and there you shall also have all for which you ask. This is the hospitality Allah will bestow on you when you arrive in the afterlife. He is the All-Forgiving, the Most Merciful.

The verses offer solace to those in pain. That is why he came to the tomb of Sunan Pojok, the saint of the teak forest. In the tomb chamber – tiled in spotless white like a bathhouse – he found moments of relief in prayer and conversation. From the tomb custodians and from other pilgrims he also got the fragments of financial help he needed to keep himself and his family afloat.

A thousand years ago Java lay under a thick fleece of jungle swarming with wildlife. Only the upper slopes of the island's many volcanoes were bare of trees. Incredibly, we have an eyewitness description of the island's forests in that distant time, painted in the vivid colours of literary hyperbole. The epic Old Javanese poem *Rāmāyaṇa* was written in Central Java some time between 856 and 930 CE. It is a retelling of the Indian *Rāmāyaṇa* originally written in Sanskrit well over two thousand years ago. The Indian environment is unmistakable in the initial chapters of the Javanese version, with flora and fauna, place names and major landmarks borrowed from Indian originals. But as the poem unfolds it becomes more and more south-east Asian. By the twenty-fourth and twenty-fifth chapters the anonymous author has sailed far away from India. He details what is in effect a biologist's catalogue of Java's living bounty. Chapter Twenty-Five consists of 117 astonishing stanzas that list more than 200 species of plants, animals, birds and fish, including more than seventy species of fruits and flowers and almost fifty different trees, most of them unique to south-east Asia.

Even after the passage of a thousand years most of the Old Javanese names are still recognisable in modern usage: fruits like *nangka* (jackfruit) and *dalima* (pomegranates); *talĕs* and *uwi* tubers; *waringin, cāmara, katapang* and *randö* trees; tiny *prenjak, prit* and *jalak* birds; graceful *kuntul* and *bango* herons; the *kuwuk* forest cat and the *luwak* palm civet, today famous for the partly digested coffee cherries collected from its droppings that supposedly add a delicious tang to a cup of coffee. The *wurangutan* also gets a mention. Today its name, slightly changed, is familiar even to speakers of English.

The author lights up the forest, species by species, in playful lines full of alliteration and internal rhyme. Here is a taste from the twenty-fifth chapter of Professor Stuart Robson's meticulous translation.

*waringin ya kengin-ingin āṛṇĕb atis*
>It is the banyan tree that is inviting, with its cool,
>thick foliage.

*kayu hambulunya ya rumambay atöb*
>The *hambulu* fig spreads luxuriantly,

*kararas tiris umuray ang kamiris*
>And the dry fronds of the coconut-palm hang loose
>over the *kamiris* rat

*alĕsĕs lĕngis-lĕngis ikāngĕrĕngös*
>The *aleses* tree is slippery, and its slipperiness gives
>a grating sensation -

*gigirĕn ng wang akri umulat muriring*
>People shudder and shiver to see it, their hair on end.

*kuyap ing kĕpuh kadi sahasramuka*
>The tangled roots of the *kepuh* are like a thousand faces,

*umingis mangang hana midĕm mukakĕm*
>Grinning and gaping, some with half-closed eyes or
>pulling a wry face.

*walū kumĕṇḍung ya kumĕṇḍĕng ing titil*
>The *walu kemendung* tree extends as far as the *titil* creeper

*kinolnya raṇḍö paḍa kapwa yākapuk*
>It embraces the *randö* tree, as both have kapok;

*pule makĕmbang hana handul ing hawan*
>The *pule* tree is in flower, there are *handul* trees on the path,

*payanggu mĕmbang paya ning kalampyayan*
>And the *payanggu* is in bloom in the swamp of the
>*kalampyayan* tree.

The *Rāmāyaṇa* even gives us an aerial view of the landscape. Warrior-king Rama boards a jewelled carriage called *Puṣpaka* and takes to the air with his wife and entourage. He looks down on mountains and valleys that are described in the poetic clichés of an Indian arcadia but unmistakably are the forested landscapes of Java.

Under its canopy the ancient Javanese forest is a sentient world full of suggestive gazing. Trees preen themselves over glassy pools, their creepers tangled with flowers like a woman's long hair. The flowers are like eyes looking into the water and the black bees sipping nectar in them are like the pupils of the eyes. The water enjoys being looked at and looks back, although from time to time the tranquillity of its gaze is rippled by darting fish.

The ambience is sensual, even erotic. Young women float on their backs naked in crystal pools well aware young men are peeping at them from rushes on the bank.

The girls' eyes turn copper-coloured, undaunted by the
   catcalls
From the boys on the edge of the grass –
The boys are happy to watch them going naked, looking
   with half-closed eyes,
Thinking of one thing only, enough to break one's heart.

The girls climb into magnolia trees, opening out their dresses to catch fragrant blossoms. They expose their smooth, curvy legs and their *subhaga* – their beautiful part – to the gaze of the boys looking up from below.

> The boys are defeated, their knees quaking and weak,
> They are filled with passion at the sight;
> They cover their eyes, but look through their fingers,
>     fumbling,
> And feeling the stiffening of their erections, they clutch at
>     their "servants".[19]

The forest is also an ornate religious retreat inhabited by learned monks whose sometimes wayward disciples are the creatures of the forest. Bees wander from flower to flower like mendicant monks. The fruit bat's leathery wings are a monk's robe wrapped around him as he hangs meditating. The python keeps a vow of silence and lives on nothing but air. The hawk puts aside the evil of its hawk-nature and strives instead to pursue *dharma*. In a parody of studious human piety, birds twitter and dispute among themselves as they study religious scriptures.

For the monks and their disciples the forest is packed with living exemplars of the moral order taught by religion. In Old Javanese *gagap* means "to reach out for, to grope for" so the *panggaga* plant is groping for goodness and reminding the monks to do the same. *Walĕs* means "to reciprocate, to repay" so the *wungli walĕs* tree reminds them to repay the good deeds of others. The soft leaves of the *lampĕs* – the medicinal basil shrub – bring calm to those suffering sickness, so in the Buddhist world of suffering they symbolise the restorative value of softness and tranquillity. These are not just models to be imitated, they also embody lessons in the equivocal character of moral virtue.

---

19   The Old Javanese reads *ya walikatĕn kol ika kalulanya*, literally "And suffering from cramp they clutch at their servant." There is a thousand-year-old double-entendre here.

It is the nature of qualities that good and bad mingle -
See how the peacock has good qualities in his tail,
But that is also the reason he has difficulties and is tired,
Weighed down and aching from carrying his tail.

The morality of the forest is a worldly morality, inseparable
from worldly order.

The *alĕr* extends along the *kulakā* hedge
Understanding their weakness, they bend down into the
     water.
This is an example to be followed by him who would be
     humble,
Who would be faithful to his vows and serve those in
     power.

The poem also speaks a sombre Javanese orientalism. The
seductive beauty of the forest is matched by its menace. It is thick,
impassable and uninhabited, with deep caves, perilous watercourses,
wide ravines and rocky crags. When Rama ventures onto the slopes
of Mount Rĕṣyamūka he learns that the impenetrable undergrowth
harbours caves full of demons and devils. Boulders come rolling
down on intruders, whirlpools catch and drown anyone who tries
to cross its wild rivers.

Many are the dangers of the fearful mountain here,
And in the cracks of the flat stones the snakes' tongues
     hang out.
Their wish is to make the tigers their prey, and their
     ferocity is ghastly -

It is no wonder that when they hiss their poison is fatal.

Today this opulence has vanished. Even in ancient times the forest was expendable, or at best collateral damage in the expansion of human civilisation. Super-hero Rama – symbolising the indifferent authority of the state – tramples and destroys the forest's beauty merely by passing through it.

> He [Rama] was to steer a course for Mount Rĕṣyamūka,
>     swift and fast,
> And his wind sighed and rushed like a gale.
> The trees that it struck were wrecked, destroyed and all
>     knocked down;
> Torn off, snapped, cracked, beaten, broken in two and
>     smashed.

To defeat the demon king Daśamukha, Rama instructs his monkey army to build a causeway across the sea to Daśamukha's realm in Lĕngkāpura (the island of Sri Langka). From a thousand years ago we are given a vision of the devastation a great construction project can visit on mountains, forests and wildlife. Like an angry modern environmentalist the *Rāmāyaṇa*'s author likens the destruction to a rape.

> There was a single monkey of fearsome size, savage and
>     wild:
> He was of a proud disposition and so was insolent and
>     unwilling to be assisted.
> He attacked the mountain slopes, marvellous to behold,
>     with a great crash the trees were crushed and broken,

And the flat stones were split and cracked, smashed with
    a thunderous sound.
Immediately he uprooted the mountain that was very big
    and tall,
Like a lover who is carried away with forceful feelings
    and knows no gentleness;
The mountain could be compared to the maiden who
    weeps at having been overpowered:
All the ponds flowed over their banks and could be called
    her tears running down.

The geese were sad and despondent, man and wife, and
    the cranes wailed as well,
Calling loudly with the bees, and flew restlessly around in
    the sky.
Birds with young called longingly and wept aloud:
They could be compared with the mountain's words,
    bewailing the fact that it had been overwhelmed.

The Javanese *Rāmāyaṇa* presages the environmental tragedy that has overwhelmed the island in the centuries since. Today unmolested wilderness has been boxed into a few enclaves amounting to around one percent of Java's area. It is a spectacular object lesson on the impact rapid population growth can have when yoked to *laissez-faire* commercial vandalism.

One of the first Europeans to visit Java saw the island's primordial forests for himself. The Portuguese apothecary, diplomat and traveller Tomé Pires reached the island in 1513 by way of Melaka, a trading city on the Malay peninsula that had fallen into Portuguese hands two years before. He sailed along the north coast of Java writing up what he saw in a travelogue titled *Suma Oriental* (A Comprehensive Account of the East). It must have been a surreal experience for him to look into a cosmopolitan but mysterious land alien to European eyes. Despite his reservations about proud and treacherous "heathens" (Hindus) and cunning "Moors" (Muslims) Pires makes no secret of his admiration for Java's wealth. He reports that the island was a lively centre of trade. He lists its commodities: good quality pepper, tamarind, gold, cloths, rice, vegetables, pigs, goats, sheep, cows, wines, fruits and slaves. He makes notes on prices, the local coinage, the system of weights and measures, portage dues and the size of port towns.

Java, he finds, is heavily forested – "well shaded" as he puts it. Describing a river that reputedly divides the island into two countries, he reports (from hearsay apparently) that there are "trees from one end [of the river] to the other, and they say the trees on each side lean over each country with the branches on the ground, large trees and beautifully tall." Describing the Sunda lands of West Java Pires reports on the exploitation of wood for buildings.

The city where the king is most of the year is the great city of Dayo. The city has well-built houses of palm leaf and wood. They say that the king's house has three hundred and thirty wooden pillars as thick as a wine cask, and five fathoms high, and beautiful timberwork on the top of the pillars, and a very well-built house.

Ship building also made big demands on Java's forests. Pires describes the aftermath of a naval expedition against Melaka in 1512-1513 in which Java's stock of wooden ships was decimated.

The newly Islamised state of Jĕpårå, a vassal of Dĕmak, joined a coalition of states determined to wrest Melaka back from its infidel conquerors. The ruler of Jĕpårå commandeered an armada of one hundred ships from ports along Java's north coast. Carrying five thousand men, the fleet sailed fifteen hundred kilometres north-west to the Malay peninsula. The distance travelled and the complement of crew and soldiers tell us these were substantial vessels. According to a Portuguese source, "the largest junk seen was an enormous troop carrier of about 1,000 tonnes, with several hulls superimposed for extra strength". Tome Pires claims even the smallest was at least two hundred tonnes in weight. But they were no match for the Portuguese who sank, burned and captured almost the entire fleet in the roadstead of Melaka. About one thousand men were killed and as many again captured. Pires notes that some formerly busy ports, Dĕmak and Jĕpårå among them, had been reduced to just a few junks. Some, including Semarang, Tuban and Gresik, had been left with none at all and their trade was at a standstill.

But Java's ship builders raided the island's forests and within decades had rebounded from the holocaust. In 1551 Jĕpårå contributed forty ships and four thousand men to a new attack on Melaka. It failed to dislodge the Portuguese, and again most of the fleet was destroyed. In 1574 an alliance of Javanese and Sumatran states tried again, this time with a contribution of three hundred ships and fifteen thousand men from Jĕpårå. This attack also failed, and yet again losses in men and materiel were heavy.

Dutch competition and military muscle strangled Java's ship building industry in the seventeenth and eighteenth centuries. Only a faint whisper of the old energy has made it into the twenty-first century in today's teak furniture factories, especially those clustered in and around modern Jepara where the old ship building industry once thrived.

The levelling of forests for building materials and export logs nevertheless continued through the seventeenth and eighteenth centuries rising to a crescendo in the nineteenth century. Rapid population growth was a principal driver of the clearances. In 1800 Java hosted less than five million people, by 1900 its population was approaching thirty million. (Today it is well over 130 million.) A human tide washed into forests, tearing them down for rice fields and gardens and dragging wood away for fuel and the construction of houses. After the Java War (1825 – 1830) Dutch settlers also fanned into the island's wilderness replacing it with cash-crop estates, including new teak plantations. The colonial authorities devised a cruel but very profitable cultivation system that forced some of Java's peasantry to work in plantations for part of the year, and others to plant a good part of their own land in cash crops – tobacco, sugar cane, rubber, coffee, tea, cacao, indigo, pepper – that Dutch entrepreneurs and the government could buy for export giving the growers ruthlessly cheap prices.

As forests dissolved into rice fields and plantations, a vicious circle developed. Rivers silted up and lost their ancient function as navigable waterways. This stoked the already frantic construction of roads and railways, which further depleted forests. A rail network was sent writhing and forking across Java chewing up wood for locomotive fuel as well as for railroad sleepers that constantly needed to be maintained and replaced. Large amounts of wood were consumed to cure and vulcanise rubber and fuel sugar factories. Between 1800 and 1900 lowland and hill forests declined by more than 50%, replaced mostly by agricultural land and cash-crop estates. In the years before World War Two around 23% of Java was still covered in non-plantation forest, but by 1973 this had dwindled to 11% and two decades later it had dropped to just 7%. Today, government figures claim a slight recovery, putting the forested area of Java at around 10%. Most of this is income-generating plantation forest – teak with smaller areas of mahogany and pine – plus protected second-growth forest.

The last scraps of untouched wilderness have been squashed into two appendages that hang off the bottom of Java at its left and right corners: the Ujung Kulon peninsula in the south-west opposite Sumatra, and the Alas Purwo peninsula in the south-east facing Bali. They are tiny, vulnerable refuges for the last survivors of Java's indigenous fauna, including the Javan rhinoceros (less than one hundred remain) and the *bantèng* ox. The incomparably beautiful Javan tiger was hounded into extinction probably some time in the 1980s.

But in the half-light of memory the Javan tiger lives on, enjoying an afterlife in the guilty nostalgia that accompanies all human-induced extinctions. Today tigers are thought to guard certain sacred sites where their ancestors once prowled. In 1860 a retired district administrator and petty aristocrat, Radèn Mas Adipati Aryå Cåndrånagårå, set off to explore Java, an island now cut open and exposed as never before by the incisions of Dutch-engineered roads. At the time Javan tigers were relatively plentiful in remote niches of the island. In the Pugĕr district on the south coast of East Java Cåndrånagårå noted that ...

> ... the area is heavily forested. Because there are so many tigers people don't dare venture out at night, and even during the day they don't like to go out alone. They go about in groups of two or more and they carry pikes or

other weapons. In fact at night it is not uncommon for tigers to come right into the square in front of the guesthouse and district office.

Tigers were abundant in the nearby Lodoyo district but, he reassures readers, "despite their great numbers, few people have been eaten by them". Every year a number of holy relics from a local village shrine were taken in ritual procession to the district administrator's headquarters in Lodoyo. The procession, he reports, "is accompanied by tigers who keep a watch over it from a distance".

One hundred and fifty years later ghost tigers still patrol Lodoyo and its surrounds. At the shrine of the holy gong Kyai Pradhah in the centre of town, two brightly coloured, life-size, plaster tigers guard the entrance. They greet visitors with a frozen snarl that somehow manages to look sheepish and friendly. According to local people the bronze gong and its guardian tigers are transformations of each other, in fact the gong is also called Kyai Macan (Sir Big-Cat).

The revered relic is at the centre of a story that allegedly happened three centuries ago. Sitting under an enormous banyan tree that hangs over the shrine, I heard one version of it, a single strand in a skein of related stories. It was told to me through laughter-filled interjections by staff from a nearby government office. A certain Prince Prabu, they told me, lived in Kartåsurå, the capital of Mataram in distant central Java. He was the eldest son and successor of Susuhunan Pakubuwånå the First (reigned 1704 – 1719) by a second-tier wife. He had reached adulthood and was looking forward succeeding his father when his father's official queen unexpectedly gave birth to a son who then took first place in the line of succession. Prince Prabu was upset at being displaced by a baby and plotted to seize the throne. His father got wind of the plot and banished him to the wilderness of Lodoyo with instructions to clear the forest and establish a settlement there. The Susuhunan must have retained some affection for his rebellious son because he gave him a holy gong that, when sounded, would protect him from the attacks of tigers as he hacked at their forest habitat.

Struggling to keep the story coherent, the khaki-uniformed staffers seemed as entranced as I was by the image of a palace-bred aristocrat squatting terrified in jungle undergrowth banging on a gong to ward off tigers. In some versions of the story the gong is a kind of telephone that will summon tigers, not repel them. Elsewhere it is described as a sacrificial object to be buried in cleared patches of forest to protect them from falling trees and the anger of wild creatures. Prince Prabu is said to have left the gong for safekeeping with his wife, telling her to strike it whenever she wanted to summon him. But when she struck the gong a white tiger appeared, echoing the ancient belief that powerful men can move easily between tiger form and the white-whiskered guise of a mystic.

Today Kyai Pradhah, alias Kyai Macan, is kept wrapped in white cambric in its shrine on the edge of Lodoyo's central *alun-alun* square. Twice a year a dense mat of people fill the square to witness the ceremonial washing of the gong and its renewed consecration with aromatic ointment. A roofed concrete platform has been built in front of the shrine to accommodate the rite. The gong is removed from the shrine and paraded around the square under swaying ceremonial umbrellas, pushing through tentacle-like masses of hands trying to touch it. On the octagonal platform discarded water from the washing rite, charged with the gong's charisma, is tipped over upturned faces in the surrounding crowd.

In the past local people saw tigers as incarnations of ancestral spirits and reverberations of this belief still haunt today's washing rite. A local functionary – usually the District Head of Blitar– strikes the gong seven times. A hush falls over the square as the gong's call ripples into an imaginary forest and summons the region's feline guardians.

In the nineteenth century tigers also "infested" (as local reports put it) the jungles east of Mount Lawu in Central Java. English traveller William Barrington D'Almeida reports they were abundant in the Ngawi-Madiun region in the 1860s, in fact were often seen crossing roads and lapping water from roadside ditches. But in the diminished world of the twenty-first century the tigers of the past have morphed into domestic moggies that have gone feral in the sacred forest of Ketonggo near Ngawi. I first heard about Ketonggo's cats in 2003 when I ventured into the forest for the first time, cringing on the pillion seat of a motorbike. The driver, a local schoolteacher, took me to the edge of the forest through a quilt of paddy fields. Young, quiet teak trees closed around us whispering in their thin voices as we entered their home and stopped to look around.

"We don't know why," the teacher murmured, "suddenly there were cats. Everywhere. After a few days they disappeared as suddenly as they had come. Then they came back. They keep coming and going."

He scratched his head and his gaze drifted to the spindly crowd of the sacred forest.

"Strange things happen here," he said. His face brightened. "But we're used to it."

In Ketonggo Forest stories grow as profusely as trees,

though they often begin with a disclaimer. "Personally I've never experienced anything unusual here, but someone once told me ..." Or "Nothing untoward has ever happened to me here, except ..."

We re-mounted the bike and fish-tailed onto a forest track. Wind grabbed at my guide's voice as he manoeuvred the machine.

"I used to be a reckless driver," he said, looking at me over his shoulder and steering with one hand. "The strange thing is I never had an accident."

The bike scrabbled for traction in a mud-filled rut.

"Then one night when I was sleeping here in Ketonggo Forest I had a funny dream. I dreamt that my shirt got ripped."

He looked around at me his eyes wide with the memory of it. The bike leaped from a massive pothole and dived into the next.

"Your shirt got ripped in a dream?"

"Yes. And the following day I had an accident. Totally unexpected. I simply fell off my bike. On a perfectly safe stretch of road like this."

The bike sailed over another open-cut hole then tore at the gravel shoulder of the track.

"I broke my collar bone and had to go to hospital. And when I left hospital I found that my shirt had been ripped in the accident. Just like in the dream!"

"Amazing."

"Yes, but that's not all." There was wonder in his voice. "I had been wearing a wind-cheater over my shirt and it was not damaged. Not a mark on it! How do you explain that? Ripped on the inside, intact on the outside."

What is surprising about the stories of strange happenings in Ketonggo Forest (and for that matter at countless other sacred places in Java) is not how unlikely or fantastic they are but how ordinary they are. A storm rages in the forest and "strangely" it does no damage. A man creeps into the forest to cut down a tree and "strangely" the tree falls on him. A visitor approaches a drinks vendor at a sacred site in the forest and "strangely" she refuses to look up at him. Again and again events that in other places would be no more than forgettable everyday trivia, in Ketonggo Forest are infused with magic. The forest is so charged with power that nothing mundane *can* happen there.

Outwardly Ketonggo is just another plantation forest, a rather small one, administered by the state forestry company Perhutani. But it is a plantation with a difference. It is guarded by phantom tigers, patrolled by demons, lit by ghostly columns of light, troubled by sounds from unseen sources, dappled with shadows of the past.

As early as the eighteenth century Ketonggo Forest was a focus of messianic expectations inherited from more distant times. People will tell you that "inwardly" a kingdom and a palace are being built there. When the time comes – when the moment is right to lift the veil that enwraps it – Ketonggo will be revealed as the majestic new capital of Java. In the meantime it is hallowed ground, a place where you can "ask for things". The very name Ketonggo shivers with mystery. In Javanese story it is a country of spirits ruled over by King Bråwijåyå of Måjåpait. It is also the place where Èrucåkrå, the messianic Righteous King, will live in hiding until the day of his emergence. In short, Ketonggo brings together the two main components of Javanese millenarianism: that the glory of pre-Islamic Måjåpait will be restored, and an Islamic messiah called the *Ratu Adil* or Righteous King, will appear there.

Reputedly founded in 1294, the Hindu-Buddhist state of Måjåpait reached the zenith of its power in the mid 1300s under King Hayam Wuruk and his chief minister Gajah Mada. Their names catch the flavour of the times: Hayam Wuruk means "strutting cock" and Gajah Mada is "rutting elephant". A few remnants of Måjåpait city and its palace can still be seen at Trowulan, near Mojokerto in East Java.

We have an eyewitness record of life at the time in the *Desawarnana* (also called the *Nāgarakrtāgama*) completed in 1365 by court poet Prapañca. With a relatively realistic eye Prapañca captures the kingdom's prosperity and the magnificence of its court. Måjåpait grew rich on the rice lands and busy harbours of east Java. It also commanded the subservience of lands beyond Java. The *Desawarnana* has a long, and probably not wholly credible, list of these lands. They include still-recognisable place names in Sumatra, the Malay Peninsula, Kalimantan, Bali, Lombok, Sumbawa, Sulawesi, Timor and Maluku. According to another source – the *Pararaton* or Book of Kings – minister Gajah Mada issued a declaration that he would never rest until he had conquered all the islands of Southeast Asia, listing targets as far flung as Papua, Singapore, Pahang and Palembang.

The lists are important in the symbolic scaffolding that props up the modern Republic. Ideologues of Indonesian nationalism have claimed that the country's borders are not arbitrary and only coincidentally the same as those of the old Dutch East Indies. Rather they are a return to those of Måjåpait (more or less). Even Indonesia's 1975 take-over of East Timor was justified as a restoration of primordial unity established under the empire of Måjåpait. When Gajah Mada declared that he would not rest until he had subdued the whole of Nusantara, he used the phrase *amukti palapa* (to enjoy a rest). It was probably a throw-away line, but twentieth century nationalism has put steel into it, interpreting the phrase as a solemn pledge – the so-called Palapa Pledge. Heavy with nationalist overtones, *palapa* was chosen as the name for Indonesia's domestic satellite system. Like the omnivorous appetite of Gajah Mada six hundred years ago, the Palapa Satellite System today reaches into the diverse extremities of the country binding them into a single nation centred in Java.

Modern nationalism has also depicted Måjåpait as a model of good government – a pinnacle of indigenous civilisation and prosperity. The spirit of this civilization, so the rhetoric goes, is (or will be) re-born under the Republic. Of all the modern ideologues who have committed themselves to history writing in the nationalist cause none surpasses Muhammad Yamin (1903-1962). Although Yamin was not a Javanese he crafted a special place for Måjåpait in the nationalist vision of the Indonesian past. In one of his works, *Tatanegara Madjapahit* (The Majapahit System of Government, 1962) he calls Måjåpait a "second Indonesia". He draws an explicit parallel between a Java-centred Republic and the ancient empire which, echoing Prapañca, he describes as a *mandala* of eight islands with Måjåpait at its centre. In his 1953 biography of Gajah Mada – more an extravagant hymn of praise than a biography – Yamin writes:

In the letter of testimony bequeathed to us by Gajah Mada and Prapañca in the 14th century, they say: "This then is Nusantara, the region that extends united over the Eight Islands. We know what regions are part of our homeland and what regions fall outside its borders!" And we of the twentieth century can likewise say to our descendants: "This is our homeland, Indonesia, united and indivisible, the legacy of Nusantara handed down to us under the aegis of Majapahit."

In at least three fundamental respects there is an undercurrent of paradox in the rose-tinted nationalist enthusiasm for Måjåpait. First, Indonesia is much more than Java, and on the whole, portraying the Republic as a recreation of a Javanese empire does not go down well with the country's non-Javanese population. Second, Indonesia is overwhelmingly Muslim. Part of the history of Islam in Indonesia is the story of its struggle to win people away from "paganism". The prospect of a restoration of Måjåpait, even if merely symbolic, is not necessarily welcome to Muslims who are proud of their faith and celebrate its victories over the pagan states of old Indonesia. And finally, there are those who reject altogether the notion that modern Indonesia must look to the past for its inspiration. On the contrary, Indonesia must throw off the shell of its backward, feudal past, take the West as its model and look forward to a completely new future rather than to one reconstituted from the dust of dead states.

Following the fall of President Soeharto in 1998 there was a flash flood of articles and small books predicting the imminent arrival of a national messiah called the *satrio piningit*. *Satrio* (spelled *satriyå* in Javanese) means "a warrior prince of noble character" and *piningit* means "hidden away".

For many, the messiah will be a descendant or reincarnation of warrior prince King Bråwijåyå the Fifth of Måjåpait. Tradition has given the name "Bråwijåyå" to all, or most, of the kings of Måjåpait, though historical scholarship has failed to find the name among the scanty texts and inscriptions of the time. The story goes that in 1478 the last ruler of Måjåpait, King Bråwijåyå the Fifth, found himself besieged in his palace by a Muslim army led by his own son Radèn Patah. The eighteenth-century historical chronicle, the *Babad Tanah Jawi*, says Bråwijåyå simply vanished into the sky but another tradition claims he escaped from the ravaged palace and fled west to Mount Lawu in Central Java.

It is the latter tradition that lives on in Ketonggo Forest. On his way to nearby Mount Lawu, King Bråwijåyå stopped in the forest at a site now called the High Seat of Srigati (*Palĕnggahan Agung Srigati*). There he rested and meditated, casting off his royal regalia including his crown, a wooden duplicate of which remains in the sanctuary. He put on the garb of an ascetic and climbed up into the fastness of Mount Lawu. After converting to Islam and living there as a hermit for a time he vanished into the sky. But many people believe his spirit stayed on, bearing the name Sunan Lawu. He became the mountain's spirit guardian.

One remarkable little book, the Indonesian-language *Satrio Piningit* (The Hidden Knight-Champion, 2003) by D. Soesetro and Zein Al Arief, draws on a rich stew of articles in newspapers and popular magazines. It claims that President Megawati Soekarnoputri (in office 2001 – 2004) inherited her power from Queen Tribhuwana Tunggadewi who ruled Måjåpait between 1329 and 1350 immediately preceding Hayam Wuruk. The strong-minded queen guided Måjåpait into the period of its greatest brilliance. In the twenty-first century her descendant in spirit, Megawati, was seen by some to be like Tribhuwana, the harbinger of a brilliant era about to dawn.

*Satrio Piningit* goes on to discuss King Hayam Wuruk's four advisers, Noyo, Gènggong, Sabdo and Palon.[20] It was thanks to

---

20  More commonly these legendary courtiers are represented as two individuals, Noyogenggong and Sabdopalon (in Javanese spelled Nåyågènggong and Sabdåpalon). Sabdopalon in particular is an enduring figure of power believed by some to be an incarnation of the guardian deity of Java, the clown-god Sĕmar. The notion that

their good advice, the book claims, that the king was able to put the finishing touches on Måjåpait's brilliance. Until, that is, the four advisers decided to collectively vanish into the sky, whereupon Måjåpait's fortunes nosedived. As the four dissolved into the infinite they promised to return in five hundred years. By not counting the years too precisely the book's authors can ask:

> We are now in the last days of their absence ... will they keep their promise? Is it really possible that Majapahit will rise again, to be known as the Republic of Indonesia, great and strong?

For centuries Javanese have been on the lookout for a messianic saviour. Like elsewhere in the world, messianism in Java seems to have been a response to unbearable injustice and the alienation wrought by social change happening too fast. On countless occasions it has materialised in stories and popular movements centred on a figure called the Righteous King. Too often hopes for the future have been dashed, so messianic prophecies are poignantly reluctant to raise expectations too high. One story, in the encyclopaedic nineteenth-century text *Sĕrat Cĕnthini* (The Book of Servant-Girl Centhini), predicts that the Righteous King will cut, but not eliminate, taxes on rice fields and the rice harvest, and he will spend not a copper more than seven thousand *réyals* a year on his own meals. He will be, moreover, a very Islamic Righteous King, so naturally he will maintain a palace in Arabia as well as in Java.

---

Noyogenggong and Sabdopalon were, in fact, four individuals can probably be attributed to the influence of the classical shadow play in which the noble warrior heroes are advised by four clown-servants, among them Sĕmar, collectively known as the *pånåkawan*.

The prophecy reassures Java's war-sickened peasantry that they will not be required to go into battle on the king's behalf but will be empowered to rout enemies with pious *dhikr* chants.

In 1810 a certain Radèn Ronggå Prawirådirjå raised the flag of rebellion against Dutch authorities and their Javanese allies in Central Java. Ronggå established his base at Maospati in the eastern foothills of Mount Lawu in a thickly forested area known as the kingdom of Ketonggo. There he quietly nurtured a belief that he was destined to rule Java as the long awaited Righteous King. The rebellion failed, Dutch troops burned the rebel redoubt and, shortly after, killed Ronggå himself. But the reputation of Ketonggo Forest as a nursery where messianic movements sprout took on new momentum. Messianic gatherings were reported there in 1817, 1819 and 1888.

Java's almost-messiah Prince Dipånagårå – leader of the anti-Dutch rebellion that raged between 1825 and 1830 – did not make his base in the Ketonggo Forest, but he did represent himself as the longed-for Righteous King. His mission was to destroy infidel power in Java, purify the land, and establish Islam as the foundation of a utopian order. He called himself Èrucåkrå but apparently made a distinction between Èrucåkrå and the Righteous King. In his autobiography, written after his capture and exile to Sulawesi, he describes a meeting he had with the Righteous King in a half-waking dream. It was 1824, a year before he took up arms against the Dutch. His recollection of the dream has been translated by historian Peter Carey.

Now we tell of the Ratu Adil who stood at the mountain
top competing in brilliance with the lordly sun which for
long glowed but palely. The prince had not the strength to

know or to look upon the countenance of the Ratu Adil, whose brilliance indeed eclipsed the sun. Only his clothing was closely observed by the prince in its entirety. His turban was green and he wore a white tabard, white trousers and a red shawl. He faced to the northwest standing at the summit of the mountain on top of a smooth stone. There were no shadows and the grass could not be seen. It was as clean as if it had been swept. The prince from below looked upwards facing to the southeast. Then the Ratu Adil spoke in a friendly way. "Ah, you Ngabdulkamid, the reason I have summoned you is for you to set my army fighting. Let Java be conquered immediately! If anyone should ask you for your mandate, it is the Qur'ān. Order them to seek it there!"

It is revealing to run a magnifying glass over the Islamic character of Dipånagårå's vision. The Righteous King is wearing Arab-style clothes: a green turban, a long *dishdasha* robe, white trousers and a red *keffiyeh* shawl. The time is the night of the twenty-first of Ramadhan, one of the dates known as a Night of Power (*laylat ul-qadr*). According to the Qur'ān the Night of Power commemorates the special night on which Allah's message was first revealed to Muhammad. It is "better than a thousand months" (Qur'ān Sūrah 97 Al-Qadr verse 3). In Islamic tradition it is a time when the piety and supplications of Muslims find special favour with Allah. The Righteous King tells Dipånagårå that his conquest of Java is authorised by the Qur'ān and he is mandated to become a ruler who will stand firm as a regulator of Islam. As he speaks the Righteous King is even facing north-west, the direction of the *qibla*. Java's new millennium – the age of Èrucåkrå – was to be a strongly

Islamic order.

The defeat of Dipånagåra in 1830 did not spell the end of Islamic messianism. It remained a persistent presence through the nineteenth and twentieth centuries, even into the post-independence era. For some, the leader of Indonesia's independence movement and the country's first president, Soekarno, was (at least for a time) the Righteous King. Certainly Soekarno saw Indonesia's independence in 1945 as the dawning of a new millennium. He was familiar with the prophecies of the *Jångkå Jåyåbåyå*. In 1930, accused of sedition by the Netherlands East Indies authorities, he delivered an impassioned courtroom defence in Dutch before a no-doubt blinking, bewildered panel of Dutch judges. Known today by the title *Indonesia Menggugat* (Indonesia Accuses) the speech has become a key document in the archives of Indonesian nationalism. Soekarno partly built his case on references to Jåyåbåyå's prophecy that a Righteous King would save Java.

> "Your Honours, please think about why the people continue to believe in a Righteous King, and always await his coming. Why is it that, right up to the present, King Jåyåbåyå still inspires hope in the hearts of our people. The reason is clear. It is because in the weeping hearts of the people, ceaselessly and continuously they hope for, and they wait for, the coming of help, just as people who are living in darkness, every hour, every minute, every second wait and hope: asking when ... when will the sun rise?"

Ketonggo Forest has remained a quietly disruptive refuge for messianic visions. In 1976 a bureaucrat in Indonesia's Department of Agriculture, Sawito Kartowibowo, was arrested and charged with subversion. The government alleged he had attempted to topple President Soeharto supernaturally. He got the signatures of several influential people on documents that criticised the government and demanded that Soeharto step down. The documents were innocuous and the VIPs who had so casually signed them quickly repudiated them. In the dramatic trial that followed it emerged that Sawito had spent several years visiting sacred sites across Java, accumulating spiritual power and collecting magically charged objects. It was this that had given him the authority to impress dignitaries and gather a small salon of followers around him. This stung the government into formally prosecuting him. One of the places Sawito had visited was Ketonggo Forest.

A member of Sawito's group, Sudjono, an ex-diplomat, gave an account of what happened in Ketonggo Forest. There was, he said, a white stone *linggam* there called Tugu Manik Kencono or Tugu Manik Kumala. When Sawito's party of spiritual wanderers reached this place the forest custodian greeted them. He told them that thirty-five days previously he had received a revelation that a party of spiritual searchers was to come. To honour them he had trimmed the bushes and cleaned up the area around the Tugu Manik Kencono. Sudjono later wrote:

What we saw there (and the witnesses included my daughter Sita) was astonishing. From afternoon and into the night we saw lights coming from all directions towards where we were sitting near the Tugu Manik Kumala. We were deep in a big teak forest, a long way from any highway or road, yet lights of various kinds were coming and going around our campsite. Some resembled the lights of cars following one another like vehicles on a highway. They seemed to be delivering guests to our ceremony. If you measured the distance between the headlights and tail lights you could only conclude that there were buses in addition to cars, each no doubt carrying dozens of passengers. Traffic was heavy. Beams from headlights sometimes dazzled us and filled the forest with bright light, yet there was no sound of engines. In the sky too there were lights, like meteors shooting back and forth. And far off among the trees we also saw campfires, though we knew there were no villages with human inhabitants in the area. Eventually, around half past one at night we saw a long row of very bright lights, as if we were being shown a distant city, lit up for a celebration as Jakarta is lit up when Independence Day is celebrated.

Later, in a ceremony at Sudjono's home in Bogor, Sawito was inaugurated as the Righteous King and future ruler of Indonesia. To confer legitimacy on him each member of the small group played the role of a king of Måjåpait. Accounts of the meeting claim that Jolono, the custodian of the royal crown of Måjåpait, materialized in their midst floating silently five metres above the ground.

Sawito's trial lasted almost two years. It provided the country's mass media with a steady diet of bizarre stories. The public responded with fascination and gasps of derisive humour directed as much at the gullible government as at Sawito. In June 1978 Sawito was found guilty and sentenced to eight years imprisonment (later reduced to seven).

Today the location of Èrucåkrå's future palace is known and is marked by a small shrine called Sultan Èrucåkrå's Palace (*Kraton Sultan Èrucåkrå*), also Sitinggil (the outer audience chamber of a

Javanese palace). It lies in the crook of a small river deep in Ketonggo Forest. An iron footbridge – guarded left and right by dragon figures – takes visitors across the river into a neat garden that leads to the shrine. As you step off the bridge the complex reveals its five main components. To the left stands a small rest pavilion with a plaster representation of a three-tiered, tree-like royal umbrella in front of it. Next to the umbrella the name of the pavilion is given in Javanese lettering on a small boulder: The "Umbrella of the World" Rest Shelter (*Cakruk Palĕrĕman Songsong Bawånå*). Above the door, also in Javanese script, is this exhortation:

The fame and good name of a nation
Resides in the nobility of its culture.
So, people of Java, don't forget your Javaneseness.
Hold fast to these three high principles:

1. Regard Javanese culture as your very own;
2. Make it your duty to hold fast to Javanese culture;
3. Look critically at yourself and have courage.

Not far from the pavilion a sacred spring called the Umbul Jambé bubbles from the edge of the stream. It is housed in a small but picturesque, open-sided, pavilion, almost classically Roman in its columned simplicity and mosaic-imprinted floor. It is topped with a bright red Chinese-style roof. Further on there is another rest pavilion with, in front of it, an obelisk rising some ten metres from the centre of a stylised lotus blossom, with a flame-like shape at its tip. A plaque in Indonesian dedicates the obelisk to "the unity of believers" (*Tugu Persatuan Umat*), but it seems to be known by other names, including the Golden Monument, the

Manik Kĕncånå Monument, and the Manik Kumålå Monument. In its appearance and symbolism the obelisk is a small echo of Indonesia's huge National Monument that stands some 180 metres in height in the centre of Medan Merdeka square in Jakarta. Built by President Soekarno in the early 1960s, it too is tipped with the representation of a flame covered in gold and, like the Ketonggo obelisk, is dedicated to the ideal of unity.

A paved path leads beyond the obelisk along the edge of a neatly clipped lawn to a modern-style split gate with serrated wings left and right decorated with images of the elephant-headed Hindu god Ganesha. Inside and up a few steps is the shrine itself standing on a paved terrace overlooking the stream. It was built in the early 1990s. Pilgrims explained to me that, many centuries ago, the Ketonggo area used to be under the rule of Hindu-Buddhist Kediri. It was descendants of these kings – "people from Kediri" – that provided funds for the shrine's construction.

The outer entrance to Sultan Èrucåkrå's palace shrine
in the depths of Ketonggo Forest.

It is a small structure about seven metres by seven metres square built from brick rendered in plaster and painted brilliant white. Inside, the floor is tiled in glossy black. The corrugated iron roof is supported by steel rafters and trusses, but there is no ceiling. From the centre of the roof a Balinese style *mèru* tower rises bringing to five the total number of tiers in the shrine's layered roof. A wide strip of cloth with a band of red and a band of white, like the Indonesian flag, hangs from the perimeter of the roof forming a tent-like wall. In the centre, on a low, step-high altar ringed with stainless steel posts, there is an arrangement of river stones with a three-tiered royal umbrella standing in it. The remnants of flower offerings lie scattered on the floor and a small clay brazier smokes with incense.

In October 2015 I stayed overnight in Ketonggo Forest, this time making my way there in a battered Toyota Xenia car with the luxury of a professional driver. My first stop, late in the afternoon, was at the High Seat of Srigati just inside the forest perimeter. It is a small house-like structure built in 1987. It commemorates King Bråwijåyå's visit as he fled from the conquest of his capital by Muslim forces. On the outside wall of the shrine, to the left and right of the door, there are stone figures of elephant-headed Ganesha. Inside, the air is heavy with the scent of perfumed oil and roses. The walls are draped with horizontal banners of red and white cloth. In the centre of the room a small hump of crusty grey earth crouches inside a rectangular tiled rim no more than one brick in height. Red and white rose petals cover it like decorative icing. People believe the mound is an extrusion from the volatile subterranean world of Java. Like that world, the mound is intelligent. When Indonesia is in trouble it registers its concern by growing, although its growth is imperceptible because pilgrims take small fragments of it away as magically charged souvenirs. And when the country is calm, the mound is calm too. Behind it, on a small table, stands a wooden replica of a Javanese king's crown and above it, two rather battered multi-tiered ceremonial umbrellas. Beside the earthen mound stands a one third size, brightly painted statuette of King Bråwijåyå. In one corner a gong hangs on a wooden frame beside an empty chair – the king's "High Seat".

Pak Marji, head custodian of Ketonggo Forest,
with his assistant Pak Gunarto.

Right beside the Srigati shrine stands the reception verandah of forest custodian Pak Marji, also known by the title Ki Among Jati, Sir Custodian-of-the-Teak. The title plays on the word *jati*, which means "teak" but also means "true" and "genuine". Pak Marji greeted me sitting cross-legged on the floor sucking on a clove-scented cigarette in a bone cigarette holder. Aged in his fifties, he was wearing a loose black cotton shirt and floppy black pants. His dark hair emerged from under a black bandana and hung to his chest. As he spoke a wispy greying beard shook and jumped over his throat. He was the epitome of an old-style key-keeper. Before long we were deep in conversation, though I was struggling to take in his simile-rich responses to my questions. Fortunately I had a dictaphone, which I laid on the floor before him. I was able to review our conversation afterwards and get a better grip on his rambling discourse.

"Ketonggo Forest is not a place of worship," he said, perhaps trying to forestall suspicion that the forest might be a hideout for un-Islamic practices. "It is in fact a barometer given to us by our ancestors. It issues warnings about changes in the social climate."

He leaned towards my dictaphone and raised his voice.

"Most people who come here are looking for their true selves, their *jati diri*, their 'teak' selves. Living in the city, working in the modern economy, they lose the hard grain of their teak selves. They become soft and empty. That's when the demon Kålånådå moves in to fill that emptiness. Kålånådå is an ancient demon but he is always with us. He is part of our heritage. Empty people get possessed by him, and from possession comes obsession. They shout and yell and think only of having a good time and chasing money. Ketonggo Forest is a quiet place of truth and genuineness – that's what *jati* means, that's what teak symbolises. People know that here they can recover their lost substance, their hardness and wholeness. They can connect with nature and find the foundations of true self-knowledge. They can pray at the Golden Monument, a symbol of mental and moral uprightness. It stands tall beside the Umbul Jambé spring where people can bathe in the water of renewal."

Pak Marji tapped the ash from his cigarette.

"That is where King Bråwijåyå of Måjåpait stopped after his own son attacked him and expelled him from his palace. It is a terrible thing for a son to attack his own father, but Bråwijåyå held no grudges. He even converted to his son's new religion. Islam teaches us that we must not hold grudges. We must compromise, forgive and adapt."

It was well after seven o'clock when I took leave of Pak Marji and headed for Ketonggo's main complex of shrines. My driver inched into the darkness of the forest. The headlights picked out two ruts in the soft earth. We slotted into them and laboured forward at walking pace. A shower of rain brought us to a stop for ten minutes before it cleared and we pressed on through bushes that flung diamond-bright droplets of water across the windscreen. Our destination was not much more than two kilometres from the High Seat of Srigati but it took us half an hour to get there. In its last one hundred meters the track dipped down a steep slope. The car skittered over rain-slicked gravel. The headlights swung from banks of bare earth on the right to a black edge on the left. In the cabin there were no handles to grip. I had no seatbelt. I braced my arms against the dashboard and pressed my feet hard to the floor.

Then we could go no further. We were at the footbridge and I was pleased to transfer my feet to terra firma. I headed at once over the bridge, past the columns of the Umbul Jambé spring up to the jagged, winged gate of Èrucåkrå's mini-palace. It was almost nine o'clock. I removed my shoes and stepped inside. I slid down to the glossy black-tiled floor and leaned back against the whitewash of the waist-high perimeter wall. It was almost totally dark and I was alone. Long sheets of slowly rippling satin filled the open sides of the shrine, brushing the back of my head. Looking right I could see the sharply serrated columns of the entry portal gleaming frosty white in the starlight. Muffled chirps and the soft buzzing of a thousand insect voices filled the trees, punctuated with a clinking call like a tiny, solitary ankle bell. I toppled slowly sideways and stretched out full length in the angle between the wall and floor. Within seconds I was asleep.

Suddenly I was awake and staring. In the darkness before me an indistinct figure – apparently a young man – was crouching with his back to me before the platform of stones. A cigarette lighter flared projecting his giant angular shadow momentarily on to the undulating cloth wall of the shrine. He lit some sticks of incense and pressed them into an ash-filled gourd on the platform. Silhouetted against a corona of dull red light from the incense he kneeled and raised his arms in a dramatic Y-shaped pose. For minutes he remained still, kneeling with his arms raised. Then he lifted a fistful of incense sticks in both hands and swept them in great circles before him. The glowing ends of the sticks printed crimson arcs in the air before they blurred and disappeared behind scarves of smoke. The figure jumped to his feet– still clutching the incense sticks – and walked rapidly around the central platform. He repeated the circumambulation seven times, his bare feet completely silent on the tiled floor. Then, like a wraith, he vanished through the entrance of the shrine.

He was the first in a steady stream of visitors. Through the night dark figures glided silently in twos and threes and fours into the shrine. The only sound was an occasional brief whisper and the rustle of plastic bags filled with bottles or small plastic jerry cans of water. The water had come from the Umbul Jambé spring. The visitors had dipped their containers into the pool and carried them dripping up the shadowy path to Èrucåkrå's shrine. They placed them on the platform under the umbrellas as they performed their prayer rites.

The following morning, as dawn brought a misty glimmer to the forest, I left the shrine and stood on the steps of the entrance looking over the slowly brightening garden. On the lawn four cats were playing, three good-sized kittens rolling and gambolling around their mother. I walked past them to the Umbul Jambé spring. Local residents use it as a public bathroom and there was a short queue at the door. It was half an hour before I made it inside. The spring water rose through a translucent pool and flowed away over my feet across a shallow rocky sluice. I undressed and splashed the tepid, soap-free freshness over me.

My damp clothes were still clinging to me as I breakfasted on instant noodles and dark sweet Javanese tea at a nearby rough-and-ready eatery. Seated on the floor under crooked bamboo walls I tried to winkle information from eight middle-aged men – office workers and small business operators – who had come from Ponorogo about seventy kilometres away. They were friendly, even exuberant, but they wouldn't tell me why they had packed into their tiny car and come swaying and nodding through the late night blackness to the shrine of Èrucåkrå. They made the trip often, they told me, around six or eight times a year. But that was all they would say. The rest was "secret".

Later one of the group approached me as I was standing on the footbridge taking photographs. He was a small, dark-skinned man, his chin blotched with grey stubble. He was wearing a threadbare woollen jumper, jeans and plastic sandals. We got talking. He told me he was a carpenter and builder. His hobby was the classical shadow theatre.

"In the shadow theatre, he said, "there is a famous play, *Babad*

*Alas Wånåmartå*, which means Clearing the Forest of Wånåmartå. In it, the great heroes of the classical shadow theatre – the five Pandawas – find themselves exiled to the Wånåmartå Forest."

Like most Javanese he seemed well aware that behind the spectacular set-piece fights and the tomfoolery of the shadow play lie complex allegories.

"Hoping to establish a new kingdom they start to cut down trees, but the trees refuse to stay down. They keep springing up again. The forest hides an invisible spirit kingdom, and the guardian demons of the forest fight back. They are hairy creatures, with red faces, bulging eyes and sharp tusks – beast-like symbols of wildness."

For a moment he looked thoughtfully at my hairy arms, my sweaty pink face, and my round Caucasian eyes.

"These creatures always fight hard," he went on, "and sometimes successfully, but eventually they are crushed by the superior power of the human invaders. Yet in defeat the primordial spirits claim a victory. Their souls flit from their dead bodies and merge with the souls of their conquerors. The forest is flattened and a city rises in its place, but the spirit of the forest lives on in the inner life – the consciences – of the city's human inhabitants."

His eyes were twinkling above a goofy grin. He explained that Ketonggo Forest is a symbol. Like the events of a shadow play, its trees hide a deeper meaning, something secret, something he called *sinandi* – concealed, hidden, incognito, disguised.

"People come to Ketonggo because here you can sense the presence of what is *sinandi*, normally hidden. Ketonggo is the secret wilderness in the heart of Indonesia. It is the secret wilderness in all our hearts. Indonesia is not as cultured and cultivated as we like to claim. In its deep heart – the treacherous depths of its social pools and its tangled forests – it is wild."

He swept his arm out over the rocky stream below us to the ranks of young teak trees on the far bank.

"One day these trees too will be chopped down. The wood will bring wealth to local people and the forest will be made habitable. A big sanctuary is going to be built here, like a town. People will live here side-by-side with our ancestors and the spirit of the past. This is the future of Indonesia. The future will begin right here. Ketonggo tells us to have confidence in that future."

He grinned his toothy grin.

"So take plenty of photos ... *mumpung wånå tĕsih wontĕn* ... while the forest is still here."

In 1997 I visited a small religious retreat, the Sanctuary of the Five Betel Trees (*Padhèpokan Jambé Limå*), on Sĕlok Hill near Cilacap on the south coast of Java. Sĕlok Hill is within walking distance of Srandil Hill, a veritable supermarket of tiny shrines and one of Java's most renowned holy places. The sanctuary lay surrounded by stands of majestic teak and mahogany trees deep in an old, but second growth, forest. The trees were alive with birds. Monkeys crashed through the foliage, from time to time making sorties on to forest paths to squat and chatter at human intruders.

President Soeharto's New Order government had designated Sĕlok Hill a recreational reserve. Local police patrolled it with their usual toughness. Villagers were allowed in to collect teak leaves for use as wrapping in local markets, and they gathered fallen branches for fuel. But the forest itself and its flourishing wildlife remained relatively untouched.

Soeharto presided over a venal system, but it is fair to say his government did more than any previous government – colonial or post-colonial – to address Java's environmental decay. During his thirty-two year rule he declared national parks at the western tip of the island (Ujung Kulon) and the eastern end (Alas Purwo and Baluran) with a good number of parks and protected reserves in between. Plagued by corruption and faced with unendurable pressure from local people to forage in forests, government officers nevertheless made a credible attempt to protect the new parks and introduce professional conservation practices. Sĕlok Hill was a beneficiary. It was in reasonably good shape.

Java's clown-god Sĕmar, with his son Nålågarèng to the left, points at an inscription reading "From the world of the past" in the Jambé Limå sanctuary on Sĕlok Hill near Cilacap.

The Sanctuary of the Five Betel Trees was a small, well-maintained, brick and plaster building looking out over the southern ocean. A flight of steps led up to a small terrace in front of a double front door. Above the door an arc of big letters in *hånåcaråkå* script announced the building's name: *Puri Giri Sagårå*, Temple of Mountain and Sea.

The first room was an antechamber with doors leading into an airy, octagonal inner chamber.

Here the back wall was filled with a larger-than-life, cartoon-like painting of the clown-god Sěmar standing in the mouth of a cave flanked left and right by his sons Nålågarèng and Pètruk. Sěmar stood pointing at an inscription that arched above him in *hånåcaråkå* script. It read *Såkå bawånå kawuri*, "From the world of the past". At the foot of the Sěmar image, there was a low, white-tiled, altar-like, square podium where flower offerings had been placed. Behind the altar, leaning against the back of a plush sofa, sat a small painting of the glamorous Ratu Kidul, spirit queen of the southern ocean. Her long hair streamed out in the ocean wind. She was wearing a low-cut, shoulderless, bright green *kěmběn* bodice above a loosely flapping, ankle-length sarong.

According to local anecdote, President Soeharto (in office 1966 – 1998) was a frequent visitor, though it is not clear exactly when he came or how often. The custodian told me that before Soeharto became president he often "used to sleep here at the Five Betel Trees sanctuary". Rumour has it that he continued to patronise the place after becoming president, but when pressed on this the custodian denied it. Soeharto had not personally returned since becoming president, he said, but he had "sent emissaries".[21]

In 1999, after the fall of Soeharto, I visited the sanctuary again. The building was still there, but now it stood alone in hectares of bare, blasted hillside. The forest had disappeared. Scarcely a twig remained standing. The downpours of the wet season had not yet arrived, but already the slopes were scarred with erosion. Here and

---

21   Soeharto also patronised the nearby Sanctuary of the Seven Betel Trees (*Padhèpokan Jambé Pitu*) reputedly built in the 1950s by a certain Råmå Sudiyat who is said to have become Soeharto's spiritual mentor.

there a few plots of newly planted manioc and dry-field rice waited for the rain, but the animals and birds had gone.

As I walked towards the Sanctuary of the Five Betel Trees – now starkly visible where once it had been hidden in dense bush – a crowd of curious villagers materialised around me. They were on their way home after a day stitching new fields into the smoking landscape. Several were shouldering short-handled, broad-bladed adze-hoes still lumpy with dirt. I asked them what had happened to the forest. They told me that the previous year, immediately after the fall of President Soeharto, a few local people had cut down a tree or two. After all, the forest was their ancestral land ... the Soeharto government had quarantined it without their permission. They were simply asserting their right to exploit what was theirs. When the police took no action more villagers moved in. Timber buyers were offering very good prices for logs. Feeling the merciless bite of the Asian Financial Crisis, no one wanted to be left out. Within weeks a sawing and chopping frenzy developed. They had to harvest the wood before outsiders turned up and beat them to it.

"And anyway," said one young man with surprising bluntness, "who has the right to criticise local people for chopping down a few hundred hectares of their own trees when Soeharto and his corrupt cronies have flattened infinitely greater areas of forest in Kalimantan and Sumatra?"

"What about the birds and monkeys," I asked. "Where are they?"

"They're still here!" he said looking vaguely left and right. "But we don't know exactly where."

Later, as I emerged from the sanctuary, the same young man was waiting for me at the foot of the entry steps. He offered me a lift back to the main road. He was quite insistent. I sensed he had something to show me. He led me to a small, whitewashed, brick-and-plaster house a few steps from the sanctuary. Glasses of tea were waiting for us in the bare front room, and parked in the middle of the room stood a brand-new, gleaming red, 180cc Honda motorcycle, its tyres freshly washed.

He brushed his hand casually and proudly over the pillion seat. But I wasn't interested. I was shocked at the disappearance of the forest and I let my anger show.

"Indonesia is losing its trees ... fast," I said through clenched teeth. "Forest fires are poisoning the air of Kalimantan and Sumatra. Animals and birds are being exterminated like they mean nothing. Indonesia has thrown a blanket of smoke over Singapore and Malaysia. That's disrespectful to your neighbours, isn't it! Beautiful forests are being burned and chopped down. And for what? For palm oil and motorbikes!?"

I slurped up a big mouthful of tea. It was sweet and delicious. For an instant I forgot that tea comes from tea plantations that were once forests filled with wildlife, ditto for sugar. Through a thousand acts of consumption I was a complicit knot in the mesh of transactions that begin with, and end with, deforestation. I took another gulp and drew a deep breath. I had more – much more – to say, but my host was staring at me, irritation scratched in vertical lines between his eyebrows. His hospitality was being tested. Tolerance of sanctimoniousness has its limits, especially in the front room of your own home.

"The trees will grow again," he murmured.

"What!? No they won't! Look at north Africa. The Romans chopped down all the forests there two thousand years ago and they haven't regrown. It's all desert now. In Australia they flattened more forest than the entire area of Java. They haven't regrown. The people of Rapanui chopped down every tree on their island. Those trees haven't regrown either, in fact we don't even know what they looked like!"

He looked bewildered, then he steadied.

"I don't know where those places are," he said. "But this is Java."

He glanced out at the stumps that now ringed his house. Bluish haze from burning plant debris hung like a frigid mist in the late afternoon air. He looked me straight in the eye.

"Here the trees will grow again."

And he was right.

In 2017, eighteen years after my previous visit, I went to Sĕlok Hill again. Again I was shocked. The government had asserted its authority and the forest had reappeared. A neat, roofed entry gate with a ticket office now straddled the road. Behind it saplings were stacked in pots ready for planting. Most were fast-growing tropical trees: *kĕtapang* almond trees, *kĕdawung* and *kĕdoyå* trees, plus a few slower growing mahogany and teak trees. There were also fruit trees: mango, *kĕmiri*, *pĕtai* and *sukun*. Official-looking roadside signs frowned in the face of visitors:

**No Felling of Trees**
**No Fires**
**No Hunting**
**Assemble Here in Case of Evacuation**

As I walked up a twisting asphalt road into the new forest it looked healthy. The trees were thin and ropey but there were plenty of them. They rose from the undergrowth like the skinny legs of a teenager. Birds were chirping in the tousled canopy. In places the trees on my left and right were already knitting their branches over the road. I passed two young men leaning against a motorbike on the leaf-strewn roadside. They didn't hear me slip pass just metres behind them. Both were staring into the foliage above them. Catapults were dangling from their hands.

A kilometre into the reserve I reached a turn-off leading to the Sanctuary of the Five Betel Trees. A roadside split gate led to another entryway guarded by two brightly painted, well-fanged *naga* snakes. Their scaly bodies flanked a ramp-like path crowded with day-trippers shuffling up to the tree-capped crest of the hill. I looked left down the hillside and saw the old Temple of Mountain and Sea. It was locked-up, its windows shuttered. It had been abandoned.

But at the far end of the ramp an extraordinary new sanctuary was emerging from the chirping leaves of the forest. At its centre stood a tall, red-brick, Balinese-style ceremonial gate. Beyond it a slow staccato of hammering and sawing rose from behind piles of sand, bamboo scaffolding and broken planks of wood. The new temple stood squat and spacious, a Javanese-style *pĕndhåpå* under a *joglo* roof of wooden shingles. Inside, across a marble-tiled floor, sat a golden image of the Buddha on a raised dais. The Sanctuary of the Five Betel Trees had morphed into a *vihara*, a centre of Buddhist devotions.

The new sanctuary had adopted the old name, *Puri Giri Sagårå*, which was embossed over the gateway in Roman-Latin script, not the beautiful but out-dated *hånåcåråkå* letters of the old sanctuary. It was striving to project an image of openness and modernity. In two places near the *vihara* the words of Albert Einstein were displayed on big placards in English with an Indonesian translation.

The religion of the future will be a cosmic religion. It should transcend a personal God and avoid dogmas and theology. Covering both the natural and the spiritual, it should be based on a religious sense arising from the experience of all things, natural and spiritual, as a meaningful unity. Buddhism answers this description.

The old sanctuary, with its images of Ratu Kidul and Sěmar, had not been forgotten. The curvaceous queen of the southern ocean now had her own shrine under the trees, with her plaster image emerging from colourfully painted waves. As in the painting of her in the old *Puri Giri Sagârâ*, she was wearing an emerald green, off-the-shoulder, *kěmběn* bodice and a tall crown. Ornamental golden ribbons entwined her body like vines. To the left and right of the shrine four white horses were frozen in play, romping over one another with looks of child-like delight on their cartoonish faces. A big banner beside the shrine drew the eye to an image of President Soekarno (in office 1945 – 1966), his face contorted with manic vehemence as he yelled his vision of modern Indonesia.

"The essence of independent Indonesia ...
Politically sovereign!
Economically self-supporting!
Culturally true to its own self!"

I walked on to the shrine of the clown-god Sěmar. There he stood, a bizarre sight on an ochre-coloured pedestal in a small *pěndhâpâ* pavilion. He was naked from the waist up, his half-female breasts bulging over a paunchy stomach and carefully painted batik sarong. His right hand was extended with an index finger pointing

towards visitors. His face looked old, his gaze half mischievous
half melancholy. A single white tooth protruded from his slightly
rouged lips. His hair was grey and a lei of flowers ringed his neck.

Not far from Sěmar's shrine a huge banner portrayed him
leading his three clown sons – Nålågarèng, Pètruk and Bagong –
across a panorama of skyscrapers symbolising modern Indonesia.
Several Javanese-language slogans marched with them along the
top of the banner:

FORWARD WE GO UNITED

HARMONY BRINGS PROSPERITY

LET'S OVERCOME OBSTACLES TOGETHER TO DEVELOP THE NATION.

Not far away, another banner drew on Java's rich store of
clichéd wisdom.

BE ASSURED, THE GOOD YOU DO WILL BE NOTICED ... AND THE EVIL TOO!
YOU HARVEST IT? YOU PLANT IT! YOU USE IT? YOU MAKE IT!

I looked around. As far as I could see there were no Islamic
places of worship. No mosque, no prayer room, no holy grave. But
the visitors were almost 100% Muslim. The ambience was relaxed
and friendly. *Hijab*-scarved girls peered into the pavilions, young
men wearing the embroidered skull-caps of faithful Muslims posed
for photos leaning on the guardian lions in front of the entry gate.
On a tiled platform in Sěmar's shrine people had left a crowd of
items to be charged – like mobile phones – with the clown-god's
power. There was a big dish of apples, glasses of tea, a packet
of Oreo biscuits, bottles of water. As I stood at the shrine, two

well-dressed middle-aged men approached. They were wearing expensive batik shirts and *taqiyah* caps. They slipped off their patent-leather sandals and stepped onto the tiled platform of the shrine. Each carefully placed an open packet of cooked rice and vegetables among the clown-god's offerings. It was their lunch. They would return in an hour to collect their meals – now spiced with the condiment of power – and eat.

Sělok Forest, with its new-born complex of religious buildings, was no longer the preserve of solitary spiritual searchers. It had become a tourist attraction, a weekend excursion for the prosperous middle-class of Cilacap. From the new *Puri Giri Sagårå* there were panoramic views over the coastline and, in the distance, the smokestacks of Cilacap's industrial estate. A cluster of *hijab*-clad teenage girls teetered on the edge of a special viewing platform, hugging each other, laughing, pulling faces, and taking selfies against the green and blue of the vista.

I sat down among them, my feet dangling over the edge of the platform. Amid the chatter I recalled my twilight conversation with Pak Marji, the custodian of Ketonggo Forest, a few weeks earlier.

"Many dangers threaten Indonesia," he had said. "But the Righteous King Èrucåkrå will emerge from the forest to save us. His name tells it all. It has two components. *Cåkrå* means "a wheel" like the great ever-turning wheel of life. It also means "the centre of things". And Èru comes from *hèra-hèruning jagad* or *hèra-hèruning bawånå* meaning "the turbulence of the world" – its unpredictable natural events, its earthquakes, its storms, its inevitable social conflicts too. So the Righteous King will be at the centre of the future's turbulence. Èrucåkrå will bring us the true Islam. He will guide us between the teeth of life's great harrow, and when we emerge we will be seeds that will sprout in the soil of the future."

"What is the true Islam?" I asked.

His answer was instantaneous and fluent, as if he had rehearsed it and spoken it many times.

"A few months ago a community leader from Kediri came here to meditate. He got an inspiring message from The Almighty instructing him to mix the soil of Medina with the soil of Ketonggo ... in other words, to blend Middle Eastern Islam with Javanese culture. This will produce beautifully mixed, very fertile soil. Ketonggo is not just Java, it represents the whole of Indonesia. There are many holy spots in Ketonggo Forest, around twenty-two, I think. Like Indonesia, there is room in the forest for all faiths and all kinds of people. If the soil of Medina and the soil of Ketonggo can be blended it will quickly make all the islands of Indonesia (he used the ancient name Nuswāntårå) peaceful, prosperous and law-abiding."

Pak Marji had peered into the gathering dusk at the adjacent High Seat of Srigati. Inside the simple shrine a dull light was shining and I could see the shadows of petitioners sitting heads bowed before the living crust of earth.

# Between mosque and holy tomb

## OF MASS MURDER, SAFE HAVENS, MAKING MONEY, AND THE NEW MOBILITY OF WOMEN

Half-a-dozen times over the last twenty years I have paid my respects to Sunan Bayat whose tomb is on Jabalkat Hill in the township of Bayat near Klaten, Central Java. At the foot of the hill, amid a jumble of scruffy shops and a *joglo*-roofed reception pavilion, the local government operates a box-office, but only half-heartedly. Entry is absurdly cheap, the equivalent of less than ten US cents. Pilgrims who come in groups march right past while their leader makes a nominal payment for everyone. On a couple of visits I found the booth unattended so I was able to glide by and get in for free.

A steep flight of 250 concrete steps leads up the hillside towards the saint's mausoleum. Left and right small shops feed off the passing torrent of visitors. At the top people leave their shoes in a special room and head barefoot – sometimes hobbling over the scorching concrete pathways – into the complex proper. In a verandah on the left they pause to record their names in the key-keeper's guest book lying open on a shin-high table. A donation is slipped between the pages of the book, but again, if you are a member of a group, your leader will do this on your behalf.

A winding path leads through a succession of walled yards filled with trees, flowering bushes and tombstones. Several of the walls are breached by ancient Balinese-style gateways open at the top. Built around five hundred years ago from rusty-coloured bricks they are decorated with stylised wings and animal heads, bas-relief whorls and diamonds, and jutting up-turned corners stacked in tiers up to the tapering, five-metre high peaks of their twin pillars. In Javanese the generic term for these gates is *candhi běntar*, split temples. Their form suggests an old-style temple-monument that has been chopped down the middle with a giant cleaver and the two halves moved apart leaving their smooth inner surfaces facing each other.

From a terrace around the hilltop mausoleum visitors look out over a murmuring vista of coconut trees filled with smoke haze and weather-darkened tiled roofs. A narrow door leads into the simple but solid mausoleum called the Diamond House (*Gědhong Intěn*). The saint's tomb is concealed under a cube-like canopy of satin in the centre of the devotions floor. A door, just big enough to crawl through, gives access to the eerie gloom of the inner sanctum where the holy grave lies.

On my last visit in 2015 the Diamond House was packed. I elbowed my way in through a mass of pilgrims choking the vice of the outer doorway. In the devotions area I tried to squat-walk into a space against the perimeter wall but I was spotted and pulled through the seated crowd to the drapes hanging over the saint's grave. The *tahlil* chant broke out. Stacked hard against me, the crowd tilted me left and right in rhythm with the chant. The holy words seemed to flow and drown in their own momentum. Eyes were shut fast, bowed heads swayed, a neighbouring hand tapped its knee in time with the rhythm, an Arabic prayer book slumped unnoticed to the floor, a young woman wound her prayer beads tight into her fingers. The chant was relaxed but strong, like insistent waves surging in a sea cave. It lasted well over half an hour: *La ilaha ilallah, La ilaha ilallah, La ilaha ilallah, La ilaha ilallah*... History, faith, place, devotions and the heat of dense-packed humanity came together in one gently quaking body. It drew me deep into a community. I was no longer a tall, fair-skinned outsider who, as a matter of courtesy, got a priority place at the saint's side. I became an unnoticed voice among many, a vibration in a chorus. Sure, I was uncomfortable bolted to the floor, sweating in the intense heat, but inwardly I felt profoundly comfortable.

The *tahlil* chant faded, faces relaxed, and everyone rose to their feet. I too struggled to my feet grimacing as I stretched my legs. The two ladies next to me covered their mouths and giggled in sympathy. The crowd spilled from the burial chamber, carrying me with them into the muggy air of mid afternoon. I looked back at the mausoleum door. To my astonishment women were emerging into the sunlight with tears glistening on their cheeks. As they descended the narrow, steep flight of steps several lifted the corners of their *hijab* scarves to wipe their faces.

"Why are they crying?" I whispered to a *pèci*-capped young man with a razor-sharp moustache stencilled along his upper lip.

"Women are emotional," he said, looking embarrassed. "When they come to a holy grave they are reminded of the dead, and of funerals past. So they feel sad."

As the crowd jostled down the steps some paused to ladle up a drink of water from two pot-bellied stone urns. The urns are irradiated by the saint's great power, so the water is sweet and spiritually refreshing. In the shadows flanking one of the lower exit doors many were pressing bank notes into the hands of two tomb functionaries sitting cross-legged left and right of the door.

At the bottom of Jabalkat Hill around thirty people – men and women – wheeled off and sauntered down the access-street and through a side alley to a mosque sitting atop a tall, solid retaining wall beside the main road through town. It was the Golo Mosque, one of the oldest in Java.

The building is small with a spartan whitewashed interior and just two tiers in its pyramid roof, but it seems to have a special place in the hearts of worshippers who enjoy the simple, friendly embrace of its walls. Some say a jinn by the name of Muhammad Harun keeps an affectionate eye on it. He has been known to pick up worshippers careless enough to fall asleep and whisk them out into the yard, gently depositing them – still asleep – under a tree.

They also say the mosque was originally built on the spine of Jabalkat Hill high above its current location. Its call to prayer boomed across the countryside deafening worshippers at the Grand Mosque in Demak, one hundred kilometres to the north. To make matters worse its lights dazzled them. The Sultan of Demak was offended that a hillbilly saint should show off in this way. When Sunan Bayat heard that the Sultan was upset he ordered his followers to shift the mosque to a less conspicuous site. As they dragged the building down to its present location it scored a track in the hillside that is still visible today (so I was told, but I couldn't see it myself).

After the intensity of devotions in the mausoleum I needed the cool of the mosque to help me gather my thoughts. Other pilgrims were looking forward to its steadying ambience too. They performed their pre-prayer *wudhu* wash in rooms just below the mosque entrance. *Rukuh* prayer smocks appeared from women's handbags. The crowd slipped off their sandals and headed into the tight confines of the prayer chamber.

I found a quiet spot on the carpeted floor at the rear and looked around. In classic Javanese style, the pyramid peak of the roof rested on four solid wooden beams that reached up into a central vault where the dark, plain rafters converged into a focal point like spokes at the hub of a wheel. There were no glass panes in the small windows, only iron bars and wooden shutters. Some bare, high-efficiency LED lights were concessions to modernity, plus a couple of fans rotating slow-motion in the roof cavity.

Before me about twenty men stood in two neat rows facing the low, domed *mihrab* niche that points west to Mecca. Beside me, at the rear of the chamber about a dozen women were also standing, hair hidden under the hoods of their white and pastel-coloured *rukuh* smocks. The congregation bowed their heads in unison, their arms folded over their midriff. Their hands rose, palms forward, to frame the face. With practised fluidity they bent forward, hands braced on their knees. They straightened and bent again, then each knelt, pressed their palms into the floor and crouched forward. For long seconds their foreheads lay pressed against the carpet. Each rose to a sitting position, stood up, and repeated the whole sequence. Then again twice more. After the four cycles (the number stipulated for the mid-afternoon '*aṣr* prayer) they remained seated. Their hands rose and wiped their faces. Their heads turned left and right, wishing peace on those beside them.

Approaching five o'clock the sky turned overcast. A silky dimness filled the corners of the prayer chamber. The congregation dispersed to buses chugging in the parking lot up the street. A fine rain began to fall with a muffled hiss. The thin beep of a car horn drifted in with the ting-a-ling of a bicycle bell and the faint shouts of children. I was alone, and the Golo Mosque wrapped its stillness around me.

In my mind's eye I tried to make sense of what I had just seen – the ragged intensity of devotions in the saint's tomb and the cool, but no less intense, discipline of *ṣalat* prayer in the mosque. As in many parts of the Islamic world (but not everywhere), in Java mosque and holy tomb represent contrasting extremities of religious ideology. In some respects, and at certain tense times, they can even be antagonists. Yet at Bayat a party of men and women had strolled across the divide between the Diamond House and the Golo Mosque, apparently without injury to their religious sensibilities.

They walked between two places that, on the face of it, are very different. The mosque is the home of unconditional surrender to the authority of Allah and His words as preserved in the verbatim accuracy of the Holy Qur'ān. The mosque echoes, sometimes thunders, with the authority of broad-ranging religious law known as *shari'a*, underpinned by the Qur'ān and the Prophet's models of right behaviour as reported in *hadith* stories. It also frames the authority of leaders like the *imam*, the *khatib*, the *modin*, the *ulama* and the *kyai*, and, behind them, the authority of the Muslim community as a whole, the *ummah*.

At the holy tomb it is local saints, local place, local history and local community that are paramount. There is no single, central authority or tradition. Of course, the "scriptures" of local pilgrimage incorporate the canon of Middle Eastern orthodoxy, but they sprawl far beyond it. They differ from place to place in genres, styles, heroes and moral messages. There are adaptations of popular stories from the Middle East and India, but equally up-front are local folk tales, accounts of dreams, personal anecdotes (especially verificatory narratives that testify to the power of a saint or site), *wayang* stories, folk etymologies and much more. Anthropologist Robert Hefner has aptly described this corpus of texts as "unfinished, open, and additive rather than fixed, exclusive and scripturalist".

A host of symbols and practices buttress the ideological walls between mosque and holy tomb. The mosque, for example, replicates the main features of the *pĕndhâpâ*, the spacious, open-sided reception pavilion at the front of public buildings and traditional houses in Java. The *pĕndhâpâ* – like the mosque – is a public gathering-place, open to the street and the outside world. Hierarchy, order and formal etiquette rule. The holy tomb, on the other hand, aligns itself with the interior of the Javanese house, in particular with the bedroom. In fact a holy tomb is called a *pasaréyan*, a sleeping place or bed. Most tombs even adopt the form of a bed with a cube-like cloth canopy hanging from a square frame above it, like an old-fashioned four-poster with its mosquito net.

The mosque is bright and airy. Its main ritual event is the *Jumatan* or *Ṣalat Jumat*, the obligatory (for men) devotional gathering held around midday every Friday. At the holy tomb, the burial chamber is usually enclosed and often quite dim. It is a private, even intimate, space. Being a "bedroom" the most ritually important events take place there at night.

*Ṣalat* prayer at the mosque is oriented outward. It flows overseas along *qibla* lines to the Ka'bah in distant Mecca, the centre-point of Islam. *Ṣalat* prayers take place at precisely determined times fixed from day to day down to the exact minute when each prayer should start. *Ṣalat* is conducted with regimented discipline and is invariable. Worshippers stand in neat *shaf* rows often marked in boxes or lines on the floor of the mosque. They move in unison behind an *imam* who leads the prayer from the front. Movements are carefully prescribed, even the positioning of hands, fingers and feet are calibrated in precise detail.

The holy tomb invites worshippers to look in the opposite direction. Prayer is directed inward, addressing local saints, whether as figures with supernatural powers in their own right or as intermediaries between humankind and Allah. Worshippers sit cross-legged in ragged circles around the grave with constant coming and going. There is considerable variation in the form, content, intensity and length of devotions. There may be multiple groups of pilgrims paying their respects at the same time, each under a different leader. They generate a babble of simultaneous prayer, with colliding recitations of Quranic verses, *tahlil* chants, and even singing.

The mosque is uncompromisingly masculine. Women and men are strictly segregated. Women follow prayers behind their menfolk, or from the side of the prayer chamber, often behind a fence or screen. Almost always there are many more men than women performing *ṣalat* prayer. Women must wear a *rukuh* (also called a *mukena*), a hooded smock that covers the entire body except for hands, face and feet. With rare exceptions, there are no female mosque functionaries – *imam*, *takmir* or *modin*.

The holy tomb couldn't be more different. Women have a high profile there. It is as feminine and domestic as the mosque is masculine and public. Research is needed on the relative numbers of male and female devotees but it is my impression women often outnumber men, especially in daylight hours. As in the mosque, devotions are almost always led by men, but behind them women and men mix indiscriminately. Women dress modestly (as men do), but I have never seen a woman wearing a *rukuh* smock in a holy tomb. They normally wear a headscarf of some kind, a long-sleeved shirt or blouse, and a sarong, kaftan or long pants, but it is also not unusual to see women wearing western-style street clothes without a head covering. Some bring small children into the burial chamber, even babes-in-arms. At a small number of holy tombs there are female key-keepers who may lead pilgrim visitors in devotions at the saint's graveside. There are even female saints, though not as many or as widely prestigious as their male counterparts.

A culture of gifts and favours dominates at holy tombs: gifts of offerings and recited verses, or favours asked of the resident saint. Devotions are often called *ngalap bĕrkah*, to pick up a favour, to grab a blessing. Some see the culture of gifts and favours as transactional: the devotee "strikes a bargain" with the saint or with Allah, undertaking to make payment in some form if a favour is granted. Requests may be candidly self-interested and materialistic, but as often as not they are vague and rather modest, asking simply for *slamĕt*, a clear run in life. In many places devotees pay their respects by making flower offerings, burning incense or sprinkling perfume. To most orthodox Muslims, trying to negotiate a deal with Allah – putting Allah under a contractual obligation – is blasphemous. Burning incense, scattering flower petals and "charging" bottles of water too are repugnant acts, or at best primitive. They would be sacrilegious in the austere surrounds of mosque or prayer house.

Robert Hefner sees parallels between the mosque-tomb axis and the spectrum that lies between two roughly defined and roughly contrasting Islamic sub-cultures in Java, *santri* and *abangan*. The Islamist *santri* ("pious students" also sometimes called *kaum putihan* or "whites") emphasise purity, exclusivism and scripture-based authority. Contrasting with them, the *abangan* ("reds") are heterodox, syncretic and relatively tolerant of diversity.

The Javanese themselves have used the terms *santri* and *abangan* since the nineteenth century. The distinction was given international currency by Clifford Geertz in his super-influential study, *The Religion of Java*, published in 1960. According to Geertz, the *santri* variant finds its home in market culture. *Santri* Muslims take seriously their five religious obligations: reciting the declaration of faith (*Kalimah Shahādah*), performing *ṣalat* prayer five times a day, putting aside alms for the poor, fasting in daylight hours during the month of Ramadhan, and making the hajj pilgrimage to the Holy Land if possible. *Santri* pay careful attention to Islamic law, dress, food, and ritual occasions, not to mention Middle Eastern derived arts and Islamic education, including study of Arabic.

The *abangan* tradition, on the other hand, is a syncretic variant of Islam centred in Java's village neighbourhoods. It revolves around a communal meal called a *slamĕtan* (that which rescues you and makes you safe) and incorporates an extensive range of spirit beliefs, curing, sorcery and magic. Although they call themselves Muslims, the *abangan* (says Geertz) are famously indifferent to the niceties of *ṣalat* prayer, fasting, dietary prohibitions, dress and other features of Islam that elsewhere are regarded as obligatory.

The holy tomb is central to the *abangan* variant, says Hefner. Rather than organising religious life around mosques as places for religious study and congregational worship

"... the spaces sacralised in *abangan* communities were those that served as points of passage to a supernatural world seen as not distant and otherworldly but accessible from the world of the living. [...] These could, without too much artifice, be assimilated to the status of a Sufi *kramat* or *punden*, a burial place for venerating the soul of a deceased Muslim saint.

Notice the past tense "were". According to Hefner, in the late decades of the twentieth century some facets of *abangan* culture collapsed, particularly its public, "institutionalised" variants centred on the ritual veneration of guardian spirits and highly visible annual celebrations. It is a view echoed with varying degrees of emphasis by many Indonesian and foreign observers.

Most agree that just half a century ago some two thirds of ethnic Javanese were followers of *abangan* Islam. It is difficult to confirm this with reliable data, but in his study *Islamisation and its Opponents*, historian Merle Ricklefs has tried. Using election results and figures on alms-giving, he estimates that in the mid 1950s at least 60% of people in Central and East Java were *abangan*. In certain places the figure went as high as 90%. Observant *santri* were on the fringes of the Muslim community, accounting for less than 10% of the population overall, though in a few places they might have reached as high as 40%.

Now a new scholarly consensus has emerged. In the early decades of the twenty-first century, *santri* and *abangan* have swapped profiles like the opposite ends of a tilting seesaw. Javanese Muslims have abandoned their *abangan* leanings and have avalanched into observant orthodoxy.

Perhaps history has repeated itself. In the 1520s, after centuries of glacially growing contact with its Muslim minority, Java reached a tipping point and its colourful, diverse Hindu-Buddhist majority crashed (not wholly, but mostly) into the arms of Islam. Fast forward almost five hundred years to the late twentieth century and again Java left behind a dominating heritage of diversity to adopt a new, more strictly defined, more internationally oriented religious order that had once been the preserve of a minority.

A veritable gusher of adjectives has poured into descriptions of the newly dominant order: orthodox, conservative, strict, standard, doctrinaire, observant, fundamentalist, legalistic, purist, scripturalist, literalist, dogmatic, exclusivist, *dakwah*-ist, Islamist. At its extreme edge it is called radical, intolerant, fanatical, hardline, *salafi, jihadi, wahhabi.*

Researchers have struggled to stiffen this imperfectly understood development with the starch of hard data. Again, Merle Ricklefs leads the way. He reports that in 1956 just 1706 Muslims from the province of Central Java undertook the hajj pilgrimage to the Holy Land, a coveted badge of *santri* piety. In 2010 this had jumped to 29,435 with a further 80,000 forced onto a waiting list because of Saudi restrictions on pilgrim numbers. Beginning in the 1980s a frenzy of mosque building broke out. In Central Java, for example, more than thirteen thousand new mosques were built between 1980 and 1992, almost doubling the total number in the province in just twelve years. In the early years of the twenty-first century Indonesian researchers were reporting that 90% or more of Javanese Muslims now performed the *ṣalat* prayer five times a day, and were strictly observing the Fast during the holy month of Ramadhan. An increasing percentage of women took to wearing *hijab* headscarfs and other items of specifically Islamic apparel.

On the face of it, a dramatic reversal of religious polarities has taken place. But why? It goes without saying, the answer is complex. It involves rising living standards, urbanisation, improved education, liberalisation of opportunities to argue the case for fundamentalist – even extremist – religious views, the internationalisation of Indonesian Islam, the massive impact of orthodox piety in the new mass media of the internet and mobile phones, and much more.

But behind the complexity looms a single ghastly ancestor: the savage anti-left pogrom that followed an attempted coup by left-wing army officers on October 1ˢᵗ, 1965. Anti-communist army units in concert with Muslim militias and vigilantes set out on a coldly organised frenzy of killing. At least half a million innocent people were murdered, most of them in Java and Bali. Suspected communists were the main targets, but for many in the electrically charged atmosphere of the time, communists and *abangan* were one and the same. As Robert Hefner accurately reports, "the intensity of religious passion, and the perception in *santri* circles that some *abangan* had declared war on Islam, contributed to the intensity of the violence".

The pogrom came after twenty years of independence. In this period religion had become fiercely politicised. Rival interests sought moral and symbolic authority, plus the brute muscle of supporter numbers, in the powerful currents of Islam. It was a high-stakes contest that, in Java, inflamed the differences between *santri* and *abangan*. Left-leaning parties – the Indonesian Communist Party (*PKI*) and the Indonesian National Party (*PNI*) – aligned themselves with *abangan* Muslims, while right-leaning parties aligned themselves with *santri* and their mass organisations like Nahdlatul Ulama (*NU*) and Muhammadiyah.

The trauma of the slaughter ran deep and is still palpable today. More than anything, simple fear was responsible for the slump in public allegiance to *abangan* culture. Many survivors sought refuge in other religions. Between 1966 and 1976 almost two million ethnic Javanese, most from *abangan* backgrounds, fled into Christianity. Another 250,000 to 400,000 converted to Hinduism. At the same time an intensive, government-backed campaign began to "Islamise" Muslims whose piety might have been tainted by the alleged ignorance and slack practices of "abanganism".

Religious education was seen as a bulwark against the reappearance of communism, and this is where the campaign was most concentrated. Islam was beefed up as a subject of study in state schools. Non-state *madrasah* schools were coordinated with the state system and modernised. Most traditional *pĕsantrèn* boarding schools were also modernised. Tertiary level academies of Islamic studies opened in most provincial capitals, and by the early years of the twenty-first century many had been turned into fully-fledged Islamic universities. The new *madrasahs*, *pĕsantrèns* and tertiary institutions were administered by the Ministry of Religion which now became a shadow provider of education, operating alongside the essentially secular Ministry of Education and Culture.

Today Islamic schools and Islamic studies programs are overflowing with students. Other signs of the new public piety can be seen everywhere: gleaming mosques on every second street corner, jam-packed gatherings on Islamic holy days, disciplined participation in the annual Fast, many hundreds of thousands on waiting lists for the annual hajj pilgrimage, heightened reverence for *ulama* scholars, enthusiastic attendance at scripture reading and prayer gatherings, prestigious local and national Qur'ān reading contests, a small army of celebrity preachers, enthusiasm for Islamic dress (for many Muslim women the *hijab* scarf – also called *jilbab* in Indonesia – is now *de rigueur* across the country), bookshops crammed with thousands of titles on Islam, *muamalat* banks operating according to sharia law, casual but studied use of pious-sounding Arabic in greetings ...

For journalists, especially easily stampeded foreign journalists, it is Islam's new public militancy that most dramatically trumpets the arrival of the transformed order. One event in particular has become an iconic case study: the electoral defeat in 2017 of

Jakarta's energetic and effective Chinese-Christian governor Basuki Tjahaja Purnama – known by the nickname Ahok – and his jailing on a charge of blasphemy.

On December 2nd, 2016 between half a million and a million Muslims held a peaceful but in-your-face demonstration in the streets of central Jakarta. It was, some said, the biggest street demonstration in the history of Indonesia. The demonstrators were overwhelmingly male, clad in the white of religious virtue. There were small squads of white-robed women too, many taking care of refreshments for their male counterparts. The crowd yelled a simple demand: arrest Ahok. They brandished banners charging him with blasphemy against Islam, besmirching the Qur'ān, belittling Muslim scholars, and insulting the Muslim community. They called their demonstration "Action in Defence of Islam". President Joko Widodo, a political ally and friend of Ahok, felt he could not ignore the massive gathering. He emerged from the nearby presidential palace and joined the Islamist leaders of the demonstration. He listened to their speeches and joined them in prayers. The event was a loud public statement that fundamentalist piety was now a force to be reckoned with in Indonesia's religious, social and political mainstream.

Ahok's alleged blasphemy occurred in an electioneering speech to a small audience on a tiny offshore island. The "blasphemy" lasted about two seconds and nobody noticed it at the time. But the speech was recorded on video and picked up by a tech-savvy supporter of his political adversaries. He snipped and edited it to misrepresent Ahok, then re-posted it online. The perpetrator, a certain Buni Yani, was later convicted of "spreading hate speech" and sentenced to eighteen months in prison, but the conviction came much too late to save Ahok.

The doctored video went viral. The Indonesian Council of Muslim Scholars (*MUI*) – the country's peak authority on Islamic law and practice – lumbered into action, prodded, so it is rumoured, by Ahok's rivals in the gubernatorial race. It issued an "opinion" and "statement of religious attitude" that fell short of a fully fledged *fatwa* but was made to look official. The "opinion" went beyond the immediate issue of Ahok's alleged blasphemy to make a partisan point relevant to the up-coming election. It claimed that verse 51 in the Qur'ān's fifth Surah, Al-Mā'ida, explicitly debars Muslims from accepting a Jew or Christian as their leader. Muslim-majority communities had to elect Muslim leaders, it said, and *ulama* were obliged to tell their congregations as much.

It was a crude but classic expression of fundamentalist purity and exclusivism. It caught the attention of opportunists who were promoting radical Islamist agendas. Among them were organisations supporting the restoration of the caliphate, the implementation of sharia law, and the establishment of an Islamic state in Indonesia. Some insisted that the pronouncements of the Council of Muslim Scholars had, or should have, the force of law.

Ahok was brought before a hastily convened court where he pleaded his innocence but also apologised. That's the custom in Indonesia, even when you're not in the wrong. You apologise to your accusers as a gesture of respect and conciliation. But it cut no ice with his Islamist tormenters. He was sent to jail for two years, and lost the election decisively.

Ahok's spectacular fall was a setback for religious tolerance, but it wasn't a disaster. There is an interesting twist in the tail of his story that alerts us to a counterforce now challenging the narrowness of Islam's neo-orthodoxy.

In the months leading up to the Jakarta election Ahok fought hard for the support of Muslim voters. He reached out to the people of north Jakarta by making at least three visits to the holy tomb of Mbah Priok, the Muslim saint of the Koja Container Terminal (see Chapter Six). On each visit he was greeted with open arms and ushered into the burial chamber where he paid his respects at the saint's graveside. Ahok confirmed that his government would designate the holy tomb a "cultural sanctuary" and would help fund a massive expansion of the site. It would become an international centre of religious tourism, he promised.

When the results of the election came in, north Jakarta was the only precinct in the Special Region of the Capital where votes for Ahok managed to match those for his victorious rival, Anies Baswedan, whose campaign had been given momentum by Islamist allies.

Ahok's warm reception at Mbah Priok's tomb may have been a matter of nuts-and-bolts self-interest for him and for the tomb's custodians. But not entirely. It was also a sincere statement of religious inclusivism, contrasting starkly with the rejection of him by Islamist forces in the community at large. It was a reminder that across Java, far beyond the mosques and public spaces of Jakarta, holy tombs reach out to embrace all comers, including Chinese-Indonesians like Ahok. At least eight busy Muslim pilgrimage sites host the remains of saintly Chinese, and extend a special welcome to Chinese visitors whether they are Muslims or not. They range from the tomb of Sunan Gunung Jati in Cirebon (the saint's wife was Chinese), to the tomb of the Chinese-Muslim artist Kyai Tĕlingsing in Kudus, and the money-spinning twin tombs of the Chinese Éyang Jugo and his adopted Muslim-Javanese son Iman Sujono high on the slopes of Mount Kawi in East Java (see Chapter Nine).

In the Gedong Batu temple complex in Semarang lies the tomb of The Honourable Helmsman, Kyai Juru Mudi, a Chinese-Muslim who – the story goes – came to Java some time in the early 1400s in a massive fleet of junks under the command of the great admiral Zheng He (Cheng Ho), also a Muslim. Today he lies under the upturned eaves of his own dazzling-red, Chinese-style mausoleum. The Islamic grave is oriented north-south so The Honourable Helmsman can lie comfortably on his side looking west towards Mecca. It is flanked by outer and inner devotions areas. Facing outward onto the teeming public pathways of the Gedong Batu complex, the grave is a focus of Chinese-style devotions. As joss sticks smoke in big brass bowls, Chinese visitors stand with hands clenched together in a single fist before their faces, paying their respects to a Chinese ancestor. Through a door at one end of the grave lies an inner devotions area. Here Muslims sit cross-legged in the subdued light offering gifts of Al-Fātiḥah to The Honourable Helmsman, their Muslim ancestor.

The counterforces of diversity and tolerance embedded in the veneration of local saints can be tracked in statistics. In 2006 an Australian student, David Armstrong, was given permission to rummage through the records of the East Java Archaeological Service. He was looking for figures on tourist numbers at archaeological ruins in the province, but in the process he turned up something interesting for our understanding of religious change in Java. Over the previous two decades visitor numbers at holy tombs administered by the Archaeological Service had risen by 873 percent, from a total of less than half a million in 1988 to three and a half million in 2005.

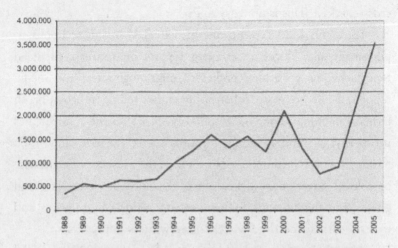

Visits to holy tombs in East Java Province, 1988 – 2005
[Armstrong 2006: 64]

He dug up figures for particular places. One of them was the tomb of Maulana Malik Ibrahim in the centre of Gresik near Surabaya. It hosted 1,556,651 visitors in 2005, up from 128,905 in 1988, a more than 10-fold increase. Visits to the tomb of Sunan Bonang in Tuban rose from 117,270 in 1988 to 618,047 in 2005, and visits to the tomb of Sunan Drajat, located halfway between Tuban and Surabaya, rose from 26,381 in 1988 to 696,858 in 2005. In the most dramatic increase, visits to the tomb of Ibrahim Asmorokondi, just east of Tuban, rose from 11,886 in 1988 to 467,896 in 2005, close to a 40-fold increase.

A decade on, and in 2014 the Indonesian Ministry of Tourism reported that 12.2 million people had visited the tombs of the Nine Saints in that year. The Ministry estimated this number would grow to around eighteen million a year by 2019. Credible? The relentless upward trend in visitor numbers makes it so, I think, but to be certain, statistical sources need to be diversified, localised and cross-checked. This is not easy to do.

The main local repositories of statistics are guest books at pilgrimage sites, local government reports on tourism, financial reports by the governing bodies of pilgrimage sites, and media reports. There are many other pointers that tell us in broad-brush terms something about the popularity of a site: the number and prosperity of vendors doing business there, the size of a site's parking lot and the number of buses in it, the presence or otherwise of a local government ticket office, the number of beggars and guides, the claims made by key-keepers, reports by pilgrims and tour operators, and the researcher's eyewitness impressions.

When I visited the Grand Mosque in Demak in 2000, custodial staff told me that in 1987 a total of 341,385 people had visited the mosque with its adjacent holy graves, but by 2000 this had jumped to 606,918 people. A million visitors a year were claimed for the tomb of Sunan Gunung Jati in Cirebon in 1997. When I visited the site in 2002, staff assured me visitor numbers were far above the 1997 figure. One sober website (managed by the Tenth of November Institute of Technology, Surabaya) reports that an average of 2,000 people a day visit the tomb of Sunan Ampel in Surabaya, rising to 4,000 a day during the first three weeks of Ramadhan, and between 10,000 and 20,000 a day in the final week of the Fasting Month. Added up, these figures produce an annual total of around 860,000 visits.

According to the Indonesian government's national Antara News Agency, Sunan Bonang's tomb in Tuban averages around 2,000 visits a day, but in the three months leading to Ramadhan this more than doubles. Another news website reports that an average of 7,000 people a day visit the tomb in the long holiday period of December and January. Mashing these rough-and-ready figures produces a total of 985,000 annual visits to Sunan Bonang's tomb, a remarkable figure given that Tuban is well away from the beaten track of arterial transport.

Indonesia's fourth president, Abdurrahman Wahid (popularly known as Gus Dur, in office 1999 – 2001) died in 2009. Today his tomb in Jombang, East Java has shot into the top rank of popular pilgrimage sites. It hosts at least 3,000 pilgrims a day, rising to 10,000 a day in the lead-up to the annual Fast. According to one carefully researched report it attracted 1,235,746 visitors in 2015. Only five years previously his tomb did not exist at all.

These are not piffling numbers. They are rubbery and patchy, sure, but they are not the aspirational fantasies of bureaucrats and key-keepers. They come from diverse sources that *in toto* add up to compelling evidence that the ancient practice of saint veneration and local pilgrimage is booming.

The banning of the Indonesian Communist Party in 1966, plus the destruction of peasants' organisations and trade unions, removed the main public institutions *abangan* had relied on for patronage and protection. In 1973 the last remaining political party tolerant of *abangan* culture, the centre-left Indonesian National Party, was neutered. The Soeharto government frog-marched it into a coalition with other non-Islamist parties that it called (with no hint of irony) the Indonesian Democratic Party. Cowed and cut adrift, *abangan* Muslims reached out to the more standard devotional practices promoted mainly through the education system, the mass media and mass religious organisations. By the 1980s observers had begun to notice a "conservative turn" in Indonesian Islam. As the East Java Archaeological Service figures show, almost simultaneously with the conservative turn, visitation to Java's pilgrimage sites began to climb.

I suppose we have to be cautious about inferring a cause-and-effect connection between the rise of observant piety and the parallel rise of pilgrimage to places that host a variety of non-standard devotional practices. Nevertheless it is striking that the two developments seem to have started at about the same time, and as the move into orthodox piety has gathered momentum pilgrim numbers have kept pace, even sky-rocketed. I think it is plausible that, for ex-*abangan* Javanese, holy tombs have become safe havens – institutions that fill a vacuum and offer protection to those whose devotional styles don't square with the rigid demands of orthodoxy.

Sacred places have cachet in Java, as they have throughout the vast expanse of the Austronesian world. In Javanese tradition, the history of a place begins with the clearing of the forest (*mbabad alas*). This creates a clearing, a safe haven that people can migrate into in the midst of a threatening wilderness. Safe havens are not just points in a landscape, they are origin points in history created by a revered and powerful ancestor-author – the *cikal-bakal* or *lĕluhur*. The story of a community, indeed its entire cultural capital, becomes attached to a place or places. To put it another way, certain places trigger memories that store the identity, knowledge and history of a community. This gives place a strong grip on people's minds that persists even into the rootlessness of the present. Some argue that modern mobility detaches people from place and weakens the authority of place-based knowledge. But mobility doesn't necessarily mean deracination. On the contrary, it can give better access to a greater number of places, thereby increasing the authority, diversity and accessibility of place-centred knowledge.

Many Islamic sites in Java – Bayat for example – are built in places that have been supernaturally charged since pre-Islamic times. A protective aura of ancient power still clings to them. They are Islamic, but filled with the power of pre-Islamic antiquity. For some this offers a reassuring umbrella of protection under which – with variation from site-to-site – *abangan* practices can survive, even flourish. Straight-laced *santri* Muslims have tended to see them as nests of idolatry and backwardness fated to disappear into the pages of history and not worth more than disdainful irritation. In this they are wrong, as the current spike in local pilgrimage is demonstrating.

But like a sceptical *santri*, I need a little more than the rhetoric of anthropology and a few statistics to convince me that holy tombs are a counter-force to the mosque. Luckily there are other sources of evidence, and they speak loud and clear. Take, for example, the burgeoning commercialisation of local pilgrimage.

As living standards rise and Indonesia's development juggernaut gathers speed, the pilgrimage business is keeping pace, generating new waves of pilgrims. A generally rising level of disposable income is making travel more affordable, especially for Java's massive rural population. Better infrastructure has smoothed the way – hotels, lodging houses, restaurants and eateries clustered around pilgrimage sites; well maintained asphalt roads to remote places; modern transport services.

A very profitable services sector has appeared calling itself pilgrimage tourism (*wisata ziarah*), also religious tourism (*wisata religi*), spiritual tourism (*wisata spiritual*), and even (this is a bizarre touch) sharia tourism (*wisata syari'a*). Most pilgrims are now whisked from tomb to tomb by chartered bus. Many trips are organised at village level by local clerics, officials or schoolteachers. Each pilgrim in a party pays a contribution towards meals, the hire of buses and accommodation, perhaps even buying souvenir bags and jackets. For tours on a shoestring, food may be the responsibility of each individual and pilgrims will sleep in the bus, in a mosque (where it is allowed), or in a rest pavilion at a pilgrimage site.

Tour operators also offer pilgrimage packages tailored to the tastes of the urban middle-class who expect their travel to be well organised and comfortable, even luxurious. Java Tours of Surabaya, for example, offers a "Nine Saints of Islam Pilgrimage Tour" lasting six days and five nights. Travelling in an air-conditioned bus, pilgrims start out from Surabaya, staying overnight in Tuban, Kudus and Cirebon. The tour takes in each of the tombs of the Nine Saints, with a stop to shop for batik in Pekalongan. The tour includes accommodation in three-star hotels, all meals, entry tickets, baggage handling and the services of a guide. For groups of fifteen or more, the cost is US$206 per person twin share.

Pilgrimage tourism has attracted government attention. For local governments it can be a source of revenue. The district government of Gresik, for example, has poured money into celebrating the birthday of Maulana Malik Ibrahim, the saint whose tomb lies just off the *alun-alun* square in the centre of town. The Birthday Funfair (*Gebyar Maulid*) highlights the traditional Islamic arts of Gresik —especially the drumming known as *bĕduk tètèr* — and promotes the sale of local goods. A similar strategy is in place in Demak, where the district government has invested heavily in revenue-generating celebrations linked to the holy graves at the Great Mosque and the mausoleum of Sunan Kalijågå. In Kudus the annual Replacing of the Cowl over the saint's grave (*Grĕbĕg Ganti Luwur*) attracts many thousands of visitors. It has become an important tourist attraction and source of revenue for the Kudus district government.

Speaking at a workshop in 2015, Minister for Tourism, Arif

Yahya, stressed the Indonesian government's view that local pilgrimage must go beyond the spiritual and generate economic value for people who live around holy tombs. Management of religious tourism must be professional, he said. He committed his government to an investment of nine trillion rupiah (around US$600,000) for immediate improvements to the tombs of the Nine Saints.

Haji Abdul Kadir, 54, is a typical small-scale *wisata ziarah* entrepreneur and guide. I met him in a crowded corridor at the tomb of Sunan Muriå, high on the slopes of Mount Muriå in Central Java. He is an ethnic Madurese from a village near Jember, East Java. He wears trendy tinted glasses, a white collarless jacket, a checked sarong, and a white *taqiyuh* skull cap. He makes a lucrative living. It has given him enough income, he says, to visit the Holy Land twice, once on the hajj pilgrimage and once with his wife on an *umroh* visit.

Haji Abdul Kadir carries a loudhailer and uses it liberally as he shepherds fifty-eight pilgrims into the reception area of Sunan Muriå's mausoleum. He does around a dozen trips a year, he says, usually taking just one busload, but sometimes two or three, occasionally more. Inside the saint's mausoleum, he wields a long, flat stick, tapping on the shoulders and backs of his charges to keep them moving through the clogged passages and walkways around the grave. Outside, he ushers his party to a counter where bottles and plastic cans are filled with water from the site's holy well. The water comes, says Haji Abdul Kadir matter-of-factly, direct from the Zamzam well in Mecca.

Haji Abdul Kadir is lucky, he has managed to do the hajj pilgrimage. This gives him authority that he exploits to take local pilgrims to local sites. It also sets him apart from a huge number of fellow Indonesians who yearn to do the hajj and can afford to do it, but are stuck in a queue managed by the Department of Religion. Unable to accommodate all hajj aspirants, the government of Saudi Arabia has imposed a quota that, for Indonesia, translates to a little over 200,000 pilgrims a year during the six days of the hajj season. In 2017 more than two million people across Indonesia had registered for the hajj, and waiting time in the queue had blown out to an average of seventeen years. Some of the impatient faithful take the *umroh* option, making devotional visits to the Holy Land outside the traditionally sanctioned hajj season in the month of Dzulhijjah. Many more assuage their longing, at least temporarily, with visits to local holy places in Java.

There is a surprising change in the composition of pilgrim groups. It is not unusual to see large parties that are predominantly female, though almost always they are chaperoned by a male leader. I don't know of any rigorously compiled statistics on the gender distribution of pilgrims but the evidence of the eye is undeniable: women are gravitating to tombs in unprecedented numbers.

Rising prosperity has given the women of Java more mobility than at any time in the past. They pursue educational opportunities far beyond their villages and suburban kampungs. They work in factories and domestic service, chase opportunities in the professions, visit dispersed families, zip from place to place on their motorbikes, drive cars and commute alone on trains, migrate to other parts of Indonesia, and sign up for contract work overseas. In all these domains they must struggle against the constraints Islamic culture tends place on female independence and mobility.

For many women – village women in particular – pilgrimage to a holy tomb offers a practical way around these constraints. It gives them the protection of devotional piety as they venture into an exotic wider world in company with other women. For many there is appeal in the intimacy of sacred sites and the perception that the saint is a community member, even perhaps a family member. For some, tombs offer an ambience that is more comfortably female-friendly than that of the male-dominated mosque with its male-dominated devotional culture.

Women crowd the devotions floor at the tomb
of Sunan Gunung Jati in Cirebon

One morning in 2016, at the tomb of Indonesia's fourth president Abdurrahman Wahid (better known as Gus Dur) in Jombang, East Java, I found myself sitting with a party of about fifty pilgrims, thirty of them women. They were wearing bright yellow t-shirts with the words *Ziarah Wali Songo* (Nine Saints Pilgrimage) stamped across the back above their place of origin, the Hibbatullah Mosque in Bangkalan on the neighbouring island of Madura.

394 GEORGE QUINN

As they wound up their devotions I managed a whispered conversation with Ibu Latif, aged around 35. She laboured to her feet, smoothing down her Nine Saints t-shirt and tugging wearily at the tassels on her lilac *hijab* headscarf.

"On this trip we are visiting all nine tombs in just six days," she said. "We've been on the road four days now and so far we've been to five tombs, plus the Grand Mosque in Demak. At night we sleep on the bus, we wash in mosques, we eat wherever we can."

She rolled her eyes.

"I wish … I just wish we could stop somewhere long enough to take in the atmosphere and really say our prayers properly. I mean, slowly. But there's never enough time."

The middle-aged male leader of the party was beckoning. She turned to go but paused politely as I asked,

"Do you think Gus Dur is a *wali* like the Nine Saints? The tenth saint?"

"Oh yes," she said emphatically. "It was only after he died that his sainthood became clear. People say his body can never decay. So he is still here."

She was looking anxiously at the exit gate but managed a brief, proud smile.

"In Bangkalan we have a saint of our own – Kyai Kholil – who was the teacher of Gus Dur's grandfather. So we feel a special connection with Gus Dur. He is like a spiritual descendant of our own learned leader. He belongs to us as much as we belong to him."

It is almost a cliché of conversations about pilgrimage that strict *santri* Muslims – members of the modernist Muhammadiyah movement, for example – never go to holy graves. I don't think that was ever entirely true, and it certainly is not true now. Observant

Muslims are now flocking to local pilgrimage sites, though it is not possible to quantify their presence with rigorous statistics. Some come from the ranks of sufi orders, study groups (*majlis taklim*), and chanting groups (*majlis dhikr*). Mainstream devotions in holy tombs – *tahlil* chants, *ṣalawat* songs, Quranic recitations – are familiar territory for members of these groups. *Majlis dhikr*, for example, chant *dhikr* phrases and fragments of text in Arabic, often with complex contrapuntal rhythmic embellishments. Devotions like this segue into those of regular pilgrims and make holy tombs a comfortable home for members of these esoteric but popular groups.

Sometimes *dhikr* and *tahlil* devotions can be emotional (as I saw at the tomb of Sunan Bayat). Julia Howell, a specialist in Indonesian sufism and new manifestations of religiosity, has noticed this. Discussing the current popularity of sufi orders, she notes:

> ... the expunging of devotions suspected of not being in conformity with the Qur'ān and Hadiths, have for many resulted in a desiccation of their faith. Eschewing idolatrous local customs, people find themselves left with empty formalism: prayers said, poor-tax paid, hajj undertaken, but simply in compliance with imposed requirements.

The director of post-graduate studies at an Islamic university – putting aside for a revealing moment his commitment to hard-hearted objectivity – puts it like this:

"The tears that flow at the tombs of the Nine Saints are a sign that we weak servants of Allah can do no more than pray to Him and plead for His help. Emotion wells up in our hearts, and shame, because we know we cannot match our saints' determination to fight hard for Islam in Java and throughout Nusantara."

Local pilgrimage, some say, recharges the batteries of those
sated with devotions in mosques. One study group – the Majlis
Taklim Al-Khasanah from a village near Blora – makes local
pilgrimage a regular part of their devotional exercises.

The Al-Khasanah *majlis taklim* group goes on religious
pilgrimages to holy tombs to combat the boredom
(*kebosanan*) members feel when they attend devotional
events at mosques. On a pilgrimage they acquire new
energy, spiritual and physical.

Push and pull factors are at work here. Frustration at the
interminable wait for a place on the hajj pilgrimage, the quest for
new markets and bigger profits in the spiritual tourism business,
and the search for relief from the tedium of mosque based devotions
– these factors are "pushing" observant Muslims into local holy
places. At the same time there are "pull" factors. Pilgrimage sites
are becoming more welcoming for *santri* Muslims wary of irregular
or blasphemous behaviour. In appearance, devotions and stories,
the old *abangan* style of sacred sites is adapting to the priorities of
a new generation of conservative pilgrims.

*Abangan*-style devotions haven't been replaced altogether, far
from it, but they are being altered, in places radically, elsewhere
subtly. Wall signs and tomb décor that promote devotional
orthodoxy are proliferating. The names of Allah and Muhammad
together with verses from the Qur'ān appear in bold Arabic lettering
on the walls of burial chambers. Other signs warn against impious
behaviour. Wagging fingers are everywhere. The most common
danger (as it has always been) is idolatry, especially prayers of

praise and pleas for help addressed to a deceased person rather than to Allah. Other signs enjoin pilgrims to be dressed in sober *Islami* fashion, to be orderly and quiet, to be serious, to be mindful of death.

**WARNING!!!**
Many people have gone astray because they hope to get blessings from the tomb, like the blessing of:
√ (magic) knowledge
√ wealth
√ personal magnetism
√ favours from someone
√ help from God
√ rank

So make the tomb a place to:
**Think about death and pray for the person buried**
God willing, you will have a smooth run in this world and the next. Amen.

Visitors must report [to the key-keeper]

A newly installed warning sign at the tomb of Jåkå Tingkir, Butuh, near Solo.

A few sites have constructed their *cungkup* frames in the form of a mini Ka'bah, with drapes resembling the Ka'bah's *kiswah* cowling, and flourishes of Quranic text in beautiful Arabic script along the upper edge reminiscent of the Ka'bah. Some sites have even been labelled "Meccas in the islands of Nusantara", drawing attention to their roles as focal points of local "*qibla*". Ka'bah-like tombs allow *santri* pilgrims to relinquish their attachment to the straight, *shaf*-like rows of the mosque with men and women strictly segregated, and sit comfortably in a circular *tawāf*-like formation – men mixing with women – in imitation of worshippers at the Ka'bah.

But the outward display of orthodox respectability almost always hides an inner eccentricity. This is neatly illustrated at the tomb of Sheikh Jumadil Kubro in Semarang. The saint's grave was renovated in 2004, key-keeper Pak Afwan told me. Each day, as the renovation proceeded, he measured the length of the grave, and each day he found it had miraculously grown a little longer. When the work was completed the new grave had become a "long grave" (*kubur panjang*) around eight metres in length, or three times its original length.[22] Today the miracle has been contained, almost literally, in the attributes of orthodox piety. A wooden paling fence now encloses the stretched grave. The tip of each paling is attractively carved with one of the ninety-nine Beautiful Names of Allah, the '*Asmā ul-Ḥusnā*, which many pious Muslims strive to learn by heart.

Devotions too are being "regularised". More and more sites are banning or discouraging dubious *abangan*-style practices like burning incense, scattering flower petals, charging bottles of water, and gobbling down food in on-site *slamĕtan* meals. Some tombs are becoming venues for devotional gatherings that are normally conducted in public places or in mosques. Take, for example, the

---

22  Some powerful figures from Islam's legendary past are thought to have been tall. Possibly this memorialises their origins among the physically bigger people of the Middle East. At the Semarang tomb of Sheikh Jumadil Kubro, I was told that the saint was "tall like you" (*jangkung kados panjĕnĕngan*, I am around 194 cm in height) and the grave was made long to physically accommodate him.

annual commemoration of Sheikh Jumadi Kubro's death at his "other" resting place in Troloyo, near Mojokerto, East Java (not his Semarang grave). In the past the commemoration has been dominated by *dhikr* recitations and *tahlil* chanting in the spacious burial chamber, followed by a colourful procession through the streets of Troloyo. The climax has been a *rĕbutan* ritual in which crowds of local people attack the procession, tearing it apart and grabbing its food and other ritually sanctified items. The riotous *rĕbutan* remains important (it is now promoted as an exotic tourist attraction), but since around 2000 the annual commemoration has been augmented with a suite of devotional events that are ritually orthodox, even rather humdrum. They include mass reading of the Qur'ān by hundreds of white-clad young men and women, reading of the Qur'ān from beginning to end by a relay of readers, and a *pengajian umum* – a mass prayer event with readings from the Qur'ān and homilies by guest speakers, interspersed with *dhikr* and *tahlil* chanting.

The stories of pilgrimage are changing too. In Chapter Nine, I mentioned the partial displacement of tales about the Chinese saint Éyang Jugo by tales of his Muslim "incarnation" Kyai Zakaria at the Mount Kawi pilgrimage site. Another striking example is the emerging sanctification of Indonesia's fourth president, Gus Dur. The late president is seen by some as a modern incarnation of the Prophet Khiḍr, the legendary "green one" of Islamic story. Khiḍr is popular throughout the Muslim world as a spiritual guide. His story is told (without actually naming him) in Surah 18 Al-Kahf verses 65 – 82 of the Qur'ān. Since 2000, at least twenty new books about Khiḍr have been published in the Indonesian language, some of them highlighting anew his connections with the saints of Java, particularly with Sunan Kalijågå. Of special interest is *Sunan*

*Gus Dur. Akrobat politik ala Nabi Khidir* (His Grace Gus Dur. A political acrobat in the same mould as the Prophet Khiḍr, 2011) by M. Mas'ud Adnan. The author draws on the Quranic story to argue that Gus Dur's political manoeuvring, his unpredictability, his eccentricity and his habit of triggering controversy all establish him as a modern Khiḍr who "engaged in political acrobatics as the Prophet Khiḍr did". Gus Dur's tomb is one of the most visited in Java. He is venerated as a devout Muslim, a political and religious activist, and president of the Republic. And now, thanks to the popularity and authority of stories about the Prophet Khiḍr, he is being redefined in terms of Islamic narrative and reconstructed as an Indonesian saint in the same mould as the Middle Eastern Khiḍr.

The up-and-coming saint Gus Dur – the pious, tolerant, Machiavellian polymath who became president of Indonesia – embodies the convergence that is being forged between, on the one hand, politically powerful, orthodox piety with its high public profile, and on the other hand the enduring charisma of Java's diverse local traditions. It is a convergence that protects rather than displaces these local traditions. And it is being exported beyond Java on powerful currents of commerce. Bali, Lombok and South Sulawesi each now hosts seven newly-invigorated Muslim pilgrimage sites that attract visitors from well beyond their immediate provincial surrounds. In Java, the tombs of female saints are growing rapidly in popularity. They are packed with women (and their children) but increasingly are drawing menfolk too. Some, like the tombs of Radèn Ajĕng Kartini (Bulu, south of Rembang, Central Java) and Cut Nyak Dien (Sumedang, West Java) have political functions. Kartini represents the hopes and the failures of government-endorsed feminism, while Cut Nyak Dien's tomb is like an uneasy Acehnese embassy in the heart of Java-dominated Indonesia.

Keeping a wary eye on these developments, the central government and the local governments of Java continue to tolerate and protect pilgrimage sites, even investing in them. Perhaps (and this demands more research) official support for the deeply-rooted practice of saint veneration and local pilgrimage is part of a strategy to counter the dangers of internationally inspired Islamic extremism.

Meanwhile, the pious Muslims of Java stand in *shaf* rows in mosques and bend west towards Mecca in *ṣalat* prayer. Behind most mosques – immediately to the west – lie the graves of the faithful. Many of the saints who speak from the pages of this book (but far from all!) sleep in tombs behind a mosque. Sunan Kalijågå, Sunan Bonang, Sunan Ampèl, the revered patriarchs of Demak, Éyang Jugo and Iman Sujono, Jumadil Kubro, Mbah Priok, Wasil Syamsuddin ... all the unruly company bequeathed to the twenty-first century by the Javanese past rest in graves on the *qibla* lines of orthodoxy, basking in the devotional attention of worshippers in an adjacent mosque. As we have seen, some started out as murderers and thieves. Others were harmless and benign, or merely eccentric. But in the context of today's religious dynamics, all of them are outlaws, low-profile presences just outside the laws of rigid orthodoxy. In the tangled Sherwood of Java's cultural interior they wait in ambush, a stubborn challenge to the well-armed soldiers of fundamentalism.

Seated against the back wall of the Golo Mosque in Bayat, I looked to my right at what used to be known as the Prophet's Door (*Pintu Rasul*). It had once been blocked off with a low fence, but now the fence was gone, the door was wide open and the doorway had been repainted. Anyone at all could use it. Blinking through horn-rimmed glasses, a young man explained.

"One of our mosque functionaries had a dream that the Prophet wanted to join us for prayers on Fridays, so as a gesture of respect we gave the Prophet exclusive use of his own doorway. It has been there for years. Nobody else could use it. But recently the mosque committee decided to cancel its special status. A door exclusively for the Prophet? That was not rational, they said. And anyway, the Golo Mosque is now heritage-protected. You are no longer allowed to add bits and pieces, like a fence across a doorway for example."

At Bayat, signs of "santrification" are starting to appear, even inside the saint's tomb. On previous visits I noticed many pilgrims carrying flower offerings into the burial chamber. Now this is discouraged ... not banned, but discouraged. When flower petals appear on the tiled floor, they are quickly swept up. High on the interior walls automatic air-fresheners shoot puffs of flowery scent into the chamber. "We don't need petals any more," said a bright-eyed teenager, smiling proudly under the visor of her *hijab* scarf as if the only function of flower offerings was to sweeten the air. And outside, down the short flight of steep steps below the burial chamber, in a small ante-room that had once been reserved for the burning of incense, a CCTV camera kept watch. There would be no more fire and smoke and mumbled prayers in front of an incense furnace.

I was reminded of an incident a few weeks before at the Ampel Mosque in Surabaya. I was standing before an ancient streetside stone gate that marks one of the entry points to the mosque. I stepped under its massive, top-heavy lintel and stood looking into a shopping alley that tapered away under a narrow, arched roof into an interior I couldn't see.

It was a scaled-down but lively likeness of a Middle Eastern *souk*. Left and right two dense lines of shops spilled their goods into a crowded corridor. Much of the merchandise was the apparatus of Islamic identity and devotions. Prayer mats, filmy head-scarves and checked sarongs hung like a profusion of medieval banners above each stall. Bottles of perfume glittered in gaudy ranks, packets of dates clambered up from the floor in crooked pillars, *peci* fez-caps lay on counters like mounds of black bread. There were religious books too, with small X-shaped folding lecterns for reading them. And garish calendars, pictures of saints, prayer beads and special wall clocks to remind the faithful of prayer times. Presiding over mini-grandstands of merchandise many of the shopkeepers had hawkish features that betrayed an Arab ancestry.

It was slow going as I weaved through the dense crowd of pilgrim shoppers. Women wearing pastel coloured headscarves and flowing kaftans browsed the stands of Islamic apparel, or rummaged among purses, or looked up to finger prayer beads hanging like bunches of grapes above them. Children stood before kaleidoscopes of plastic toys tugging at their parents' hands and pointing at balloons. An elderly gentleman – spectacular in loose black pants, black collarless shirt and a snowy white skull cap – pulled aside his wispy beard as he crouched over a table sipping a glass of tea. A soft light made it through the curved glass of the overhead vault. Here and there the softness was slashed by shafts of sun that picked out the whiteness of a pilgrim's shirt or the oil glistening on a tray of tennis-ball pastries.

At the far end of the alley a massive, lime-green roofed gate ushered me into the more airy world of Java. Opposite the gate stood the solid immensity of the Ampel Mosque, capable, so it is claimed, of accommodating more than five thousand worshippers. The roof was a shallow-sloping three-tiered pyramid in traditional *joglo* style. A minaret protruded like a slightly tapering lighthouse from the western side of the roof. Possibly at one time the minaret stood outside the mosque but the building had been renovated and extended so many times the roof now lapped around the tower and enclosed its base.

I left my sandals on the verandah, walked quietly into the mosque, and slid to the floor against an internal pillar. I had come during an interval between regular prayer times, and the broad gleaming floor was almost empty. But this time, as I took in the hushed ambience and the tiny creaks and echoes of the chamber, I had an unpleasant surprise. A young man appeared from behind a pillar and squatted abruptly beside me. He was dressed simply: a white *taqiyah* skull cap, a plain white shirt and dark, carefully creased trousers.

"Are you a Muslim?" he said in Indonesian without preliminaries and without a smile or outstretched hand.

"No, I'm just a visitor."

"Well, I must ask you to leave."

"Why?"

"You are not a Muslim."

"But I have been here before. Several times, in fact. And I have always been welcome."

"This is a holy place. We must keep it unpolluted. You will have to leave."

I thought his choice of the word "unpolluted" (*suci*) was indelicate, but I didn't argue. Outside I faced the young man and tried to look puzzled.

"Where is the mosque office?"

"I will take you there," he said, his hostility suddenly replaced with politeness.

It was a single tiny room opposite the entrance that brought visitors in from the shopping alley. There I was introduced to an older man, a senior mosque attendant or *takmir*. His black *peci* cap leaned over his forehead as he confirmed the rule.

"Yes," he said, looking defensive. "Non-Muslims are not allowed into the mosque. It is a holy place."

"I am interested in mosque architecture," I said. "Do you have any printed information or photographs I can take away with me?"

He looked shiftily around the room and lifted a dog-eared calendar off the wall.

"There are pictures of the mosque in this."

"Wonderful. Can I buy a copy?"

"No. This is our last one, we want to keep it. But you're welcome to look at it."

The calendar was several years old. Its single picture of the mosque's interior was blotched with fly specks and coffee stains. I stared at it meekly.

"Hmmm. Interesting. What about the grave of Sunan Ampel? Can I go there and pay my respects?"

The tension vanished. A toothy smile struggled through the bristles of the *takmir's* moustache. He waved his hand dismissively.

"Of course! No problem. Let me take you there."

A few moments later he delivered me into a broad enclosure to the west of the mosque where the grave lay. I sank to the ground in a roofed shelter against the perimeter wall. The mosque official disappeared and I looked around. The saint's simple grave, beside that of his wife, lay open to the sky in a small square plot surrounded by a stainless steel fence in the middle of the compound. Around it, amid ranks of stubby headstones, more than a hundred pilgrims

– men and women – were sitting with bowed, swaying heads. At the saint's grave they sat pressed against the fence, gripping its bars and peering in. The murmur of prayers and subdued *tahlil* chants hung in the air.

As I savoured the atmosphere I thought about what had just happened. On the face of it, the mosque and holy graves at Ampel had been side-swiped by the struggle between fundamentalist purity and *abangan*-tinged eclecticism. At least for the moment, the mosque was to be a tiny echo of Mecca and Medina, the forbidden cities in Islam's holy heart (forbidden, that is, to unbelievers). But perhaps it had always been thus. When Dutch theologian and prolific writer Francois Valentijn visited the mosque in 1706 he reported that it was "very big and, in their opinion, very magnificent, but no unbeliever, even if he washed his feet in the stone water trough, was allowed to enter." So the prohibition at Ampel may be a long-standing one, though as I discovered on previous visits, it had not always been strictly enforced.

Perhaps, I thought, I should have paid more attention to the grave of Mbah Solèh on the other side of the mosque. According to tradition Mbah Solèh was a simple man who lived in the time of Sunan Ampèl. He dedicated himself to the saint by keeping the mosque clean. After his death he was buried outside its northeast corner. One day Sunan Ampèl noticed the mosque was not as clean as it had once been, and he wished that Mbah Solèh were still alive. Thanks to the power of the saint's words, at that instant Mbah Solèh materialised and resumed work sweeping and cleaning. The mosque regained its old sparkle. After a time he again died and was buried beside his previous burial place. Again the mosque lost its sparkle, again the saint wished that Mbah Solèh were still alive, and again he returned to life. In fact he died and was returned to life a total of eight times. When Sunan Ampèl himself died, Mbah Solèh was alive, but when he too later died (for the ninth time) there was no saint to revive him and he stayed dead.

Mbah Solèh's remarkable resting place is in fact nine burial slabs, each with two headstones, that lie one beside the other like a bar code. Eight of them are empty, but the two headstones on the ninth, where the remains of the faithful retainer lie, are respectfully wrapped in white cotton. For those who know the story (and that means almost everyone who enters the mosque precinct) the grave is an icon that signals "Be Humble, Be Pious, Be Clean". Unfortunately I had walked past it too quickly as I entered the mosque and had not heard the ancient admonition that still speaks from it loud and clear.

But the adjacent cemetery? Its holy graves with their cheerfully diverse devotions and clientele had been dismissed by mosque staff as not pure enough to be worth protecting from the intrusion of a non-Muslim. Nevertheless some feeble gestures were being made in the direction of orthodoxy. At the entrance to the burial ground signs tried to separate male visitors from female, and in the cemetery enclosure itself a length of cloth tied to a low fence was supposed to keep the sexes apart. But male and female pilgrims sat intermingled. The bonds of family and common company were far stronger than the wedges of orthodox regulation.

After my visit to Sunan Ampèl's grave I left the complex and walked back down the shopping arcade. Halfway along I stopped at a small eatery for a snack. Seeing me seated alone the manager joined me. He was young and thin. A lick of dark hair emerged like a brush-stroke from under his white *taqiyah* cap. As he pushed the lock back from his eyes I saw a dark red circle gleaming on the skin in the centre of his forehead. It was the mark left by piety, a souvenir of the hundred thousand times he had pressed his forehead hard into the floor during the prostration of *ṣalat* prayer.

He asked me what I thought of the Ampel Mosque. I told him I had been asked to leave before I could really take it in. For a moment he stared, then he was on his feet, anger bulging in his eyes.

"Come with me!" he shouted.

He gripped my arm and yanked it.

"You are coming with me to the mosque as my guest! Right now!"

I protested, but he wouldn't listen. Holding fast to my arm he led me back past the merchandise-stuffed stalls, through the lime-green entrance gate, past the mosque office with the *takmir* staring glassily at us from the doorway, past Mbah Solèh's immaculately clean row of graves, and into the hushed magnificence of the mosque. We folded ourselves to the floor and sat cross-legged.

The interior was dramatic. Supporting the roof, a quartet of teak beams rose seventeen metres from the polished marble floor into a square central vault. Around them twelve fatter pillars were arranged in an outer square, each resting on a squat, polished stone plinth. High up, two levels of crossbeams extended horizontally from pillar to pillar. Each beam, whether upright or horizontal, was made from a single giant teak trunk. The overall effect was of a spacious interior patterned in a variety of rectangular and triangular planes formed by the criss-crossing of strong, dark, interior scaffolding. The whole space was washed with delicate natural light from a band of windows in the roof and from the many arched doors in the perimeter walls. It was a masterpiece of old-style Javanese architecture.

We sat side-by-side for half an hour, companions in silence, dissolving slowly into the quiet ambience that breathed stories from every pillar and tile.

# Acknowledgements

Many generous hearts have buoyed me during the long preparation of this book. I owe a special word of thanks to the key-keepers at the pilgrimage sites of Java and Madura who, without exception, made me feel welcome and were lavish in their responses to my questions. Warmest *panuwun* to Bapak Afwan (Makam Jumadil Kubro, Semarang), Bapak Amir (Makam Wasil Syamsudin, Kediri), Bapak Fodli (Makam Mbah Panggung, Tegal), Habib Ali Alaydrus (Makam Mbah Priok, Jakarta), Bapak Hadi Suparto (Pasareyan Nyai Agĕng Bagĕlèn, Purworejo), Bapak Heri Suworo (Pundhen Ki Boncolono, Kediri), Ibu Kardikem (Pundhen Mbah Båndhå, Bero, Klaten), Bapak Marji and Bapak Gunarto (Alas Ketonggo, Ngawi), Bapak Mohammad Lazim (Makam Sunan Bonang, Tuban), Bapak Nanang Yuwono Hadi Projo (Makam Éyang Jugo and Iman Sujono, Gunung Kawi), Ibu Sidem (Makam Ki Agĕng Balak, Bekonang), Bapak Sugeng (Makam Sunan Pojok, Blora), Bapak Sukarmen (Pamuksan Sri Aji Jåyåbåyå, Kediri), and Bapak Zainal Ilyas (Asta Tinggi, Sumenep).

During visits to pilgrimage sites I enjoyed the company and insider knowledge of Ahmad Muriadi (Mbah Karimah, Surabaya), Azzam Anwar (Kyai Nur Iman, Mlangi), Dwi Elyono (Alas Ketonggo, Ngawi), Iwan Dzulvan Amir (Makam Mbah Priok, Jakarta), Nur Lailatur Rofiah (Makam Sunan Giri and Makam Nyi Agĕng Pinatih, Gresik), Nyoman Riasa (Makam Keramat Karang Rupit, Temukus, Bali), Paul Stange (Gua Langse, Parangtritis),

Puspo Endah (Pundhen Ki Boncolono, Kediri), Rizal Abdi (Makam Sunan Pandanaran, Bayat), Suprapti (Gunung Kawi, Malang) and Taufiq Urrohim (Makam Sunan Pandanaran, Bayat). I owe a special debt of gratitude to two companions in particular. Dr Tommy Christomy of the University of Indonesia accompanied me on visits to the Makam Sheikh Abdul Muhyi in Pamijahan, Makam Cut Nyak Dien in Sumedang, Room 308 (Kamar Nyai Rårå Kidul) at the Samudra Beach Hotel in Pelabuhan Ratu, Makam Nike Ardilla in Ciamis, Makam Godog in Garut, Situ Lengkong Panjalu south of Ciamis, and the tombs of Sultan Maulana Yusuf and Sultan Hasanudin in Banten Lama. Ibu Dr Daru Winarti of Gadjah Mada University was my long-suffering and very helpful companion on visits to Bayat, Gunung Srandil and Gunung Selok near Cilacap, Gunung Tidar in Magelang, Makam Nyi Agěng Serang south of Muntilan, Makam Mbah Dalhar and Raden Santri at Gunung Pring in Muntilan, Makam Sunan Geseng in the village of Tirto near Magelang, the Pamuksan Sri Aji Jåyåbåyå near Kediri, Makam Wasil Syamsudin in Kediri, Makam Tambak south of Kediri, Makam Mbah Prawiro Purbo in Jogjakarta, and the burned out home of Mbah Maridjan in Kinahrejo and his grave at Srunen on the slopes of Mount Merapi.

Many academic colleagues were generous with their advice and encouragement, and patient with my shortcomings. I am particularly grateful for the feedback and support of colleagues at the Australian National University: Syamsul Rijal, Kathy Robinson, Campbell McKnight, Amrih Widodo, Greg Fealy, Tony Reid, France Meyer, Ronit Ricci and Jim Fox. A very special word of thanks to Emeritus Professor Virginia Hooker, who overlooked my tortoise-like progress and gave me patient, very valued support.

*Makasih Mbak Nia!* Further afield I have benefited from the advice of Minako Sakai, Willem van der Molen, Stuart Robson, Merle Ricklefs, Bob Hefner, Martin Slama, Tom Hogarth, Sumit Mandal and Iqbal Nurul Azhar.

I am indebted to Professor Stuart Robson for extracts from his English translation of the Old Javanese *Rāmāyaṇa* quoted in Chapter 10, and Professor Peter Carey for his translation of an extract from Prince Dipånagårå's *Babad Dipånagårå* also quoted in Chapter 10. Karina Pelling of the CartoGIS cartography service in the ANU's College of Asia and the Pacific prepared the maps quickly and accurately. Thanks Karina. I spent a lot of time in Menzies Library at the ANU, the National Library of Australia, Fisher Library at the University of Sydney, and the library of the Koninklijk Instituut voor Taal-, Land- en Volkenkunde in Leiden, Netherlands. Huge thanks to these often taken-for-granted institutions!

My ragged manuscript improved thanks to the advice of Lliane Clarke and Kit Carstairs and many others who read fragments of it or attended my seminars at the ANU. Thanks also to Philip Tatham of Monsoon Books, and my agent Thomas Nung Atasana of the Borobudur Agency, Jakarta, for their unfailing support and professionalism, and especially for alerting me to many unsuspected challenges of writing communicatively about history and religion in a little-known corner of the world.

In the early stages of this project, funded in part with a small grant from the Australian Research Council, my wife Emmy prepared digests of hundreds of newspaper and magazine reports on sacred places. She also accompanied me on visits to several sites (most memorably to Luar Batang in Jakarta) and patiently answered my innumerable questions on language matters. She proofread the entire manuscript, reading parts of it over and over. Her advice was sometimes blunt, often revelatory, and always invaluable. This book would not have been possible without her. *Kamsia*, Mie!

None of the above bear responsibility for the final outcome of my research. I know some will disagree with my findings and my style of reporting them. *Nyuwun ngapuntĕn*. Needless to say, only I am responsible for the mistakes and shortcomings of the book.

# Sources and sites

Many tributaries of information and analysis feed into this book. Conversations with key-keepers and countless pilgrims, plus my own eyewitness observations, were the sources of much that it reports. A big variety of written sources were also crucial, including accounts of sainthood in guidebooks sold at pilgrimage sites, and hagiographic stories told and retold in websites, newspapers and popular magazines. Scholarly studies were equally important, many of them recent, but some going back to Dutch colonial times.

For general and contextual studies on Javanese religion and particular pilgrimage sites visit this book's website at www.saintsofjava. net. Sources that I cited or consulted directly, including the sources of direct quotes, are detailed in narrative form under their relevant chapter headings below.


## The Holy Qur'ān

Certain verses from the Qur'ān are important to the practice of pilgrimage in Java and are often cited or recited by pilgrims and key-keepers. In this book I quote the following: **Surah 1 Al Fātiḥah (The Opening)** The short first book of the Qur'ān is often said to encapsulate the essence of Allah's message. It is normally recited at holy tombs as a "gift" to the deceased. **Surah 2 Al Baqarah (The Cow) verses 143-144** These verses establish Muslims as a single community of faith, an Islamic "nation" distinguishing themselves from non-Muslims by facing the Sacred Mosque in Mecca when performing ṣalat prayers. **Surah 2 Al Baqarah (The Cow) verse 255** The sonorous Throne Verse is so-called for its reference to the heavens and the earth as the limitless "seat" of Allah. It is one of the most popular verses recited in devotions at holy tombs. **Surah 5 Al Mā'idah (The Table) verse 35** This verse mentions the key term wasīlah "the means of access" (to Allah). This is conventionally taken to mean good works and obedience to the will of Allah. But in the rhetoric of sainthood wasīlah is also understood to be an intermediary – the Prophet or a saint – who intercedes to help one approach Allah. **Surah 5 Al Mā'idah (The Table) verse 51** This verse was the basis for the campaign to unseat incumbent governor of Jakarta Basuki Tjahaja Purnama (Ahok) in the election for governor in 2017. **Surah 7 Al A'rāf (The Ramparts) verses 63-64 and 77-78** Quranic verses describing natural disasters have special impact in Indonesia where catastrophic disasters – volcanic eruptions, earthquakes, tsunamis – are relatively common. Some pilgrimage sites play a role in memorialising natural disasters and linking them to expressions of piety. **Surah 17 Al Isra' (The Night Journey) verse 59** The book is also called Bani Isrā'il, the Children of Israel. It makes reference to the authority of divinely bestowed signs, an important concept in the culture of pilgrimage and sainthood. They include warning signs, signs of Allah's greatness, signs of Allah's presence in the world, and *patilasan* or "traces" of a saint's presence or visit. **Surah 18 Al Kahf (The Cave) verses 65-82** Tells the story of the encounter between the Prophet Musa (Moses) and a mysterious figure known in the Qur'ān as "One of Our Servants". Tradition has named him Khiḍr, also "The Green One". In Indonesia the Prophet Khiḍr appears in folk stories, including stories involving local saints. **Surah 21 Al Anbiya' (The Prophets) verses 68-69** In these verses the story is told of the prophet Ibrahim who was saved from death when Allah intervened to cool the fire of execution burning around him. This echoes other stories well known in Java in which fire is a purifying element. **Surah 24 Al Nūr (The Light) verse 30** which admonishes Muslim males to respect women by lowering their gaze and "guarding their modesty". **Surah 35 Fātir (The Originator) verse 29** Holy tombs are invariably centres of commerce. Almost everywhere, alms boxes (*kotak sĕdĕkah*) invite pilgrims to make charitable donations. The key word in this verse is *tijarat*, commerce. The verse emphasises the certain reward that comes from "investment" in reading the Qur'ān, performing ṣalat prayers and spending money in the service of charity. **Surah 36 Ya Sin** The mysteriously titled Ya Sin (the name of the book is untranslatable) is said to confer special blessings on those who recite it during devotional visits to holy graves. If it is recited on the night before Friday (*malam Jĕmuah*) it is said that Allah will lighten the torments of the deceased. **Surah 41 Fussilat (Well-Expounded) verses 30-32** Graves are "doorways" to the hereafter. Pilgrimage to holy graves, it is believed, reminds one of death's constant presence and inevitability. These verses – inscribed on the wall above the grave of a Javanese saint – remind pilgrims of the rewards that await them when they too pass through that doorway. **Surah 61 Al-Saff (The Lineup) verses 10-12** The relentlessly commercial character of many pilgrimage sites sends pilgrims and key-keepers to the Qur'ān to seek justifications for the "transactional" character of devotions at holy tombs. In these verses piety is likened to investment. **Surah 87 Al A'la (The Most High) verse 1** The pious exhortations of the Qur'ān are appearing with increasing frequency in guidebooks and on the walls of Java's pilgrimage sites. **Surah 97 Al Qadr (The Power) verse 3** This very short *surah* refers to the Night of Power (*laylatul qadr*) on which verses of the Qur'ān were initially revealed to Muhammad by the angel Jibril.

It is not known when exactly the Night of Power falls, but it is thought by many to be on one of the odd-numbered dates towards the end of the fasting month of Ramadhan. On these dates many pilgrimage sites across Java are crowded with visitors because, as this verse says, the Night of Power "is better than a thousand months".

## Javanese-language sources

This book could not have been written without drawing on sources in Javanese. Today Javanese is spoken by at least eighty million people. Tragically, it is now withering in the shadow of Indonesian and English and is little studied in Java's schools and universities. Javanese-language sources are also fading from studies on Indonesian society, and this impoverishes the field. It obliterates much of the cultural and historical context that remains essential to a deep and nuanced understanding of the country in the twenty-first century.

From a treasure-trove of Javanese texts I summarise parts of, or directly quote from, the following: *Babad Cirĕbon, Babad Dĕmak, Babad Dipånagårå, Babad Tanah Jawi, Bhāratayuddha Kakawin, Cariyos Bab Lampah-lampahipun Radèn Mas Aryå Purwålĕlånå* (a travelogue by Radèn Mas Adipati Aryå Cåndranagårå), *Desawarnana* (also called the *Nāgarakrtāgama*), *Jångkå Jåyåbåyå* (also called the *Pralambang Jåyåbåyå*), *Kitab Musarar, Lampahan Babat Alas Wånåmartå* (the text of a shadow play), *Pararaton, Préwangan Gunung Måndhålikå* (a novel by Dyaning Wiratmoko), *Rāmāyaṇa Kakawin, Sĕrat Centhini, Sĕrat Darmågandhul, Sĕrat Kålåtidhå* (by R.Ng. Rånggåwarsitå), *Sĕrat Sèh Sitijĕnar, Sĕrat Suluk Sèh Malåyå, Suluk Gatholoco, Suluk Linglung Sunan Kalijågå, Suluk Malang Sumirang,* and *Suluk Wujil.* In the bibliographic notes that follow I give the published sources of these works, where possible citing editions with English and/or Indonesian translations.

### NOTES AND SOURCES FOR EACH CHAPTER

## Prologue. Java's inner archipelago

The Caliph Ali's remarks on pilgrimage appear in *Mutiara Nahjul Balaghah, Wacana dan Surat-Surat Imam Ali R.A.* translated from Arabic and edited by Muhammad Al-Baqir, Penerbit Mizan (1990, eighth printing 2000) p.54. The story of Tumĕnggung Cåkrånagårå's encounter with Nyai Agĕng Bagĕlèn in a dream is digested from Radix Penadi *Nyai Agĕng Bagelen, Patih Semono – Patih Lowo Ijo,* Lembaga Study dan Pengembangan Sosial Budaya (1998, revised edition 1991).

## 1. Drawing a line to Mecca

For studies and reports on the *qibla* issue at Demak's Grand Mosque and the nearby mosque of Sunan Kalijågå see "Determination of what is lawful" (*Ketentuan Hukum*) no.3, *Fatwa Majelis Ulama Indonesia no.03 2010 tentang Kiblat*, available at http://mui.or.id/wp-content/uploads/2017/02/Fatwa-Kiblat_PDF.pdf. Also *Analisis Kontroversi dalam Penetapan Arah Kiblat Masjid Agung Demak*, Masters thesis by Ahmad Munif, Semarang: Institut Agama Islam Negeri Walisongo (2013) available at http://eprints.walisongo.ac.id/47/; *Studi Analisis Arah Kiblat Masjid Sunan Kalijaga Kadilangu Demak*, Undergraduate (S1) thesis by Jauharotun Nafis, Semarang: Institut Agama Islam Negeri Walisongo (2012) available at http://eprints.walisongo.ac.id/1370/; "Arah kiblat Masjid Agung Demak dibahas" *NU Online*, 14 December, 2011, accessable at http://www.nu.or.id/post/read/35288/arah-kiblat-masjid-agung-demak-dibahas; and Arjuna Rinaldy "Mitos arah kiblat Masjid Agung Demak, yang sempat diubah" *KCD News*, 29 May 2016 29 accessable at http://www.kcdnews.com/2016/05/mitos-arah-kiblat-masjid-agung-demak.html. The miraculous fixing of the *qibla* by Sunan Kalijågå is narrated in many sources including the *Babad Tanah Jawi*, Batavia: Balai Pustaka #1024 (1939 – 1941) vol. 3 canto 18 verses 11-12 pp.16-17, and the *Babad Děmak* see Atmodarminto *Babad Demak dalam Tafsir Sosial Politik*, Jakarta: Millennium (2000) pp.59-62. Popularised accounts of Sunan Kalijågå's life can be found in Achmad Chodjim's best-selling *Sunan Kalijaga Mistik dan Makrifat*, Jakarta: Serambi (2013, fourth printing 2014), and Purwadi *Sejarah Sunan Kalijaga: Sintesis Ajaran Wali Sanga vs Seh Siti Jenar*, Jogjakarta: Persada (2003). In his bandit persona of Brandhal Lokåjåyå, Sunan Kalijågå's forest encounter with Sunan Bonang is narrated in the *Sěrat Suluk Sèh Malåyå*, canto 1 verses 1-11 written around 1900 and available on the Sastra.org website at https://www.sastra.org/agama-dan-kepercayaan/suluk/1416-suluk-seh-malaya-angabei-iv-c-1900-1313. A variant version of this text, the *Suluk Linglung*, describes the saint's meeting with the prophet Khiḍr, see Kasmiran W. Sanadji (ed.) *Suluk Linglung Sunan Kalijaga (Syeh Melaya)* translated by M. Khafid Kasri and colleagues, Jakarta: Balai Pustaka (1993). Sunan Kalijågå's prowess as a puppeteer is mentioned in Umar Hasyim *Sunan Kalijaga*, Kudus: Menara (1974) p.27, and Effendy Zarkasi *Unsur Islam Dalam Pewayangan*, Bandung: Alma'arif (?1978). The building of Demak's Grand Mosque with its *såkå tatal* pillar is described in many sources, including the *Babad Tanah Jawi op.cit.* canto 18 verses 1-7 pp.14-16, and Atmodarminto *op.cit.* pp.62-63. The 1983 feature film *Sunan Kalijaga* directed by Sofyan Sharna opens with a romanticised but vivid scene showing the *såkå tatal* pillar being assembled and put in place as Demak's Grand Mosque is built. Sunan Kalijågå explains to his missionary elder, Sunan Ampèl, "If these off-cuts of wood are banded together into one, the pillar will be strong. So it is with us ... if we are united we will be a real force." See YouTube https://www.youtube.com/watch?v=mB1tbE0K_es . The story of Islam's origins in the mission exploits of Sheikh Jumadil Kubro who went to "Rum" is told in Moch. Cholil Nasiruddin *Punjer Wali Songo, Silsilah Sayyid Jumadil Kubro*, Jombang: SEMMA (no date), and *Syeikh Maulana Jumadil Kubro*, pamphlet issued to commemorate the construction of the Jumadil Kubro Mosque in Semarang and renovation of the adjacent tomb complex (no date, probably 2012). The place of Demak's Grand Mosque and its famous pillar in the nationalist rhetoric of modern Indonesia is reported in Atmodarminto *op.cit.* p.63, and in Nancy K. Florida *Writing the Past, Inscribing the Future: History as Prophecy in Colonial Java*, Durham NC: Duke University Press (1995) p.324.

## 2. "Thirsty? You can drink my piss!"

The thoughts of Sunan Bonang, the "saint without a history" who may have travelled to western China, appear in various texts including the *Suluk Wujil* and its variants, see Sri Harti Widyastuti *Suluk Wujil, Suntingan Teks dan Tinjauan Semiotik*, Semarang: Mekar (2001); G.W.J. Drewes *The Admonitions of Seh Bari*, The Hague: Martinus Nijhoff (1969); B.J.O. Schrieke *Het Boek van Bonang*, Utrecht: P. den Boer (1916); Poerbatjaraka *Kapustakan Djawi*, Jakarta/Amsterdam: Djambatan (1952) pp.98-100. The story of Wujil and Satpådå peering into the mirror of existence is popularised in Sri Harti Widyastuti's edition of the *Suluk Wujil op.cit.* pp.111-113. Sunan Bonang's encounter with the Hindu holy man Sakyakirti is told in Mas Bilal *Kisah Para Sunan*, Bandung: Mizan (1993). The *Sěrat Darmågandhul* has appeared in several recensions including Tandhanagara *Darmagandul: Carita adege nagara Islam ing Demak bedhahe nagara Majapahit kang salugune wiwite wong Jawa ninggal agama Buddha banjur salin agama Islam*, Surakarta: Toko Buku Sadu-Budi (fourth printing 1959), and Damar Shashangka *Darmagandhul: Kisah kehancuran Jawa dan ajaran-ajaran rahasia*, Jakarta: Dolphin (2011, fourth impression 2012). The controversial figure of Gatholoco appears in Philippus van Akkeren's doctoral dissertation *Een Gedrocht en Toch de Volmaakte Mens*, s'Gravenhage: Excelsior (1951). In his English translation of the *Suluk Gatholoco* Ben Anderson records something of the checkered publishing history of the text, see Benedict R.O'G. Anderson "The Suluk Gatoloco" part one *Indonesia* 32 (October 1981) pp.109-150, part two *Indonesia* 33 (April 1983) pp.31-88. The place of the two texts in the evolution of religion in Java is discussed in G.W.J. Drewes "The struggle between Javanism and Islam as illustrated by the Sěrat Děrmagandul" *Bijdragen tot de Taal-, Land- en Volkenkunde* vol.122 no.3 (1966) pp.309-365, and in Merle C. Ricklefs *Polarising Javanese Society, Islamic and other visions c.1830-1930*, Singapore: NUS Press (2007) pp.189-211. Sunan Bonang's encounter with Bută Locåyå is discussed in G.W.J Drewes *op.cit.* especially pp.339-342. The story of Sunan Bonang's outraged shifting of the Brantas River is told in the *Sĕrat Darmågandhul* (Damar Shashangka *op.cit.* p.155) and Fajar, M. "Brantas pindhah ngetan" *Panjebar Semangat* March 26, 1994, pp.2 and 49-51.


### 3. Where the ancestor of Java's kings vanished into the sky

The twelfth century king of Kediri, Jåyåbåyå, is glorified in the Old Javanese version of the Indian *Bhāratayuddha* epic, see S. Soepomo *Bhāratayuddha: An old Javanese poem and its Indian sources*, New Delhi: International Academy of Indian Culture and Aditya Prakashan (1993). My translation of an extract from the poem is based on Sutjipto Wirjosuparto *Kakawin Bharata-Yuddha*, Jakarta: Bhratara (1968) canto 52 verses 6-9, pp.180-181. The origins of King Jåyåbåyå's Vanishing Place are narrated in a guidebook sold at the site, *Petilasan Sang Prabu Sri Aji Joyoboyo*, Yogyakarta: Yayasan Hondodento (no date) p.8. On the prophetic *Jångkå Jåyåbåyå* or *Pralambang Jåyåbåyå* Th.G.Th. Pigeaud writes, "In the eighteenth and nineteenth centuries a peculiar kind of messianic texts, in the form of prophecies of coming events and future kingdoms, became popular all over Java. They were called *Pralambang Jaya Baya*, after a king of Kadhiri, belonging to the pre-Islamic period. In Old Javanese literature as yet no prototype of eighteenth century Jaya Baya prophecies has been found. So the connection with the pre-Islamic Kadhiri is not yet accounted for." See Th.G.Th. Pigeaud *Literature of Java* (three volumes), The Hague: Martinus Nyhoff (1967) vol.1 p.155. Mohammad Hari Soewarno lists many *jångkå* texts attributed to King Jåyåbåyå, none of which date from before the eighteenth century, see Mohammad Hari Soewarno *Ramalan Jayabaya Versi Sabda Palon*, Jakarta: PT Yudha Gama Corporation (no date) chapter 1 pp.9-10. See also Mugihardjo & Mbah Lantip *Ramalan Djangka Djojobojo Kawedar*, Semarang: Penerbit Keng (1966), and *Hikmah-Hikmah Hidup Serat Jayabaya* interpreted by Hariwijaya, Yogyakarta?: Nirwana (2003). The 1945 visit to Jåyåbåyå's Vanishing Place by the future President Soekarno is reported by Sindhunata in *Bayang-Bayang Ratu Adil*, Jakarta: Gramedia Pustaka Utama (1999) p.22. My English translation of two stanzas predicting the Japanese occupation of Java and the rise of Soekarno comes from a version of Jåyåbåyå's prophecies in Mohammad Hari Soewarno *op.cit.* pp.33-34. For information about Tirto Kamandanu, the baths adjacent to the Vanishing Place of King Jåyåbåyå, see *Loka Muksa Sang Prabu Sri Aji Jayabaya dan Sendang Tirto Kamandanu*, Jogjakarta: Yayasan Hondodento (no date). The story of the tall, well-built Persian perfume dealer and wise healer, Wasil

Syamsuddin, who helped King Jåyåbåyå write his prophecies is told in Nono Emje *Sekilas Tentang Syech Wasil Ali Syamsudjien*, Kediri: Kajian Lingkungan dan Budaya Masyarakat Kota (no date). The version of the king's prophecies known as the *Kitab Musarar* (The Book of Musarar) has been published in several versions including the *Jangka Jayabaya "Musarar"*, Jogjakarta: Penerbit Buku Eyang Brata (third impression, no date). The tomb of Wasil Syamsuddin is a popuar destination for "religious tourists" as is reported in "Jejak Mbah Wasil Setono Gedong" *andikafm*, August 14, 2011, available at http://www.andikafm.com/news/detail/2737/12/jejak-mbah-wasil-setono-gedong.

## 4. Bandit saints of the borderlands

John Pemberton's colourful and insightful study *On the Subject of "Java"*, Ithaca and London: Cornell University Press (1994) describes the fearsome appearance of Ki Agěng Balak (pp.293-294). For an excellent overview of Java's opium economy in the nineteenth century see James Rush *Opium to Java: Revenue farming and Chinese enterprise in colonial Indonesia, 1860-1910*, Ithaca and London: Cornell University Press (1990). For a sharply critical, often sarcastic view, of the opium business see J.F. Scheltema "The opium trade in the Dutch East Indies" *American Journal of Sociology* (in two parts, 1907). See also "Jawa dalam politik candu (opium) kolonial Belanda" *Phesolo*, 18 January 2012, https://phesolo.wordpress.com/2012/01/18/jawa-dalam-politik-candu-opium-kolonial-belanda/. See also Peter Carey "Changing perceptions of the Chinese communities in Central Java, 1755-1825" in *Indonesia* (Cornell University) no.37 (April 1984). For press reports on Ki Agěng Balak's modern functions as a "Mr Fix-it" for people in trouble with the law see, for example, "'Warga asing' di Makam Balakan disorot" *Suara Merdeka*, 21 May, 2004, and Herryanto Honggo "Tolak balak dan pesugihan di Makam Ki Agěng Balak" *Liberty* no.1837, 1–10 May, 1994. Also John Pemberton *op.cit.* p.293 and George Quinn "A double life: Ki Agěng Balak, a friend for those in trouble with the law" *Inside Indonesia* no.87, July-September 2006. The story of Roroyono's kidnapping is digested from Suroadi Menggolo "Ki Agěng Ngerang I dan istrinya Nyai Ngerang" *Sejatininghidup*, 14 February, 2014, http://sejatininghidup.blogspot.com.au/2014/02/, and Ferry Riyandika "Sejarah kisah para maling sakti (Aguno) dari masa ke masa" *Melancong Watu*, 30 July, 2011, http://tatkalam.blogspot.com.au/2011/07/sejarah-kisah-para-maling-sakti-aguno.html. For some, Maling Gěntiri is a modern hero despite his criminal record, see Mayshiza Widya "Maling Gentiri ternyata pahlawan di Blora" *Indonesia Nan Elok*, 6 March, 2014, http://indonesiananelok.blogspot.com.au/2014/03/maling-gentiri-ternyata-pahlawan-di.html,

and "Ki Boncolono (maling genthiri)" *Kediri Raya*, August 2011, http://
www.kediriraya.com/2011/08/ki-boncolono-maling-genthiri.html. The
story of Sitijå, the shadow theatre "Son of the Earth" who, like Ki
Boncolono, returns from death by reconnecting with the earth, is told in
the *Ensiklopedi Wayang Purwa I (Compendium)*, no place of publication:
Proyek Pembinaan Kesenian, Direktorat Pembinaan Kesenian, Dit.Jen.
Kebudayaan Departemen P & K (no date) pp.403-406. Loren Ryter
has documented Japto Soerjosoemarno's checkered career, see "Pemuda
Pancasila: The last loyalist free men of Soeharto's order?" *Indonesia* no.66
(October 1998) pp.46-47. In a series of (Indonesian-language) television
interviews with Peter Gontha, Japto gave his own account of his life, see
*Impact*, broadcast on Q Channel, 27 August 2008, https://www.youtube.
com/watch?v=FyAl4HC_i-c&list=PL08C147FFD42FC149.  Japto  is
proud of Pancasila Youth's problematic reputation as *préman*, once
saying that the defence of Indonesia's 1945 Constitution must be in the
hands of people of courage (*pemberani*), see "Japto: Pemuda Pancasila
memang preman" *Kaskus.com*, 8 May 2012, https://m.kaskus.co.id/
thread/14351732/japto-quotpemuda-pancasila-memang-premanquot/.
The recent, less-than-convincing steps by Pancasila Youth to project
a contrite view of themselves can be seen on one of the organisation's
webpages, "Sejarah Pemuda Pancasila: Selayang Pandang Pemuda
Pancasila" *Pemuda Pancasila* 30, July 2012, http://pemudapancasila04.
blogspot.com.au/. *Jagal,* the Indonesian-language version of Joshua
Oppenheimer's chilling documentary *The Act of Killing* (2012) about
killers in the ranks of the Pancasila Youth, can be viewed on YouTube at
https://www.youtube.com/watch?v=3tILiqotj7Y.

## 5. Dogs in the mosque

My retelling of Prince Panggung's story is based on a version of the *Suluk
Malang Sumirang* in D.A. Rinkes "De heiligen van Java V, Pangeran
Panggoeng, zijne honden en het wayangspel" *Tijdscrift voor Indische
Taal-, Land- en Volkenkunde* vol.54 (1912) pp.135-207, and a version
of the text in G.W.J. Drewes "Het document uit den brandstapel" *Djåwå*
vol.7 (1927) pp.97-109. The extracts from the *suluk* directly translated
in this chapter are drawn from the version of the *Suluk Malang Sumirang*
in G.W.J. Drewes' article. Nancy Florida offers a nuanced and insightful
discussion of the *suluk* in her *Writing the Past, Inscribing the Future:
History as Prophecy in Colonial Java*, Durham NC: Duke University
Press (1995), pp.366-384. See also S. Soebardi *The Book of Cabolek*,
The Hague: Martinus Nijhoff (1975) canto VI verses 6-18 pp.107 and
canto XI verses 3-25 pp.147-152. The vignette of Mansur Al-Hallaj's
execution is quoted (with some small modifications) from A.J. Arberry
*Muslim Saints and Mystics. Episodes from the Tadhkirat Al-Auliya'*
(Memorial of the Saints) *by Farid Al-Din Attar*, Routledge and Keagan

Paul (1966) pp.270-271. Biographies of Sheikh Siti Jenar, with accounts of his supposed teachings, are popular in Indonesia. Two of the biggest sellers have been *Syekh Siti Jenar, Makna Kematian* by Achmad Chodjim, Jakarta: Serambi Ilmu Semesta (2002, twelfth impression 2007), and *Syekh Siti Jenar, Pergumulan Islam-Jawa* by Abdul Munir Mulkhan, Yogyakarta: Yayasan Bentang Budaya (1999, fifth impression August 2000). Michael Feener presents a scholarly and critical view of the relationship between Al-Hallaj and Siti Jĕnar in "A re-examination of the place of Al-Hallaj in the development of Southeast Asian Islam" *Bijdragen tot de Taal-, Land- en Volkenkunde* 154 no.4 (1998) pp.571-592. The atheistic tendencies in Sheikh Siti Jĕnar's teachings are prominent in the *Sĕrat Siti Jĕnar*. The version consulted for this book appeared as a supplement titled *Sĕrat Sèh Sitijĕnar* in the 1920 edition of an Almanac published in Batavia by H. Buning. The Javanese text is available on the website of the Sastra Lestari Foundation at https://www.sastra.org/katalog/judul?ti_id=436. The book is summarised in *Falsafah Sitidjenar* by Bratakesawa, Surabaya: Djojobojo (?1954) pp.27-29. An Indonesian translation of a variant version of the book appears as a supplement in Abdul Munir Mulkhan *op.cit.* pp.223-347. Bratakesawa reports his personal experience of the atheistic Red Union whose followers accepted certain teachings of Siti Jĕnar (*op.cit.* p.10) and his report is echoed in the view that followers of Sheikh Siti Jenar "would also become total unbelievers" in the *Ensiklopedi Islam Indonesia* compiled by a team of writers at IAIN Syarif Hidayatullah chaired by Prof. Dr. H.Harun Nasution, three volumes, Jakarta: Penerbit Djambatan (1992, revised edition 2002) vol.3 p.1052-1053. See also Takashi Shiraishi *An Age in Motion, Popular Radicalism in Java, 1912-1926*, Ithaca & London: Cornell University Press (1990). The harrowing but poetic account of Siti Jĕnar's death appears in Muhammad Sholikhin *Sufisme Syekh Siti Jenar: Kajian Kitab Serat dan Suluk Siti Jenar*, Yogyakarta: Narasi (2004) p.133.

## 6. "We plead for your grace O prophet of Medina, O saints of Tarim!"

There are conflicting accounts of what happened at the tomb of Mbah Priok on April 14th 2010. Several eyewitness accounts estimate that close to 3,000 police were involved, but later reports suggest the number was below 2,000. My account is digested from a number of reasonably trustworthy contemporary press reports, including "Ditebas, lengan petugas Satpol PP nyaris putus" *Kompas.com* 14 April 2010; "Insiden Priok, korban Satpol PP lebih banyak" *Kompas.com* 14 April 2010; "59 korban bentrokan Priok dirawat RS Koja" *Kompas.com* 14 April 2010; "Perang batu kembali terjadi di makam Mbah Priok" *Kompas.com* 14

April 2010; "Tiga nyawa tumbal makam Mbah Priok" *Warta Kota* 16 April 2010; "Indonesia begins search for blame after bloody port battle" *The Jakarta Globe* 15 April 2010; "Mediasi Priok berhasil" *Republika* April 16 2010; "Makam keramat banyak versi" *Tempo* 3 May 2010; "Sebelum tragedi, belum ada kata sepakat" *Gatra* 28 April 2010. For a thumbnail account of the conflict at Mbah Priok's tomb from the point of view of workers in the Pelindo II container terminal see Sanjiv Pandita and Fahmi Panimbang "Global supply chains: Struggle within or against them" in *Lessons for Social Change in the Glocal Economy: Voices from the Field* edited by Shae Garwood, Sky Croeser and Cristalla Yakinthou, Lanham MD: Lexington Books (2014) pp.134-135. My sketch of the Tanjung Priok Incident (1984) is based mainly on Peter Burns "The post-Priok trials: religious principles and legal issues" *Indonesia* no.47 (April 1989) pp.61-88. My account of the rebuilding of Mbah Priok's tomb after 1998 and the findings of the research team appointed by the Indonesian Council of Muslim Scholars to investigate the riot of 2010 is drawn from the team's report *Kasus "Mbah Priok", Studi bayani-wa-tahqiq terhadap masalah makam eks TPU Dobo* by Ahmad Syafi'i Mufid et.al. Jakarta: Madani Institute (2010) especially pp.31ff and pp.101-102. The "official" biography of Mbah Priok appears on pages 4-10 of the *Risalah Manaqib Keramat Syech Sayyid Mbah Priuk* (no place of publication, publisher or date of publication), a small booklet on sale at the saint's tomb in 2015. For more on the story's sources in the conventions of Javanese storytelling see George Quinn "Faith comes from the sea, Maritime symbolism in the origin stories of three Muslim pilgrimage sites in Java" accessable at https://www.academia.edu/8275141/Faith_comes_from_the_sea_Maritime_symbolism_in_the_origin_stories_of_three_Muslim_pilgrimage_sites_in_Java. The "Ratib Al Haddad", the centrepiece of *pengajian* devotions at Mbah Priok's tomb, also appears in the *Risalah Manaqib Keramat Syech Sayyid Mbah Priuk*, as well as in *Risalah Qoshidatul Mubarokah*, a hard cover book (no publisher, no date) on sale at Mbah Priok's tomb, pp.37-57.

## 7. The guardian of the mountain and his advertising contract
My description of the annual Labuhan Merapi rite is drawn mostly from Lucas Sasongko Triyoga *Merapi dan Orang Jawa: Persepsi dan Kepercayaannya*, Jakarta: Grasindo (2010) especially pp.76-82 and pp.120-123. Triyoga's study originally appeared in 1991. Public interest in Mbah Maridjan after his gruesome death in 2010 led to its revision and republication in the same year. See also "Labuhan Keraton Ngayogyakarta ing Gunung Merapi" *Panjebar Semangat* 10 August 2011. *The White Banyan* by Elizabeth D. Prasetyo and Heri Dono, Yogyakarta: Babad Alas (1998) has snippets of insight into the life of Mbah Maridjan and the exotic stories surrounding Mount Merapi. It is also illustrated

with beautiful line drawings. Radèn Ngabei Rånggåwarsitå's nineteenth century warning about an "age of madness" is set out in (among many editions) Wiwin Widyawati R. *Serat Kalatidha, Tafsir Sosiologis dan Filosofis Pujangga Jawa terhadap Kondisi Sosial*, Yogyakarta: Pura Pustaka (2009), and *Ronggowarsito Zaman Edan*, edited and translated by Ahmad Norma, Yogyakarta: Bentang Budaya (1998). Stories surrounding Mount Merapi and its mythic denizens are legion. My account begins with Harnaeni Hamdan Hs *Sang Penjaga Merapi: Cerita dari Jawa*, Bandung: Citra Budaya (no date) pp.5-6, also Trijoto *Gunung Merapi; Antara Legenda, Mitos, dan Penanggulangan Bencana*, Jakarta: Mitra Gama Widya (1996). The Kuku Bima advertising campaign is sketched in Muhammad Iqbal's "Marketing mix: Studi pada Kuku Bima Ener-G" *Pharm Marketing* 22 November 2009, reposted in *Moko Apt* 22 November 2009, https://moko31.wordpress.com/2009/11/22/evaluasi-hubungan-strategi-marketing-mix-dan-kepuasan-pelanggan-studi-kasus-pada-kuku-bima-ener-g/. An example of a TV commercial for Kuku Bima starring Mbah Maridjan can be viewed on YouTube at https://www.youtube.com/watch?v=Bd4tMQBGVy8. The story of the singed saint Sunan Gĕsĕng appears in many versions, among them S. Padmasoekotjo *Memetri Basa Jawi*, Surabaya: Citra Jaya (1979) volume 1, p.94; Radix Penadi *Babad Sunan Geseng: Mubaligh Tanah Bagelen*, Purworejo: Lembaga Study dan Pengembangan Sosial Budaya (1998); and D.A. Rinkes "Soenan Geseng" in *De Heiligen van Java III*, Batavia: Albrecht & Co. (1911). The song *Lontang-lantung* ... refers to the tube-like container made from a segment of bamboo that dangles beneath the palm tapper as he fills it with nectar or sap from the tree he is tapping. There are several variants of the song, see for example, Radix Penadi *op.cit.* p.7.

## 8. How to be a queen in Madura

For a good account of Madurese arts, including ludrug, see Hélène Bouvier *Lèbur!: Seni Musik dan Pertunjukan Dalam Masyarakat Madura*, Jakarta: Yayasan Obor Indonesia (2002). For an overview of ludrug see James L. Peacock's now a little dated but still very insightful *Rites of Modernization: Symbolic and Social Aspects of Indonesian Proletarian Drama*, Chicago: University of Chicago Press (1968). For good accounts of Madura's history see M.C. Ricklefs *A History of Modern Indonesia since c. 1200*, Palgrave Macmillan (fourth edition 2008); H.J. de Graaf *Geschiedenis van Indonesië*, W. van Hoeve, (1949); H.J. de Graaf and Th.G.Th Pigeaud *De Eerste Moslimse Vorstendommen op Java*, s'Gravenhage: Martinus Nijhoff (1974) chapters 13 and 14; and Luc Nagtegaal "The legitimacy of rule in early modern Madura" in Kees Van Dijk, Huub de Jonge and Elly Towen-Bouwsma (eds.)

*Across Madura Strait: The Dynamics of an Insular Society*, Leiden: KITLV Press (1995). A readily accessible traditional history of Madura is Werdisastra *Babad Sumenep* translated into Indonesian by Moh. Thoha Hadi, Pasuruan: Garoeda Buana Indah (1996). My reconstruction of the career of Prince Jimat is based mostly on Nagtegaal *op.cit.* especially pp. 40 and 62. The death of Captain Tack and his men in Surakarta is described in H.J. de Graaf *De Moord op Kapitein Francois Tack, 8 Februari 1686*, Amsterdam: H.J. Paris (1935). Arifin Mansurnoor gives a good overview of Madurese Islam in his *Islam in an Indonesian World: Ulama of Madura*, Yogyakarta: Gadjah Mada University Press (1990). Legends surrounding Prince Pulangjiwå and Bindårå Saud are narrated in *Legenda Bindara Saod & Joko Tole*, Sumenep: booklet compiled by Tim YAPASTI on sale at the Asta Tinggi royal burial ground (dated 2010), and R.B.Abd. Rasyid *Diktat Sejarah Bindara Saued*, booklet on sale at the Asta Tinggi burial ground (dated 1984). The moral panic in 2015-2016 over LGBT culture is reported (among many sources) in "Hukuman bagi pelaku penyimpangan seksual dalam fatwa MUI" *Republika.co.id* 15 January, 2015, http://www.republika.co.id/berita/dunia-islam/islam-nusantara/15/01/15/ni76pd-hukuman-bagi-pelaku-penyimpangan-seksual-dalam-fatwa-mui, and "Menhan nilai LGBT bagian dari 'Proxy War' yang harus diwaspadai" *Kompas.com* 23 February 2016, https://nasional.kompas.com/read/2016/02/23/22085741/Menhan.Nilai.LGBT.Bagian.dari.Proxy.War.yang.Harus.Diwaspadai. My history of the Aer Mata burial ground is drawn partly from Soegiyono MS "Pasarean Aer Mata Madura: Syarifah Ambami ngerti sadurunge dumadi" *Mekar Sari* vol.29 no.19 (1 December 1985) p.31, and partly from Iqbal Nurul Azhar *Mortéka Dâri Madhurâ. Antologi Cerita Rakyat Madura Edisi Kabupaten Bangkalan*, Balai Bahasa Jawa Timur (2016) pp.84-88. The story of the magic gamelan at Aer Mata comes from "De legende der Mata-ajer Ajer-mata" in Jos. Meijboom-Haliaander *Javaansche Sagen Mythen en Legenden*, Zutphen: W.J. Thieme & Cie (1928) pp.162-165.

## 9. Where money comes from

Dyaning Wiratmoko's Javanese-language novel *Préwangan Gunung Måndhålikå* was serialised in *Djaka Lodang* nos.441-446 (28 February 1981 – 4 April 1981). G.W.J. Drewes reports the existence of the *blorong* creature in "Verboden rijkdom" *Djawa* no.9 (1929) p.23. A very readable account of the role of cash in the peasant society of nineteenth century Java appears in *The Thugs, The Curtain Thief, and the Sugar Lord: Power, Politics and Culture in Colonial Java* by Onghokham, Jakarta: Metaphor (2003) especially pp.124, 193, 194. The extract from a short story about toddler-demons comes from "Memuja setan tuyul" by Ki Damar in *Misteri* no.66 (February 1987) pp.52-56. My description of the *tour de tuyul* incident is adapted from George Quinn "An excursion to Java's get-rich-quick tree" in Jan van der Putten and Mary Kilcline Cody (eds.) *Lost Times and Untold Tales from the Malay World*, Singapore: National University of Singapore Press (2009) pp.33-40. David Reeve gives a vivid account of Onghokham's involvement in the 1985 seminar on the "Non-Physical Realm" and his interpretation of the *tuyul* phenomenon as "an incipient rural proletarian rejection of the accumulation of wealth", see "Ong and tuyul" in David Reeve, J.J. Rizal and Wasmi Alhaziri (eds.) *Onze Ong, Onghokham dalam Kenangan*, Depok: Komunitas Bambu (2007) pp.95-101. The main sources for my account of events in Bero are "Ribuan pengunjung 'Kerajaan Tuyul' di Klaten kemarin dibubarkan Muspika" *Suara Merdeka* 28 October 1985, and "'Tour de Tuyul' ke 'Kerajaan Tuyul' gagal" *Suara Karya* 28 October 1985. See also an Indonesian-language TV report from the tree "Menguak mitos pohon ketos di Trucuk" by *SoloposTV* dated June 2nd, 2014 posted on YouTube at https://www.youtube.com/watch?v=bC__V44I0kY. The example of commentary on commerce in a Quranic verse comes from an edition of the Holy Qur'ān published in Saudi Arabia and distributed worldwide: *The Holy Qur-ān, English Translation of the Meanings and Commentary* issued by the custodian of the two holy mosques, King Fahd complex for the printing of the Holy Qur-ān (1413H) pp.1307-1308, note 3915. On devotions at the Mount Kawi tomb of Éyang Jugo and Iman Sujono and the history of the site see Raden Soelardi Soeryowidagdo *Pesarean Gunung Kawi: Tata Cara Ziarah dan Riwayat Makam Eyang Penembahan Djoego Eyang Raden Mas Iman Soedjono di Gunung Kawi Malang*, Wonosari: Yayasan Ngesti Gondo (no date, c.1989). Im Yang Tju's early biography of Éyang Jugo, *Riwajat Ejang Djugo Panembahan Gunung Kawi*, was published in Surabaya by Toko Astagina (no date, probably c.1953-1954). The vignettes of Éyang Jugo's life and thought are found in *op.cit.* pages 27 and 45-47. The "secret" history of the relationship between Éyang Jugo, alias Kyai Zakaria the Second, and Prince Dipånagårå is reported in George Quinn "Where history meets pilgrimage: The graves of Sheikh Yusuf Al-Maqassari and Prince Dipanagara in Madura" *The Journal of Indonesian Islam*. vol.3 no.2 (2009) pp.249-266. The commercial operations of Mount Kawi's chief benefactor, Liem Sioe Liong (Sudono Salim), are reported in Richard Borsuk and Nancy Chng *Liem Sioe Liong's Salim Group: The Business Pillar of Soeharto's Indonesia*. Singapore: Institute of Southeast Asian Studies (2014).

## 10. In the forests of the future

Sunan Pojok's biography is given in a booklet sold at his tomb in Blora, *Riwayat Sunan Pojok Blora, Pejabat Pemerintah Gemar Ibadah*, Blora:

Dinas Pendidikan Nasional Kab. Blora, UPTD Perpustakaan Umum Kab. Blora, bekerjasama dengan Yayasan Sunan Pojok Blora (2008). The extracts from the *Rāmāyaṇa* with their English translations come from Stuart Robson *The Old Javanese Rāmāyaṇa*, Tokyo: Research Institute for Languages and Cultures of Asia and Africa, Tokyo University of Foreign Studies (2015). For discussion of Java's natural environment as depicted in the Old Javanese *Rāmāyaṇa* see Stuart Robson *op.cit.* pp.21-22, and P.J. Zoetmulder *Kalangwan, A Survey of Old Javanese Literature*, Martinus Nijhoff (1974) pp.232-233. Anthony Reid's classic study *Southeast Asia in the Age of Commerce 1450-1680*, two vols. Chiang Mai: Silkworm Books (vol.1 1988, vol.2 1993) is an essential beginning point for the reading of Tome Pires' account of his visit to Java in the second decade of the 1500s. Pires reports his visit in exotic and fascinating detail in his *Suma Oriental* published as Tome Pires and Fransisco Rodrigues *The Suma Oriental of Tome Pires and The Book of Francisco Rodrigues*, edited by Armando Cortesao, 2 vols. New Delhi, Chennai: Asian Educational Services (2005). Anthony Reid's study reports on the shipping of the time. On the size of vessels, for example, see Reid *op.cit.* vol.2 p.38. The current condition of Java's natural environment is detailed in Tony Whitten, Roehayat Emon Soeriaatmadja and Suria A. Afiff *The Ecology of Java and Bali*, Periplus Editions (1996), and in "Luas hutan di pulau Jawa tinggal 11 persen" *Antara* 26 Januari 2006, http://www.antaranews.com/berita/26789/luas-hutan-di-pulau-jawa-tinggal-11-persen . The survival of Java's now extinct tigers as symbols is discussed in Robert Wessing "The last tiger in East Java: symbolic continuity in ecological change" *Asian Folklore Studies* (1995). Nineteenth century sightings of tigers in the vicinity of Ketonggo Forest are mentioned in Peter Carey *The Power of Prophecy: Prince Dipanagara and the End of the Old Order in Java, 1785-1855*, Leiden: KITLV Press (2007) p.12 note 35. One of Java's earliest indigenous travelogues mentions Java's tigers, see Radèn Mas Adipati Aryå Cåndranagårå *Cariyos Bab Lampah-lampahipun Radèn Mas Aryå Purwålělånå*, Semarang: G.C.T. van Dorp & Co. (1877) p.165. Cåndranagårå's fascinating book has been translated into French by Marcel Bonnef under the title *Pérégrinations javanaises: Les voyages de R.M.A. Purwa Lelana*, Paris: Editions de la Maisons des sciences de l'homme (1986), and into Dutch by Judith Bosnak and Hans Koot *Op reis met een Javaanse edelman*, Walburg Pers, 2013. Historian Merle Ricklefs has documented what few facts are known about the court of Kartåsurå at the beginning of the eighteenth century. The facts are more bizarre than the fictions I heard in Lodoyo, see Merle.C. Ricklefs *The Seen and Unseen Worlds in Java, 1726-1749: History, Literature and Islam in the Court of Pakubuwana II*, University of Hawaii Press (1998). The most complete contemporary portrait we have of fourteenth century Måjåpait appears in the *kakawin* poem *Desawarnana* translated by Stuart Robson as *Desawarnana (Nāgarakrtāgama) of Mpu Prapañca*, Leiden: KITLV Press Verhandelingen 169 (1995). Coloured by the imperatives of modern Indonesian nationalism Muhammad Yamin's *Tatanegara Madjapahit* (4 volumes), Jakarta: Prapantja (1962) attempts a comprehensive description of Måjåpait's history and government. His *Gadjah Mada: Pahlawan Persatuan Nusantara*, Jakarta: Balai Pustaka (1953) likewise views Måjåpait through the ideological glasses of Indonesian nationalism. Another source, The Book of Kings or *Pararaton* has been translated into English in I Gusti Putu Phalgunadi *The Pararaton: A Study of the Southeast Asian Chronicle*, New Delhi: Sundeep Prakashan (1996). Accounts of the fall of Måjåpait are confused and incomplete. In popular tradition, the capital was sacked by a Muslim army from Demak in 1478. Scholarly studies dispute this, suggesting (though not with absolute confidence) that the events of 1478 were part of a civil war within Måjåpait and the Hindu-Buddhist state was not snuffed out by Muslims until as late as 1527. For a brief, balanced scholarly account see Merle C. Ricklefs *A History of Modern Indonesia since c.1200*, Palgrave Macmillan (2008). Two of many books predicting the appearance of a Righteous King in modern Indonesia are *Satrio Piningit* by D. Soesetro and Zein al Arief, Jogjakarta: Narasi (2003), and *Ratu Adil Segera Datang!* by Otto Sukatno CR, Jogjakarta: Penerbit IRCiSoD (2014). Sartono Kartodirjo's *Ratu Adil*, Jakarta: Sinar Harapan (1984) is a fine scholarly study of twentieth century messianism in Java. See also Peter Carey "Waiting for the 'Just King': The agrarian world of South-Central Java from Giyanti (1755) to the Java War (1825-30)" in *Modern Asian Studies* vol.20 no.1 (1986) pp.59-137. The modest expectations Javanese have of their Righteous King are mentioned in *Serat Centhini kalatinaken miturut aslinipun dening Kamajaya*, Jogjakarta: Yayasan Cĕnthini (vol.4 1988) p.5 verses 4-6, available at https://www.sastra.org/kisah-cerita-dan-kronikal/serat-centhini/964-centhini-kamajaya-1986-1988-92-761-jilid-041. For a view of the Righteous King phenomenon coloured by Catholicism see *Javanese Popular Belief in the Coming of Ratu-Adil, a Righteous Prince* by Andrea Corsini Harjaka Hardjamardjaja, Rome: Pontificia Universitas Gregoriana (1962). Peter Carey's *The Power of Prophecy: Prince Dipanagara and the End of the Old Order in Java, 1785-1855*. Leiden: KITLV Press (2007) discusses Prince Dipånagårå as a messianic figure, see especially pp.564-591. On modern manifestations of millenarianism see, for example, Tjantrik Mataram on Soekarno and the prophecies of Jåyåbåyå in *Peranan Ramalan Djojobojo Dalam Revolusi Kita*, Bandung: Masa Baru (1954), also *Indonesia Menggugat: Pidato Pembelaan Bung Karno Di Muka Hakim Kolonial*, Jakarta: S.K. Seno (1956) p.75, and the case of Sawito Kartowibowo detailed in David Bourchier *Dynamics of Dissent in Indonesia: Sawito and the Phantom*

*Coup*, Ithaca, New York: Cornell Modern Indonesia Project (Interim Reports Series no.63) Southeast Asia Program, Cornell University (1984), as well as in Titania *Sawito: Siapa Mengapa & Bagaimana*, Solo: Sasongko (1978). The shadow play *Babad Alas Wånåmartå* (Clearing the Forest of Wånåmartå) has been published in shortened form in Purwadi *Serat Pedhalangan Lampahan Babat Wanamarta*, Sukoharjo Surakarta: CV Cendrawasih, no date. For a glimpse of President Soeharto's visits to sacred places on Selok Hill see George Quinn "National legitimacy through a regional prism: Local pilgrimage and Indonesia's Javanese presidents" in Minako Sakai, Greg Banks and John Walker (eds.) *The Politics of the Periphery in Indonesia: Social and Geographical Perspectives*. National University of Singapore Press (2009).

## Epilogue. Between mosque and holy tomb

The Islamisation of Java and the contest between theological and devotional variants of Islam have been the subject of innumerable scholarly studies. By far the most outstanding and most comprehensive is a sequence of three books by Merle C. Ricklefs, each scrupulously grounded in Javanese-language primary sources and very detailed:

*Mystic Synthesis in Java: A history of Islamization from the fourteenth to the early nineteenth centuries*, EastBridge (2006); *Polarising Javanese Society: Islamic and other visions (c.1830-1930)*, Singapore: NUS Press (2007); and *Islamisation and its Opponents in Java: c.1930 to the present*, Singapore: NUS Press (2012). The latter presents rare documentary evidence of religious change in Java since Indonesia's independence, see for example pp.84-85 and 272-273. The terms *santri* and *abangan* were first made known to an international audience by Clifford Geertz in his agenda-setting study *The Religion of Java*, Chicago, London: University of Chicago Press (1960). Recent changes in theological and devotional orientations are well documented in Robert Hefner's "Where have all the *abangan* gone? Religionization and the decline of non-standard Islam in Indonesia" in Rémy Madinier and Michel Picard (eds.) *The Politics of Religion in Indonesia: Syncretism, Orthodoxy and Religious Contention in Java and Bali*, London and New York: Routledge (2011) pp.71-91.

One of the best short accounts of the transformation of Indonesian Islam since the 1980s is Martin van Bruinessen's "Introduction" (pp.1-20) in Martin van Bruinessen (ed.) *Contemporary Developments in Indonesian Islam: Explaining the "Conservative Turn"*, Singapore: Institute of Southeast Asian Studies, 2013. See also R.W. Liddle "The Islamic turn in Indonesia: a political explanation" *Journal of Asian Studies* vol.55 no.3 (1996) pp.613–634. For an excellent short account of the anti-left, anti-*abangan* killings of 1965-1966 see Robert Cribb "The Indonesian massacres" in Samuel Totten and William S. Parsons (eds.) *Century of Genocide: Critical Essays and Eyewitness Accounts*, New York and London: Routledge (updated edition 2009, originally published 1997) pp.193-217. The role of the Indonesian army in orchestrating the killings is carefully documented in Jess Melvin's *The Army and the Indonesian Genocide, The Mechanics of Mass Murder*, London: Routledge (2018). Robert Hefner *op.cit.* pp. 84-86 reports on the impact of these killings on religious affiliations.

The extraordinary rise in the popularity of local pilgrimage since the 1980s is documented in David Armstrong *Tingkat Kunjungan Wisatawan ke Situs Purbakala di Jawa Timur: Data Selama 18 Tahun 1988–2005*, Malang: Program ACICIS, Fakultas Sosial dan Ilmu Politik, Universitas Muhammadiyah Malang (2006), especially pp.6 and 64-65, accessable at http://1073zb3xfs20yv98x228do7r.wpengine.netdna-cdn.com/wp-content/uploads/2015/03/ARMSTRONG-David.pdf. See also news reports, including "Wisata ziarah Walisongo sejaterahkan umat" *Aktual.com*, November 25, 2015, http://www.aktual.com/wisata-ziarah-walisongo-sejaterahkan-umat/; "Mesjid dan makam Sunan Ampel" *Pesona Wisata Indonesia*, Institut Teknologi Sepuluh Nopember, December 2014 http://ekspedisiwisata.blogspot.com.au/2014/12/masjid-dan-makam-sunan-ampel-tinjauan.html; "Pengunjung Makam Sunan Bonang Tuban membeludak" *AntaraNews.com*, 3 June, 2016 https://www.antaranews.com/berita/564921/pengunjung-makam-sunan-bonang-tuban-membeludak; Khusni Nubarok "Penziarah padati makam Sunan Bonang" *Pojok Pitu*, 25 December 2016 http://pojokpitu.com/baca.php?idurut=38687&&top=1&&ktg=J%20Pantura&&keyrbk=Mlaku%20-%20Mlaku&&keyjdl=sunan%20bonang; and "Makam Gus Dur diserbu ribuan peziarah" *Tribun Jateng*, 5 June, 2016 http://jateng.tribunnews.com/2016/06/05/makam-gus-dur-diserbu-ribuan-peziarah. On religious pilgrimage to the brand-new tomb of Indonesia's fourth president, Abdurrahman Wahid, see Sri Mulyani & Daryono "Kajian terhadap daerah asal, motivasi pengunjung dan fasilitas penunjang obyek wisata religi makam KH. Abdurrahman Wahid di Kecamatan Diwek Kabupaten Jombang" *Swara Bhumi* vol.4 no.2, 2016, p.79. The commercial character of local pilgrimage is examined in George Quinn "Throwing money at the holy door: Commercial aspects of popular pilgrimage in Java" in Greg Fealy and Sally White (eds.) *Expressing Islam: Religious Life and Politics in Indonesia*, Singapore: Institute of Southeast Asian Studies (2007) pp.63-79. For an example of the commercialisation of local pilgrimage by the tourism industry see the website of Java Tours at http://www.javatours.com/front/index.php/about-visitors/pilgrimage-tour and http://www.javatours.com/front/index.php/tour-program/sacred-tour/jvt-zia-03. For an example of government interest in pilgrimage sites as sources of revenue see "Retribusi ziarah makam segera ditertibkan" *Kompas*, 18 April 2002, and "Wisata Ziarah ..." above. For reports on the connection between local pilgrimage and manifestations of sufism, especially *majlis dhikr* groups, see Arif Zamhari *Rituals of Islamic Spirituality: A study of majlis dhikr groups in East Java*, Canberra: ANU Press (2010) especially Chapter 3, also Julia Day Howell "Sufism and the Indonesian Islamic revival" *The Journal of Asian Studies* vol.60 no.3 (August 2001) p.711. The director of postgraduate studies at the Walisongo State Islamic University in Semarang alludes to the emotional impact of pilgrimage in "Milad UIN Semarang napak tilasi Wali Songo" *Republika*, 16 April 2017, and a glimpse of its liberating function appears in *Metode Dakwah Melalui Wisata Religi (Studi Kasus di Majelis Ta'lim Al-Khasanah Desa Sukolilo Kecamatan Ngawen Kabupaten Blora)* by Ainur Rohmah, Yogyakarta: Undergraduate (S1) thesis, UIN Walisongo (2015), especially p.5. On the emerging sanctification of Abdurrahman Wahid see, for example, Imam Turmudzi *Gus Dur Wali Kesepuluh*, Jombang: Zahra Book (2011) and Mas'ud Adnan *Sunan Gus Dur: Akrobat Politik ala Nabi Khidir*, Surabaya: Harian Bangsa (2011), as well as George Quinn "The tenth saint and his antecedents: Continuity in a Javanese narrative trope" in Yumi Sugahara and Willem van der Molen (eds) *Transformations of Religions as Reflected in Javanese Texts*, Tokyo: Research Institute for Languages and Cultures of Asia and Africa, Tokyo University of Foreign Studies (2018) pp.142-159. On the spread of Java's Islamic pilgrimage culture to Bali see Syaifudin Zuhri "Inventing Balinese Muslim sainthood" in *Indonesia and the Malay World* vol.41 no.119 (2013) pp.1-13, and George Quinn "The Muslim saints of Bali" *Bali in Global Asia Conference*, Udayana University, Denpasar (July 16–18, 2012) accessable at https://www.academia.edu/2547994/The_Muslim_Saints_of_Bali. On the rise of pilgrimage to the tombs of saints in Lombok and South Sulawesi, see "7 wisata religi di Lombok yang biasa dikunjungi peziarah" *Pak.Wis* (no date) http://paketwisata.id/wisata-religi-di-lombok/, and "Wali Pitu (Wali Tujuh) Sulawesi Selatan" *Sejarah dan Peristiwa* (31 May 2013) http://agungpambudi72-sejarahdanperistiwa.blogspot.com/2013/05/wali-pitu-wali-tujuh-7-sulawesi.html. The "feminisation" of pilgrimage is sketched in George Quinn "The veneration of female saints in Indonesia" in Suad Joseph et.al. (eds) *Encyclopedia of Women and Islamic Cultures*, Brill (2012). Quinn also reports on a brand-new female saint in "Nike Ardilla: Instant pop saint" *RIMA (Review of Indonesian and Malaysian Affairs)* vol.41 no.2 (2007) pp.205-221. On Francois Valentijn's visit to the Ampel Mosque in 1705 see Francois Valentijn *Oud en Nieuw Oost-Indien*, 's-Gravenhage: H.C. Susan, C.Hzoon (3 vols 1856-1858) vol.3 p.304.

## The location of sites and how to access them

The locations of the pilgrimage sites visited in this book – including their GPS coordinates – and detailed directions for accessing them can be found on the book's website at www.saintsofjava.net. The website also sketches the etiquette of pilgrimage – the general rules visitors should follow when visiting holy places in Java and Madura.